SAS® Certified Professional Prep Guide: Advanced Programming Using SAS® 9.4

SAS® Documentation

The correct bibliographic citation for this manual is as follows: SAS Institute Inc. 2019. *SAS® Certified Professional Prep Guide: Advanced Programming Using SAS® 9.4*. Cary, NC: SAS Institute Inc.

SAS® Certified Professional Prep Guide: Advanced Programming Using SAS® 9.4

Copyright © 2019, SAS Institute Inc., Cary, NC, USA

ISBN 978-1-64295-691-7 (Hardcover)
ISBN 978-1-64295-467-8 (Paperback)
ISBN 978-1-64295-468-5 (PDF)
ISBN 978-1-64295-469-2 (Epub)
ISBN 978-1-64295-470-8 (Kindle)

All Rights Reserved. Produced in the United States of America.

For a hard copy book: No part of this publication may be reproduced, stored in a retrieval system, or transmitted, in any form or by any means, electronic, mechanical, photocopying, or otherwise, without the prior written permission of the publisher, SAS Institute Inc.

For a web download or e-book: Your use of this publication shall be governed by the terms established by the vendor at the time you acquire this publication.

The scanning, uploading, and distribution of this book via the Internet or any other means without the permission of the publisher is illegal and punishable by law. Please purchase only authorized electronic editions and do not participate in or encourage electronic piracy of copyrighted materials. Your support of others' rights is appreciated.

U.S. Government License Rights; Restricted Rights: The Software and its documentation is commercial computer software developed at private expense and is provided with RESTRICTED RIGHTS to the United States Government. Use, duplication, or disclosure of the Software by the United States Government is subject to the license terms of this Agreement pursuant to, as applicable, FAR 12.212, DFAR 227.7202-1(a), DFAR 227.7202-3(a), and DFAR 227.7202-4, and, to the extent required under U.S. federal law, the minimum restricted rights as set out in FAR 52.227-19 (DEC 2007). If FAR 52.227-19 is applicable, this provision serves as notice under clause (c) thereof and no other notice is required to be affixed to the Software or documentation. The Government's rights in Software and documentation shall be only those set forth in this Agreement.

SAS Institute Inc., SAS Campus Drive, Cary, NC 27513-2414

October 2019

SAS® and all other SAS Institute Inc. product or service names are registered trademarks or trademarks of SAS Institute Inc. in the USA and other countries. ® indicates USA registration.

Other brand and product names are trademarks of their respective companies.

P1:certprpg

Contents

How to Prepare for the Exam vii
Using Sample Data xi
Accessibility Features of the Prep Guide xiii

PART 1 SQL Processing with SAS   1

Chapter 1 • PROC SQL Fundamentals 3
PROC SQL Basics 4
The PROC SQL SELECT Statement 5
The FROM Clause 9
The WHERE Clause 10
The GROUP BY Clause 19
The HAVING Clause 29
The ORDER BY Clause 32
PROC SQL Options 35
Validating Query Syntax 38
Quiz 39

Chapter 2 • Creating and Managing Tables 43
The CREATE TABLE Statement 43
Using the LIKE Clause 48
Using the AS Keyword 49
The INSERT Statement 51
The DESCRIBE TABLE Statement 59
Using Dictionary Tables 60
Chapter Quiz 63

Chapter 3 • Joining Tables Using PROC SQL 65
Understanding Joins 66
Generating a Cartesian Product 66
Using Inner Joins 68
Using Natural Joins 77
Using Outer Joins 78
Comparing SQL Joins and DATA Step Match-Merges 84
Quiz 89

Chapter 4 • Joining Tables Using Set Operators 95
Understanding Set Operators 96
Using the EXCEPT Set Operator 103
Using the INTERSECT Set Operator 109
Using the UNION Set Operator 114
Using the OUTER UNION Set Operator 120
Quiz 123

Chapter 5 • Using Subqueries 131
Subsetting Data Using Subqueries 131
Creating and Managing Views Using PROC SQL 141

Quiz 149

Chapter 6 • Advanced SQL Techniques **155**
Creating Data-Driven Macro Variables with PROC SQL 155
Accessing DBMS Data with SAS/ACCESS 161
The FedSQL Procedure 165
Quiz 171

PART 2 SAS Macro Language Processing   177

Chapter 7 • Creating and Using Macro Variables **179**
Introducing Macro Variables 179
The SAS Macro Facility 181
Using Macro Variables 188
Troubleshooting Macro Variable References 190
Delimiting Macro Variable References 193
Quiz 194

Chapter 8 • Storing and Processing Text **197**
Processing Text with Macro Functions 198
Using SAS Macro Functions to Manipulate Character Strings 198
Using SAS Functions with Macro Variables 203
Using SAS Macro Functions to Mask Special Characters 207
Creating Macro Variables during PROC SQL Step Execution 214
Creating Macro Variables during DATA Step Execution 217
Referencing Macro Variables Indirectly 226
Quiz 228

Chapter 9 • Working with Macro Programs **231**
Defining and Calling a Macro 232
Passing Information into a Macro Using Parameters 237
Controlling Variable Scope 240
Debugging Macros 245
Conditional Processing 247
Iterative Processing 252
Quiz 254

Chapter 10 • Advanced Macro Techniques **259**
Storing Macro Definitions in External Files 259
Understanding Session Compiled Macros 261
Using the Autocall Facility 262
Data-Driven Macro Calls 266
Quiz 268

PART 3 Advanced SAS Programming Techniques   271

Chapter 11 • Defining and Processing Arrays **273**
Defining and Referencing One-Dimensional Arrays 273
Expanding Your Use of One-Dimensional Arrays 283
Defining and Referencing Two-Dimensional Arrays 288
Quiz 293

Chapter 12 • Processing Data Using Hash Objects 297
Declaring Hash Objects 297
Defining Hash Objects 300
Finding Key Values in a Hash Object 302
Writing a Hash Object to a Table 304
Hash Object Processing 306
Using Hash Iterator Objects 311
Quiz 314

Chapter 13 • Using SAS Utility Procedures 317
Creating Picture Formats with the FORMAT Procedure 317
Creating Functions with PROC FCMP 328
Quiz 334

Chapter 14 • Using Advanced Functions 337
Using a Variety of Advanced Functions 337
Performing Pattern Matching with Perl Regular Expressions 344
Quiz 355

PART 4 Workbook 359

Chapter 15 • Practice Programming Scenarios 361
Differences between the Workbook and Certification Exam 362
Scenario 1 362
Scenario 2 363
Scenario 3 363
Scenario 4 364
Scenario 5 365
Scenario 6 366
Scenario 7 366
Scenario 8 367
Scenario 9 368
Scenario 10 368

PART 5 Solutions 371

Chapter 16 • Chapter Quiz Answer Keys 373
Chapter 1: PROC SQL Fundamentals 373
Chapter 2: Creating and Managing Tables 374
Chapter 3: Joining Tables Using PROC SQL 375
Chapter 4: Joining Tables Using Set Operators 376
Chapter 5: Using Subqueries 377
Chapter 6: Advanced SQL Techniques 378
Chapter 7: Creating and Using Macro Variables 379
Chapter 8: Storing and Processing Text 380
Chapter 9: Working with Macro Programs 381
Chapter 10: Advanced Macro Techniques 382
Chapter 11: Defining and Processing Arrays 383
Chapter 12: Processing Data Using Hash Objects 384
Chapter 13: Using SAS Utility Procedures 384
Chapter 14: Using Advanced Functions 385

Chapter 17 • Programming Scenario Solutions 387
- Scenario 1 388
- Scenario 2 389
- Scenario 3 390
- Scenario 4 392
- Scenario 5 393
- Scenario 6 395
- Scenario 7 396
- Scenario 8 398
- Scenario 9 399
- Scenario 10 400

Recommended Reading 403
Index 405

How to Prepare for the Exam

Requirements and Details

Requirements

To complete examples in this book, you must have access to the SAS windowing environment, SAS Enterprise Guide, SAS Studio, or SAS University Edition.

Exam Objectives and Updates to This Book

The current exam objectives and a list of any updates to this book are available at www.sas.com/certify (https://www.sas.com/certify). Exam objectives are subject to change.

Take a Practice Exam

Practice exams are available for purchase through SAS and Pearson VUE. For more information about practice exams, see https://www.sas.com/certification/sas-practice-exams.html (https://www.sas.com/certification/sas-practice-exams.html)

Registering for the Exam

To register for the SAS 9.4 Advanced Programming Performance-Based Exam, see the SAS Global Certification website at www.sas.com/certify (https://www.sas.com/certify).

Additional Resources for Learning SAS Programming

From SAS Software	
Help	• SAS®9: Select **Help** ⇨ **SAS Help and Documentation**. • SAS Enterprise Guide: Select **Help** ⇨ **SAS Enterprise Guide Help**. • SAS Studio: Select the Help icon ⓘ.
Documentation	• SAS®9: Select **Help** ⇨ **SAS Help and Documentation**. • SAS Enterprise Guide: Access documentation on the web. • SAS Studio: Select the Help icon ⓘ and then click **Help**.

On the Web	
Base SAS Glossary	support.sas.com/baseglossary (http://support.sas.com/baseglossary)
Bookstore	www.sas.com/books (http://www.sas.com/books/)
Certification	www.sas.com/certify (https://www.sas.com/certify)
Communities	communities.sas.com (https://communities.sas.com)
Knowledge Base	support.sas.com/notes (https://support.sas.com/notes/)
Learning Center	www.sas.com/learn (https://www.sas.com/learn)
SAS Documentation	support.sas.com/documentation (https://support.sas.com/documentation/) documentation.sas.com (https://documentation.sas.com)
SAS OnDemand	support.sas.com/ondemand/ (https://support.sas.com/ondemand/)
Technical Support	support.sas.com (https://support.sas.com/en/technical-support.html). and click **Technical Support**.
Tip Sheets	support.sas.com/professional-tipsheet (https://support.sas.com/professional-tipsheet)
Training	www.sas.com/training (https://www.sas.com/training)

Syntax Conventions

In this book, SAS syntax looks like this example:

DATA *output-SAS-data-set*
    (**DROP**=*variables(s)* | **KEEP**=*variables(s)*);
  SET *SAS-data-set* <*options*>;
  BY *variable(s)*;
RUN;

Here are the conventions that are used in the example:

- **DATA**, **DROP=**, **KEEP=**, **SET**, **BY**, and **RUN** are in uppercase bold because they must be spelled as shown.
- *output-SAS-data-set*, *variable(s)*, *SAS-data-set*, and *options* are in italics because each represents a value that you supply.
- *<options>* is enclosed in angle brackets because it is optional syntax.
- **DROP=** and **KEEP=** are separated by a vertical bar (|) to indicate that they are mutually exclusive.

The example syntax that is shown in this book includes only what you need to know in order to prepare for the certification exam. For complete syntax, see the appropriate SAS reference guide.

Using Sample Data

Setting Up Practice Data for SAS OnDemand for Academics

To set up your sample data program in SAS OnDemand:

1. Navigate to https://github.com/sassoftware/sas-cert-prep-data.
2. Click the professional-prep-guide directory.
3. Open the **cre8data.sas** program and click **Raw**. Right-click anywhere on the screen and select **Save As**. Save the **cre8data.sas** program to a location that is accessible to SAS.
4. Open the **cre8premdata.sas** program and click **Raw**. Right-click anywhere on the screen and select **Save As**. Save the **cre8premdata.sas** program to the same location as **cre8data.sas**.
5. Log on to SAS OnDemand for Academics and open SAS Studio.
6. Right-click the **Files** (Home) folder, and then select **New→Folder**.
7. Name the new folder **certadv** and click **Save**.
8. Right-click the **certadv** folder and select **Upload Files**.
9. Click **Choose Files** and navigate to the **certadv** folder within the practice-data folder on your local machine.
10. Select all program files and click **Open**. All available programs are listed under **Select Files**. Click **Upload**.
11. Open and edit the **cre8data.sas** program.
12. In the Path macro variable, replace **/folders/myfolders** with the path to the **certadv** folder. Right-click the **certadv** folder in SAS Studio and click **Properties**. Copy the path in the Location box and paste it into your %LET statement.
13. Save and then run the **cre8data.sas** program.

Your practice data is now created and ready for you to use.

Note: When you end your SAS session, the Path macro variable in the **cre8data.sas** program is reset. To avoid having to rerun **cre8data.sas** every time, run the **libname.sas** program from your sample data folder to restore the libraries.

Setting Up Practice Data in Other SAS Environments

To complete examples in this book, you must have access to the SAS windowing environment, SAS Enterprise Guide, or SAS Studio (or SAS University Edition). To access the sample data files and create your practice data:

1. Navigate to https://github.com/sassoftware/sas-cert-prep-data.

2. Click the professional-prep-guide directory.

3. Open the **cre8data.sas** program and click **Raw**. Right-click anywhere on the screen and select **Save As**. Save the **cre8data.sas** program to a location that is accessible to SAS. It is recommended that you create a new folder named **Certadv** in the location that is accessible to SAS and save the **cre8data.sas** program in the **Certadv** folder. The librefs that are associated with this book use Certadv as the libref name.

4. Open the **cre8premdata.sas** program and click **Raw**. Right-click anywhere on the screen and select **Save As**. Save the **cre8premdata.sas** program to the same location as **cre8data.sas**.

5. Open the **cre8data.sas** program in the SAS environment of your choice. SAS windowing environment: Click File→ **Open Program**, and then navigate to the **Certadv** folder in the practice-data folder. SAS Studio: In the Navigation pane, expand **Files and Folders** and then navigate to the **Certadv** folder within the practice-data folder. SAS Enterprise Guide: In the **Servers** list, expand **Servers → Local → Files**, and then navigate to the **Certadv** folder in the practice-data folder.

6. In the Path macro variable, replace **/folders/myfolders** with the path to the folder where you saved your practice data and run the program **%let path=/folders/myfolders/my-folder-name;**

Important: The location that you specify for the Path macro variable and the location of your downloaded SAS programs should be the same location. Otherwise, the **cre8data.sas** program cannot create the practice data.

Your practice data is now created and ready for you to use.

Note: When you end your SAS session, the Path macro variable in the **cre8data.sas** program is reset. To avoid having to rerun **cre8data.sas** every time, run the **libname.sas** program from your sample data folder to restore the libraries.

Accessibility Features of the Prep Guide

Overview

The *SAS Certified Professional Prep Guide: Advanced Programming Using SAS 9.4* is a test preparation document that uses the following environments and products:

- SAS windowing environment
- SAS Enterprise Guide
- SAS Studio or SAS University Edition

Accessibility Documentation Help

The following table contains accessibility information for the listed products:

Accessibility Documentation Links

Product or Environment	Where to Find Accessibility Documentation
Base SAS (Microsoft Windows, UNIX, and z/OS)	https://support.sas.com/en/software/base-sas-support.html (https://support.sas.com/en/software/base-sas-support.html)
SAS Enterprise Guide	https://support.sas.com/content/support/en/software/enterprise-guide-support.html (https://support.sas.com/content/support/en/software/enterprise-guide-support.html)
SAS Studio	support.sas.com/studioaccess (https://support.sas.com/studioaccess)

Documentation Format

Contact accessibility@sas.com if you need this document in an alternative digital format.

Part 1

SQL Processing with SAS

Chapter 1
PROC SQL Fundamentals *3*

Chapter 2
Creating and Managing Tables *43*

Chapter 3
Joining Tables Using PROC SQL *65*

Chapter 4
Joining Tables Using Set Operators *95*

Chapter 5
Using Subqueries *131*

Chapter 6
Advanced SQL Techniques *155*

Chapter 1
PROC SQL Fundamentals

PROC SQL Basics 4
    What Is PROC SQL? 4
    PROC SQL Syntax 5

The PROC SQL SELECT Statement 5
    A Brief Overview 5
    SELECT Statement Syntax 5
    Example: Selecting Columns 6
    Example: Displaying All Columns Using SELECT * 7
    Example: Using the FEEDBACK Option 7
    Example: Creating a New Column 8
    Example: Eliminating Duplicate Rows from Output 9

The FROM Clause 9
    FROM Clause Syntax 9
    Example: Querying a Single Table Using the FROM Clause 9

The WHERE Clause 10
    A Brief Overview 10
    WHERE Clause Syntax 10
    Example: Using the WHERE Clause 10
    Subsetting Rows by Using Calculated Values 11
    Example: Using Calculated Values in a SELECT Clause 12
    Subsetting Rows Using Conditional Operators 13

The GROUP BY Clause 19
    A Brief Overview 19
    GROUP BY Clause Syntax 20
    Example: Determine Total Number of Miles Using the SUM Function 20
    Number of Argument and Summary Function Processing 21
    Groups and Summary Function Processing 22
    SELECT Clause Columns and Summary Function Processing 23
    Example: Using a Summary Function with a Single Argument (Column) 23
    Example: Using a Summary Function with Multiple Arguments (Columns) 24
    Example: Using a Summary Function with Columns outside the Function 24
    Example: Using a Summary Function with a GROUP BY Clause 25
    Counting Values by Using the COUNT Summary Function 26
    Example: Counting All Rows in a Table 27
    Example: Counting Rows within Groups of Data 27
    Counting All Nonmissing Values in a Column 28
    Example: Counting All Unique Values in a Column 28
    Example: Listing All Unique Values in a Column 28

The HAVING Clause	**29**
A Brief Overview	29
HAVING Clause Syntax	29
Subsetting Grouped Data	30
Example: Selecting Groups by Using the HAVING Clause	30
Understanding Data Remerging	31
The ORDER BY Clause	**32**
A Brief Overview	32
ORDER BY Clause Syntax	32
Example: Ordering Rows by the Values of a Single Column	33
Example: Ordering by Multiple Columns	34
Example: Ordering Columns by Position	34
PROC SQL Options	**35**
A Brief Overview	35
PROC SQL Statement Syntax	35
Using Invocation Options	36
Validating Query Syntax	**38**
A Brief Overview	38
Example: Using the NOEXEC Option	38
Example: Using the VALIDATE Keyword	39
Quiz	**39**

PROC SQL Basics

What Is PROC SQL?

PROC SQL is the SAS implementation of Structured Query Language (SQL). SQL is a standardized language that is widely used to retrieve and update data in tables and in views that are based on those tables.

The following table compares terms that are used in data processing, SAS, and SQL.

This book uses all of these terms.

Data Processing	SAS	SQL
file	SAS data set	table or view
record	observation	row
field	variable	column

PROC SQL can often be used as an alternative to other SAS procedures or the DATA step. Use PROC SQL for tasks such as these:

- retrieve data from and manipulate SAS tables
- add or modify data values in a table
- add, modify, or drop columns in a table
- create tables and views

- join multiple tables (when they contain columns with the same name)
- generate reports

PROC SQL Syntax

The SQL procedure is initiated with a PROC SQL statement. You can use multiple statements within a PROC SQL step. Each statement defines a process and is executed immediately. Each statement must end with a semicolon. The SQL procedure is terminated with a QUIT statement.

Syntax, SQL procedure:

PROC SQL <*options*>;
   statements;
QUIT;

The PROC SQL SELECT Statement

A Brief Overview

The SELECT statement retrieves and displays data. It consists of a SELECT clause and several optional clauses that can be used within the SELECT statement. Each clause begins with a keyword and is followed by one or more components. The optional clauses name the input data set, subset, group, or sort the data.

A PROC SQL step that contains one or more SELECT statements is referred to as a *PROC SQL query*. The SELECT statement is only one of several statements that can be used with PROC SQL.

SELECT Statement Syntax

The SELECT statement is the primary tool of PROC SQL. Using the SELECT statement, you can identify, manipulate, and retrieve columns of data from one or more tables and views. The SELECT statement must contain a SELECT clause and a FROM clause, both of which are required in a PROC SQL query.

Syntax, SELECT statement:

PROC SQL <*options*>;
   SELECT *column-1* <,...*column-n*>
      FROM *input-table*
      <WHERE clause>
      <GROUP BY clause>
      <HAVING clause>
      <ORDER BY clause>
   ;
QUIT;

When you construct a SELECT statement, you must specify the clauses in the following order:

- The SELECT clause selects columns.
- The FROM clause selects one or more source tables or views.
- The WHERE clause enables you to filter your data.
- The GROUP BY clause enables you to process data in groups.
- The HAVING clause works with the GROUP BY clause to filter grouped results.
- The ORDER BY clause specifies the order of the rows.

Example: Selecting Columns

To specify which columns to display in a query, write a SELECT clause. After the keyword SELECT, list one or more column names and separate the column names with commas. The SELECT clause specifies existing columns and can create columns. The existing columns are already stored in a table.

The following SELECT clause specifies the columns EmpID, JobCode, Salary, and bonus. The columns EmpID, JobCode, and Salary are existing columns. The column named Bonus is a new column. The column alias appears as a column heading in the output and matches the case that you used in the SELECT clause.

```
proc sql;
   select empid, jobcode, salary, salary*.06 as bonus
       from certadv.payrollmaster
       where salary<32000
       order by jobcode;
quit;
```

Output 1.1   PROC SQL Query Result

EmpID	JobCode	Salary	bonus
1970	FA1	$31,661	1899.66
1422	FA1	$31,436	1886.16
1113	FA1	$31,314	1878.84
1132	FA1	$31,378	1882.68
1094	FA1	$31,175	1870.5
1789	SCP	$25,656	1539.36
1564	SCP	$26,366	1581.96
1354	SCP	$25,669	1540.14
1101	SCP	$26,212	1572.72
1658	SCP	$25,120	1507.2
1405	SCP	$25,278	1516.68
1104	SCP	$25,124	1507.44

Example: Displaying All Columns Using SELECT *

Use an asterisk (*) in the SELECT clause to display all columns in the order in which they are stored in a table. All rows are displayed, by default, unless you limit or subset them.

The following SELECT statement displays all columns and rows in the table Certadv.Staffchanges. Certadv.Staffchanges lists all employees in a company who have had changes in their employment status.

```
proc sql;
   select *
       from certadv.staffchanges;
quit;
```

*Output 1.2   PROC SQL Query Result of SELECT **

EmpID	LastName	FirstName	City	State	PhoneNumber
1639	CARTER	KAREN	STAMFORD	CT	203/781-8839
1065	CHAPMAN	NEIL	NEW YORK	NY	718/384-5618
1561	SANDERS	RAYMOND	NEW YORK	NY	212/588-6615
1221	WALTERS	DIANE	NEW YORK	NY	718/384-1918
1447	BRIDESTON	AMY	NEW YORK	NY	718/384-1213
1998	POWELL	JIM	NEW YORK	NY	718/384-8642

Example: Using the FEEDBACK Option

When you specify SELECT * you can use the FEEDBACK option in the PROC SQL statement to write the expanded list of columns to the SAS log. For example, the PROC SQL query shown below contains the FEEDBACK option:

```
proc sql feedback;
   select *
       from certadv.staffchanges;
quit;
```

The following is written to the SAS log.

Log 1.1   SAS Log

```
NOTE: Statement transforms to:

      select STAFFCHANGES.EmpID, STAFFCHANGES.LastName, STAFFCHANGES.FirstName,
STAFFCHANGES.City, STAFFCHANGES.State, STAFFCHANGES.PhoneNumber
         from CERTADV.STAFFCHANGES;
```

The FEEDBACK option is a debugging tool that lets you see exactly what is being submitted to the SQL processor. The resulting message in the SAS log expands asterisks (*) into column lists. It also resolves macro variables and places parentheses around expressions to show their order of evaluation.

Example: Creating a New Column

You can create new columns that contain either text or a calculation. New columns appear in output, along with any existing columns that are selected. The new columns exist only for the duration of the query, unless a table or a view is created.

To create a new column, include any valid SAS expression in the SELECT clause list of columns. You can assign a column alias, a name, to a new column by using the keyword AS followed by the name that you would like to use.

Note: A column alias must follow the rules for SAS names.

In the following example, an expression is used to calculate the new column, Bonus. The value of the new column is Salary multiplied by 0.06. The keyword AS is used to assign the column alias Bonus to the new column.

```
proc sql;
   select empid, jobcode, salary, salary*.06 as bonus
      from certadv.payrollmaster
      where salary<32000
      order by jobcode;
quit;
```

Output 1.3 PROC SQL Query Result: New Column – Bonus

EmpID	JobCode	Salary	bonus
1970	FA1	$31,661	1899.66
1422	FA1	$31,436	1886.16
1113	FA1	$31,314	1878.84
1132	FA1	$31,378	1882.68
1094	FA1	$31,175	1870.5
1789	SCP	$25,656	1539.36
1564	SCP	$26,366	1581.96
1354	SCP	$25,669	1540.14
1101	SCP	$26,212	1572.72
1658	SCP	$25,120	1507.2
1405	SCP	$25,278	1516.68
1104	SCP	$25,124	1507.44

A column alias is useful because it enables you to reference the column elsewhere in the query. The column alias appears as a column heading in the output and matches the case that you used in the SELECT clause. You can specify a label for an existing or a new column in the SELECT clause. If both a label and a column alias are specified for a new column, the label is displayed as the column heading in the output[1]. If only a column alias is specified, specify the column alias exactly as you want it to appear in the output.

---

[1] Displaying labels for a column is further determined by the LABEL|NOLABEL system option. If this option is set to NOLABEL, the label not displayed as the column heading in the output. This option can be set by your site administrator.

Example: Eliminating Duplicate Rows from Output

You can use the DISTINCT keyword to eliminate duplicate rows. The DISTINCT keyword applies to all columns, and only those columns, that are listed in the SELECT clause.

```
proc sql;
    select distinct flightnumber, destination
        from certadv.internationalflights;
quit;
```

Note: The DISTINCT keyword is identical to UNIQUE. Although the UNIQUE keyword is identical to DISTINCT, it is not an ANSI standard.

Output 1.4 PROC SQL Query Result: Unique Values

FlightNumber	Destination
132	YYZ
182	YYZ
219	LHR
271	CDG
387	CPH
622	FRA
821	LHR

The FROM Clause

FROM Clause Syntax

After writing the SELECT clause, use the FROM clause to specify the tables or views to be queried. Enter the keyword FROM, followed by the name of the table.

Syntax, FROM clause:

PROC SQL <*options*>;
    SELECT *column-1* <,...*column-n*>
        FROM *input-tables*;
QUIT;

Example: Querying a Single Table Using the FROM Clause

Suppose you want to query a permanent SAS table called Payrollmaster, which is stored in the Certadv library. The FROM clause specifies Certadv.Payrollmaster to be queried.

```
proc sql;
```

```
          select empid, jobcode, salary, salary*0.06 as bonus
             from certadv.payrollmaster
             where salary<32000
             order by jobcode;
       quit;
```

The WHERE Clause

A Brief Overview

The WHERE clause enables you to subset data based on a condition that each row of the table must satisfy. PROC SQL output includes only those rows that satisfy the condition. The WHERE clause is used within the SELECT statement in a PROC SQL step. The expression in the WHERE clause can be any valid SQL expression. In the WHERE clause, you can specify any columns from the underlying tables that are specified in the FROM clause. The columns that are specified in the WHERE clause do not have to be specified in the SELECT clause.

WHERE Clause Syntax

The WHERE clause must come after the SELECT and FROM clauses.

Syntax, WHERE clause:

PROC SQL *<options>*;
   SELECT *column-1 <,...column-n>*
      FROM *input-tables*
      WHERE *expression*;
QUIT;

expression
   can be either character or numeric values. Character values are case sensitive and must be enclosed in single or double quotation marks. Double quotation marks are a SAS enhancement and typically are not allowed in database systems. Numeric values are not enclosed in quotation marks and must be standard numeric values. You cannot include special symbols such as commas or dollar signs when referencing numeric values.

To reference date and time values, use one of the following forms:

- A SAS date value is a date written in the following form: '*ddmmm<yy>yy*'d or "*ddmmm<yy>yy*"d.
- A SAS time constant is a time written in the following form:'*hh:mm<:ss.s>*'t or "*hh:mm<:ss.s>*"t.
- A SAS datetime constant is a datetime value written in the following form: '*ddmmm<yy>yy:hh:mm<:ss.s>*'dt or "*ddmmm<yy>yy:hh:mm<:ss.s>*"dt.

Example: Using the WHERE Clause

In the following PROC SQL query, the WHERE clause selects rows in which the value of Salary is less than $32,000.

```
proc sql;
   select empid, jobcode, salary, salary*0.06 as bonus
      from certadv.payrollmaster
      where salary<32000
      order by jobcode;
quit;
```

Output 1.5 PROC SQL Query Result: Subset of Payroll with Salaries Less Than $32,000

EmpID	JobCode	Salary	bonus
1970	FA1	$31,661	1899.66
1422	FA1	$31,436	1886.16
1113	FA1	$31,314	1878.84
1132	FA1	$31,378	1882.68
1094	FA1	$31,175	1870.5
1789	SCP	$25,656	1539.36
1564	SCP	$26,366	1581.96
1354	SCP	$25,669	1540.14
1101	SCP	$26,212	1572.72
1658	SCP	$25,120	1507.2
1405	SCP	$25,278	1516.68
1104	SCP	$25,124	1507.44

Subsetting Rows by Using Calculated Values

Understanding How PROC SQL Processes Calculated Columns

An earlier example showed how to define a new column by using the SELECT clause and performing a calculation. The following PROC SQL query creates the new column Total by adding the values of three existing columns: Boarded, Transferred, and Nonrevenue.

```
proc sql outobs=10;
   select flightnumber, date, destination,
          boarded + transferred + nonrevenue as Total
      from certadv.marchflights;
quit;
```

You can also use a calculated column in the WHERE clause to subset rows. However, because of the way in which SQL queries are processed, you cannot just specify the column alias in the WHERE clause. To see what happens, take the preceding PROC SQL query and add a WHERE clause in the SELECT statement to reference the calculated column Total.

```
proc sql outobs=10;
   select flightnumber, date, destination,
          boarded + transferred + nonrevenue as Total
      from certadv.marchflights
      where total < 100;
quit;
```

When this query is executed, the following error message is displayed in the SAS log.

```
ERROR: The following columns were not found in the contributing tables: total.
```

This error message is generated because, in SQL queries, the WHERE clause is processed before the SELECT clause. The SQL processor looks in the table for each column named in the WHERE clause. The table Certadv.Marchflights does not contain a column named Total, so SAS generates an error message.

Note: To avoid the error message, you must use the CALCULATED keyword.

Example: Using Calculated Values in a WHERE Clause

Use the column alias and the CALCULATED keyword in the WHERE clause to refer to a calculated value. The CALCULATED keyword tells PROC SQL that the value is calculated within the query.

```
proc sql outobs=10;
   select flightnumber, date, destination,
         boarded + transferred + nonrevenue as Total
      from certadv.marchflights
      where calculated total < 100;
quit;
```

Output 1.6 PROC SQL Query Result: Using the CALCULATED Keyword

FlightNumber	Date	Destination	Total
982	01MAR2013	DFW	70
416	01MAR2013	WAS	93
829	01MAR2013	WAS	96
416	02MAR2013	WAS	90
302	02MAR2013	WAS	93
132	03MAR2013	YYZ	88
921	03MAR2013	DFW	85
290	05MAR2013	WAS	55
523	05MAR2013	ORD	59
416	05MAR2013	WAS	31

Note: As an alternative to using the keyword CALCULATED, repeat the calculation in the WHERE clause. However, this method is inefficient because PROC SQL must perform the calculation twice. It is the ANSI method that recalculates the WHERE clause. In the preceding query, here is what the alternate WHERE statement would be:

```
where boarded + transferred + nonrevenue <100;
```

Example: Using Calculated Values in a SELECT Clause

You can also use the CALCULATED keyword in other parts of a query. In the following example, the SELECT clause calculates the new column Total and then calculates a second new column based on Total. To create the second calculated column, you must specify the keyword CALCULATED in the SELECT clause.

```
proc sql outobs=10;
   select flightnumber, date, destination,
          boarded + transferred + nonrevenue as Total,
          calculated total/2 as Half
      from certadv.marchflights;
quit;
```

This query produces the following output.

Output 1.7 PROC SQL Query Result: Using the CALCULATED Keyword

FlightNumber	Date	Destination	Total	Half
182	01MAR2013	YYZ	123	61.5
114	01MAR2013	LAX	196	98
202	01MAR2013	ORD	167	83.5
219	01MAR2013	LHR	222	111
439	01MAR2013	LAX	185	92.5
387	01MAR2013	CPH	163	81.5
290	01MAR2013	WAS	119	59.5
523	01MAR2013	ORD	200	100
982	01MAR2013	DFW	70	35
622	01MAR2013	FRA	227	113.5

Subsetting Rows Using Conditional Operators

A Brief Overview

In the WHERE clause, you can specify any valid SAS expression to subset or restrict the data that is displayed in output. The expression might contain any of various types of operators, such as the following.

Type of Operator	Example
comparison	where membertype='GOLD'
logical	where visits<=3 or status='new'
concatenation	where name=trim(last) ||', '||first

Using Operators in PROC SQL

Comparison, logical, and concatenation operators are used in PROC SQL in the same way as they are used in other SAS procedures.

In PROC SQL queries, you can also use the following conditional operators. All of these operators can be used in other SAS procedures.

Conditional Operator	Looks for These Values	Example
BETWEEN-AND	values that occur within an inclusive range	`where salary between 70000 and 80000`
CONTAINS or ?	values that contain a specified string	`where name contains 'ER'` `where name ? 'ER'`
IN	values that match one of a list of values	`where code in ('PT' , 'NA', 'FA')`
IS MISSING or IS NULL	missing values	`where dateofbirth is missing` `where dateofbirth is null`
LIKE (with %,)	values that match a specified pattern	`where address like '% P%PLACE'`
=*	values that sound like a specified value	`where lastname=* 'Smith'`

TIP To create a negative condition, you can precede any of these conditional operators with the NOT operator.

Using the BETWEEN-AND Operator to Select within a Range of Values

Use the BETWEEN-AND operator in the WHERE clause to select rows that are based on a range of numeric or character values. The BETWEEN-AND operator is inclusive. The values that you specify as limits for the range of values are included in the query results, in addition to any values that occur between the limits.

Syntax, BETWEEN-AND operator:

BETWEEN *value-1* **AND** *value-2*

value-1
  is the value at one end of the range.

value-2
  is the value at the other end of the range.

Note: When specifying the limits for the range of values, it is not necessary to specify the smaller value first.

Here are a few examples of WHERE clauses.

Example	Returns Rows That Contain These Values
`where date between '01mar2018'd and '07mar2018'd` In this example, the values are specified as date constants.	the value of Date is `01mar2018`, `07mar2018`, or any date value in between
`where salary between 70000 and 80000`	the value of Salary is `70000`, `80000`, or any numeric value in between

Example	Returns Rows That Contain These Values
`where salary not between 70000 and 80000`	the value of Salary is not between or equal to **70000** and **80000**

Using the CONTAINS Operator to Select a String

The CONTAINS or question mark (?) operator is usually used to select rows for which a character column includes a particular string. These operators are interchangeable.

Syntax, CONTAINS operator:

SQL-expression **CONTAINS** *SQL-expression*

SQL-expression **?** *SQL-expression*

SQL-expression
> is a character column, string (character constant), or expression. A string is a sequence of characters to be matched that must be enclosed in quotation marks.

Note: PROC SQL retrieves a row for output no matter where the string (or second SQL-expression) occurs within the column's (or first SQL-expression's) values. Matching is case sensitive when making comparisons.

Note: The CONTAINS or question mark (?) operator is not part of the ANSI standard; it is a SAS enhancement.

The following PROC SQL query uses CONTAINS to select rows in which the Name column contains the string `ER`. As the output shows, all rows that contain `ER` anywhere within the Name column are displayed.

```
proc sql;
   select name
      from certadv.frequentflyers
      where name contains 'ER';
quit;
```

Output 1.8 *PROC SQL Query Result: Name Containing String 'ER' (partial output)*

Name
COOPER, LESLIE
COOPER, ANTHONY
COOK, JENNIFER
FOSTER, GERALD
BRADLEY, JEREMY
BURKE, CHRISTOPHER
AVERY, JERRY
EDGERTON, JOSHUA
SAYERS, RANDY
WANG, CHRISTOPHER

Using the IN Operator to Select Values from a List

Use the IN operator to select only the rows that match one of the values in a list of fixed values, either numeric or character.

Syntax, IN operator:

column **IN** (*constant-1*<,...*constant-n*>)

column
: specifies the selected column name.

constant-1 and *constant-n*
: represent a list that contains one or more specific values. The list of values must be enclosed in parentheses and separated by either commas or spaces. Values can be either numeric or character. Character values must be enclosed in quotation marks.

Here are examples of WHERE clauses that contain the IN operator.

Example	Returns Rows That Contain These Values
`where jobcategory in ('PT','NA','FA')`	the value of JobCategory is **PT**, **NA**, or **FA**.
`where dayofweek in (2,4,6)`	the value of DayOfWeek is **2**, **4**, or **6**.
`where chesspiece not in ('pawn','king','queen')`	the value of Chesspiece is anything but **pawn**, **king**, or **queen**.

Using the IS MISSING or IS NULL Operator to Select Missing Values

Use the IS MISSING or IS NULL operator to select rows that contain missing values, both character and numeric. These operators are interchangeable.

Syntax, IS MISSING or IS NULL operator:

column **IS MISSING**

column **IS NULL**

column
: specifies the selected column name.

Note: The IS MISSING operator is not part of the ANSI standard for SQL. It is a SAS enhancement.

Suppose you want to find out whether the table Certadv.Marchflights has any missing values in the column Boarded. You can use the following PROC SQL query to retrieve rows from the table that have missing values:

```
proc sql;
   select boarded, transferred, nonrevenue, deplaned
      from certadv.marchflights
      where boarded is missing;
quit;
```

The following output displays two rows in the table that have missing values for Boarded.

Output 1.9   PROC SQL Query Result: IS MISSING

Boarded	Transferred	NonRevenue	Deplaned
.	9	0	210
.	16	5	79

TIP   Alternatively, you can specify missing values without using the IS MISSING or IS NULL operator, as shown in the following examples:

```
where boarded = .
where flight = ' '
```

However, the advantage of using the IS MISSING or IS NULL operator is that you do not have to specify the data type (character or numeric) of the column.

Using the LIKE Operator to Select a Pattern

To select rows that have values that match a specific pattern of characters rather than a fixed character string, use the LIKE operator. For example, using the LIKE operator, you can select all rows in which the LastName value starts with H. (If you wanted to select all rows in which the last name contains the string HAR, you would use the CONTAINS operator.)

Syntax, LIKE operator:

column **LIKE** *'pattern'*

column
   specifies the column name.

pattern
   specifies the pattern to be matched and contains one or both of the special characters underscore (_) and percent sign (%). The entire pattern must be enclosed in quotation marks and matching is case sensitive.

When you use the LIKE operator in a query, PROC SQL uses pattern matching to compare each value in the specified column with the pattern that you specify using the LIKE operator. The query output displays all rows in which there is a match.

You specify a pattern using one or both of the special characters shown below.

Special Character	Represents This Pattern
underscore (_)	any single character
percent sign (%)	any sequence of zero or more characters

Note: The underscore (_) and percent sign (%) are sometimes referred to as wildcard characters.

To specify a pattern, combine one or both of the special characters with any other characters that you want to match. The special characters can appear before, after, or on both sides of other characters.

The following PROC SQL query uses the LIKE operator to find all frequent-flyer club members whose street name begins with P and ends with the word PLACE. The following PROC SQL step performs this query:

```
proc sql;
   select ffid, name, address
      from certadv.frequentflyers
      where address like '%P%PLACE';
quit;
```

The pattern `'%P%PLACE'` specifies the following sequence:

- any number of characters (%)
- a space
- the letter P
- any number of characters (%)
- the word PLACE

Output 1.10 PROC SQL Query Result: PLACE

FFID	Name	Address
WD8375	COOPER, ANTHONY	12 PIEDPIPER PLACE
WD6271	MORGAN, GEORGE	39 PEPPER PLACE
WD6184	STARR, WILLIAM	12 PINEY PLACE
WD2118	JOHNSON, ANTHONY	78 PIPER PLACE
WD3827	KING, WILLIAM	14 PICTURE PLACE
WD8789	HOWARD, LEONARD	45 PECAN PLACE
WD6169	WILDER, NEIL	78 PUMPKIN PLACE
WD8667	YOUNG, DEBORAH	53 PINE PLACE
WD5687	EDWARDS, JENNIFER	3 PEGBOARD PLACE
WD1673	MURPHY, ALICE	15 HUMPHREY PLACE

Using the Sounds-Like (=*) Operator to Select a Spelling Variation

Use the sounds-like (=*) operator in the WHERE clause to select rows that contain a value that sounds like another value that you specify.

Syntax, sounds-like (=*) operator:

SQL-expression =* *SQL-expression*

SQL-expression
 is a character column, string (character constant), or expression. A string is a sequence of characters to be matched that must be enclosed in quotation marks.

The sounds-like (=*) operator uses the SOUNDEX algorithm to compare each value of a column (or other SQL-expression) with the word or words (or other SQL-expression) that you specify. Any rows that contain a spelling variation of the value that you specified are selected for output.

For example, here is a WHERE clause that contains the sounds-like operator:

```
where lastname =* 'Smith';
```

The sounds-like operator does not always select all possible values. For example, suppose you use the preceding WHERE clause to select rows from the following list of names that sound like Smith:

- Schmitt
- Smith
- Smithson
- Smitt
- Smythe

Two of the names in this list will not be selected: Schmitt and Smithson.

Note: The SOUNDEX algorithm is English-biased and is less useful for languages other than English.

The GROUP BY Clause

A Brief Overview

Use the GROUP BY clause to group your data for summarization. You can use the GROUP BY clause to do the following:

- classify the data into groups based on the values of one or more columns.
- group multiple columns, or separate the column names with commas within the GROUP BY clause. You can use aggregate functions with any of the columns that you select.

Note: If you specify a GROUP BY clause in a query that does not contain a summary function, your clause is changed to an ORDER BY clause, and a message is written to the SAS log.

To summarize data, you can use the following summary functions with PROC SQL. Notice that some functions have more than one name to accommodate both SAS and SQL conventions. Where multiple names are listed, the first name is the SQL name.

Note: The summary functions listed below are limited for the purposes of this book.

AVG, MEAN	mean or average of values
COUNT, FREQ, N	number of nonmissing values
CSS	corrected sum of squares
CV	coefficient of variation (percent)
MAX	largest value
MIN	smallest value
NMISS	number of missing values

PRT	probability of a greater absolute value of student's *t*
RANGE	range of values
STD	standard deviation
STDERR	standard error of the mean
SUM	sum of values
T	student's *t* value for testing the hypothesis that the population mean is zero
USS	uncorrected sum of squares
VAR	variance

PROC SQL calculates summary functions and writes output results in different ways, depending on a combination of factors. Here are four key factors:

- whether the summary function specifies one or multiple columns as arguments
- whether the query contains a GROUP BY clause
- if the summary function is specified in a SELECT clause, whether there are additional columns listed that are outside a summary function
- whether the WHERE clause, if there is one, contains only columns that are specified in the SELECT clause

GROUP BY Clause Syntax

Syntax, GROUP BY clause:

PROC SQL <*options*>;
    SELECT *column-1* <,...*column-n*>
        FROM *input-tables*
        WHERE *expression*
        GROUP BY *column-name* <,*column-name*>;
QUIT;

Example: Determine Total Number of Miles Using the SUM Function

Suppose you want to determine the total number of miles traveled by frequent-flyer program members in each of three membership classes (Gold, Silver, and Bronze). Frequent-flyer program information is stored in the table Certadv.Frequentflyers. To summarize your data, you can submit the following PROC SQL step:

```
proc sql;
    select membertype, sum(milestraveled) as TotalMiles   /*1*/
        from certadv.frequentflyers
```

```
        group by membertype;                              /* 2 */
quit;
```

1. The SUM function totals the values of the MilesTraveled column to create the TotalMiles column.

2. The GROUP BY clause groups the data by the values of MemberType.

The results show total miles by membership class (MemberType).

Output 1.11 PROC SQL Query Result: Total Number of Miles by MemberType

MemberType	TotalMiles
BRONZE	3229225
GOLD	2903569
SILVER	4345169

Number of Argument and Summary Function Processing

Summary functions specify one or more arguments in parentheses. In the examples shown in this chapter, the arguments are always columns in the table being queried.

Note: The ANSI-standard summary functions, such as AVG and COUNT, can be used only with a single argument. The SAS summary functions, such as MEAN and N, can be used with either single or multiple arguments.

The following table shows how the number of columns that are specified as arguments affects the way that PROC SQL calculates a summary function.

Summary Function Behavior	Calculation	Sample Code and Result
specifies one column as argument	performed down the column	```proc sql;
select sum(boarded), sum(transferred),sum(nonrevenue)
as Total
from certadv.marchflights;
quit;```

Partial View of Certadv.Marchflights

Boarded	Transferred	Nonrevenue
104	16	3
172	18	6
151	11	5

Partial Output: SQL Query Result

		Total
83782	9148	2612

Summary Function Behavior	Calculation	Sample Code and Result
| specifies multiple columns as arguments | performed across columns for each row | ```
proc sql;
   select sum(boarded,transferred,nonrevenue)
          as Total
      from certadv.marchflights;
quit;
```  Partial View of Certadv.Marchflights  | Boarded | Transferred | Nonrevenue | | --- | --- | --- | | 104 | 16 | 3 | | 172 | 18 | 6 | | 151 | 11 | 5 |  Boarded + Transferred + Nonrevenue = Total  Partial Output: SQL Query Result  | Total | | --- | | 123 | | 196 | | 167 | |

Groups and Summary Function Processing

Summary functions perform calculations on groups of data. When PROC SQL processes a summary function, it looks for a GROUP BY clause:

GROUP BY Clause Presence	PROC SQL Behavior	Example
| is not present in the query | applies the function to the entire table | ```
proc sql;
   select jobcode, avg(salary)
          as AvgSalary
      from certadv.payrollmaster;
quit;
``` |
| is present in the query | applies the function to each group specified in the GROUP BY clause | ```
proc sql;
   select jobcode, avg(salary)
          as AvgSalary
      from certadv.payrollmaster
      group by jobcode;
quit;
```  If a query contains a GROUP BY clause, all columns in the SELECT clause that do not contain a summary function should typically be listed in the GROUP BY clause. Otherwise, unexpected results might be returned. |
```

SELECT Clause Columns and Summary Function Processing

A SELECT clause that contains a summary function can also list additional columns that are not specified in the summary function. The presence of these additional columns in the SELECT clause list causes PROC SQL to display the output differently.

SELECT Clause Contents	PROC SQL Behavior	Example
| contains summary functions and no columns outside summary functions | calculates a single value by using the summary function for the entire table. However, if groups are specified in the GROUP BY clause, for each group it combines the information into a single row of output for the entire table. | ```
proc sql;
   select avg(salary)
          as AvgSalary
      from certadv.payrollmaster;
quit;
``` |
| contains summary functions and additional columns outside summary functions | calculates a single value for the entire table. However, if groups are specified, for each group it displays all rows of output within the single grouped value. If the data in the table is grouped by more than one value, then grouped values are repeated. | ```
proc sql;
   select EmpId,
          jobcode,
          dateofhire,
          avg(salary)
          as AvgSalary
      from certadv.payrollmaster
      group by jobcode;
quit;
``` |

Example: Using a Summary Function with a Single Argument (Column)

The following example illustrates a PROC SQL query that calculates the average salary for all employees who are listed in Certadv.Payrollmaster.

```
title 'Average Salary for All Employees';
proc sql;
   select avg(salary) as AvgSalary
      from certadv.payrollmaster;
quit;
```

The SELECT statement contains the summary function AVG with Salary as its argument. Because there is only one column as an argument, the function calculates the statistic down the Salary column to display a single value: the average salary for all employees.

Output 1.12 PROC SQL Query Result: Calculating Average Salary for All Employees

Average Salary for All Employees

AvgSalary
54079.62

Example: Using a Summary Function with Multiple Arguments (Columns)

Consider a PROC SQL query that contains a summary function with multiple columns as arguments. This query calculates the total number of passengers for each flight in March by adding the number of boarded, transferred, and nonrevenue passengers:

```
proc sql;
   select sum(boarded, transferred, nonrevenue) as Total
      from certadv.marchflights;
quit;
```

The SELECT clause contains the summary function SUM with three columns as arguments. Because the function contains multiple arguments, the statistic is calculated across the three columns for each row to produce the following output.

Output 1.13 PROC SQL Query Result: Calculating Total for 3 Arguments (partial output)

Total
123
196
167
222
185
163
119
200
70
227

Example: Using a Summary Function with Columns outside the Function

The following example illustrates calculating an average for each job group. The result is grouped by JobCode. Your first step is to add an existing code, Jobcode, to the SELECT clause list.

```
proc sql;
   select jobcode, avg(salary) as AvgSalary
      from certadv.payrollmaster;
quit;
```

As this result shows, adding a column to the SELECT clause that is not within a summary function causes PROC SQL to display all rows instead of a single value. To generate this output:

- PROC SQL calculated the average salary down the column as a single value (**54079.62**).
- PROC SQL displayed all rows in the output, because JobCode is not specified in a summary function.

Therefore, the single value for AvgSalary is repeated for each row. When you submit the query, SAS remerges the summary information with the JobCode values.

Note: The SAS log displays a message indicating that data remerging has occurred.

Output 1.14 *PROC SQL Query Result: Summary Function with Jobcode (partial output)*

JobCode	AvgSalary
TA2	54079.62
ME2	54079.62
ME1	54079.62
FA3	54079.62
TA3	54079.62
ME3	54079.62
SCP	54079.62
PT2	54079.62
TA2	54079.62
TA3	54079.62

Log 1.2 *SAS Log*

```
NOTE: The query requires remerging summary statistics back with the original
data.
```

Example: Using a Summary Function with a GROUP BY Clause

Using the query from the previous example, add a GROUP BY clause. The GROUP BY clause groups rows by JobCode, which results in one row per JobCode value. For example, you might have multiple JobCode values for FA2 but only one value of FA2 displayed in the output. In the SELECT clause, JobCode is specified but is not used as a summary function argument. Other changes to the query include specifying a format for the AvgSalary column.

```
proc sql;
   select jobcode, avg(salary) as AvgSalary format=dollar11.2
      from certadv.payrollmaster
      group by jobcode;
quit;
```

The summary function has been calculated for each JobCode group, and the results are grouped by JobCode.

Output 1.15 PROC SQL Query Result Grouped by JobCode

JobCode	AvgSalary
BCK	$36,111.89
FA1	$32,255.18
FA2	$39,181.50
FA3	$46,107.57
ME1	$39,900.50
ME2	$49,807.64
ME3	$59,374.86
NA1	$58,845.00
NA2	$73,336.00
PT1	$95,071.13
PT2	$122,253.40
PT3	$154,706.50
SCP	$25,632.14
TA1	$38,809.89
TA2	$47,004.90
TA3	$55,551.42

Counting Values by Using the COUNT Summary Function

Sometimes you want to count the number of rows in an entire table or in groups of rows. There are three main ways to use the COUNT function.

Form for COUNT	Result	Example
COUNT(*)	the total number of rows in a group or in a table	`select count(*) as Count`
COUNT(*column*)	the total number of rows in a group or in a table for which there is a nonmissing value in the selected column	`select count(jobcode) as Count`
COUNT(DISTINCT *column*)	the total number of unique values in a column	`select count(distinct jobcode)` `    as Count`

Note: When given a column entry, the COUNT summary function counts only the nonmissing values. Missing values are ignored. Many other summary functions also ignore missing values. When you use a summary function with data that contains missing values, the results might not provide the information that you expect.

> *TIP* To count the number of missing values, use the NMISS function.

Example: Counting All Rows in a Table

Suppose you want to know how many employees are listed in the table Certadv.Payrollmaster. This table contains a separate row for each employee, so counting the number of rows in the table gives you the number of employees.

```
proc sql;
   select count(*) as Count
      from certadv.payrollmaster;
quit;
```

Note: The COUNT summary function is the only function that enables you to use an asterisk (*) as an argument.

Output 1.16 PROC SQL Query Result: Counting All Rows in Certadv.Payrollmaster

Count
148

Example: Counting Rows within Groups of Data

You can also use COUNT(*) to count rows within groups of data. To do this, you specify the groups in the GROUP BY clause. Consider a more complex PROC SQL query that uses COUNT(*) with grouping. This time, the goal is to find the total number of employees within each job category, using the same table that was used previously.

```
proc sql;
   select substr(jobcode,1,2)      /*1*/
      label='Job Category',
      count(*) as Count             /*2*/
      from certadv.payrollmaster
      group by 1;                   /*3*/
quit;
```

This query defines two new columns in the SELECT clause.

1. The first column, which is labeled JobCategory, is created by using the SAS function SUBSTR. The SUBSTR function extracts the two-character job category from the existing JobCode field.

2. The second column, Count, is created by using the COUNT function.

3. The GROUP BY clause specifies that the results are to be grouped by the first defined column, which is referenced by 1 because the column was not assigned a name.

Output 1.17 PROC SQL Query Result: Count Rows within Groups of Data

Job Category	Count
BC	9
FA	34
ME	29
NA	8
PT	20
SC	7
TA	41

CAUTION:
> **Columns should not contain missing values.** When a column contains missing values, PROC SQL treats the missing values as a single group. This can produce unexpected results.

Counting All Nonmissing Values in a Column

Suppose you want to count all of the nonmissing values in a specific column instead of in the entire table. To do this, you specify the name of the column as an argument of the COUNT function.

If the table has no missing data, you get the same output as you would by using COUNT(*). However, if the variable column contained missing values, the query would produce a lower value of Count than the number of values in a column.

Example: Counting All Unique Values in a Column

To count all unique values in a column, add the keyword DISTINCT before the name of the column that is used as an argument.

```
proc sql;
   select count(distinct jobcode) as Count
      from certadv.payrollmaster;
quit;
```

This query counts 16 unique values for JobCode.

Output 1.18 PROC SQL Query Result: Counting Unique Values

Count
16

Example: Listing All Unique Values in a Column

To display the unique JobCode values, you can apply the method of eliminating duplicates, which was discussed earlier. The following query lists only the unique values for JobCode.

```
proc sql;
```

```
     select distinct jobcode
        from certadv.payrollmaster;
quit;
```

There are 16 job codes, so the output contains 16 rows.

Output 1.19 *PROC SQL Query Result: Displaying Distinct Values*

JobCode
BCK
FA1
FA2
FA3
ME1
ME2
ME3
NA1
NA2
PT1
PT2
PT3
SCP
TA1
TA2
TA3

The HAVING Clause

A Brief Overview

The HAVING clause tells PROC SQL how to filter the data after summarization. You can use a HAVING clause with a GROUP BY clause to filter grouped data. The HAVING clause affects groups in a way that is similar to how a WHERE clause affects individual rows. When you use a HAVING clause, PROC SQL displays only the groups that satisfy the HAVING expression.

Note: You can use summary functions in a HAVING clause but not in a WHERE clause. The HAVING clause is used with groups, but a WHERE clause can be used only with individual rows.

HAVING Clause Syntax

Syntax, HAVING clause:

PROC SQL *<options>*;
    SELECT *column-1 <,...column-n>*
        FROM *input-tables*
        WHERE *expression*
        GROUP BY *column-name <,column-name>*
        HAVING *expression*;
QUIT;

expression
    produces a value from a sequence of operands and operators.

Subsetting Grouped Data

The HAVING clause is used with at least one summary function and a GROUP BY clause to summarize groups of data in a table. A HAVING clause can be used in any valid SQL expression that is evaluated as either true or false for each group in a query. Alternatively, if the query involves remerged data, then the HAVING clause is evaluated for each row that participates in each group. The query must include one or more summary functions.

Typically, the GROUP BY clause is used with the HAVING clause and defines the group or groups to be evaluated. If you omit the GROUP BY clause, the summary function and the HAVING clause treat the table as one group.

Example: Selecting Groups by Using the HAVING Clause

Suppose you want to select only a subset of groups for your query output.

```
proc sql;
   select jobcode, avg(salary) as AvgSalary format=dollar11.2
      from certadv.payrollmaster
      group by jobcode
      having avg(salary)>56000;
quit;
```

TIP Alternatively, because the average salary is already calculated in the SELECT clause, the HAVING clause could specify the column alias AvgSalary:

```
having AvgSalary > 56000
```

The query output is shown below. This output is smaller than the previous output because only the values of JobCode that meet the condition in the HAVING clause are displayed.

Output 1.20 PROC SQL Query Result: Average Salaries over $56,000

JobCode	AvgSalary
ME3	$59,374.86
NA1	$58,845.00
NA2	$73,336.00
PT1	$95,071.13
PT2	$122,253.40
PT3	$154,706.50

Without a GROUP BY clause, the HAVING clause calculates the average salary for the table as a whole for all jobs in the company. The output contains either all the rows in the table if the average salary for the entire table is greater than $56,000, or none of the rows in the table if the average salary for the entire table is less than $56,000.

Understanding Data Remerging

Sometimes, when you use a summary function in a SELECT clause or a HAVING clause, PROC SQL must remerge the data (that is, it makes two passes through the table). You can modify your query to avoid remerging.

Consider a PROC SQL query that requires remerging. This query calculates each navigator's salary as a percentage of all navigators' salaries:

```
proc sql;
   select empid, salary,(salary/sum(salary)) as Percent format=percent8.2
      from certadv.payrollmaster
      where jobcode contains 'NA';
quit;
```

When you submit this query, the SAS log displays the following message.

Log 1.3 SAS Log

```
NOTE: The query requires remerging summary statistics back with the original
data.
```

Remerging occurs whenever any of the following conditions exist:

- The values returned by a summary function are used in a calculation.
- The SELECT clause specifies a column that contains a summary function and other columns that are not listed in a GROUP BY clause.
- The HAVING clause specifies one or more columns or column expressions that are not included in a subquery or a GROUP BY clause.

During remerging, PROC SQL makes two passes through the table:

1. PROC SQL calculates and returns the value of summary functions. PROC SQL also groups data according to the GROUP BY clause.

2. PROC SQL retrieves any additional columns and rows that it needs to display in the output. It uses the result from the summary function to calculate any arithmetic expressions in which the summary function participates.

The ORDER BY Clause

A Brief Overview

The order of rows in the output of a PROC SQL query cannot be guaranteed, unless you specify a sort order with the ORDER BY clause. Specify the keywords ORDER BY, followed by one or more column names separated by commas.

Figure 1.1 SORT Methods for ORDER BY

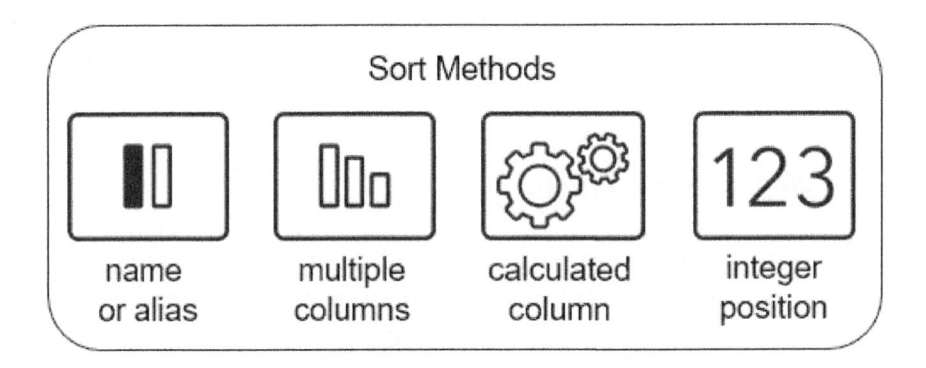

Sort Methods: name or alias, multiple columns, calculated column, integer position

Without an ORDER BY clause, the order of the output rows is determined by the internal processing of PROC SQL, the default collating sequence of SAS, and your operating environment. Therefore, if you want your result table to appear in a particular order, use the ORDER BY clause. Here are details about sort order:

- The PROC SQL default sort order is ascending.
- PROC SQL sorts missing values before nonmissing values. Therefore, when you specify ascending order, missing values appear first in the query results.
- When you use an ORDER BY clause, you change the order of the results but not the order of the rows that are stored in the source table.
- If multiple ORDER BY columns are specified, the first one determines the major sort order.

ORDER BY Clause Syntax

Syntax, ORDER BY clause:

PROC SQL <*options*>;
    SELECT *column-1* <,...*column-n*>
        FROM *input-tables*
        WHERE *expression*
        GROUP BY *column-name* <,*column-name*>
        ORDER BY *column-name* <DESC> <,*column-name*>;
QUIT;

Example: Ordering Rows by the Values of a Single Column

In the following PROC SQL query, the ORDER BY clause sorts rows by values of the column JobCode. The ORDER BY clause is the last clause in the SELECT statement, so the ORDER BY clause ends with a semicolon.

```
proc sql;
   select empid,jobcode,salary,
          salary*.06 as bonus
     from certadv.payrollmaster
     where salary<32000
     order by jobcode;
quit;
```

In the sample query output shown below, the rows are sorted by the values of JobCode. By default, the ORDER BY clause sorts rows in ascending order.

Output 1.21 *PROC SQL Query Result Sorted by JobCode*

EmpID	JobCode	Salary	bonus
1970	FA1	$31,661	1899.66
1422	FA1	$31,436	1886.16
1113	FA1	$31,314	1878.84
1132	FA1	$31,378	1882.68
1094	FA1	$31,175	1870.5
1789	SCP	$25,656	1539.36
1564	SCP	$26,366	1581.96
1354	SCP	$25,669	1540.14
1101	SCP	$26,212	1572.72
1658	SCP	$25,120	1507.2
1405	SCP	$25,278	1516.68
1104	SCP	$25,124	1507.44

Example: Ordering by Multiple Columns

To sort rows by the values of two or more columns, list multiple column names or numbers in the ORDER BY clause. Use commas to separate the column names or numbers.

```
proc sql;
   select empid,jobcode,salary,
         salary*.06 as bonus
      from certadv.payrollmaster
      where salary<32000
      order by jobcode,empid;
quit;
```

The rows are sorted by JobCode and then by EmpID, as shown in the following output.

Output 1.22   PROC SQL Query Result Sorted by JobCode and EmpID

EmpID	JobCode	Salary	bonus
1094	FA1	$31,175	1870.5
1113	FA1	$31,314	1878.84
1132	FA1	$31,378	1882.68
1422	FA1	$31,436	1886.16
1970	FA1	$31,661	1899.66
1101	SCP	$26,212	1572.72
1104	SCP	$25,124	1507.44
1354	SCP	$25,669	1540.14
1405	SCP	$25,278	1516.68
1564	SCP	$26,366	1581.96
1658	SCP	$25,120	1507.2
1789	SCP	$25,656	1539.36

Example: Ordering Columns by Position

You can order columns by their position in the SELECT clause. In the following PROC SQL query, the ORDER BY clause sorts the values of the fourth column and the second column.

```
proc sql;
   select empid, jobcode, salary, dateofhire
      from certadv.payrollmaster
      where salary<32000
      order by 4, 2;
quit;
```

The following SQL query result is sorted by the fourth position, which is DateofHire and then by the second position, which is JobCode.

Output 1.23   PROC SQL Query Result: Ordering by Position

EmpID	JobCode	Salary	DateOfHire
1422	FA1	$31,436	09APR1999
1405	SCP	$25,278	29JAN2000
1094	FA1	$31,175	20APR2002
1132	FA1	$31,378	26OCT2003
1564	SCP	$26,366	05JUL2005
1354	SCP	$25,669	20JUN2007
1970	FA1	$31,661	15MAR2008
1104	SCP	$25,124	13JUN2009
1658	SCP	$25,120	04MAR2010
1113	FA1	$31,314	20OCT2010
1789	SCP	$25,656	14APR2016
1101	SCP	$26,212	04OCT2018

PROC SQL Options

A Brief Overview

The SQL procedure offers a variety of options that control processing. Some options control execution. For example, you can limit the number of rows that are read or written during a query. Other options control output. For example, you can control the number of rows to be displayed in your output.

PROC SQL Statement Syntax

Syntax, PROC SQL statement:

PROC SQL <*option(s)*>;

option(s)
   names the option(s) to be used.

After you specify an option, it remains in effect until you change it or you reset it.

The following tables list the options that are covered in this section. A description and an example of each option appear in the following sections.

Table 1.1 Controlling Execution Options

Desired Result	Option
Restrict the number of input rows.	INOBS=
Restrict the number of output rows.	OUTOBS=
Specify whether PROC SQL prints the query's result.	PRINT	NOPRINT
Include a column of row numbers.	NUMBER	NONUMBER

Table 1.2 SAS Data Set Options

Desired Result	Option
Specify the names of columns to be kept.	KEEP=
Specify the names of columns to be dropped.	DROP=
Specify the last observations that SAS processes in a data set.	OBS=
Change the name of a variable.	RENAME=

Using Invocation Options

Restricting Row Processing

When you are developing queries against large tables, you can shorten the time that it takes for the queries to run by reducing the number of rows that PROC SQL processes. Subsetting the tables with WHERE clauses is one way to do this. Using the INOBS= and OUTOBS= options in PROC SQL is another way.

You already know that you can use the OUTOBS= option to restrict the number of rows that PROC SQL displays or writes to a table. However, the OUTOBS= option does not restrict the rows that are read. The INOBS= option restricts the number of rows that PROC SQL takes as input from any single source. The INOBS= option is similar to the SAS data set option OBS= and is useful for debugging queries on large tables.

In the following PROC SQL set operation, INOBS=5 is specified. As indicated in the log, only five rows from the source table Certadv.Mechanicslevel1 are read. The resulting table contains five rows.

```
proc sql inobs=5;
   select *
      from certadv.mechanicslevel1;
quit;
```

Log 1.4 SAS Log

```
WARNING: Only 5 records were read from CERTADV.MECHANICSLEVEL1 due to INOBS=
option.
```

Output 1.24 PROC SQL Query Result: INOBS= Option

EmpID	JobCode	Salary
1400	ME1	$41,677
1403	ME1	$39,301
1120	ME1	$40,067
1121	ME1	$40,757
1412	ME1	$38,919

Example: Limiting the Number of Rows Displayed

Suppose you want to quickly review the types of values that are stored in a table, without printing out all the rows. The following PROC SQL query selects data from the table Certadv.Payrollmaster, which contains more than 100 rows. The query prints only the first ten rows that are ordered by Salary in descending order.

```
proc sql outobs=10;
   select *
      from certadv.payrollmaster
      order by Salary desc;
quit;
```

When you limit the number of rows, a warning is written to the SAS log.

Log 1.5 SAS Log

```
WARNING: Statement terminated early due to OUTOBS=10 option.
```

Output 1.25 PROC SQL Query Result Using the OUTOBS Option

EmpID	JobCode	Salary	DateOfBirth	DateOfHire
1118	PT3	$155,931	19JAN1982	22DEC2008
1777	PT3	$153,482	26SEP1969	25JUN2001
1404	PT2	$127,926	28FEB1971	04JAN2018
1107	PT2	$125,968	12JUN1962	13FEB2017
1928	PT2	$125,801	19SEP1962	16JUL2002
1106	PT2	$125,485	10NOV1965	20AUG1996
1333	PT2	$124,048	03APR1989	14FEB2019
1890	PT2	$120,254	23JUL1979	28NOV2012
1410	PT2	$118,559	06MAY1975	10NOV2000
1442	PT2	$118,350	08SEP1974	16APR2011

TIP You can also use the INOBS= option to restrict the number of rows that PROC SQL takes as input from any single source.

Example: Including a Column of Row Numbers

The NUMBER | NONUMBER option specifies whether the output from a query should include a column named ROW, which displays row numbers. NONUMBER is the default. The option is similar to the NOOBS option in the PRINT procedure.

The following PROC SQL step specifies the NUMBER option. Output from the step includes a column named Row, which contains row numbers.

```
proc sql inobs=10 number;
   select flightnumber, destination
      from certadv.internationalflights;
quit;
```

Output 1.26   PROC SQL Query Result: NUMBER Option

Row	FlightNumber	Destination
1	182	YYZ
2	219	LHR
3	387	CPH
4	622	FRA
5	821	LHR

Validating Query Syntax

A Brief Overview

When you are building a PROC SQL query, you might find it more efficient to check your query without actually executing it. To verify the syntax and the existence of columns and tables that are referenced in the query without executing the query, use either of the following combinations:

- the NOEXEC option in the PROC SQL statement
- the VALIDATE keyword before a SELECT statement

Example: Using the NOEXEC Option

The NOEXEC option is specified in the following PROC SQL statement:

```
proc sql noexec;
   select empid, jobcode, salary
      from certadv.payrollmaster
      where jobcode contains 'NA'
      order by salary;
quit;
```

If the query is valid and all referenced columns and tables exist, the SAS log displays the following message.

Log 1.6 SAS Log

```
NOTE: Statement not executed due to NOEXEC option.
```

Or, if there are any errors in the query, SAS displays the standard error messages in the log.

When you use the NOEXEC option, SAS checks the syntax of all queries in that PROC SQL step for accuracy but does not execute them.

Example: Using the VALIDATE Keyword

You specify the VALIDATE keyword just before a SELECT statement; it is not used with any other PROC SQL statement.

You can modify the preceding PROC SQL query by using the VALIDATE keyword instead of the NOEXEC option:

```
proc sql;
   validate
   select empid, jobcode, salary
      from certadv.payrollmaster
      where jobcode contains 'NA'
      order by salary;
quit;
```

Note: The VALIDATE keyword is not followed by a semicolon.

If the query is valid, the SAS log displays the following message.

Log 1.7 SAS Log

```
NOTE: PROC SQL statement has valid syntax.
```

If there are errors in the query, SAS displays the standard error messages in the log.

The main difference between the VALIDATE keyword and the NOEXEC option is that the VALIDATE keyword affects the SELECT statement that immediately follows it, whereas the NOEXEC option applies to all queries in the PROC SQL step. If you are working with a PROC SQL query that contains multiple SELECT statements, the VALIDATE keyword must be specified before each SELECT statement that you want to check.

Quiz

Select the best answer for each question. After completing the quiz, check your answers using the answer key in the appendix.

1. Which of the statements or clauses in the PROC SQL program below is written incorrectly?

   ```
   proc sql;
      select style sqfeet bedrooms
         from certadv.houses
         where sqfeet ge 800;
   quit;
   ```

a. SELECT

b. FROM

c. WHERE

d. Both a and c.

2. How many statements does the program below contain?

```
proc sql;
   select grapes,oranges,
          grapes + oranges as sumsales
       from certadv.produce
       order by sumsales;
quit;
```

a. two

b. three

c. four

d. five

3. Complete the following PROC SQL query to select the columns Address and SqFeet from the table Certadv.Size and to select Price from the table Certadv.Price. (Only the Address column appears in both tables.)

```
proc sql;
   _____
       from certadv.size left join certadv.price;
       on size.address = price.address;
quit;
```

a.   select address,sqfeet,price

b.   select size.address,sqfeet,price

c.   select price.address,sqfeet,price

d. Either b or c.

4. Which of the clauses below correctly sorts rows by the values of the columns Price and SqFeet?

a.   order price, sqfeet

b.   order by price,sqfeet

c.   sort by price sqfeet

d.   sort price sqfeet

5. Which clause below specifies that the two tables Produce and Hardware be queried? Both tables are located in a library to which the libref Sales has been assigned.

a.   select sales.produce sales.hardware

b.   from sales.produce sales.hardware

c.   from sales.produce,sales.hardware

d.   where sales.produce, sales.hardware

6. Complete the SELECT clause below to create a new column named Profit by subtracting the values of the column Cost from those of the column Price.

```
select fruit,cost,price,
       _____
```

a. `Profit=price-cost`
   b. `price-cost as Profit`
   c. `profit=price-cost`
   d. `Profit as price-cost`

7. What happens if you use a GROUP BY clause in a PROC SQL step without a summary function?

   a. The step does not execute.
   b. The first numeric column is summed by default.
   c. The GROUP BY clause is changed to an ORDER BY clause.
   d. The step executes but does not group or sort data.

8. Which clause in the following program is incorrect?

   ```
   proc sql;
      select age,mean(weight) as avgweight
         from certadv.employees certadv.health
         where employees.id=health.id
         group by age;
   quit;
   ```

   a. SELECT
   b. FROM
   c. WHERE
   d. GROUP BY

Chapter 2
Creating and Managing Tables

The CREATE TABLE Statement **43**
    A Brief Overview 43
    CREATE TABLE Statement Syntax 44
    Example: Creating an Empty Table by Defining Column Structure 45
    Specifying Data Types for Columns 46
    Specifying Column Widths 47
    Specifying Column Modifiers 48
    Example: Using Column Modifiers 48

Using the LIKE Clause **48**
    LIKE Clause Syntax 48
    Example: Creating an Empty Table That Is like Another 49

Using the AS Keyword **49**
    AS Keyword Syntax 49
    Example: Creating a Table from a Query Result 50

The INSERT Statement **51**
    A Brief Overview 51
    The SET Clause 52
    The VALUES Clause 54
    The INSERT Statement with SELECT and FROM Clauses 57

The DESCRIBE TABLE Statement **59**
    A Brief Overview 59
    DESCRIBE TABLE Statement Syntax 59
    Example: Displaying the Structure of a Table 59

Using Dictionary Tables **60**
    A Brief Overview 60
    Example: Exploring and Using Dictionary Tables 61

Chapter Quiz **63**

The CREATE TABLE Statement

A Brief Overview

PROC SQL offers you three ways to create a table. The CREATE TABLE statement is used for all three methods, although the statement syntax varies for each method.

Method of Creating a Table	Example
| create an empty table by defining columns | ```
proc sql;
    create table work.discount
        (Destination char(3),
        BeginDate num Format=date9.,
        EndDate num format=date9.,
        Discount num);
quit;
``` |
| create an empty table that is like (has the same columns and attributes as) an existing table | ```
proc sql;
    create table work.flightdelays2
        like certadv.flightdelays;
quit;
``` |
| create a populated table (a table with both columns and rows of data) from a query result | ```
proc sql;
    create table work.ticketagents as
        select lastname, firstname,
            jobcode, salary
        from certadv.payrollmaster,
            certadv.staffmaster
        where payrollmaster.empid
            = staffmaster.empid
            and jobcode contains 'TA';
quit;
``` |

The CREATE TABLE statement generates a table only as output, not as a report. The SAS log displays a message that indicates that the table has been created as well as the number of rows and columns that it contains.

Log 2.1 SAS Log

```
NOTE: Table WORK.FLIGHTDELAYS2 created, with 0 rows and 8 columns.
```

Note: You can display additional information about a table's structure in the SAS log by using the DESCRIBE TABLE statement in PROC SQL.

CREATE TABLE Statement Syntax

Use the CREATE TABLE statement to create an empty table and define the table's columns and attributes. The empty table will not contain any rows.
```

Syntax, CREATE TABLE statement with column specifications:

CREATE TABLE *table-name*
        (*column-specification-1<*,
        ...*column-specification-n>***);**

table-name
    specifies the name of the table to be created.

column-specification
    specifies a column to be included in the table. The following constraints are available for the columns, using this form:

    column-definition consists of the following:
        column-name data-type<(column-width)> <column-modifier-1> <column-modifier-n>

    column-name
        specifies the name of the column. The column name is stored in the table in the same case that is used in *column-name*.

    data-type
        is enclosed in parentheses and specifies one of the following: CHARACTER (or CHAR) | VARCHAR | INTEGER (or INT) | SMALLINT | DECIMAL (or DEC) | NUMERIC (or NUM) | FLOAT | REAL | DOUBLE PRECISION | DATE.

    column-width
        which is enclosed in parentheses, is an integer that specifies the width of the column. (PROC SQL processes this value only for the CHARACTER and VARCHAR data types.)

    column-modifier
        is one of the following: INFORMAT= | FORMAT= | LABEL= . More than one column-modifier can be specified.

Note: The entire set of column-specifications must be enclosed in parentheses. Multiple column-specifications must be separated by commas. Elements within a column-specifications must be separated by spaces.

Example: Creating an Empty Table by Defining Column Structure

Suppose you want to create the temporary table Work.Discount, which contains data about discounts that are offered by an airline. There is no existing table that contains the four columns, and column attributes, that you would like to include: Destination, BeginDate, EndDate, and Discount.

You use the following PROC SQL step to create the table, based on column definitions that you specify:

```
proc sql;
   create table work.discount
         (Destination char(3),
         BeginDate num Format=date9.,
         EndDate num format=date9.,
         Discount num);
quit;
```

The SAS log confirms that the table has been created.

Log 2.2 *SAS Log*

```
NOTE: Table WORK.DISCOUNT created, with 0 rows and 4 columns.
```

TIP In this example, and all other examples in this chapter, you are instructed to save your data to a temporary table (in the library Work) that will be deleted at the end of the SAS session. To save the table permanently in a different library, use the appropriate libref instead of the libref Work in the CREATE TABLE statement.

Specifying Data Types for Columns

When you create a table by defining columns, you must specify a data type for each column, following the column name:

column-name **data-type** *<(column-width)> <column-modifier-1<...column-modifier-n>>*

The following PROC SQL step defines four columns: a one-character column, Destination, and three numeric columns, BeginDate, EndDate, and Discount.

```
proc sql;
   create table work.discount
      (Destination char(3),
       BeginDate num format=date9.,
       EndDate num format=date9.,
       Discount num);
quit;
```

SAS tables use two data types: numeric and character. However, PROC SQL supports additional data types (many, but not all, of the data types that SQL-based databases support). Therefore, in the CREATE TABLE statement, you can specify any of 10 different data types. When the table is created, PROC SQL converts the supported data types that are not SAS data types to either numeric or character format.

Table 2.1 Character Data Types Supported by PROC SQL

Specified Data Type	SAS Data Type
CHARACTER (or CHAR)	CHARACTER
VARCHAR	CHARACTER

Table 2.2 Numeric Data Types Supported by PROC SQL

Specified Data Type	Description	SAS Data Type
NUMERIC (or NUM)	floating-point	NUMERIC
DECIMAL (or DEC)	floating-point	NUMERIC
FLOAT	floating-point	NUMERIC
REAL	floating-point	NUMERIC
DOUBLE PRECISION	floating-point	NUMERIC
INTEGER (or INT)	integer	NUMERIC

Specified Data Type	Description	SAS Data Type
SMALLINT	integer	NUMERIC
DATE	date	NUMERIC with a DATE.7 informat and format

The following PROC SQL step specifies three supported data types other than CHAR and NUM: VARCHAR, DATE, and FLOAT.

```
proc sql;
   create table work.discount2
      (Destination varchar(3),
       BeginDate date,
       EndDate date,
       Discount float);
quit;
```

PROC SQL converts these data types to either character or numeric. Because it supports data types other than SAS data types, PROC SQL can save you time. In many cases, you can copy native code from an implementation of SQL that is external to SAS without having to modify the data types.

Specifying Column Widths

In SAS, the default column width for both character and numeric columns is 8 bytes. However, character and numeric data values are stored differently:

- Character data is stored one character per byte.
- Numeric data is stored as floating-point numbers in real binary representation, which allows for 15- or 16-digit precision within 8 bytes.

PROC SQL enables you to specify a column width for character columns but not for numeric columns.

Note: PROC SQL allows the WIDTH and NDEC (decimal places) arguments to be included in the column specification for the DECIMAL, NUMERIC, and FLOAT data types. However, PROC SQL ignores this specification and uses the SAS defaults.

In a column specification, the column width follows the data type and is specified as an integer enclosed in parentheses:

column-name data-type <(column-width)> <column-modifier-1<...column-modifier-n>>

In the following PROC SQL step, the first column specification indicates a column width of 3 for the character column Destination:

```
proc sql;
   create table work.discount
      (Destination char(3),
       BeginDate num format=date9.,
       EndDate num format=date9.,
       Discount num);
quit;
```

Because the last three columns are numeric, no width is specified and these columns will have a default column width of 8 bytes.

Specifying Column Modifiers

In the CREATE TABLE statement, a column specification might include one or more of the following SAS column modifiers: INFORMAT=, FORMAT=, and LABEL=. Column modifiers, if used, are specified at the end of the column specification.

column-name data-type <(column-width)> <...column-modifier-1 <...column-modifier-n>>

Note: A fourth SAS column modifier, LENGTH=, is not allowed in a CREATE TABLE statement. It can be used in a SELECT clause.

Example: Using Column Modifiers

The following PROC SQL step creates the table Work.Departments by specifying four columns. The column modifiers LABEL= and FORMAT= are used to specify additional column attributes.

```
proc sql;
   create table work.departments
      (Dept varchar(20) label='Department',
       Code integer label='Dept Code',
       Manager varchar(20),
       AuditDate num format=date9.);
quit;
```

The SAS log verifies that the table was created.

Log 2.3 *SAS Log*

```
NOTE: Table WORK.DEPARTMENTS created, with 0 rows and 4 columns.
```

Using the LIKE Clause

LIKE Clause Syntax

Suppose you need to create a new table. The new table must contain the same columns and attributes as an existing table, but no rows. You can use a CREATE TABLE statement with a LIKE clause to create an empty table that is like another table.

Syntax, CREATE TABLE statement with a LIKE clause:

CREATE TABLE *table-name*
    LIKE *table-1*;

table-name
    specifies the name of the table to be created.

table-1
    specifies the table whose columns and attributes will be copied to the new table.

Example: Creating an Empty Table That Is like Another

Suppose you want to create a new table, Work.Flightdelays2, that contains data about flight delays. You would like the new table to contain the same columns and attributes as the existing table Certadv.Flightdelays, but you do not want to include any of the existing data. The following PROC SQL step uses a CREATE TABLE statement and a LIKE clause to create Work.Flightdelays2:

```
proc sql;
   create table work.flightdelays2
      like certadv.flightdelays;
quit;
```

Work.FlightDelays2 contains 0 rows and 8 columns.

Using the AS Keyword

AS Keyword Syntax

Suppose you want to create a new table that contains both columns and rows that are derived from an existing table or set of tables. In this situation, you can submit one PROC SQL step that does both of the following:

- creates a new table
- populates the table with data from the result of a PROC SQL query

To create a table from a query result, use a CREATE TABLE statement that includes the keyword AS and the clauses that are used in a query: SELECT, FROM, and any optional clauses, such as ORDER BY.

Syntax, CREATE TABLE statement with query clauses:

CREATE TABLE *table-name* **AS**
    SELECT *column-1<, ... column-n>*
        FROM *table-1 | view-1<, ... table-n | view-n>*
            <optional query clauses>;

table-name
    specifies the name of the table to be created.

SELECT
    specifies the columns that will appear in the table.

FROM
    specifies the tables or views to be queried.

optional query clauses
    are used to refine the query further and include WHERE, GROUP BY, HAVING, and ORDER BY.

Here are the results of creating a table from a query result:

- The new table is populated with data that is derived from one or more tables or views that are referenced in the query's FROM clause.
- The new table contains the columns that are specified in the query's SELECT clause.

- The new table's columns have the same column attributes (type, length, informat, and format) as those of the selected source columns.

Note: When you are creating a table, if you do not specify a column alias for a calculated column, SAS assigns a column name, such as _TEMA001.

When query clauses are used within a CREATE TABLE statement, that query's automatic report generation is turned off. Only the new table is generated as output.

Example: Creating a Table from a Query Result

Suppose you want to create a new, temporary table that contains data for ticket agents who are employed by an airline. The data that you need is a subset of the data contained in two existing tables, Certadv.Payrollmaster and Certadv.Staffmaster. The following PROC SQL step creates the new table Work.Ticketagents from the result of a query on the two existing tables. The WHERE clause joins the table by matching EMPID and selects the subset of rows for employees whose JobCode contains **TA**.

```
proc sql;
   create table work.ticketagents as
      select lastname, firstname, jobcode, salary
         from certadv.payrollmaster,
              certadv.staffmaster
         where payrollmaster.empid
             = staffmaster.empid
             and jobcode contains 'TA';
quit;
```

Note: Because this query lists two tables in the FROM clause and subsets rows based on a WHERE clause, the query is actually a PROC SQL inner join.

The new table Work.Ticketagents is not empty; it contains rows of data. Therefore, you can submit a SELECT statement to display Work.Ticketagents as a report.

```
proc sql;
   select *
      from work.ticketagents;
quit;
```

Output 2.1   PROC SQL Query Result: Work.Ticketagents (partial output)

LastName	FirstName	JobCode	Salary
ADAMS	GERALD	TA2	$48,126
AVERY	JERRY	TA3	$54,351
BLALOCK	RALPH	TA2	$45,661
BOSTIC	MARIE	TA3	$54,299
CARTER	KAREN	TA3	$56,364
CHIN	JACK	TA3	$55,545

... more observations ...

WELCH	DARIUS	TA3	$57,201
WELLS	NADINE	TA2	$45,605
WHALEY	CAROLYN	TA2	$47,664
WONG	LESLIE	TA3	$55,149
WOOD	SANDRA	TA2	$46,215

The SAS log also displays a message, indicating that the table has been created.

Log 2.4   SAS Log

```
NOTE: Table WORK.TICKETAGENTS created, with 41 rows and 4 columns.
```

The INSERT Statement

A Brief Overview

You can use the INSERT statement in three ways to insert rows of data into existing, empty, or populated tables.

Method of Inserting Row	Example

insert values by column name by using the SET clause	```proc sql;
	    insert into work.discount
	        set destination='LHR',
	            begindate='01MAR2018'd,
	            enddate='05MAR2018'd,
	            discount=.33
	        set destination='CPH',
	            begindate='03MAR2018'd,
	            enddate='10MAR2018'd,
	            discount=.15;
	quit;```

Method of Inserting Row	Example
| insert lists of values by using the VALUES clause | ```
proc sql;
    insert into work.discount (destination,
            begindate,enddate,discount)
        values ('LHR','01MAR2018'd,
            '05MAR2018'd,.33)
        values ('CPH','03MAR2018'd,
            '10MAR2018'd,.15);
quit;
``` |
| insert rows that are copied from another table by using a query result | ```
proc sql;
    insert into payrollchanges2
        select empid,salary,dateofhire
            from certadv.payrollmaster
            where empid in ('1919','1350','1401');
quit;
``` |

In each method, the INSERT statement inserts new rows of data into the table. To indicate that the rows have been inserted, the SAS log displays a message similar to the following.

Log 2.5 SAS Log

```
NOTE: 2 row was inserted into WORK.DISCOUNT.
```

The SET Clause

A Brief Overview

Suppose you need to add rows of data to a table, but the data is not currently contained in any table. In this situation, you can use either the SET clause or the VALUES clause in the INSERT statement to specify the data to be added.

The SET clause in the INSERT statement enables you to specify new data to be added to a table. The SET clause specifies column names and values in pairs. PROC SQL reads each column name-value pair and assigns the value to the specified column. A separate SET clause is used for each row to be added to the table.

SET Clause Syntax

The syntax of the INSERT statement that contains the SET clause is shown below.

Syntax, INSERT statement containing the SET clause:

INSERT INTO *table-name* <(*target-column-1*<, ... *target-column-n*)>
    SET *column-1=value-1*<, ... *column-n=value-n*>
    <... SET *column-1=value-1*<, ... *column-n=value-n*>>;

table-name
    specifies the name of the table to which rows will be inserted.

target-column
    specifies the name of a column into which data will be inserted.

each SET clause
    specifies one or more values to be inserted in one or more specified columns in a row. Multiple SET clauses are not separated by commas.

column
    specifies the name of a column into which data will be inserted.

value
    specifies a data value to be inserted into the specified column. Character values must be enclosed in quotation marks.

multiple *column=value* pairs in a SET clause
    are separated by commas.

Note: It is optional to include a list of target column names after the table name in the INSERT TABLE statement that includes a SET clause. The list can include the names of all or only a subset of columns in the table. If you specify an optional list of target column names, then you can specify values only for columns that are in the list. You can list target columns in any order, regardless of their position in the table. Any columns that are in the table but not listed are given missing values in the inserted rows.

Note: Although it is recommended that the SET clause list column-value pairs in order (as they appear in the table or the optional column list), it is not required.

Example: Inserting Rows by Using the SET Clause

Consider the table Work.Discount, which was presented in the last topic. Work.Discount stores airline discounts for certain flight destinations and time periods in March.

The following example illustrates these points:

- adding two rows of new data to Work.Discount by using an INSERT statement that contains two SET clauses, one for each row

- generating a report that displays Work.Discount, with its two new rows, by using a SELECT statement

In this situation, you do not need to include an optional list of column names.

```
proc sql;
   insert into work.discount
      set destination='LHR',
          begindate='01MAR2018'd,
          enddate='05MAR2018'd,
          discount=.33
      set destination='CPH',
          begindate='03MAR2018'd,
          enddate='10MAR2018'd,
          discount=.15;
   select *
```

```
         from work.discount;
quit;
```

Because SELECT * was used in the query, the displayed output includes all six rows of data. If you ran the previous examples, Work.Discount displays six rows of data and not just the two that were inserted.

Output 2.2   PROC SQL Query Result: Inserting Two Rows

Destination	BeginDate	EndDate	Discount
LHR	01MAR2018	05MAR2018	0.33
CPH	03MAR2018	10MAR2018	0.15
LHR	01MAR2018	05MAR2018	0.33
CPH	03MAR2018	10MAR2018	0.15
LHR	01MAR2018	05MAR2018	0.33
CPH	03MAR2018	10MAR2018	0.15

The following is printed to the SAS log.

Log 2.6   SAS Log

```
NOTE: 2 rows were inserted into WORK.DISCOUNT.
```

The VALUES Clause

A Brief Overview

You can use the VALUES clause to insert a value for all or only some of the columns in the table.

Desired Result	Steps to Take	Example

insert a value for all columns in the table	You can omit the optional list of column names in the INSERT statement.
	
	PROC SQL actions:
	
	• reads values in the order in which they are specified in the VALUES clause.
	
	• inserts the values into columns in the order in which the columns appear in the table.
		`insert into work.newtable`
		`    values ('WI','FLUTE',6)`
		`    values ('ST','VIOLIN',3);`

Desired Result	Steps to Take	Example
| insert a value for only some of the columns in the table | You must include a list of column names in the INSERT statement.<br><br>PROC SQL actions:<br><br>• reads values in the order in which they are specified in the VALUES clause.<br><br>• inserts the values into columns in the order in which the columns are specified in the column list. | ```
insert into work.newtable
     (item,qty)
  values ('FLUTE',6)
  values ('VIOLIN',3);
``` |

You must list a value for every column into which PROC SQL will insert values (as specified in either the table or the optional list of column names). To specify that a value is missing, use a space enclosed in single quotation marks for character values and a period for numeric values.

For example, the following VALUES clause specifies values to be inserted in three columns. The first two values are missing:

```
values (' ', ., 45)
```

In the example above, the first value that is specified is a missing value for a character column. The second value is a missing value for a numeric column, and the third value is the numeric **45**.

VALUES Clause Syntax

The INSERT statement uses the VALUES clause to insert a list of values into a table. Unlike the SET clause, the VALUES clause does not specify a column name for each value, so the values must be listed in the correct order. Values must be specified in the order in which the columns appear in the table or, if an optional column list is specified, in the order in which the columns appear in that list. A separate VALUES clause is used for each row to be added to the table.

Syntax, INSERT statement containing the VALUES clause:

INSERT INTO *table-name* <(*target-column-1*<, ... *target-column-n*)>
      VALUES (*value-1*<, ... *value-n*)>
      <... VALUES (*value-1*<, ... *value-n*)>**;**

table-name
   specifies the name of the table to which rows will be inserted.

target-column
   specifies the name of a column into which data will be inserted.

each VALUES clause
   lists the values to be inserted in some or all columns in one row. The values are enclosed in parentheses. Multiple VALUES clauses are not separated by commas.

value
   specifies a data value to be added. Character values must be enclosed in quotation marks. Multiple values must be separated by commas. Values must be listed in positional order, either as they appear in the table or, if the optional column list is specified, as they appear in the column list.
```

Note: It is optional to include a list of target column names after the table name in the INSERT TABLE statement that includes a VALUES clause. The list can include the names of all or only a subset of columns in the table. If an optional list of target column names is specified, then only those columns are given values by the statement. Target columns can be listed in any order, regardless of their position in the table. Any columns that are in the table but not listed are given missing values in the inserted rows.

Example: Inserting Rows Using the VALUES Clause

Suppose you want to insert two more rows into the table Work.Discount, which stores airline discounts for certain flight destinations and time periods in March. In the previous section, you inserted two rows into Work.Discount by using the SET clause, so the table now looks like the following table.

Output 2.3   PROC SQL Query Result: Work.Discount

Destination	BeginDate	EndDate	Discount
LHR	01MAR2018	05MAR2018	0.33
CPH	03MAR2018	10MAR2018	0.15
LHR	01MAR2018	05MAR2018	0.33
CPH	03MAR2018	10MAR2018	0.15
LHR	01MAR2018	05MAR2018	0.33
CPH	03MAR2018	10MAR2018	0.15

Add two more rows, by using the VALUES clause. The following PROC SQL step adds two rows of new data to Work.Discount and generates a report that displays the updated table.

```
proc sql;
   insert into work.discount (destination,
         begindate,enddate,discount)
      values ('ORD', '05MAR2018'd, '15MAR2018'd, .25)
      values ('YYZ', '06MAR2018'd, '20MAR2018'd, .10);
   select *
      from work.discount;
quit;
```

Output 2.4   PROC SQL Query Result: Inserting Rows

Destination	BeginDate	EndDate	Discount
LHR	01MAR2018	05MAR2018	0.33
CPH	03MAR2018	10MAR2018	0.15
ORD	05MAR2018	15MAR2018	0.25
YYZ	06MAR2018	20MAR2018	0.1

The two rows that were just inserted by using the VALUES clause are the third and fourth rows above.

You might have noticed that the INSERT statement in this example includes an optional list of column names. In this example, data is being inserted into all columns of the table, and the values are listed in the order in which the columns appear in the table. Therefore, it is not strictly necessary to use a column list. However, including the list of column names makes it easier to read the code and understand what the code is doing.

The INSERT Statement with SELECT and FROM Clauses

A Brief Overview

The fastest way to insert rows of data into a table is to use a query to select existing rows from one or more tables or views and to insert the rows into another table. You can insert rows from a query result into either an empty table or a table that already contains rows of data. When you add rows of data to a table that already contains rows, the new rows are added at the end of the table.

To insert rows from a query result, use an INSERT statement that includes the clauses that are used in a query: SELECT, FROM, and any optional clauses, such as ORDER BY. Values from the query result are inserted into columns in the order in which the columns appear in the table or, if an optional column list is specified, in the order in which the columns appear in that list.

INSERT Statement with SELECT and FROM Clause Syntax

Syntax, INSERT statement containing query clauses:

INSERT INTO *table-name* <*(target-column-1<, ... target-column-n)*>
    SELECT *column-1<, ... column-n>*
        FROM *table-1 | view-1<, ... table-n | view-n>*
        <*optional query clauses*>;

table-name
    specifies the name of the table to which rows will be inserted.

target-column
    specifies the name of a column into which data will be inserted.

SELECT
    specifies the columns that will be inserted.

FROM
    specifies the tables or views to be queried.

optional query clauses
    are used to refine the query further. These include the WHERE, GROUP BY, HAVING, and ORDER BY clauses.

Note: It is optional to include a list of target column names after the table name in the INSERT TABLE statement that includes query clauses. The list can include the names of all or only a subset of columns in the table. If an optional list of target column names is specified, then only those columns are given values by the statement. Target columns might be listed in any order, regardless of their position in the table. Any columns that are in the table but not listed are given missing values in the inserted rows.

Example: Inserting Rows from a Query Result

A mechanic at a company has been promoted from level 2 to level 3, and you need to add this employee to Certadv.Mechanicslevel3, a table that lists all level-3 mechanics. Create a temporary copy of Certadv.Mechanicslevel3 called Work.Mechanicslevel3_New, and display the new table in a report:

```
proc sql;
   create table work.mechanicslevel3_new as
   select *
      from certadv.mechanicslevel3;
quit;
```

Output 2.5 PROC SQL Query Result: Work.Mechanicslevel3_New

EmpID	JobCode	Salary
1499	ME3	$60,235
1409	ME3	$58,171
1379	ME3	$59,170
1521	ME3	$58,136
1385	ME3	$61,460
1420	ME3	$60,299
1882	ME3	$58,153

Next, insert a row into Work.Mechanicslevel3_New for the new level-3 employee, whose EmpID is 1653. This employee is currently listed in Certadv.Mechanicslevel2, so your INSERT statement queries the table Certadv.Mechanicslevel2. Your PROC SQL step ends with a SELECT statement that creates an output of the revised table Work.Mechanicslevel3_New.

```
proc sql;
   insert into work.mechanicslevel3_new
   select empid, jobcode, salary
      from certadv.mechanicslevel2
         where empid='1653';
   select *
      from work.mechanicslevel3_new;
quit;
```

Output 2.6 PROC SQL Query Result: One Row Inserted

EmpID	JobCode	Salary
1499	ME3	$60,235
1409	ME3	$58,171
1379	ME3	$59,170
1521	ME3	$58,136
1385	ME3	$61,460
1420	ME3	$60,299
1882	ME3	$58,153
1653	ME2	$49,151

Note: Although the new row is shown above, the order of rows in a PROC SQL query cannot be guaranteed if an ORDER BY clause is not used.

The DESCRIBE TABLE Statement

A Brief Overview

Suppose you want to view the table structure of a table which you or someone else created. The structure of a table includes the columns and the column attributes. When you create a table, the CREATE TABLE statement writes a message to the SAS log, which indicates the number of rows and columns in the table that was created. However, the message does not contain information about column attributes.

If you are working with an existing table that contains rows of data, you can use a PROC SQL query to generate a report that shows all of the columns in a table. However, the report does not list the column attributes, and a PROC SQL query will not generate output for an empty table.

The DESCRIBE TABLE statement writes to the SAS log a CREATE TABLE statement that includes column definitions for the specified table, regardless of how the table was originally created. For example, if the DESCRIBE TABLE statement specifies a table that was created with the DATA step, a CREATE TABLE statement is still displayed.

DESCRIBE TABLE Statement Syntax

To display a list of columns and column attributes for one or more tables in the SAS log, regardless of whether the tables contain rows of data, you can use the DESCRIBE TABLE statement in PROC SQL.

Syntax, DESCRIBE TABLE statement:

DESCRIBE TABLE *table-name-1*<, ... *table-name-n*>;

table-name
specifies the table to be described as one of the following:
- a one-level name
- a two-level *libref.table* name
- a physical pathname that is enclosed in single quotation marks

TIP As an alternative to the DESCRIBE TABLE statement, you can use other SAS procedures, like PROC CONTENTS, to list a table's columns and column attributes. PROC CONTENTS generates a report instead of writing a message to the SAS log, as the DESCRIBE TABLE statement does.

Example: Displaying the Structure of a Table

The empty table Work.Discount was created by using the CREATE TABLE statement and column specifications shown below:

```
proc sql;
   create table work.discount
        (Destination char(3),
         BeginDate num format=date9.,
         EndDate num format=date9.,
```

                    Discount num);
       quit;

The following DESCRIBE TABLE statement writes a CREATE TABLE statement to the SAS log for the table Work.Discount:

```
proc sql;
   describe table work.discount;
quit;
```

Log 2.7 *SAS Log*

```
NOTE: SQL table WORK.DISCOUNT was created like:

create table WORK.DISCOUNT( bufsize=65536 )
  (
   Destination char(3),
   BeginDate num format=DATE9.,
   EndDate num format=DATE9.,
   Discount num
  );
```

Using Dictionary Tables

A Brief Overview

Metadata is a description or definition of data or information.

SAS session metadata is stored in Dictionary tables, which are special, Read-Only SAS tables that contain information about SAS libraries, SAS data sets, SAS macros, and external files that are available in the current SAS session. Dictionary tables also contain the settings for SAS system options and SAS titles and footnotes that are currently in effect. Dictionary tables are commonly used to monitor and manage SAS sessions because the data is easier to manipulate than the output from procedures. You can use the SQL procedure to access the metadata stored in Dictionary tables. For example, you can query a Dictionary table to find out which tables in a SAS library contain a specified column.

The following statements are true about Dictionary tables:

- They are created each time they are referenced in a SAS program.
- They are updated automatically.
- They are limited to Read-Only access.

Accessing a Dictionary table causes SAS to determine the current state of the SAS session and return the information that you want. Dictionary tables can be accessed by running a PROC SQL query against the table, using the Dictionary libref. Though SAS librefs are usually limited to eight characters, Dictionary is an automatically assigned, reserved word. You can also access a Dictionary table by referring to the PROC SQL view of the table that is stored in the Sashelp library.

The following table describes some of the Dictionary tables that are available and lists the corresponding Sashelp views. For a complete list of Dictionary tables, see the SAS documentation for the SQL procedure.

Dictionary Table	Sashelp View	What the Table Contains
Catalogs	Vcatalg	information about catalog entries
Columns	Vcolumn	detailed information about variables and their attributes
Extfiles	Vextfl	currently assigned filerefs
Indexes	Vindex	information about indexes defined for data files
Macros	Vmacro	information about both user and system defined macro variables
Members	Vmember Vsacces Vscatlg Vslib Vstable Vstabvw Vsview	general information about data library members
Options	Voption	current settings of SAS system options
Tables	Vtable	detailed information about data sets
Titles	Vtitle	text assigned to titles and footnotes
Views	Vview	general information about data views

Example: Exploring and Using Dictionary Tables

You can query Dictionary tables the same way that you query any other table, including subsetting with a WHERE clause, ordering the results, creating tables, and creating PROC SQL views. Because Dictionary tables are Read-Only objects, you cannot insert rows or columns, alter column attributes, or add integrity constraints to them.

To see how each Dictionary table is defined, submit a DESCRIBE TABLE statement. The DESCRIBE TABLE statement writes a CREATE TABLE statement to the SAS log for the table that is specified in the DESCRIBE TABLE statement. After you know how a table is defined, you can use its column names in a subsetting WHERE clause in order to retrieve specific information.

The Dictionary.Tables table contains detailed information about tables. The following DESCRIBE TABLE statement displays information about the Dictionary.Tables table in the log window. The information includes the names of the columns that are stored in the table.

```
proc sql;
   describe table dictionary.tables;
quit;
```

Log 2.8 *SAS Log*

```
create table DICTIONARY.TABLES
  (
    libname char(8) label='Library Name',
    memname char(32) label='Member Name',
    memtype char(8) label='Member Type',
    memlabel char(256) label='Dataset Label',
    typemem char(8) label='Dataset Type',
    crdate num format=DATETIME informat=DATETIME label='Date Created',
  ...);
```

To display information about the files in a specific library, specify the column names in a SELECT statement and the Dictionary table name in the FROM clause.

For example, the following PROC SQL step displays these columns:

- Memname (name)
- Nobs (number of observations)
- Nvar (number of variables)
- Crdate (creation date) of the tables in the Certadv library

The Dictionary column names are specified in the SELECT statement, and the Dictionary table name, Dictionary.Tables, is specified in the FROM clause. The library name, Certadv, is specified in the WHERE clause.

Note: You must specify the library name in the WHERE clause in uppercase letters, because that is how it is stored within SAS, and enclose it in quotation marks.

```
proc sql;
   select memname format=$20., nobs, nvar, crdate
      from dictionary.tables
      where libname='CERTADV';
quit;
```

Output 2.7 *Dictionary.Tables of Certadv (partial output)*

Member Name	Number of Physical Observations	Number of Variables	Date Created
ACITIES	50	4	17JUL19:15:31:54
ALL	.	12	17JUL19:15:31:57
ALLEMPS	50	5	17JUL19:15:31:56
BONUS	3	2	01JUL19:15:23:07

... *more observations* ...

Note: The number of physical observations value for ALL is missing because ALL is a view, not a table.

Note: Your output might differ from that shown above, depending on the contents of your Certadv library.

You can also use Dictionary tables to determine more specific information such as which tables in a SAS library contain a specific column.

Chapter Quiz

Select the best answer for each question. After completing the quiz, check your answers using the answer key in the appendix.

1. If you specify a CREATE TABLE statement in your PROC SQL step, which of the following happens?

    a. The results of the query are displayed, and a new table is created.

    b. A new table is created, but it does not contain any summarization that was specified in the PROC SQL step.

    c. A new table is created, but no report is displayed.

    d. Results are grouped by the value of the summarized column.

2. Which of the following PROC SQL steps creates a new table by copying only the column structure (but not the rows) of an existing table?

    a.
    ```
    proc sql;
        create table work.newpayroll as
            select *
                from certadv.payrollmaster;
    quit;
    ```

    b.
    ```
    proc sql;
        create table work.newpayroll
            like certadv.payrollmaster;
    quit;
    ```

    c.
    ```
    proc sql;
        create table work.newpayroll
            copy certadv.payrollmaster;
    quit;
    ```

    d.
    ```
    proc sql;
        create table work.newpayroll
            describe certadv.payrollmaster;
    quit;
    ```

3. Which of the following PROC SQL steps creates a table that contains rows for the level-1 flight attendants only?

    a.
    ```
    proc sql;
        create table work.newpayroll as
            select *
                from certadv.payrollmaster
                where jobcode='FA1';
    quit;
    ```

    b.
    ```
    proc sql;
        create work.newpayroll as
            select *
                from certadv.payrollmaster
                where jobcode='FA1';
    quit;
    ```

    c.
    ```
    proc sql;
        create table work.newpayroll
    ```

```
                    copy certadv.payrollmaster
                        where jobcode='FA1';
            quit;

      d.    proc sql;
                create table work.newpayroll as
                    certadv.payrollmaster
                    where jobcode='FA1';
            quit;
```

4. Which of the following statements is used to add new rows to a table?

   a. INSERT

   b. LOAD

   c. VALUES

   d. CREATE TABLE

5. Which of the following displays the structure of a table in the SAS log?

   a.
   ```
   proc sql;
       describe as
           select *
               from certadv.payrollmaster;
   quit;
   ```

   b.
   ```
   proc sql;
       describe contents certadv.payrollmaster;
   quit;
   ```

   c.
   ```
   proc sql;
       describe table certadv.payrollmaster;
   quit;
   ```

   d.
   ```
   proc sql;
       describe * from certadv.payrollmaster;
   quit;
   ```

6. Which of the following creates an empty table that contains the two columns FullName and Age?

   a.
   ```
   proc sql;
       create table work.names
               (FullName char(25), Age num);
   quit;
   ```

   b.
   ```
   proc sql;
       create table work.names as
               (FullName char(25), Age num);
   quit;
   ```

   c.
   ```
   proc sql;
       create work.names
               (FullName char(25), Age num);
   quit;
   ```

   d.
   ```
   proc sql;
       create table work.names
           set (FullName char(25), Age num);
   quit;
   ```

Chapter 3
Joining Tables Using PROC SQL

Understanding Joins 66
Generating a Cartesian Product 66
Using Inner Joins 68
    A Brief Overview 68
    Inner Join Syntax 68
    Understanding How Joins Are Processed 69
    Example: Using a FROM Clause with the INNER JOIN Keyword 70
    Example: Eliminating Duplicate Columns 70
    Example: Renaming a Column by Using a Column Alias 71
    Example: Joining Tables That Have Rows with Matching Values 72
    Specifying a Table Alias 72
    Example: Complex PROC SQL Inner Join 74
    Example: PROC SQL Inner Join with Summary Functions 75
Using Natural Joins 77
    A Brief Overview 77
    Natural Join Syntax 77
    Example: Using a Natural Join 77
Using Outer Joins 78
    A Brief Overview 78
    Outer Join Syntax 79
    Example: Using a Left Outer Join 79
    Example: Eliminating Duplicate Columns in a Left Outer Join 80
    Example: Using a Right Outer Join 81
    Example: Using a Full Outer Join 81
    Example: Complex Outer Join 82
Comparing SQL Joins and DATA Step Match-Merges 84
    A Brief Overview 84
    When All of the Values Match 85
    When Only Some of the Values Match 86
    COALESCE Function Syntax 87
    Example: Using the COALESCE Function 87
    Understanding the Advantages of PROC SQL Joins 88
Quiz 89

Understanding Joins

You combine data horizontally by merging or joining multiple data sets into one data set. This process is called *horizontal combination* because, in the final data set, each observation (or horizontal row) has variables from more than one input data set.

Figure 3.1 PROC SQL: Understanding Joins

```
proc sql;
   select *
      from a,b
         where a.x=b.x
;
quit;
```

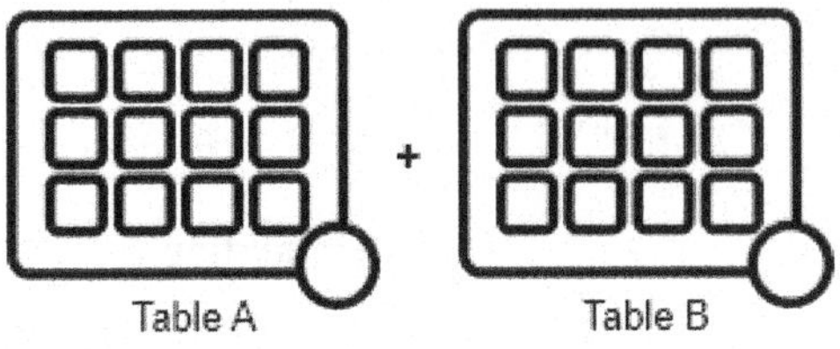

Table A   Table B

A *PROC SQL join* is a query that specifies multiple tables or views to be combined based on the conditions under which rows match and return a result set.

Joins combine tables horizontally, side by side, by combining rows. The tables being joined are not required to have the same number of rows or columns.

Note: You can use a join to combine views as well as tables. Most of the following references to tables are also applicable to views; any exceptions are noted.

When you use a PROC SQL query to join tables, you must decide how you want the rows from the various tables to be combined. There are two main types of joins, as shown below.

Type of Join	Output
Inner join 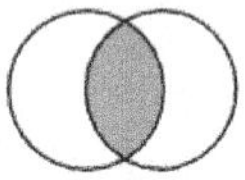	only the rows that match across all table or tables
Outer join 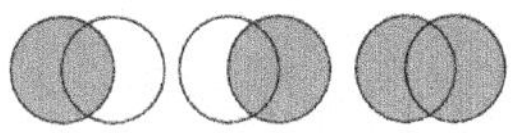	rows that match across tables (as in the inner join) plus nonmatching rows from one or more tables

When any type of join is processed, PROC SQL starts by generating a Cartesian product, which contains all possible combinations of rows from all tables.

Generating a Cartesian Product

The most basic type of join combines data from two tables that are specified in the FROM clause of a SELECT statement. When you specify multiple tables in the FROM clause but do not include a WHERE statement to subset data, PROC SQL returns the

Cartesian product of the tables. In a Cartesian product, each row in the first table is combined with every row in the second table. The following example illustrates a Cartesian product where table One and table Two are joined using a FROM clause.

```
proc sql;
   select *;
      from certadv.one, certadv.two
   ;
quit;
```

The output shown below displays all possible combinations of each row in table One with all rows in table Two. Note that each table has a column named X, and both of these columns appear in the output. A Cartesian product includes all columns from the source tables. Columns that have common names are not overlaid.

Output 3.1 *Cartesian Product of Tables Certadv.One and Certadv.Two*

Certadv.One

x	a
1	a
2	b
4	d

Certadv.Two

x	b
2	x
3	y
5	v

Cartesian Product

x	a	x	b
1	a	2	x
1	a	3	y
1	a	5	v
2	b	2	x
2	b	3	y
2	b	5	v
4	d	2	x
4	d	3	y
4	d	5	v

In most cases, generating all possible combinations of rows from multiple tables does not yield useful results, so a Cartesian product is rarely the query outcome that you want. For example, in the Cartesian product of two tables that contain employee information, each row of output might contain information about two different employees. Usually, you want your join to return only a subset of rows from the tables.

The size of a Cartesian product can also be problematic. The number of rows in a Cartesian product is equal to the product of the number of rows in the contributing tables.

Tables One and Two, used in the preceding example, contain three rows each. The number of rows in the Cartesian product of tables One and Two is calculated as follows:

```
3 x 3 = 9 rows
```

Joining small tables such as One and Two results in a relatively small Cartesian product. However, the Cartesian product of large tables can be huge and can require a large amount of system resources for processing.

For example, joining two tables of 1,000 rows each results in output of the following size:

```
1,000 x 1,000 = 1,000,000 rows
```

When you run a query that involves a Cartesian product that cannot be optimized, PROC SQL writes the following warning message to the SAS log.

Log 3.1 SAS Log

```
NOTE: The execution of this query involves performing one or more Cartesian
product joins that cannot be optimized.
```

Although you will not often choose to create a query that returns a Cartesian product, it is important to understand how a Cartesian product is generated. In all types of joins, PROC SQL generates a Cartesian product first, and then eliminates rows that do not meet any subsetting criteria that you have specified.

Note: In many cases, PROC SQL can optimize the processing of a join, thereby minimizing the resources that are required to generate a Cartesian product.

Using Inner Joins

A Brief Overview

An SQL inner join combines matching rows between two tables. You can perform an inner join on tables using two methods:

- Specify the two tables to be joined in a FROM clause separated by the INNER JOIN keyword. Next, specify an ON clause that indicates how rows should be matched.

- Join the two tables based on the matching criteria, known as *join conditions*, that you specify in a WHERE clause.

The following diagram illustrates an inner join of two tables. The shaded area of overlap represents the matching rows (the subset of rows) that the inner join returns as output.

Figure 3.2 Venn Diagram, Inner Join for Table 1 and Table 2

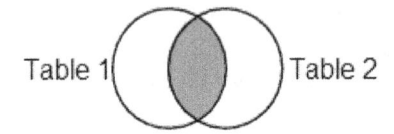

Note: An inner join is sometimes called a *conventional join*.

This book focuses on joining tables using the INNER JOIN keyword with the ON clause in the FROM clause.

Inner Join Syntax

In the FROM clause, specify the first table, the keyword INNER JOIN, and then the second table. Following the table names and join type, the syntax requires an ON clause to describe the join criteria for matching rows in the tables. Omitting the ON clause produces a syntax error.

Syntax, SELECT statement for inner join:

SELECT *column-1<,...column-n>*

    FROM *table-1 | view-1* **INNER JOIN** *table-2 | view-2* <INNER JOIN...*table-n | view-n*>

    ON *table1.column=table2.column*

    <other clauses>;

INNER JOIN
: specifies the join type.

table
: specifies the name of the source table.

ON
: specifies join conditions, which are expressions that specify the column or columns on which the tables are to be joined.

table.column
: refers to the source table and the column name on which the join occurs.

<other clauses>
: refers to optional PROC SQL clauses.

Note: The maximum number of tables that you can combine in a single inner join depends on your version of SAS.

Understanding How Joins Are Processed

Understanding how PROC SQL processes inner and outer joins will help you to understand which output is generated by each type of join. PROC SQL follows these steps to process a join:

- Builds a Cartesian product of rows from the indicated tables.

- Evaluates each row in the Cartesian product, based on the join conditions specified in the WHERE clause, along with any other subsetting conditions, and removes any rows that do not meet the specified conditions.

- If summary functions are specified, summarizes the applicable rows.

- Returns the rows that are to be displayed in output.

Note: The PROC SQL query optimizer follows a more complex process than the conceptual approach described here, by breaking the Cartesian product into smaller pieces. For each query, the optimizer selects the most efficient processing method for the specific situation.

By default, PROC SQL joins do not overlay columns with the same name. Instead, the output displays all columns that have the same name. To avoid having columns with the same name in the output from an inner or outer join, you can eliminate or rename the duplicate columns.

TIP You can also use the COALESCE function with an inner or outer join to overlay columns with the same name.

Example: Using a FROM Clause with the INNER JOIN Keyword

The following example illustrates an inner join. Inner joins are also known as *equijoins* because of the equality in the ON clause. The ON clause specifies that only rows with identical values in the column produce a match.

```
proc sql;
   select *
      from certadv.one inner join certadv.two
      on one.x=two.x;
quit;
```

Output 3.2 Inner Join Output: INNER JOIN Keyword

x	a	x	b
2	b	2	x

The FROM clause, along with the INNER JOIN keyword and the ON clause, specifies that the result set should include only these rows: those whose values of column X in table One are equal to values in column X of table Two. Only one row from table One and one row from table Two have matching values of X. Therefore, those two rows are combined into one row of output.

Note: PROC SQL will not perform a join unless the columns that are compared in the join condition have the same data type. However, the two columns are not required to have the same name. For example, the join condition shown in the following ON clause is valid if ID and EmpID have the same data type:

```
on table1.id = table2.empid
```

Note: The join condition that is specified in the ON clause often contains the equal (=) operator, but the expression might contain one or more other operators instead. You can use other comparison operators, such as greater than, less than, or special WHERE operators.

Example: Eliminating Duplicate Columns

The following example uses an inner join to combine the tables One and Two.

```
proc sql;
   select *
      from certadv.one inner join certadv.two
      on one.x=two.x;
quit;
```

Output 3.3 Inner Join, Tables One and Two

x	a	x	b
2	b	2	x

The two tables have a column with an identical name, X. Because the SELECT clause in the query shown above contains an asterisk, the output displays all columns from both tables.

To eliminate a duplicate column, you can specify just one of the duplicate columns in the SELECT statement. The SELECT statement in the preceding PROC SQL query can be modified as follows:

```
proc sql;
   select one.x, a, b
      from certadv.one inner join certadv.two
      on one.x=two.x;
quit;
```

Here, the SELECT clause specifies that only column X from table One will be included in output. The output, which now displays only one column X, is shown below.

Output 3.4   Table One Output

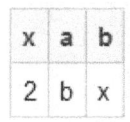

x	a	b
2	b	x

Note: In an inner equijoin, like the one shown here, it does not matter which of the same-named columns is listed in the SELECT statement. The SELECT statement in this example could have specified Two.X instead of One.X.

Another way to eliminate the duplicate X column in the preceding example is shown below:

```
proc sql;
   select one.*, b
      from certadv.one inner join certadv.two
      on one.x=two.x;
quit;
```

By using the asterisk (*) to select all columns from table One, and only B from table Two, this query generates the same output as the preceding version.

Example: Renaming a Column by Using a Column Alias

If you are working with several tables that have a column with a common name but slightly different data, you might want both columns to appear in output. To avoid the confusion of displaying two different columns with the same name, you can rename one of the duplicate columns by specifying a column alias in the SELECT statement.

```
proc sql;
   select one.x as ID, two.x, a, b
      from certadv.one inner join certadv.two
      on one.x=two.x;
quit;
```

The output of the modified query is shown here.

Output 3.5   PROC SQL Result: Modified Query Output

ID	x	a	b
2	2	b	x

The column One.X has been renamed to ID and the output clearly indicates that ID and X are two different columns.

Example: Joining Tables That Have Rows with Matching Values

Consider what happens when you join two tables in which multiple rows have duplicate values of the column on which the tables are being joined. Each of the tables Three and Four has multiple rows that contain the value 2 for column X.

Figure 3.3 Original Tables: Certadv.Three and Certadv.Four

Certadv.Three

X	A
1	a1
1	a2
2	b1
2	b2
4	d

Certadv.Four

X	B
2	x1
2	x2
3	y
5	v

The following PROC SQL inner join matches rows from the two tables based on the common column X.

```
proc sql;
   select *
      from certadv.three inner join certadv.four
      on three.x=four.x;
quit;
```

The output shows how this inner join handles the duplicate values of X.

Output 3.6 PROC SQL Inner Join

X	A	X	B
2	b1	2	x1
2	b1	2	x2
2	b2	2	x1
2	b2	2	x2

All possible combinations of the duplicate rows are displayed. There are no matches on any other values of X, so no other rows are displayed in output.

Note: A DATA step match-merge would write output to only two rows because it processes data sequentially from top to bottom.

Specifying a Table Alias

To enable PROC SQL to distinguish between same-named columns from different tables, you use qualified column names. To create a qualified column name, you prefix the column name with its table name. The following PROC SQL inner join contains several qualified column names.

```
proc sql;
title 'Employee Names and Job Codes';
   select staffmaster.empid, lastname, firstname, jobcode
      from certadv.staffmaster inner join certadv.payrollmaster
      on staffmaster.empid=payrollmaster.empid;
quit;
```

It can be time consuming and difficult to read PROC SQL code that contains lengthy qualified column names. You can use a temporary, alternate name for any or all tables in any PROC SQL query. This temporary name, which is called a *table alias*, is specified after the table name in the FROM clause. The keyword AS is often used, although its use is optional.

The following modified PROC SQL query specifies table aliases in the FROM clause, and then uses the table aliases to qualify column names in the SELECT and ON clauses.

```
proc sql;
title 'Employee Names and Job Codes';
   select s.empid, lastname, firstname, jobcode
      from certadv.staffmaster as s inner join
           certadv.payrollmaster as p
      on s.empid=p.empid;
quit;
```

In this query, the optional keyword AS is used to define the table aliases in the FROM clause. The FROM clause would be equally valid without the keyword AS.

```
from certadv.staffmaster s,
     certadv.payrollmaster p
```

Note: While using table aliases helps you to work more efficiently, the use of table aliases does not cause SAS to execute the query more quickly.

Table aliases are usually optional. However, there are two situations that require their use.

When Are Table Aliases Required?	Example
a table is joined to itself (called a *self-join* or *reflexive join*)	`from certadv.staffmaster as s1,` `     certadv.staffmaster as s2`

you need to reference columns from same-named tables in different libraries	`from certadv.flightdelays as af,`
	`     certadvf.flightdelays as wf`
	`on af.delay > wf.delay`

Thus far, you have seen relatively simple examples of inner joins. However, as in any other PROC SQL query, inner joins can include more advanced components, such as these:

- titles and footers
- functions and expressions in a SELECT clause
- multiple conditions in a WHERE clause
- an ORDER BY clause for sorting
- summary functions with grouping

Example: Complex PROC SQL Inner Join

Suppose you want to create a report where the name is displayed with first initial and last name (R. Long), JobCode, and ages of all employees who live in New York. The report also should be sorted by JobCode and Age.

The data that you need is stored in the two tables below.

Table	Relevant Columns
Certadv.Staffmaster	EmpID, LastName, FirstName, State
Certadv.Payrollmaster	EmpId, JobCode, DateOfBirth

Of the three columns that you want to display, JobCode is the only column that already exists in the tables. The other two columns must be created from existing columns.

The PROC SQL query shown here uses an inner join to generate the output that you want:

```
proc sql outobs=15;
   title 'New York Employees';
   select substr(firstname,1,1) || '. ' || lastname    /*1*/
      as Name,
      jobcode,
      int((today() - dateofbirth)/365.25)
      as Age
      from certadv.payrollmaster as p inner join       /*2*/
         certadv.staffmaster as s
      on p.empid =                                     /*3*/
         s.empid
      where state='NY'                                 /*4*/
      order by 2,3                                     /*5*/
   ;
quit;
```

1   The SELECT clause specifies the new column Name, the existing column JobCode, and the new column Age.

   The SELECT clause uses functions and expressions to create two new columns.

   - To create Name, the SUBSTR function extracts the first initial from FirstName. Then the concatenation operator combines the first initial with a period, a space, and then the contents of the LastName column. Finally, the keyword AS names the new column.

   - To calculate Age, the INT function returns the integer portion of the result of the calculation. In the expression that is used as an argument of the INT function, the employee's birth date (DateOfBirth) is subtracted from today's date (returned by the TODAY function), and the difference is divided by the number of days in a year (365.25).

2   The FROM clause lists the tables to select from. The FROM clause uses the AS keyword to distinguish a table alias from other table names. The FROM clause also specifies the INNER JOIN keyword to specify the join type.

3   The ON clause describes the join criteria for matching rows in the tables. The ON clause produces a match for the rows with identical values in the EmpID column.

4   The WHERE clause subsets the data further by selecting only the rows where State is **NY**.

5   The ORDER BY clause specifies the order in which rows are displayed in the result table.

This query writes to output only those rows that have matching values of EmpID and rows in which the value of State is **NY**. You do not need to prefix the column name State with a table name because State occurs in only one of the tables.

Output 3.7   PROC SQL Query Result: Inner Join

New York Employees

Name	JobCode	Age
T. BURNETTE	BCK	33
R. LONG	BCK	39
N. JONES	BCK	44
J. MARKS	BCK	44
R. VANDEUSEN	BCK	50
L. GORDON	BCK	51
J. PEARSON	BCK	51
C. PEARCE	FA1	39
D. WOOD	FA1	40
C. RICHARDS	FA1	41
R. MCDANIEL	FA1	43
L. JONES	FA1	43
A. PARKER	FA1	46
D. FIELDS	FA1	52
M. CAHILL	FA2	31

Example: PROC SQL Inner Join with Summary Functions

You can use summary functions to summarize and group data in a PROC SQL join. The following example summarizes columns for New York employees in each job code: number of employees and average age.

```
proc sql outobs=15;
   title 'Average Age of New York Employees';
   select jobcode,count(p.empid) as Employees,            /*1*/
                avg(int((today() - dateofbirth)/365.25))
                format=4.1 as AvgAge
      from certadv.payrollmaster as p inner join          /*2*/
           certadv.staffmaster as s
         on p.empid=                                      /*3*/
            s.empid
```

```
                where state='NY'                            /* 4 */
                group by jobcode                            /* 5 */
                order by jobcode                            /* 6 */
        ;
        quit;
```

1. The SELECT clause uses summary functions to create two new columns.
   - To create Employees, the COUNT function is used with p.EmpID (Payrollmaster.EmpID) as its argument.
   - To create AvgAge, the AVG function is used with an expression as its argument. As described in the previous example, the expression uses the INT function to calculate each employee's age.
2. The FROM clause lists the tables to select from. The FROM clause uses the AS keyword to distinguish a table alias from other table names. The FROM clause also specifies the INNER JOIN keyword to specify the join type.
3. The ON clause describes the join criteria for matching rows in the tables. The ON clause produces a match for the rows with identical values in the EmpID column.
4. The WHERE clause subsets the data further by selecting only the rows where State is **NY**.
5. The GROUP BY clause specifies what variable to group the data by for summarization.
6. The ORDER BY clause specifies the order in which rows are displayed in the result table.

Output 3.8   PROC SQL Query Result: Inner Join with Summary Functions

Average Age of New York Employees

JobCode	Employees	AvgAge
BCK	7	44.6
FA1	7	43.4
FA2	9	44.8
FA3	4	38.8
ME1	5	40.2
ME2	9	44.8
ME3	2	50.5
NA1	1	40.0
NA2	1	50.0
PT1	5	40.2
PT2	5	50.2
PT3	2	43.0
SCP	6	42.3
TA1	5	45.8
TA2	12	45.2

Using Natural Joins

A Brief Overview

A natural join automatically selects columns from each table to match rows. With a natural join, PROC SQL identifies columns in each table that have the same name and type, and uses those as the join criteria. The advantage of using a natural join is that the coding is streamlined. The ON clause is implied, and you do not need to use table aliases to qualify column names that are common to both tables.

If you specify a natural join on tables that do not have at least one column with a common name and type, the result is a Cartesian product. You can use a WHERE clause to limit the output. Because the natural join makes certain assumptions about what you want to accomplish, you should examine your data thoroughly before using it.

Natural Join Syntax

Syntax, SELECT statement for outer join:

SELECT *column-1<,...column-n>*
      FROM *table-1 | view-1* **NATURAL JOIN** *table-2 | view-2*
  <other clauses>;

NATURAL JOIN
  specifies the type of join.

table
  specifies the name of the source table.

<other clauses>
  refers to optional PROC SQL clauses.

Note: Do not use an ON clause with a natural join. When using a natural join, an ON clause is implied, matching all like columns. You can use a WHERE clause to subset the query results. A natural join functions the same as a qualified join with the USING clause. A natural join is a shorthand form of USING. As is the case with USING, like columns appear only once in the result set.

Example: Using a Natural Join

A natural join assumes that you want to base the join on equal values of all pairs of all common columns. The following example selects all columns from Certadv.Schedule and Certadv.Courses and creates an output using a natural join.

```
proc sql;
   select *
      from certadv.schedule natural join
           certadv.courses
   ;
quit;
```

PROC SQL identified Course_Code as the common column between Certadv.Schedule and Certadv.Courses. Based on that column, the natural join selected columns from each table to match the rows.

Output 3.9 PROC SQL Query Result: Natural Join

Course_Code	Description	Course Length	Course Fee	Course Number	Location	Begin	Instructor
C001	Basic Telecommunications	3	$795	1	Seattle	23OCT2018	Hallis, Dr. George
C002	Structured Query Language	4	$1150	2	Dallas	04DEC2018	Wickam, Dr. Alice
C003	Local Area Networks	3	$650	3	Boston	08JAN2019	Forest, Mr. Peter
C004	Database Design	2	$375	4	Seattle	22JAN2019	Tally, Ms. Julia
C005	Artificial Intelligence	2	$400	5	Dallas	26FEB2019	Hallis, Dr. George
C006	Computer Aided Design	5	$1600	6	Boston	02APR2019	Berthan, Ms. Judy
C001	Basic Telecommunications	3	$795	7	Dallas	21MAY2019	Hallis, Dr. George
C002	Structured Query Language	4	$1150	8	Boston	11JUN2019	Wickam, Dr. Alice
C003	Local Area Networks	3	$650	9	Seattle	16JUL2019	Forest, Mr. Peter
C004	Database Design	2	$375	10	Dallas	13AUG2019	Tally, Ms. Julia
C005	Artificial Intelligence	2	$400	11	Boston	17SEP2019	Tally, Ms. Julia
C006	Computer Aided Design	5	$1600	12	Seattle	01OCT2019	Berthan, Ms. Judy
C001	Basic Telecommunications	3	$795	13	Boston	12NOV2019	Hallis, Dr. George
C002	Structured Query Language	4	$1150	14	Seattle	03DEC2019	Wickam, Dr. Alice
C003	Local Area Networks	3	$650	15	Dallas	07JAN2020	Forest, Mr. Peter
C004	Database Design	2	$375	16	Boston	21JAN2020	Tally, Ms. Julia
C005	Artificial Intelligence	2	$400	17	Seattle	05FEB2020	Hallis, Dr. George
C006	Computer Aided Design	5	$1600	18	Dallas	25FEB2020	Berthan, Ms. Judy

Using Outer Joins

A Brief Overview

An outer join returns nonmatching rows as well as matching rows.

Type of Outer Join	Output
Left	Returns all rows from the left table (first table) and matching rows from the right table (second table) that are specified in the FROM clause.

Type of Outer Join	Output
Right	Returns all rows from the right table (second table) and matching rows from the left table (first table).
Full	Returns all matching and nonmatching rows from all the tables.

Outer Join Syntax

Syntax, SELECT statement for outer join:

SELECT *column-1<,...column-n>*

   FROM *table-1 | view-1* **LEFT JOIN | RIGHT JOIN | FULL JOIN** *table-2 | view-2*

   ON *table1.column = table2.column*

   <other clauses>;

LEFT JOIN, RIGHT JOIN, FULL JOIN
   are keywords that specify the type of outer join.

table
   specifies the name of the source table.

ON
   specifies join conditions, which are expressions that specify the column or columns on which the tables are to be joined.

table.column
   refers to the source table and the column name on which the join occurs.

<other clauses>
   refers to optional PROC SQL clauses.

Note: To further subset the rows in the query output, you can follow the ON clause with a WHERE clause. The WHERE clause subsets the individual detail rows before the outer join is performed. The ON clause then specifies how the remaining rows are to be selected for output.

Note: You can perform an outer join on only two tables or views at a time.

Example: Using a Left Outer Join

A left outer join retrieves all rows that match across tables, based on the join conditions, plus nonmatching rows from the left table (the first table specified in the FROM clause).

Suppose you are using a PROC SQL left join to combine the two tables One and Two. The join condition is stated in the expression following the ON keyword.

```
proc sql;
   select *
      from certadv.one left join
         certadv.two
         on one.x=two.x
   ;
quit;
```

The two tables and the three rows of output are shown below:

Output 3.10   PROC SQL Query Result: Left Outer Join Output

Certadv.One

x	a
1	a
2	b
4	d

+

Certadv.Two

x	b
2	x
3	y
5	v

=

Left Join

x	a	x	b
1	a	.	.
2	b	2	x
4	d	.	.

In each row of output, the first two columns correspond to table One (the left table) and the last two columns correspond to table Two (the right table).

Because this is a left join, all rows, both matching and nonmatching, from table One are included in the output. Rows from table Two are included in the output only if they match a row from table One. In the output, the rows from table One are the first two columns and the rows from table Two are the last two columns.

The second row of output is the only row in which the row from table One matched a row from table Two, based on the join conditions specified in the ON clause. In the first and third rows of output, the row from table One had no matching row in table Two.

Note: In all three types of outer joins (left, right, and full), the columns in the result (combined) row that are from the unmatched row are set to missing values.

Example: Eliminating Duplicate Columns in a Left Outer Join

To eliminate one of the duplicate columns in any outer join, you can modify the SELECT clause to list the specific columns that will be displayed. The SELECT clause from the preceding query has been modified to remove the duplicate X column.

```
proc sql;
   select one.x, a, b
      from certadv.one left join
         certadv.two
         on one.x=two.x
   ;
quit;
```

Output 3.11 PROC SQL Query Result: Left Outer Join without Duplicate Rows

Certadv.One   Certadv.Two

x	a
1	a
2	b
4	d

\+

x	b
2	x
3	y
5	v

=

x	a	b
1	a	
2	b	x
4	d	

Example: Using a Right Outer Join

A right outer join retrieves all rows that match across tables, based on the join conditions, plus nonmatching rows from the second table that are specified in the FROM clause. The following PROC SQL query uses a right join to combine rows from tables One and Two, based on the join conditions that were specified in the ON clause.

```
proc sql;
   select *
      from certadv.one right join
           certadv.two
           on one.x=two.x
;
quit;
```

Output 3.12 PROC SQL Query Result: Right Outer Join Output

Certadv.One   Certadv.Two   Right Join

x	a
1	a
2	b
4	d

\+

x	b
2	x
3	y
5	v

=

x	a	x	b
2	b	2	x
.		3	y
.		5	v

In each row of output, the first two columns correspond to table One and the last two columns correspond to table Two.

Because this is a right join, all rows, both matching and nonmatching, from table Two are included in the output. Rows from table One are displayed in the output only if they match a row from table Two. There is only one row in table One that matches a value of X in table Two, and these two matching rows combine to form the first row of output. In the remaining rows of output, there is no match and the columns corresponding to table One are set to missing values.

Example: Using a Full Outer Join

A full outer join retrieves both matching rows and nonmatching rows from both tables.

```
proc sql;
   select *
      from certadv.one full join
           certadv.two
           on one.x=two.x
;
```

82 Chapter 3 • Joining Tables Using PROC SQL

```
quit;
```

Output 3.13   PROC SQL Query Result: Full Outer Join Output

Certadv.One

x	a
1	a
2	b
4	d

+

Certadv.Two

x	b
2	x
3	y
5	v

=

Full Join

x	a	x	b
1	a	.	.
2	b	2	x
.	.	3	y
4	d	.	.
.	.	5	v

Because this is a full join, all rows, both matching and nonmatching, from both tables are included in the output. There is only one match between table One and table Two, so only one row of output displays values in all columns. All remaining rows of output contain only values from table One or table Two, with the remaining columns set to missing values.

Example: Complex Outer Join

Suppose you want to list all of an airline's flights that were scheduled for March, along with any available corresponding delay information. Each flight is identified by both a flight date and a flight number. Your output should display the following data: flight date, flight number, destination, and length of delay in minutes.

The data that you need is stored in the two tables shown below. The applicable columns from each table are identified.

Table	Relevant Columns
Certadv.Marchflights	Date, FlightNumber, Destination
Certadv.Flightdelays	Date, FlightNumber, Destination, Delay

Your output should include the columns that are listed above and all of the following rows:

- rows that have matching values of Date and FlightNumber across the two tables
- rows from Certadv.Marchflights that have no matching row in Certadv.Flightdelays

To generate the output that you want, the following PROC SQL query uses a left outer join, with Certadv.Marchflights specified as the left table.

```
proc sql outobs=20;
title 'All March Flights';
   select m.date,                                        /*1*/
          m.flightnumber label='Flight Number',
          m.destination  label='Left',
          f.destination  label='Right',
          delay label='Delay in Minutes'
   from certadv.marchflights as m left join              /*2*/
        certadv.flightdelays as f
```

```
      on m.date=f.date                              /*3*/
         and m.flightnumber=f.flightnumber
   order by delay;                                  /*4*/
quit;
```

1. The SELECT clause eliminates the duplicate Date and FlightNumber columns by specifying their source as Certadv.Marchflights. However, the SELECT clause list specifies the Destination columns from both tables and assigns a table alias to each to distinguish between them.

2. The FROM clause lists the tables to select from. The FROM clause uses the AS keyword to distinguish a table alias from other table names. The FROM clause also specifies the LEFT JOIN keyword to specify the join type.

3. The ON clause contains two join conditions, which match the tables on the two columns Date and FlightNumber.

4. The ORDER BY clause specifies the order in which rows are displayed in the result table.

The first 12 rows in the output display rows from Certadv.Marchflights. The rows that have no matching values with Certadv.Flightdelays display missing values for those columns. Therefore, the first 12 rows have missing values.

Output 3.14 PROC SQL Query Result: Outer Join

All March Flights

Date	Flight Number	Left	Right	Delay in Minutes
14MAR2013	271	CDG		.
16MAR2013	622	FRA		.
.	132	YYZ		.
22MAR2013	183	WAS		.
11MAR2013	290	WAS		.
27MAR2013	982	DFW		.
29MAR2013	829	WAS		.
11MAR2013	202	ORD		.
08MAR2013	182	YYZ		.
17MAR2013	182	YYZ		.
03MAR2013	416	WAS		.
25MAR2013	872	LAX		.
09MAR2013	821	LHR	LHR	-10
25MAR2013	829	WAS	WAS	-10
02MAR2013	387	CPH	CPH	-10
10MAR2013	523	ORD	ORD	-10
07MAR2013	523	ORD	ORD	-10
18MAR2013	219	LHR	LHR	-10
14MAR2013	829	WAS	WAS	-10
27MAR2013	182	YYZ	YYZ	-9

Note: The same results could be generated by using a right outer join, with Certadv.Marchflights specified as the right (second) table.

Comparing SQL Joins and DATA Step Match-Merges

A Brief Overview

DATA step match-merges and PROC SQL joins can produce the same results. However, there are important differences between these two techniques. For example, a join does not require that you sort the data first; a DATA step match-merge requires that the data be sorted.

It is useful to compare the use of SQL joins and DATA step match-merges in the following situations:

- when all of the values of the selected variable match
- when only some of the values of the selected variable match

When All of the Values Match

When all of the values of the BY variable match, you can use a PROC SQL inner join to produce the same results as a DATA step match-merge.

Suppose you want to combine tables Five and Six.

Figure 3.4 Tables Certadv.Five and Certadv.Six

Certadv.Five

X	A
1	a
2	b
3	c

Certadv.Six

X	B
1	x
2	y
3	z

These two tables have column X in common, and all values of X in each row match across the two tables. Both tables are already sorted by X.

The following DATA step match-merge (followed by a PROC PRINT step) and the PROC SQL inner join produce identical reports.

DATA Step Match-Merge	PROC SQL Inner Join
| ```
data merged;
   merge certadv.five certadv.six;
   by x;
run;
proc print data=merged noobs;
   title 'Table Merged';
run;
``` | ```
proc sql;
title 'Table Merged';
   select five.x, a, b
      from certadv.five, certadv.six
      where five.x = six.x
      order by x;
quit;
``` |

Table Merged

X	A	B
1	a	x
2	b	y
3	c	z

Table Merged

X	A	B
1	a	x
2	b	y
3	c	z

Note: The DATA step match-merge creates a data set. By contrast, the PROC SQL inner join, as shown here, creates only a report as output. To make these two programs completely identical, the PROC SQL inner join could be rewritten to create a table.

86 Chapter 3 • *Joining Tables Using PROC SQL*

Note: If the order of rows in the output does not matter, the ORDER BY clause can be removed from the PROC SQL join. Without the ORDER BY clause, this join is more efficient, because PROC SQL does not need to make a second pass through the data.

When Only Some of the Values Match

When only some of the values of the BY variable match, you can use a PROC SQL full outer join to produce the same result as a DATA step match-merge. Unlike the DATA step match-merge, however, a PROC SQL outer join does not overlay the two common columns by default. To overlay common columns, you must use the COALESCE function in the PROC SQL full outer join.

Note: The COALESCE function can also be used with inner join operators.

Consider what happens when you use a PROC SQL full outer join without the COALESCE function. Suppose you want to combine tables Three and Four. These two tables have the column X in common, but most of the values of X do not match across tables. Both tables are already sorted by X. The following DATA step match-merge (followed by a PROC PRINT step) and the PROC SQL outer join combine these tables, but do not generate the same output. The COALESCE function can also be used with inner join operators.

DATA Step Match-Merge	PROC SQL Full Outer Join
| ```
data merged;
   merge certadv.three certadv.four;
   by x;
run;

proc print data=merged noobs;
   title 'Table Merged';
run;
``` | ```
proc sql;
title 'Table Merged';
   select three.x, a, b
      from certadv.three
      full join
      certadv.four
      on three.x = four.x
      order by x;
quit;
``` |

Table Merged

X	A	B
1	a1	
1	a2	
2	b1	x1
2	b2	x2
3		y
4	d	
5		v

Table Merged

X	A	B
.		y
.		v
1	a2	
1	a1	
2	b1	x1
2	b2	x2
2	b2	x1
2	b1	x2
4	d	

The DATA step match-merge automatically overlays the common column, X. The PROC SQL outer join selects the value of X from just one of the tables, table Three, so that no X values from table Four are included in the PROC SQL output. However, the PROC

SQL outer join cannot overlay the columns by default. The values that vary across the two merged tables are highlighted.

COALESCE Function Syntax

When you add the COALESCE function to the SELECT clause of the PROC SQL outer join, the PROC SQL outer join can produce the same result as a DATA step match-merge.

Syntax, COALESCE function in a SELECT clause:

SELECT COALESCE *(column-1<,...column-n>)*

column-1 through *column-n*
    are the names of two or more columns to be overlaid. The COALESCE function requires that all arguments have the same data type.

The COALESCE function overlays the specified columns:

- It checks the value of each column in the order in which the columns are listed.
- It returns the first value that is a SAS nonmissing value.

Note: If all returned values are missing, COALESCE returns a missing value.

Example: Using the COALESCE Function

When the COALESCE function is added to the preceding PROC SQL full outer join, the DATA step match-merge (with PROC PRINT step) and the PROC SQL full outer join combine rows in the same way. The two programs, the tables, and the output are shown below.

DATA Step Match-Merge	PROC SQL Full Outer Join
| ```
data merged;
    merge certadv.three certadv.four;
    by x;
run;
proc print data=merged noobs;
    title 'Table Merged';
run;
``` | ```
proc sql;
 title 'Table Merged';
   select coalesce(three.x, four.x)
       as X, a, b
       from certadv.three
       full join
       certadv.four
       on three.x = four.x;
``` |

Table Merged

X	A	B
1	a1	
1	a2	
2	b1	x1
2	b2	x2
3	y	
4	d	
5	v	

Table Merged

X	A	B
1	a2	
1	a1	
2	b1	x1
2	b1	x2
2	b2	x1
2	b2	x2
3	y	
4	d	
5	v	

Understanding the Advantages of PROC SQL Joins

DATA step match-merges and PROC SQL joins both have advantages and disadvantages. Here are some of the advantages of PROC SQL joins.

Advantage	Example
| PROC SQL joins do not require sorted or indexed tables. | ```
proc sql;
    select table1.x, a, b
        from table1
            full join
            table2
            on table1.x = table2.x;
quit;
```  Note that *table-1* is sorted by column X and *table-2* is not. |
| PROC SQL joins do not require that the columns in join expressions have the same name. | ```
proc sql;
    select table1.x, lastname,
            status
        from table1, table2
        where table1.id =
            table2.custnum;
``` |

Advantage	Example
| PROC SQL joins can use comparison operators other than the equal sign (=). | ```
proc sql;
   select a.itemnumber, cost,
          price
      from table1 as a,
           table2 as b
      where a.itemnumber = b.itemnumber
            and a.cost>b.price;
quit;
``` |

Note: Join performance can be substantially improved when the tables are indexed on the columns on which the tables are being joined.

Quiz

Select the best answer for each question. After completing the quiz, check your answers using the answer key in the appendix.

1. When is a Cartesian product returned?

   a. When join conditions are not specified in a PROC SQL join.

   b. When join conditions are not specified in a PROC SQL set operation.

   c. When more than two tables are specified in a PROC SQL join.

   d. When the keyword ALL is used with the OUTER UNION operator.

2. Given the PROC SQL query and tables shown below, which output is generated?

   Store1

Wk	Sales
1	$515.07
2	$772.29
3	$888.88
4	$1000.01

   Store2

Wk	Sales
1	$1368.99
2	$1506.23
3	$1200.57
4	$1784.11
5	$43.00

   ```
   proc sql;
      select *
         from certadv.store1, certadv.store2
         where store1.wk=store2.wk;
   quit;
   ```

   a.
   ```

Wk	Sales	Wk	Sales
1	$515.07	1	$1368.99
2	$772.29	2	$1506.23
3	$888.88	3	$1200.57
4	$1000.01	4	$1784.11
.	.	5	$43.00

b.

Wk	Sales	Wk	Sales
1	$515.07	1	$1368.99
2	$772.29	2	$1506.23
3	$888.88	3	$1200.57
4	$1000.01	4	$1784.11

c.

Wk	Sales
1	$515.07
2	$772.29
3	$888.88
4	$1000.01

d.

Wk	Sales	Wk	Sales
1	$515.07	1	$1368.99
1	$515.07	2	$1506.23
1	$515.07	3	$1200.57
1	$515.07	4	$1784.11
1	$515.07	5	$43.00
2	$772.29	1	$1368.99
2	$772.29	2	$1506.23
2	$772.29	3	$1200.57
2	$772.29	4	$1784.11
2	$772.29	5	$43.00
3	$888.88	1	$1368.99
3	$888.88	2	$1506.23
3	$888.88	3	$1200.57
3	$888.88	4	$1784.11
3	$888.88	5	$43.00
4	$1000.01	1	$1368.99
4	$1000.01	2	$1506.23
4	$1000.01	3	$1200.57
4	$1000.01	4	$1784.11
4	$1000.01	5	$43.00

3. Which output will the following PROC SQL query generate?

```
proc sql;
   select *
      from table1 left join table2
         on table1.g3=table2.g3;
quit;
```

Table 1

G3	Z
89	FL
46	UI
47	BA

Table 2

G3	R
46	BC
85	FL
99	BA

a.

G3	Z	G3	R
46	UI	46	BC
47	BA	.	.
89	FL	.	.

b.

G3	Z	G3	R
46	UI	46	BC
.		85	FL
.		99	BA

c.

G3	Z
46	UI

d.

G3	Z	G3	R
46	UI	46	BC

4. What is needed in order for PROC SQL to perform an inner join?

    a. The tables being joined must contain the same number of columns.

    b. The tables must be sorted before they are joined.

    c. The columns that are specified in a join condition in the WHERE clause must have the same data type.

    d. The columns that are specified in a join condition in the WHERE clause must have the same name.

5. Which PROC SQL query will generate the same output as the DATA step match-merge and PROC PRINT step shown below?

```
data merged;
   merge certadv.table1 certadv.table2;
      by g3;
run;
proc print data=merged noobs;
   title 'Merged';
run;
```

Table 1

G3	Z
89	FL
46	UI
47	BA

Table 2

G3	R
46	BC
85	FL
99	BA

Merged

G3	Z	R
46		BC
85		FL

a.
```
proc sql;
   title 'Merged';
      select a.g3, z, r
         from table1 as a full join table2 as b
            on a.g3 = b.g3
```

```
        order by 1;
   quit;
```

b.
```
proc sql;
   title 'Merged';
      select a.g3, z, r
         from table1 as a table2 as b
            on a.g3 = b.g3
         order by 1;
quit;
```

c.
```
proc sql;
   title 'Merged';
      select coalesce(a.g3, b.g3)
            label='G3', z, r
         from table1 as a full join table2 as b
            on a.g3 = b.g3
         order by 1;
quit;
```

d.
```
proc sql;
   title 'Merged';
      select g3, z, r
         from table1 as a full join table2 as b
            on a.g3 = b.g3
         order by 1;
quit;
```

6. Which statement about the use of table aliases is false?

   a. Table aliases must be used when referencing identical table names from different libraries.

   b. Table aliases can be referenced by using the keyword AS.

   c. Table aliases or full table names must be used when referencing a column name that is the same in two or more tables.

   d. Table aliases must be used when using summary functions.

7. Which statement is true regarding the use of the PROC SQL step to query data that is stored in two or more tables?

   a. When you join multiple tables, the tables must contain a common column.

   b. You must specify the table from which you want each column to be read.

   c. The tables that are being joined must come from the same type of data source.

   d. If two tables that are being joined contain a same-named column, you must specify the table from which you want the column to be read.

Chapter 4
Joining Tables Using Set Operators

Understanding Set Operators **96**
    Introducing Set Operators 96
    Set Operator Syntax 97
    Example: The Basics of Using a Set Operator 98
    Using Multiple Set Operators 98
    Processing Unique versus Duplicate Rows 101
    Combining and Overlaying Columns 101
    Modifying Results Using Keywords 102

Using the EXCEPT Set Operator **103**
    A Brief Overview 103
    Example: Using the EXCEPT Operator Alone 104
    Example: Using the Keyword ALL with the EXCEPT Operator 106
    Example: Using the Keyword CORR with the EXCEPT Operator 106
    Example: Using the Keywords ALL and CORR with the EXCEPT Operator ... 107
    Example: EXCEPT Operator 108

Using the INTERSECT Set Operator **109**
    A Brief Overview 109
    Example: Using the INTERSECT Operator Alone 110
    Example: Using the Keyword ALL with the INTERSECT Set Operator 110
    Example: Using the Keyword CORR with the INTERSECT Set Operator 111
    Example: Using the Keywords ALL and CORR with the
       INTERSECT Set Operator 112
    Complex Example Using the INTERSECT Operator 112

Using the UNION Set Operator **114**
    A Brief Overview 114
    Example: Using the UNION Operator Alone 114
    Example: Using the Keyword ALL with the UNION Operator 115
    Example: Using the Keyword CORR with the UNION Operator 116
    Example: Using the Keywords ALL and CORR with the UNION Operator 117
    Example: Using the UNION Set Operator 118
    Example: Using a UNION Operator and Summary Functions 119

Using the OUTER UNION Set Operator **120**
    A Brief Overview 120
    Example: Using the OUTER UNION Operator Alone 121
    Example: Using the Keyword CORR with One OUTER UNION Operator 122
    Example: Using Two OUTER UNION Operators with the Keyword CORR 122

Quiz **123**

Understanding Set Operators

Introducing Set Operators

You can combine the results of two or more queries by using set operators. Each of the four set operators—EXCEPT, INTERSECT, UNION, and OUTER UNION—selects rows and handles columns in a different way, as described below.

Note: In the comparison below, Table 1 is the table that is referenced in the first query, and Table 2 is the table that is referenced in the second query.

Set Operator	Treatment of Rows	Treatment of Columns	Example
EXCEPT	Selects unique rows from the first table that are not found in the second table.	Overlays columns based on their position in the SELECT clause without regard to the individual column names.	```proc sql;
select *
from table1
except
select *
from table2;```
INTERSECT	Selects unique rows that are common to both tables.	Overlays columns based on their position in the SELECT clause without regard to the individual column names.	```proc sql;
select *
from table1
intersect
select *
from table2;
quit;```
UNION	Selects unique rows from both tables.	Overlays columns based on their position in the SELECT clause without regard to the individual column names.	```proc sql;
select *
from table1
union
select *
from table2;
quit;```

Set Operator	Treatment of Rows	Treatment of Columns	Example

OUTER UNION	Selects all rows from both tables.
	
	The OUTER UNION operator concatenates the results of the queries.
		Does not overlay columns.	`proc sql;`
			`    select *`
			`        from table1`
			`    outer union`
			`    select *`
			`        from table2;`
			`quit;`

A set operation contains the following elements:

- two queries (each beginning with a SELECT clause)
- a set operator
- one or both of the keywords ALL and CORR (CORRESPONDING)

Set Operator Syntax

Syntax of an SQL query using a set operator:

SELECT *column-1<, ... column-n>*

> **FROM** *table-1 | view-1<, ... table-n | view-n>*
> *<optional query clauses>*

set-operator <ALL> <CORR>

SELECT *column-1<, ... column-n>*

> **FROM** *table-1 | view-1<, ... table-n | view-n>*
> *<optional query clauses>*;

SELECT
: specifies the column(s) to appear in the result.

FROM
: specifies the table(s) or view(s) to be queried.

optional query clauses
: are used to refine the query further and include the clauses WHERE, GROUP BY, HAVING, and ORDER BY.

- the *set-operator* is one of the following: EXCEPT|INTERSECT|UNION|OUTER UNION.
- the optional keywords ALL and CORR (CORRESPONDING) further modify the set operation.

Note: Place a semicolon after the last SELECT statement only.

Set operators combine columns from two queries based on their position in the referenced tables without regard to the individual column names. Columns in the same relative position in the two queries must have the same data type. The column names of the tables in the first query become the column names of the output table.

The following optional keywords give you more control over set operations:

ALL
> does not suppress duplicate rows. When the keyword ALL is specified, PROC SQL does not make a second pass through the data to eliminate duplicate rows. Thus, using ALL is more efficient than not using it. ALL is not allowed with the OUTER UNION operator.

CORR
> overlays columns that have the same name in both tables. When used with EXCEPT, INTERSECT, and UNION, CORR suppresses columns that are not in both tables.

Example: The Basics of Using a Set Operator

When a PROC SQL step evaluates a SELECT statement with one set operator, it does the following:

- evaluates each query to produce an intermediate, internal, result table
- makes each intermediate result table become an operand that is linked with a set operator to form an expression
- evaluates the entire expression to produce a single output result set

In the following PROC SQL step, the SELECT statement contains one set operation. The set operation uses the set operator UNION to combine the result of a query on the table Certadv.Stress17 with the result of a query on the table Certadv.Stress18.

```
proc sql;
   select *
      from certadv.stress17 union
   select *
      from certadv.stress18;
quit;
```

Using Multiple Set Operators

A Brief Overview

A single SELECT statement can contain more than one set operation. Each additional set operation includes a set operator and a group of query clauses.

```
proc sql;
   select *
      from table1
   set-operator
   select *
      from table2
   set-operator
   select *
      from table3;
quit;
```

This SELECT statement uses two set operators to link together three queries. Regardless of the number of set operations in a SELECT statement, the statement contains only one semicolon, which is placed after the last query.

Example: Using Multiple Set Operators
The following PROC SQL step contains two set operators that combine three queries.

```
proc sql;
    select *
        from certadv.mechanicslevel1
    outer union
    select *
        from certadv.mechanicslevel2
    outer union
    select *
        from certadv.mechanicslevel3;
quit;
```

The PROC SQL query result displays all the columns from Certadv.MechanicsLevel1, Certadv.MechanicsLevel2, and Certadv.MechanicsLevel3. The OUTER UNION operator selects all the rows from all from the tables and displays them in the query result. It does not overlay the columns. Because Certadv.MechanicsLevel1, Certadv.MechanicsLevel2, and Certadv.MechanicsLevel3 do not have columns with the same values, there are missing values displayed in some columns.

Output 4.1   PROC SQL Query Result

EmpID	JobCode	Salary	EmpID	JobCode	Salary	EmpID	JobCode	Salary
1400	ME1	$41,677	.		.			.
1403	ME1	$39,301	.		.			.
1120	ME1	$40,067	.		.			.
1121	ME1	$40,757	.		.			.
1412	ME1	$38,919	.		.			.
1200	ME1	$38,942	.		.			.
1995	ME1	$40,334	.		.			.
1418	ME1	$39,207	.		.			.
		.	1653	ME2	$49,151			.
		.	1782	ME2	$49,483			.
		.	1244	ME2	$51,695			.
		.	1065	ME2	$49,126			.
		.	1129	ME2	$48,901			.
		.	1406	ME2	$49,259			.
		.	1356	ME2	$51,617			.
		.	1292	ME2	$51,367			.
		.	1440	ME2	$50,060			.
		.	1900	ME2	$49,147			.
		.	1423	ME2	$50,082			.
		.	1432	ME2	$49,458			.
		.	1050	ME2	$49,234			.
		.	1105	ME2	$48,727			.
		.			.	1499	ME3	$60,235
		.			.	1409	ME3	$58,171
		.			.	1379	ME3	$59,170
		.			.	1521	ME3	$58,136
		.			.	1385	ME3	$61,460
		.			.	1420	ME3	$60,299
		.			.	1882	ME3	$58,153

Processing Multiple Set Operators

When PROC SQL evaluates a SELECT statement that contains multiple set operations, an additional processing step, step 3 below, is required:

1. Each query is evaluated to produce an intermediate (internal) result table.

2. Each intermediate result table then becomes an operand that is linked with a set operator to form an expression (for example, `Table1 UNION Table2`).

3. If the set operation contains more than two queries, the result from the first two queries (enclosed in parentheses in the following examples) becomes an operand for the next set operator and operand.
   - with two set operators: `(Table1 UNION Table2) EXCEPT Table3`
   - with three set operators: `((Table1 UNION Table2) EXCEPT Table3) INTERSECT Table4`
4. PROC SQL evaluates the entire expression to produce a single output result set.

Note: When processing set operators, PROC SQL follows a default order of precedence, unless this order is overridden by parentheses in the expressions. By default, INTERSECT is evaluated first. OUTER UNION, UNION, and EXCEPT all have the same level of precedence.

Processing Unique versus Duplicate Rows

When processing a set operation that displays only unique rows (a set operation that contains the set operator EXCEPT, INTERSECT, or UNION), PROC SQL makes two passes through the data, by default:

1. PROC SQL eliminates duplicate, nonunique, rows in the tables.
2. PROC SQL selects the rows that meet the criteria and, where requested, overlays columns.

For set operations that display both unique and duplicate rows, only one pass through the data, step 2 above, is required.

Combining and Overlaying Columns

A Brief Overview

You can use a set operation to combine tables that have different numbers of columns and rows or that have columns in a different order.

By default, the set operators EXCEPT, INTERSECT, and UNION overlay columns based on the relative position of the columns in the SELECT clause. Column names are ignored. You control how PROC SQL maps columns in one table to columns in another table by specifying the columns in the appropriate order in the SELECT clause. The first column that is specified in the first query's SELECT clause and the first column that is specified in the second query's SELECT clause are overlaid, and so on.

When columns are overlaid, PROC SQL uses the column name from the first table. If there is no column name in the first table, the column name from the second table is used. When the SELECT clause contains an asterisk (*) instead of a list of column names, the set operation combines the tables based on the positions of the columns in the tables.

Example: Overlaying Columns

The following example takes the first column from Certadv.Col1 and overlays it in Certadv.Col2.

```
title 'PROC SQL Query Result';
proc sql;
   select *                       /* 1 */
      from certadv.col1 except    /* 2 */
```

```
       select *
          from certadv.col2;
   quit;
```

1 The SELECT clause in each query uses an asterisk (*) to overlay columns based on their positions in the tables.

2 The EXCEPT set operator overlays columns.

Output 4.2 PROC SQL Query Result: Overlaying Columns

Col1		Col2		PROC SQL Query Result	
X	A	X	B	X	A
1	a	1	x	1	a
1	a	2	y	1	b
1	b	3	z	2	c
2	c	3	v	4	e
3	v	5	w	6	g
4	e				
6	g				

In order to be overlaid, columns in the same relative position in the two SELECT clauses must have the same data type. If they do not, PROC SQL generates a warning message in the SAS log and stops executing. For example, in the tables shown above, if the data type differed in column Col1.X and Col2.X, the SAS log would display the following error message.

Log 4.1 SAS Log

```
ERROR: Column 1 from the first contributor of EXCEPT
is not the same type as its counterpart from the second.
```

Modifying Results Using Keywords

To modify the behavior of set operators, you can use either or both of the keywords ALL and CORR immediately following the set operator:

```
proc sql;
   select *
      from table1
   set-operator <all> <corr>
   select *
      from table2;
quit;
```

The use of each keyword is described below.

Keyword	Action	Situation
ALL	Makes only one pass through the data and does not remove duplicate rows.	It does not matter whether there are duplicates. Duplicates are not possible. ALL cannot be used with OUTER UNION.
CORR (or CORRESPONDING)	Compares and overlays columns by name instead of by position: • When used with EXCEPT, INTERSECT, and UNION, removes any columns that do not have the same name in both tables. • When used with OUTER UNION, overlays same-named columns and displays columns that have nonmatching names without overlaying. If an alias is assigned to a column in the SELECT clause, CORR uses the alias instead of the permanent column name.	Two tables have some or all columns in common, but the columns are not in the same order.

Using the EXCEPT Set Operator

A Brief Overview

The set operator EXCEPT does both of the following:

- selects unique rows from the first table (the table specified in the first query) that are not found in the second table
- overlays columns

Figure 4.1 EXCEPT Set Operator Relationship

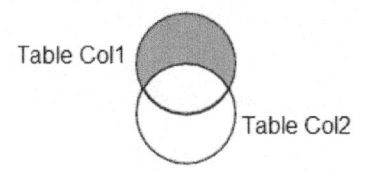

Table Col1

Table Col2

Example: Using the EXCEPT Operator Alone

Suppose you want to display the unique rows in table Col1 that are not found in table Col2. The PROC SQL set operation that includes the EXCEPT operator, the tables Col1 and Col2, and the output of the set operation are shown below.

```
proc sql;
   select *
      from certadv.col1 except
   select *
      from certadv.col2;
quit;
```

Output 4.3 PROC SQL Query Result Illustration

Certadv.Col1

X	A
1	a
1	a
1	b
2	c
3	v
4	e
6	g

Certadv.Col2

X	B
1	x
2	y
3	z
3	v
5	w

PROC SQL Query Result

X	A
1	a
1	b
2	c
4	e
6	g

The set operator EXCEPT overlays columns by their position. In this output, the following columns are overlaid:

- the first columns, Col1.X and Col2.X, both of which are numeric
- the second columns, Col1.A and Col2.B, both of which are character

The column names from table Col1 are used, so the second column of output is named A rather than B.

In the first pass, PROC SQL eliminates any duplicate rows from the tables. As shown below, there is one duplicate row: in table Col1, the second row is a duplicate of the first row. All remaining rows in table Col1 are still candidates in PROC SQL's selection process.

```
proc sql;
   select *
      from certadv.col1 except
   select *
      from certadv.col2;
quit;
```

Output 4.4 Tables Certadv.Col1 and Certadv.Col2

Certadv.Col1

X	A
1	a
1	a
1	b
2	c
3	v
4	e
6	g

Certadv.Col2

X	B
1	x
2	y
3	z
3	v
5	w

In the second pass, PROC SQL identifies any rows in table Col1 for which there is a matching row in table Col2 and eliminates them. The one matching row in the two tables, as shown below, is eliminated.

```
proc sql;
   select *
      from certadv.col1 except
   select *
      from certadv.col2;
quit;
```

Output 4.5 Tables Certadv.Col1 and Certadv.Col2

Certadv.Col1

X	A
1	a
1	a
1	b
2	c
3	v
4	e
6	g

Certadv.Col2

X	B
1	x
2	y
3	z
3	v
5	w

The five remaining rows in table Col1, the unique rows, are displayed in the output.

106 Chapter 4 • *Joining Tables Using Set Operators*

Output 4.6 PROC SQL Query Result: Overlaying Tables

PROC SQL Query Result

X	A
1	a
1	b
2	c
4	e
6	g

Example: Using the Keyword ALL with the EXCEPT Operator

To select all rows in the first table, both unique and duplicate, that do not have a matching row in the second table, add the keyword ALL after the EXCEPT set operator. The modified PROC SQL set operation, the tables Col1 and Col2, and the output are shown below.

```
proc sql;
   select *
       from certadv.col1 except all
   select *
       from certadv.col2;
quit;
```

Output 4.7 PROC SQL Query Result Illustration

Certadv.Col1

X	A
1	a
1	a
1	b
2	c
3	v
4	e
6	g

Certadv.Col2

X	B
1	x
2	y
3	z
3	v
5	w

PROC SQL Query Result

X	A
1	a
1	a
1	b
2	c
4	e
6	g

The output now contains six rows. PROC SQL has again eliminated the one row in table Col1, the fifth row, that has a matching row in table Col2, the fourth row. Remember that when the keyword ALL is used with the EXCEPT operator, PROC SQL does not make an extra pass through the data to remove duplicate rows within table Col1. Therefore, the second row in table Col1, which is a duplicate of the first row, is now included in the output.

Example: Using the Keyword CORR with the EXCEPT Operator

Add the keyword CORR after the set operator to display both of the following:

- only columns that have the same name

- all unique rows in the first table that do not appear in the second table

The modified PROC SQL set operation, the tables Col1 and Col2, and the output are shown below:

```
proc sql;
   select *
      from certadv.col1 except corr
   select *
      from certadv.col2;
quit;
```

Output 4.8 PROC SQL Query Result Illustration

Certadv.Col1			Certadv.Col2			PROC SQL Query Result
X	A		X	B		X
1	a		1	x		4
1	a		2	y		6
1	b		3	z		
2	c		3	v		
3	v		5	w		
4	e					
6	g					

X is the only column that has the same name in both tables, so X is the only column that PROC SQL examines and displays in the output.

In the first pass, PROC SQL eliminates the second and third rows of table Col1 from the output because they are not unique within the table. They contain values of X that duplicate the value of X in the first row of table Col1. In the second pass, PROC SQL eliminates the first, fourth, and fifth rows of table Col1 because each contains a value of X that matches a value of X in a row of table Col2.

The output displays the two remaining rows in table Col1, the rows that are unique in table Col1 and that do not have a row in table Col2 that has a matching value of X.

Example: Using the Keywords ALL and CORR with the EXCEPT Operator

If the keywords ALL and CORR are used together, the EXCEPT operator displays all unique and duplicate rows in the first table that do not appear in the second table, and overlays and displays only columns that have the same name.

The modified PROC SQL set operation, the tables Col1 and Col2, and the output are shown below:

```
proc sql;
   select *
      from certadv.col1 except all corr
   select *
      from certadv.col2;
quit;
```

Output 4.9 PROC SQL Query Result Illustration

Certadv.Col1

X	A
1	a
1	a
1	b
2	c
3	v
4	e
6	g

Certadv.Col2

X	B
1	x
2	y
3	z
3	v
5	w

PROC SQL Query Result

X
1
1
4
6

Once again, PROC SQL examines and displays only the column that has the same name in the two tables: X. Because the keyword ALL is used, PROC SQL does not eliminate any duplicate rows in table Col1. Therefore, the second and third rows in table Col1, which are duplicates of the first row in table Col1, appear in the output. PROC SQL does eliminate the first, fourth, and fifth rows in table Col1 from the output because for each one of these three rows there is a corresponding row in table Col2 that has a matching value of X.

When the keyword ALL is used with the EXCEPT operator, a row in table Col1 cannot be eliminated from the output unless it has a separate matching row in table Col2. Table Col1 contains three rows in which the value of X is **1**, but table Col2 contains only one row in which the value of X is **1**. That one row in table Col2 causes the first of the three rows in table Col1 that have a matching value of X to be eliminated from the output. However, table Col2 does not have two additional rows in which the value of X is **1**. Therefore, the other two rows in table Col1 are not eliminated, and do appear in the output.

Example: EXCEPT Operator

Suppose you want to display the names of all new employees of a company. Because no table exists that contains information for only the new employees, you use data from the following two tables.

Table	Relevant Columns
Certadv.Staffchanges lists information for all new employees and existing employees who have had a change in salary or job code.	FirstName, LastName
Certadv.Staffmaster lists information for all existing employees.	FirstName, LastName

The relationship between these two tables is shown in the diagram below:

Figure 4.2 EXCEPT Operator Relationship

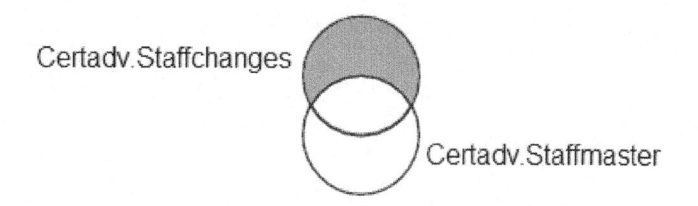

The intersection of these two tables includes information for all existing employees who have had changes in job code or salary. The shaded portion, the portion of Certadv.Staffchanges that does not overlap with Certadv.Staffmaster, includes information for the people that you want: new employees.

The following PROC SQL step separates the new employees from the existing employees in Certadv.Staffchanges to create a set operation that displays all rows from Certadv.Staffchanges that do not exist in the Certadv.Staffmaster.

```
proc sql;
   select firstname, lastname
      from certadv.staffchanges except all
   select firstname, lastname
      from certadv.staffmaster;
quit;
```

This PROC SQL set operation includes the operator EXCEPT and the keyword ALL. Although you do not want the output to contain duplicate rows, you already know that there are no duplicates in these two tables. Therefore, ALL is specified to prevent PROC SQL from making an extra pass through the data. This speeds up the processing of this query.

PROC SQL compares only the columns that are specified in the SELECT clauses, and these columns are compared in the order in which they are specified. The output displays the first and last names of the two new employees.

Output 4.10 PROC SQL Query Result: Using EXCEPT Operator and Keyword ALL

FirstName	LastName
AMY	BRIDESTON
JIM	POWELL

Note: In a set operation that uses the EXCEPT operator, the order in which the tables are listed in the SELECT statement makes a difference. If the tables in this example were listed in the opposite order, the output would display all existing employees who have had no changes in salary or job code.

Using the INTERSECT Set Operator

A Brief Overview

The set operator INTERSECT does both of the following:

- selects unique rows that are common to both tables

110 Chapter 4 • *Joining Tables Using Set Operators*

- overlays columns

Figure 4.3 INTERSECT Set Operator Relationship

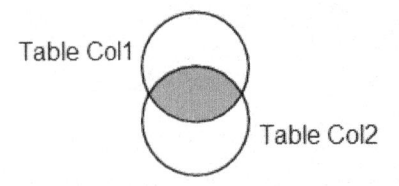

Example: Using the INTERSECT Operator Alone

The INTERSECT operator compares and overlays columns in the same way as the EXCEPT operator, by column position instead of column name. However, INTERSECT selects rows differently and displays in output the unique rows that are common to both tables.

The following PROC SQL set operation uses the INTERSECT operator to combine the tables Col1 and Col2.

```
proc sql;
   select *
      from certadv.col1 intersect
   select *
      from certadv.col2;
quit;
```

Output 4.11 PROC SQL Query Result Illustration

Certadv.Col1

X	A
1	a
1	a
1	b
2	c
3	v
4	e
6	g

Certadv.Col2

X	B
1	x
2	y
3	z
3	v
5	w

PROC SQL Query Result

X	A
3	v

Tables Col1 and Col2 have only one unique row in common and this row is displayed in the output.

Example: Using the Keyword ALL with the INTERSECT Set Operator

Adding the keyword ALL to the preceding PROC SQL query prevents PROC SQL from making an extra pass through the data. If there were any rows common to tables Col1 and Col2 that were duplicates of other common rows, they would also be included in output. However, as you have seen, there is only one common row in these tables.

```
proc sql;
   select *
```

```
            from certadv.col1 intersect all
      select *
            from certadv.col2;
   quit;
```

Output 4.12 PROC SQL Query Result Illustration

Certadv.Col1			Certadv.Col2			PROC SQL Query Result	
X	A		X	B		X	A
1	a		1	x		3	v
1	a		2	y			
1	b		3	z			
2	c		3	v			
3	v		5	w			
4	e						
6	g						

Example: Using the Keyword CORR with the INTERSECT Set Operator

To display the unique rows that are common to the two tables based on the column name instead of the column position, add the keyword CORR to the PROC SQL set operation.

```
proc sql;
   select *
        from certadv.col1 intersect corr
   select *
        from certadv.col2;
quit;
```

Output 4.13 PROC SQL Query Result Illustration

Certadv.Col1			Certadv.Col2			PROC SQL Query Result
X	A		X	B		X
1	a		1	x		1
1	a		2	y		2
1	b		3	z		3
2	c		3	v		
3	v		5	w		
4	e					
6	g					

X is the only column name that is common to both tables, so X is the only column that PROC SQL examines and displays in the output. In the first pass, PROC SQL eliminates the rows that are duplicated within each table: the second and third rows in table Col1 contain the same value for X as the first row, and the fourth row in table Col2 contains the same value for X as the third row. In the second pass, PROC SQL eliminates any

112 Chapter 4 • *Joining Tables Using Set Operators*

rows that are not common across tables: the fourth and fifth rows in table Col1 and the fifth row in table Col2 do not have a matching value of X in the other table. The output displays the three rows with unique values of X that are also common to both tables.

Example: Using the Keywords ALL and CORR with the INTERSECT Set Operator

If the keywords ALL and CORR are used together, the INTERSECT operator displays all unique and duplicate rows that are common to the two tables, based on columns that have the same name.

```
proc sql;
   select *
      from certadv.col1 intersect all corr
   select *
      from certadv.col2;
quit;
```

Output 4.14 PROC SQL Query Result Illustration

Certadv.Col1

X	A
1	a
1	a
1	b
2	c
3	v
4	e
6	g

Certadv.Col2

X	B
1	x
2	y
3	z
3	v
5	w

PROC SQL Query Result

X
1
2
3

PROC SQL examines and displays only the column with the same name, X. There are three common rows across the two tables, which are highlighted above. These three rows are displayed in the output.

Each of the tables contains at least one other row that duplicates a value of X in one of the common rows. For example, in the second and third rows in table Col1, the value of X is 1, and only one row is displayed in the output. However, in order to be considered a common row and to be included in the output, every duplicate row in one table must have a separate duplicate row in the other table. In this example, there are no rows that have duplicate values and that are also common across tables. Therefore, in this example, the set operation with the keywords ALL and CORR generates the same output as with the keyword CORR alone.

Complex Example Using the INTERSECT Operator

Suppose you want to display the names of the existing employees who have changed their salary or job code.

Using the INTERSECT Set Operator

Table	Relevant Columns
Certadv.Staffchanges lists information for all new employees and existing employees who have had a change in salary or job code.	`FirstName, LastName`
Certadv.Staffmaster lists information for all existing employees.	`FirstName, LastName`

The relationship between these two tables is shown in the diagram.

Figure 4.4 INTERSECT Set Operator

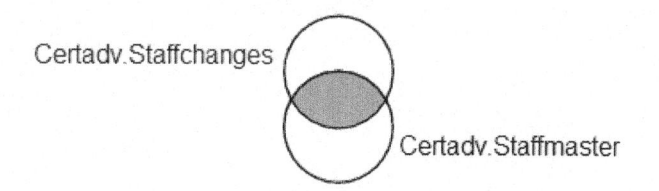

To display the unique rows that are common to both tables, you use a PROC SQL set operation that contains INTERSECT. It is known that these tables contain no duplicates, so ALL is used to speed up query processing.

```
proc sql;
   select firstname, lastname
      from certadv.staffchanges
   intersect all
   select firstname, lastname
      from certadv.staffmaster;
quit;
```

Output 4.15 PROC SQL Query Result: Using INTERSECT Operator and Keyword ALL

FirstName	LastName
DIANE	WALTERS
KAREN	CARTER
NEIL	CHAPMAN
RAYMOND	SANDERS

In this PROC SQL step, which contains just one INTERSECT set operator, the order in which you list the tables in the SELECT statement does not make a difference. However, in a more complex PROC SQL step that contains multiple stacked INTERSECT set operators, it is important to think through the table order carefully, depending on when you want the nonmatching rows to be eliminated. The output shows that there are four existing employees who have changed their salary or job code.

Using the UNION Set Operator

A Brief Overview

The set operator UNION does both of the following:

- selects unique rows from both tables
- overlays columns

Figure 4.5 *UNION Set Operator Relationship*

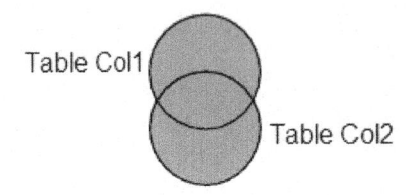

Example: Using the UNION Operator Alone

To display all rows from the tables Col1 and Col2 that are unique in the combined set of rows from both tables, use a PROC SQL set operation that includes the UNION operator.

```
proc sql;
   select *
      from certadv.col1 union
   select *
      from certadv.col2;
quit;
```

Output 4.16 PROC SQL Query Result Illustration

Certadv.Col1

X	A
1	a
1	a
1	b
2	c
3	v
4	e
6	g

Certadv.Col2

X	B
1	x
2	y
3	z
3	v
5	w

PROC SQL Query Result

X	A
1	a
1	b
1	x
2	c
2	y
3	v
3	z
4	e
5	w
6	g

With the UNION operator, PROC SQL first concatenates and sorts the rows from the two tables, and eliminates any duplicate rows. In this example, two rows are eliminated: the second row in table Col1 is a duplicate of the first row, and the fourth row in table Col2 matches the fifth row in table Col1. All remaining rows, the unique rows, are included in the output. The columns are overlaid by position.

Example: Using the Keyword ALL with the UNION Operator

When the keyword ALL is added to the UNION operator, the output displays all rows from both tables, both unique and duplicate.

```
proc sql;
   select *
      from certadv.col1 union all
   select *
      from certadv.col2;
quit;
```

Output 4.17 PROC SQL Query Result Illustration

Certadv.Col1	Certadv.Col2	PROC SQL Query Result
X A	X B	X A
1 a	1 x	1 a
1 a	2 y	1 a
1 b	3 z	1 b
2 c	3 v	2 c
3 v	5 w	3 v
4 e		4 e
6 g		6 g
		1 x
		2 y
		3 z
		3 v
		5 w

When the keyword ALL is used, PROC SQL does not remove duplicates or sort the rows. The output now includes the two duplicate rows that were eliminated in the previous example: the second row in table Col1 and the fourth row in table Col2. Note that order of the rows in this output differs from the order of the rows in the output from the previous set operation.

Example: Using the Keyword CORR with the UNION Operator

To display all rows from the tables Col1 and Col2 that are unique in the combined set of rows from both tables, based on columns that have the same name rather than the same position, add the keyword CORR after the set operator.

```
proc sql;
   select *
      from certadv.col1 union corr
   select *
      from certadv.col2;
quit;
```

Output 4.18 PROC SQL Query Result Illustration

Certadv.Col1		Certadv.Col2		PROC SQL Query Result
X	A	X	B	X
1	a	1	x	1
1	a	2	y	2
1	b	3	z	3
2	c	3	v	4
3	v	5	w	5
4	e			6
6	g			

X is the only column name that is common to both tables, so X is the only column that PROC SQL examines and displays in the output. In the combined set of rows from the two tables, there are duplicates of the values **1**, **2**, and **3**, and these duplicate rows are eliminated from the output. The output displays the six unique values of X.

Example: Using the Keywords ALL and CORR with the UNION Operator

If the keywords ALL and CORR are used together, the UNION operator displays all rows in the two tables both unique and duplicate, based on the columns that have the same name. In this example, the output displays all 12 values for X, the one column that has the same name in both tables.

```
proc sql;
   select *
      from certadv.col1 union all corr
   select *
      from certadv.col2;
quit;
```

Output 4.19 PROC SQL Query Result Illustration

Certadv.Col1		Certadv.Col2		PROC SQL Query Result
X	A	X	B	X
1	a	1	x	1
1	a	2	y	1
1	b	3	z	1
2	c	3	v	2
3	v	5	w	3
4	e			4
6	g			6
				1
				2
				3
				3
				5

Example: Using the UNION Set Operator

Suppose you are generating a report based on data from a health clinic. You want to display the results of individual patient stress tests taken in 2017, followed by the results from stress tests taken in 2018. To do this, you use the UNION operator to combine the tables Certadv.Stress17 and Certadv.Stress18. These two tables have similar structure:

- Both tables contain nine columns that have the same names.
- Each row contains data for an individual patient.

You are not sure whether the tables contain duplicate records, but you do not want duplicates in your output. Because the tables have the same column structure, you can overlay the columns by position, and the keyword CORR is not necessary.

```
proc sql;
   select *
      from certadv.stress17 union
   select *
      from certadv.stress18;
quit;
```

Output 4.20 PROC SQL Query Result: UNION Set Operator

ID	Name	RestHR	MaxHR	RecHR	TimeMin	TimeSec	Tolerance	Year
2458	Murray, W	72	185	128	12	38	D	2018
2462	Almers, C	68	171	133	10	5	I	2018
2501	Bonaventure,	78	177	139	11	13	I	2017
2523	Johnson, R	69	162	114	9	42	S	2018
2539	LaMance, K	75	168	141	11	46	D	2018
2544	Jones, M	79	187	136	12	26	N	2017
2552	Reberson, P	69	158	139	15	41	D	2017
2555	King, E	70	167	122	13	13	I	2018
2563	Pitts, D	71	159	116	10	22	S	2018
2568	Eberhardt, S	72	182	122	16	49	N	2017
2571	Nunnelly, A	65	181	141	15	2	I	2017
2572	Oberon, M	74	177	138	12	11	D	2018
2574	Peterson, V	80	164	137	14	9	D	2018
2575	Quigley, M	74	152	113	11	26	I	2018
2578	Cameron, L	75	158	108	14	27	I	2017
2579	Underwood, K	72	165	127	13	19	S	2017
2584	Takahashi, Y	76	163	135	16	7	D	2018
2586	Derber, B	68	176	119	17	35	N	2018
2588	Ivan, H	70	182	126	15	41	N	2017
2589	Wilcox, E	78	189	138	14	57	I	2018
2595	Warren, C	77	170	136	12	10	S	2017

TIP If you can determine that these tables have no duplicate records, you could add the keyword ALL to speed up processing by avoiding an extra pass through the data.

Example: Using a UNION Operator and Summary Functions

Suppose you want to display the following summarized data for members of a frequent-flyer program: total points earned, total points used, and total miles traveled. All three values can be calculated from columns in the table Certadv.Frequentflyers by using summary functions.

You might wonder why set operations are needed when only one table is involved. If you wanted to display the three summarized values horizontally, in three separate columns, you could solve the problem without a set operation, using the following simple SELECT statement:

```
proc sql;
   select sum(pointsearned) format=comma12.
          label='Total Points Earned',
          sum(pointsused) format=comma12.
          label='Total Points Used',
```

```
              sum(milestraveled) format=comma12.
              label='Total Miles Traveled'
       from certadv.frequentflyers;
quit;
```

Output 4.21   PROC SQL Query Result

Total Points Earned	Total Points Used	Total Miles Traveled
10,583,463	4,429,670	10,477,963

Assume, however, that you want the three values to be displayed vertically in a single column. To generate this output, you create three different queries on the same table, and then use two UNION set operators to combine the three query results:

```
proc sql;
title 'Points and Miles Traveled';
title2 'by Frequent Flyers';
   select 'Total Points Earned:',
          sum(PointsEarned) format=comma12.
      from certadv.frequentflyers union
   select 'Total Points Traveled:',
          sum(MilesTraveled) format=comma12.
      from certadv.frequentflyers union
   select 'Total Points Used:',
          sum(PointsUsed) format=comma12.
      from certadv.frequentflyers
;
quit;
```

Each SELECT clause defines two columns: a character constant as a label and the summarized value. The output is shown below.

Output 4.22   PROC SQL Query Result: Using a UNION Operator and Summary Functions

**Points and Miles Traveled
by Frequent Flyers**

Total Points Earned:	10,583,463
Total Points Traveled:	10,477,963
Total Points Used:	4,429,670

Using the OUTER UNION Set Operator

A Brief Overview

The set operator OUTER UNION concatenates the results of the queries:

- It selects all rows (both unique and nonunique) from both tables.
- It does not overlay columns.

Figure 4.6 Outer Union Set Operator Relationship

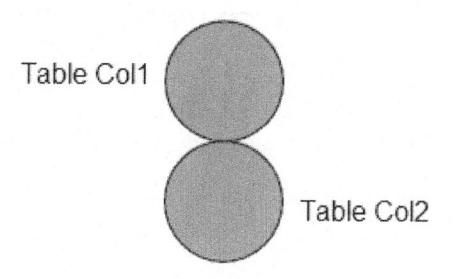

Table Col1

Table Col2

The following examples demonstrate how OUTER UNION works when used alone and with the keyword CORR. The keyword ALL is not used with OUTER UNION because this operator's default action is to include all rows in output.

Example: Using the OUTER UNION Operator Alone

Suppose you want to display all rows from both of the tables Col1 and Col2, without overlaying columns.

```
proc sql;
   select *
      from certadv.col1 outer union
   select *
      from certadv.col2;
quit;
```

Output 4.23 PROC SQL Query Result Illustration

Col1			Col2			PROC SQL Query Result			
X	A		X	B		X	A	X	B
1	a		1	x		1	a	.	.
1	a		2	y		1	a	.	.
1	b		3	z		1	b	.	.
2	c		3	v		2	c	.	.
3	v		5	w		3	v	.	.
4	e					4	e	.	.
6	g					6	g	.	.
						.	.	1	x
						.	.	2	y
						.	.	3	z
						.	.	3	v
						.	.	5	w

In the output, the columns have not been overlaid. Instead, all four columns from both tables are displayed. Each row of output contains missing values in the two columns that correspond to the other table.

Example: Using the Keyword CORR with One OUTER UNION Operator

The output from the preceding set operation contains two columns with the same name. To overlay the columns with a common name, add the keyword CORR to the set operation:

```
proc sql;
   select *
      from certadv.col1 outer union corr
   select *
      from certadv.col2
;
quit;
```

The output from the modified set operation contains only three columns because the two columns named X are overlaid.

Output 4.24   PROC SQL Query Result Illustration

Col1			Col2			PROC SQL Query Result		
X	A		X	B		X	A	B
1	a		1	x		1	a	
1	a		2	y		1	a	
1	b		3	z		1	b	
2	c		3	v		2	c	
3	v		5	w		3	v	
4	e					4	e	
6	g					6	g	
						1		x
						2		y
						3		z
						3		v
						5		w

Example: Using Two OUTER UNION Operators with the Keyword CORR

Suppose you want to display the employee ID numbers, job codes, and salaries of all mechanics working for an airline. The mechanic job has three levels, and there is a separate table containing data for the mechanics at each level: Certadv.Mechanicslevel1, Certadv.Mechanicslevel2, and Certadv.Mechanicslevel3. These tables all contain the same three columns.

The following PROC SQL step uses two OUTER UNION operators to concatenate the tables and the keyword CORR to overlay the columns that have common names:

```
proc sql;
   select *
```

```
           from certadv.mechanicslevel1 outer union corr
      select *
           from certadv.mechanicslevel2 outer union corr
      select *
           from certadv.mechanicslevel3;
quit;
```

Output 4.25 PROC SQL Query Result: Using OUTER UNION Operator and Keyword CORR (partial output)

EmpID	JobCode	Salary
1400	ME1	$41,677
1403	ME1	$39,301
1120	ME1	$40,067
1121	ME1	$40,757

... more observations ...

1385	ME3	$61,460
1420	ME3	$60,299
1882	ME3	$58,153

Quiz

Select the best answer for each question. After completing the quiz, check your answers using the answer key in the appendix.

1. Which statement is false with respect to a set operation that uses the EXCEPT, UNION, or INTERSECT set operator without a keyword?

    a. Column names in the result set are determined by the first table.

    b. To be overlaid, columns must be of the same data type.

    c. To be overlaid, columns must have the same name.

    d. By default, only unique rows are displayed in the result set.

2. The keyword ALL cannot be used with which of the following set operators?

    a. EXCEPT

    b. INTERSECT

    c. UNION

    d. OUTER UNION

3. Which PROC SQL step combines the tables Certadv.Summer and Certadv.Winter to produce the output displayed below?

Summer

Month	Temp	Precip
7	78	0.05
8	85	0.04
9	83	0.15

Winter

Month	Temp	Precip
1	29	0.15
2	32	0.17
3	38	0.20
2	32	0.17

PROC SQL Query Result

Month	Temp	Precip
1	29	0.15
2	32	0.17
3	38	0.2
7	78	0.05
8	85	0.04
9	83	0.15

a.
```
proc sql;
   select *
      from certadv.summer intersect all
   select *
      from certadv.winter;
quit;
```

b.
```
proc sql;
   select *
      from certadv.summer outer union
   select *
      from certadv.winter;
quit;
```

c.
```
proc sql;
   select *
      from certadv.summer union corr
   select *
      from certadv.winter;
quit;
```

d.
```
proc sql;
   select *
      from certadv.summer union
   select *
      from certadv.winter;
quit;
```

4. Which PROC SQL step combines tables but does not overlay any columns?

a.
```
proc sql;
   select *
      from groupa outer union
   select *
      from groupb;
```

```
       quit;
b.     proc sql;
          select *
             from groupa as a outer union corr
          select *
             from groupb as b;
       quit;
c.     proc sql;
          select coalesce(a.obs, b.obs)
                 label='Obs', med, duration
             from groupa as a full join groupb as b
                on a.obs=b.obs;
       quit;
d.     proc sql;
          select *
             from groupa as a intersect
          select *
             from groupb as b;
       quit;
```

5. Which statement is false regarding the keyword CORR (CORRESPONDING)?

   a. It cannot be used with the keyword ALL.

   b. It overlays columns by name, not by position.

   c. When used in EXCEPT, INTERSECT, and UNION set operations, it removes any columns that are not found in both tables.

   d. When used in OUTER UNION set operations, it causes same-named columns to be overlaid.

6. Which PROC SQL step generates the following output from the tables Certadv.Dogs and Certadv.Pets?

Dogs

Name	Price
FIFI	$101
GEORGE	$75
SPARKY	$136
TRUFFLE	$250

Pets

Name	Price	Arr
ANA	$25	08OCT2018
FIFI	$101	20JUL2018
GAO	$57	08DEC2017
GAO	$57	08DEC2017
SPARKY	$136	16SEP2018
TRUFFLE	$250	18AUG2018
ZEUS	$500	03APR2018

PROC SQL Query Result

Name	Price
ANA	$25
GAO	$57
ZEUS	$500

a.
```
proc sql;
    select name, price
        from certadv.pets except all
    select *
        from certadv.dogs;
quit;
```

b.
```
proc sql;
    select name, price
        from certadv.pets except
    select *
        from certadv.dogs;
quit;
```

c.
```
proc sql;
    select name, price
        from certadv.pets except corr all
    select *
        from certadv.dogs;
quit;
```

d.
```
proc sql;
    select *
        from certadv.dogs except corr
    select name, price
        from certadv.pets;
quit;
```

7. The PROG1 and PROG2 tables list students who took the PROG1 and PROG2 courses, respectively. Which PROC SQL step will give you the names of the students who took only the PROG1 class?

PROG1

FName	LName
Pete	Henry
Mary	Johnson
Alex	Kinsley
Dori	O'Neil

PROG2

FName	LName
Clara	Addams
Pete	Henry
Dori	O'Neil
Cindy	Phillips
Mandi	Young

PROC SQL Query Result: PROG1 Only

FName	LName
Alex	Kinsley
Mary	Johnson

a.
```
proc sql;
    select fname, lname
        from certadv.prog1 intersect
    select fname, lname
        from certadv.prog2;
quit;
```

b.
```
proc sql;
    select fname, lname
        from certadv.prog1 except all
    select fname, lname
        from certadv.prog2;
quit;
```

c.
```
proc sql;
    select *
        from certadv.prog2 intersect corr
    select *
        from certadv.prog1;
quit;
```

d.
```
proc sql;
    select *
        from certadv.prog2 union
    select *
        from certadv.prog1;
quit;
```

8. Which PROC SQL step returns the names of all the students who took PROG1, PROG2, or both classes?

PROG1

FName	LName
Pete	Henry
Mary	Johnson
Alex	Kinsley
Dori	O'Neil

PROG2

FName	LName
Clara	Addams
Pete	Henry
Dori	O'Neil
Cindy	Phillips
Mandi	Young

PROC SQL Query Result: PROG1, PROG2, or Both

FName	LName
Alex	Kinsley
Cindy	Phillips
Clara	Addams
Dori	O'Neil
Mandi	Young
Mary	Johnson
Pete	Henry

a.
```
proc sql;
    select fname, lname
        from certadv.prog1 intersect
    select fname, lname
        from certadv.prog2;
quit;
```

b.
```
proc sql;
    select fname, lname
        from certadv.prog1 outer union corr
    select fname, lname
        from certadv.prog2;
quit;
```

c.
```
proc sql;
    select fname, lname
        from certadv.prog1 union
    select fname, lname
        from certadv.prog2;
quit;
```

d.
```
proc sql;
    select fname, lname
        from certadv.prog1 except corr
    select fname, lname
        from certadv.prog2;
quit;
```

9. Which PROC SQL step returns the names of all the students who took both the PROG1 and PROG2 classes?

PROG1

FName	LName
Pete	Henry
Mary	Johnson
Alex	Kinsley
Dori	O'Neil

PROG2

FName	LName
Clara	Addams
Pete	Henry
Dori	O'Neil
Cindy	Phillips
Mandi	Young

PROC SQL Query Result: PROG1 & PROG2

FName	LName
Dori	O'Neil
Pete	Henry

a.
```
proc sql;
    select fname, lname
        from certadv.prog1 union
    select fname, lname
        from certadv.prog2;
quit;
```

b.
```
proc sql;
    select fname, lname
        from certadv.prog1 except corr
    select fname, lname
        from certadv.prog2;
quit;
```

c.
```
proc sql;
    select fname, lname
        from certadv.prog1 intersect all
    select fname, lname
        from certadv.prog2;
quit;
```

d.
```
proc sql;
    select fname, lname
        from certadv.prog1 union corr
    select fname, lname
        from certadv.prog2;
quit;
```

Chapter 5
Using Subqueries

Subsetting Data Using Subqueries **131**
    Introducing Subqueries 131
    Subsetting Data by Using Noncorrelated Subqueries 132
    Subsetting Data by Using Correlated Subqueries 138

Creating and Managing Views Using PROC SQL **141**
    A Brief Overview 141
    The CREATE VIEW Statement 141
    The DESCRIBE VIEW Statement 143
    Managing PROC SQL Views 144
    Updating PROC SQL Views 146
    The DROP VIEW Statement 148

Quiz **149**

Subsetting Data Using Subqueries

Introducing Subqueries

A Brief Overview
A subquery selects rows from one table based on values in another table. Subqueries are also known as *nested queries* or *inner queries*. A *subquery* is a query expression that is nested as part of another query expression. Depending on the clause that contains it, a subquery can return a single value or multiple values. Subqueries are most often used in WHERE and HAVING clauses. Subqueries are enclosed in parentheses.

The following PROC SQL query contains a subquery in the HAVING clause that returns all jobcodes where the average salary for that jobcode is greater than the company average salary.

```
proc sql;
   select jobcode, avg(salary) as AvgSalary
         format=dollar11.2
      from certadv.payrollmaster
      group by jobcode
      having avg(salary)>(select avg(salary)
         from certadv.payrollmaster);
quit;
```

The subquery shown above is a single-value subquery; it returns a single value, the average salary from the table Certadv.Payrollmaster, to the outer query. A subquery can return values for multiple rows but only for a single column.

The table that a subquery references can be either the same as or different from the table that is referenced by the outer query. In the PROC SQL query shown above, the subquery selects data from the same table as the outer query.

Using SAS Functions

PROC SQL supports almost all of the SAS DATA step functions. You can use SAS functions as a part of subqueries to subset your data. For example, you can use date functions in PROC SQL to summarize amounts by quarter and month.

The Two Types of Subqueries

Type	Description
noncorrelated	A *noncorrelated subquery* is a self-contained subquery that executes independently of the outer query. The simplest type of subquery is a noncorrelated subquery that returns a single value.
correlated	A *dependent subquery* is one that requires one or more values to be passed to it by the outer query before the subquery can return a value to the outer query.

Both noncorrelated and correlated subqueries can return either single or multiple values to the outer query.

Subsetting Data by Using Noncorrelated Subqueries

Example: Using Single-Value Noncorrelated Subqueries

The following PROC SQL query displays job codes for which a group's average salary exceeds the company's average salary. The HAVING clause contains a noncorrelated subquery. PROC SQL always evaluates a noncorrelated subquery before the outer query. If a query contains noncorrelated subqueries at more than one level, PROC SQL evaluates the innermost subquery first and works outward, evaluating the outermost query last.

```
proc sql;
   select jobcode, avg(salary) as AvgSalary format=dollar11.2
      from certadv.payrollmaster
      group by jobcode
      having avg(salary) >                 /* 1 */
         (select avg(salary)               /* 2 */
            from certadv.payrollmaster);
quit;
```

1 The HAVING clause completes the expression by calculating the subquery. The subquery calculates the average salary for the entire company, all rows in the table, using the AVG summary function with Salary as an argument. The subquery returns the value of the average salary to the outer query.

2   In the SELECT clause, the outer query calculates the average salary for each JobCode group as defined by the GROUP BY clause. It selects only the groups whose average salary is greater than the company's average salary.

The PROC SQL query result is displayed below.

Output 5.1   *PROC SQL Query Result: Average Salary for Each JobCode*

JobCode	AvgSalary
ME3	$59,374.86
NA1	$58,845.00
NA2	$73,336.00
PT1	$95,071.13
PT2	$122,253.40
PT3	$154,706.50
TA3	$55,551.42

This noncorrelated subquery returns only a single value, the average salary for the whole company, to the outer query. Both the subquery and the outer query use the same table as a source.

Using Multiple-Value Noncorrelated Subqueries

Some subqueries are multiple-value subqueries: they return more than one value, or row, to the outer query. If your noncorrelated subquery might return a value for more than one row, be sure to use one of the following operators in the WHERE or HAVING clause that can handle multiple values:

- the conditional operator IN
- a comparison operator that is modified by ANY or ALL
- the conditional operator EXISTS

Note: If you create a noncorrelated subquery that returns multiple values, but the WHERE or HAVING clause in the outer query contains an operator other than one of the operators that are specified above, the query will fail. An error message is displayed in the SAS log, which indicates that the subquery evaluated to more than one row. For example, if you use the equal (=) operator with a noncorrelated subquery that returns multiple values, the query will fail. The equal operator can handle only a single value.

Consider a query that contains both the conditional operator IN and a noncorrelated subquery that returns multiple values.

Example: Using a Conditional Operator in a Noncorrelated Subquery

Suppose you want to send cards to employees who have birthdays coming up. Create a PROC SQL query that lists the names and addresses of all employees who have birthdays in February. This query selects data from two different tables:

- employee names and addresses in the table Certadv.Staffmaster
- employee birth dates in the table Certadv.Payrollmaster

In both tables, the employees are identified by their employee identification number, EmpID.

In the following PROC SQL query, the WHERE clause contains the conditional operator IN followed by a noncorrelated subquery:

```
proc sql;
   select empid, lastname, firstname, city, state
      from certadv.staffmaster
         where empid in                              /* 1 */
            (select empid from certadv.payrollmaster /* 2 */
               where month(dateofbirth)=2);          /* 3 */
quit;
```

1. The WHERE expression selects the employees whose birthday is in the month of February. Note that the MONTH function is used in the subquery.

2. The subquery returns the EmpID values of the selected employees to the outer query.

3. The outer query displays data for the employees identified by the subquery.

The output, shown below, lists the six employees who have February birthdays.

Output 5.2 PROC SQL Query Result: Employees with February Birthdays

EmpID	LastName	FirstName	City	State
1403	BOWDEN	EARL	BRIDGEPORT	CT
1404	CARTER	DONALD	NEW YORK	NY
1834	LONG	RUSSELL	NEW YORK	NY
1103	MCDANIEL	RONDA	NEW YORK	NY
1420	ROUSE	JEREMY	PATERSON	NJ
1390	SMART	JONATHAN	NEW YORK	NY

Although an inner join would have generated the same results, it is better to use a subquery in this example since no columns from the Certadv.Payrollmaster table were in the output.

Using Comparisons with Subqueries

Sometimes it is helpful to compare a value with a set of values returned by a subquery. When a subquery might return multiple values, you must use one of the conditional operators ANY or ALL to modify a comparison operator in the WHERE or HAVING clause immediately before the subquery. For example, the following WHERE clause contains the less than (<) comparison operator and the conditional operator ANY:

```
where dateofbirth < any
   <subquery...>
```

Note: If you create a noncorrelated subquery that returns multiple values, and if the WHERE or HAVING clause in the outer query contains a comparison operator that is not modified by ANY or ALL, the query will fail.

When the outer query contains a comparison operator that is modified by ANY or ALL, the outer query compares each value that it retrieves against the value or values that are returned by the subquery. All values for which the comparison is true are then included in the query output. If ANY is specified, the comparison is true if it is true for any one of the values that are returned by the subquery. If ALL is specified, the comparison is true only if it is true for all values that are returned by the subquery.

Note: The operators ANY and ALL can be used with correlated subqueries, but they are usually used only with noncorrelated subqueries.

In PROC SQL queries, you can use the following comparisons with subqueries. ANY, ALL, and EXISTS cannot be used in other SAS procedures.

Conditional Operator	Operator Looks for These Values	Example

ANY	values that meet a specified condition with respect to any one of the values returned by a subquery	`where dateofbirth < any`
		`    (select dateofbirth`
		`        from certadv.payrollmaster`
		`        where jobcode='FA3')`

ALL	values that meet a specified condition with respect to all the values returned by a subquery	`where dateofbirth < all`
		`    (select dateofbirth`
		`        from certadv.payrollmaster`
		`        where jobcode='FA3')`

EXISTS	values that are returned by a subquery	`where exists`
		`    (select *`
		`        from certadv.flightschedule`
		`        where fa.empid=`
		`            flightschedule.empid)`

Using the ANY Operator

An outer query that specifies the ANY operator selects values that pass the comparison test with any of the values that are returned by the subquery.

For example, suppose you have an outer query containing the following WHERE clause:

```
where dateofbirth < any
    <subquery...>
```

This WHERE clause specifies that DateofBirth (the operand) should be less than any (the comparison operator) of the values returned by the subquery.

The following comparison shows the effect of using ANY with these common comparison operators: greater than (>), less than (<) and equal to (=).

Comparison Operator with ANY	Outer Query Action	Example
> ANY	Selects values that are greater than any value returned by the subquery.	If the subquery returns the values 20, 30, 40, the outer query selects all values that are > 20 (the lowest value that was returned by the subquery).
< ANY	Selects values that are less than any value returned by the subquery.	If the subquery returns the values 20, 30, 40, the outer query selects all values that are < 40 (the highest value that was returned by the subquery).

Comparison Operator with ANY	Outer Query Action	Example
= ANY	Selects values that are equal to any value returned by the subquery.	If the subquery returns the values 20, 30, 40, the outer query selects all values that are = 20 or = 30 or = 40.

TIP Instead of using the ANY operator with a subquery, there are some SAS functions that you can use to achieve the same result with greater efficiency. Instead of > ANY, use the MIN function in the subquery. Instead of < ANY, use the MAX function in the subquery.

Example: Using the ANY Operator

Suppose you want to identify any flight attendants at level 1 or level 2 who are older than any of the flight attendants at level 3. Job type and level are identified in JobCode; each flight attendant has the job code FA1, FA2, or FA3. The following PROC SQL query accomplishes this task by using a subquery and the ANY operator.

```
proc sql;
   select empid, jobcode, dateofbirth
      from certadv.payrollmaster
         where jobcode in ('FA1', 'FA2')
            and dateofbirth <any      /*1*/
               (select dateofbirth   /*2*/
                  from certadv.payrollmaster
                  where jobcode='FA3');
quit;
```

1 The subquery returns the birth dates of all level-3 flight attendants.

2 The outer query selects only level-1 and level-2 flight attendants whose birth dates indicate that they are older than any of the others whose birth dates are returned by the subquery.

Note that both the outer query and subquery use the same table.

Note: Internally, SAS represents a date value as the number of days from January 1, 1960, to the given date. For example, the SAS date for 17 October 1991 is 11612. Representing dates as the number of days from a reference date makes it easy for the computer to store them and perform calendar calculations. These numbers are not meaningful to users, however, so several formats are available for displaying dates and datetime values in most of the commonly used notations.

Output 5.3 PROC SQL Query Result: Level-1 and Level-2 Flight Attendants

EmpID	JobCode	DateOfBirth
1574	FA2	01MAY1988
1125	FA2	12NOV1976
1475	FA2	19DEC1969
1368	FA2	15JUN1969
1411	FA2	31MAY1969
1441	FA2	23NOV1977
1477	FA2	25MAR1972
1424	FA2	08AUG1977
1413	FA2	20SEP1973
1555	FA2	20MAR1976
1434	FA2	14JUL1970
1390	FA2	23FEB1973
1135	FA2	24SEP1968
1415	FA2	12MAR1966
1221	FA2	25SEP1975
1122	FA2	04MAY1971

TIP Using the ANY operator to solve this problem results in a large number of calculations, which increases processing time. For this example, it would be more efficient to use the MAX function in the subquery. Here is an alternative WHERE clause:

```
where jobcode in ('FA1','FA2')
      and dateofbirth <
         (select max(dateofbirth)
             from [...]
```

Using the ALL Operator

An outer query that specifies the ALL operator selects values that pass the comparison test with all of the values that are returned by the subquery.

The following comparison shows the effect of using ALL with these common comparison operators: greater than (>) and less than (<).

Comparison Operator with ALL	Sample Values Returned by Subquery	Effect
> ALL	(20, 30, 40)	> 40 (greater than the highest number in the list)
< ALL	(20, 30, 40)	< 20 (less than the lowest number in the list)

Example: Using the ALL Operator

Substitute ALL for ANY in the previous query example. The following query identifies level-1 and level-2 flight attendants who are older than all of the level-3 flight attendants.

```
proc sql;
   select empid, jobcode, dateofbirth
      from certadv.payrollmaster
         where jobcode in ('FA1', 'FA2')
            and dateofbirth < all     /* 1 */
               (select dateofbirth    /* 2 */
                  from certadv.payrollmaster
                  where jobcode='FA3');
quit;
```

1   The subquery returns the birth dates of all level-3 flight attendants.

2   The outer query selects only level-1 and level-2 flight attendants whose birth dates indicate that they are older than any of the others whose birth dates are returned by the subquery.

The following query results show that only two level-1 or level-2 flight attendants are older than all of the level-3 flight attendants.

Output 5.4   PROC SQL Query Result: Level-1 and Level-2 Flight Attendants

EmpID	JobCode	DateOfBirth
1475	FA2	19DEC1969
1368	FA2	15JUN1969
1411	FA2	31MAY1969
1477	FA2	25MAR1972
1434	FA2	14JUL1970
1135	FA2	24SEP1968
1415	FA2	12MAR1966
1122	FA2	04MAY1971

TIP   For this example, it would be more efficient to solve this problem using the MIN function in the subquery instead of the ALL operator. Here is an alternative WHERE clause:

```
where jobcode in ('FA1','FA2')
    and dateofbirth <
       (select min(dateofbirth)
          from [...]
```

Subsetting Data by Using Correlated Subqueries

A Brief Overview

Correlated subqueries are not evaluated independently because they depend on the values passed to them by the outer query for results. Correlated subqueries evaluate each row in the outer query and often require more processing time than noncorrelated subqueries. Because correlated subqueries are resource intensive, they reduce system performance. A PROC SQL join is a more efficient alternative to a correlated subquery.

Example: Using Correlated Subqueries

The following PROC SQL query displays the names of all navigators who are also managers. The WHERE clause in the subquery specifies the column Staffmaster.EmpID, which is the column that the outer query must pass to the correlated subquery.

```
proc sql;
   select lastname, firstname
      from certadv.staffmaster
         where 'NA'=
            (select jobcategory
               from certadv.supervisors
               where staffmaster.empid =
               supervisors.empid);
quit;
```

Note: When a column appears in more than one table, the column name is preceded by the table name or alias to avoid ambiguity. In this example, EmpID appears in both tables, so the appropriate table name is specified in front of each reference to that column.

The output from this query is shown below. There are three navigators who are also managers.

Output 5.5 PROC SQL Query Result: Navigators Who Are Also Managers

LastName	FirstName
FERNANDEZ	KATRINA
NEWKIRK	WILLIAM
RIVERS	SIMON

Using the EXISTS and NOT EXISTS Conditional Operators

In the WHERE clause or in the HAVING clause of an outer query, you can use the EXISTS or NOT EXISTS conditional operators to test for the existence or non-existence of a set of values returned by a subquery.

Condition	Requirement
EXISTS	the subquery returns at least one row
NOT EXISTS	the subquery returns no data

Note: The operators EXISTS and NOT EXISTS can be used with both correlated and noncorrelated subqueries.

Example: Correlated Subquery with NOT EXISTS

Consider a sample PROC SQL query that includes the NOT EXISTS conditional operator. Suppose you are working with the following tables:

140 *Chapter 5* • *Using Subqueries*

- Certadv.Flightattendants contains the names and employee ID numbers of all flight attendants.
- Certadv.Flightschedule contains one row for each crew member who is assigned to a flight for each date.

As shown in the diagram below, the intersection of these two tables contains data for all flight attendants who have been scheduled to work.

Figure 5.1 Flight Attendants and Employees Scheduled to Work

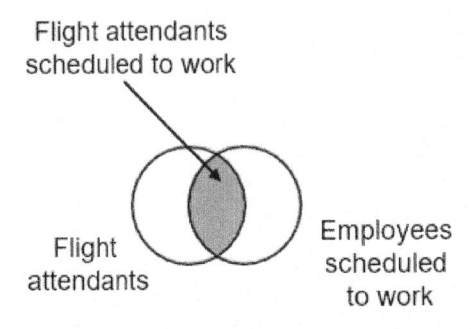

Now suppose you want to list by name the flight attendants who have not been scheduled. That is, you want to identify the data in the area highlighted below.

Figure 5.2 Flight Attendants Not Scheduled to Work

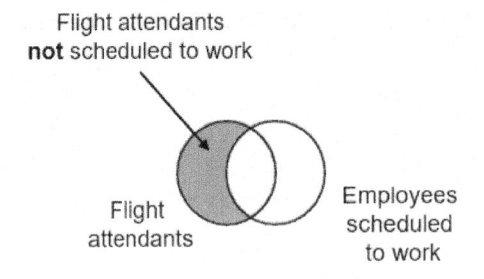

The following PROC SQL query accomplishes this task by using a correlated subquery and the NOT EXISTS operator.

```
proc sql;
   select lastname, firstname
      from certadv.flightattendants
         where not exists
            (select * from certadv.flightschedule
               where flightattendants.empid=
                  flightschedule.empid);
quit;
```

Output 5.6 PROC SQL Query Result: List of Employees Not Scheduled for a Flight

LastName	FirstName
PATTERSON	RENEE
VEGA	FRANKLIN

Creating and Managing Views Using PROC SQL

A Brief Overview

A *PROC SQL view* is a stored query expression that reads data values from its underlying files, which can include SAS data files, DATA step views, other PROC SQL views, or DBMS data. A view contains only the descriptor and other information required to retrieve the data values from other SAS files or external files. The view contains only the logic for accessing the data, but not the data itself.

Because PROC SQL views are not separate copies of data, they are referred to as *virtual tables*. They do not exist as independent entities like real tables. However, views use the same naming conventions as tables and can be used in SAS programs instead of an actual SAS table. Like tables, views are considered to be SAS data sets. The view derives its data from the tables or views that are listed in its FROM clause. The data that is accessed by a view is a subset or superset of the data that is in its underlying tables or views.

The following statements are true about PROC SQL views:

- They can be used in SAS programs in place of an actual SAS data file.
- They can be joined with tables or other views.
- They can be derived from one or more tables, PROC SQL views, or DATA step views.
- They can access data from a SAS data set, a DATA step view, a PROC SQL view, or a relational database table.
- They extract underlying data, which enables you to access the most current data.

Views are useful because for these reasons:

- They often save space (a view is usually quite small compared with the data that it accesses).
- They prevent users from continually submitting queries to omit unwanted columns or rows.
- They ensure that input data sets are always current, because data is derived from tables at execution time.
- They shield sensitive or confidential columns from users while enabling the same users to view other columns in the same table.
- They hide complex joins or queries from users.

The CREATE VIEW Statement

CREATE VIEW Statement Syntax

You use the CREATE VIEW statement to create a view.

Syntax, CREATE VIEW statement:

CREATE VIEW *proc-sql-view* **AS**
    SELECT *column-1<, ... column-n>*
        FROM *table-1 | view-1<, ... table-n | view-n>*
        <optional query clauses>;

- *proc-sql-view* specifies the name of the PROC SQL view that you are creating.
- SELECT specifies the column(s) to appear in the table.
- FROM specifies the table(s) or view(s) to be queried.
- *optional query clauses* are used to refine the query further and include the WHERE, GROUP BY, HAVING, and ORDER BY clauses.

A PROC SQL view derives its data from the tables or views that are listed in the FROM clause. The data that is accessed by a view is a subset or superset of the data that is in its underlying tables or views. When a view is referenced by a SAS procedure or in a DATA step, it is executed and, conceptually, an internal table is built. PROC SQL processes this internal table as if it were any other table.

Example: Creating a PROC SQL View

The following PROC SQL step creates a view that contains information for flight attendants. The view always returns the employee's age as of the current date.

The view Certadv.Faview creates a virtual table from the accompanying SELECT statement. Although the underlying tables, Certadv.Payrollmaster and Certadv.Staffmaster, can change, the instructions that make up the view stay constant.

The libref specified in the FROM clause is optional. It is assumed that the contributing tables are stored in the same library as the view itself, unless otherwise specified.

```
proc sql;
   create view certadv.faview as
      select lastname, firstname ,
             int((today()-dateofbirth)/365.25) as Age,
             substr(jobcode,3,1) as Level,
             salary
        from certadv.payrollmaster,
             certadv.staffmaster
       where jobcode contains 'FA' and
             staffmaster.empid=
             payrollmaster.empid;
quit;
```

When this PROC SQL step is submitted, SAS does not actually execute the SELECT statement that follows the AS keyword, but partially compiles and stores the SELECT statement in a data file with a member type of VIEW. A message in the SAS log confirms that the view has been defined.

Log 5.1 *SAS Log*

```
NOTE: SQL view CERTADV.FAVIEW has been defined.
```

TIP It is helpful to give a PROC SQL view a name that easily identifies it as a view (for example, Faview or Fav).

Note: In the Windows and UNIX operating environments, the default extension for PROC SQL views and DATA step views is .sas7bvew.

Example: Using a PROC SQL View

You can use a view in a subsequent PROC SQL step, or later in the same step, just as you would use an actual SAS table.

In the following example, the PROC SQL view Certadv.Faview is used in a query. Because the query that is stored in the view calculates the age of each flight attendant based on the current date, the resulting output from this PROC SQL step shows each flight attendant's age as of the current date. If Certadv.Faview were a static table, instead of a view, the age shown for each flight attendant would never change.

```
proc sql;
   select *
      from certadv.faview;
quit;
```

Output 5.7 *PROC SQL Query Result: Certadv.Faview (partial output)*

LastName	FirstName	Age	Level	Salary
ARTHUR	BARBARA	36	3	$46,040
CAHILL	MARSHALL	31	2	$40,001
CARTER	DOROTHY	30	3	$46,346
COOPER	ANTHONY	41	3	$45,104
DEAN	SHARON	39	3	$46,787

TIP You can use PROC SQL views in other SAS procedures and DATA steps.

The DESCRIBE VIEW Statement

DESCRIBE VIEW Statement Syntax

You can use a DESCRIBE VIEW statement to display a definition of a view in the SAS log.

Syntax, DESCRIBE VIEW statement:

DESCRIBE VIEW *proc-sql-view-1<,...proc-sql-view-n>*;

proc-sql-view
  specifies a PROC SQL view and can be one of the following:
  - a one-level name
  - a two-level libref.view name
  - a physical pathname that is enclosed in single quotation marks

TIP If you use a PROC SQL view in a DESCRIBE VIEW statement that is based on or derived from another view, then you might want to use the FEEDBACK option in the PROC SQL statement. This option displays in the SAS log how the underlying view is defined and expands any expressions that are used in this view definition.

Example: Displaying the Definition of a PROC SQL View

The following PROC SQL step writes the view definition for Certadv.Faview to the SAS log.

```
proc sql;
   describe view certadv.faview;
quit;
```

Log 5.2 SAS Log

```
NOTE: SQL view CERTADV.FAVIEW is defined as:

       select lastname, firstname,  INT((TODAY() - dateofbirth) / 365.25) as
Age,
SUBSTR(jobcode, 3, 1) as Level, salary
         from CERTADV.PAYROLLMASTER, CERTADV.STAFFMASTER
         where jobcode contains 'FA' and (staffmaster.empid =
payrollmaster.empid);
```

Managing PROC SQL Views

Guidelines for Using PROC SQL Views

- Avoid using an ORDER BY clause in a view definition, which causes the data to be sorted every time the view is executed. Users of the view might differ in how or whether they want the data to be sorted, so it is more efficient to specify an ORDER BY clause in a query that references the view.

- If the same data is used many times in one program or in multiple programs, it is more efficient to create a table rather than a view because the data must be accessed at each view reference. This table can be a temporary table in the Work library.

- Avoid creating views that are based on tables whose structure might change. A view is no longer valid when it references a nonexistent column.

- If a view resides in the same SAS library as the contributing tables, it is best to specify a one-level name in the FROM clause.

Omitting the Libref

The default libref for the table or tables in the FROM clause is the libref of the library that contains the view. Using a one-level name in the FROM clause prevents you from having to change the view if you assign a different libref to the SAS library that contains the view and its contributing table or tables.

The following PROC SQL step creates the view Certadv.Payrollv. The FROM clause specifies a two-level name for the contributing table, Certadv.Payrollmaster. However, it is not necessary to specify the libref Certadv because the contributing table is assumed to be stored in the same library as the view.

```
proc sql;
   create view certadv.payrollv as
      select *
         from certadv.payrollmaster;
quit;
```

When the one-level name Payrollmaster is used in the FROM clause, Certadv.Payrollmaster is being specified, even though it appears that Work.Payrollmaster is being specified.

```
proc sql;
   create view certadv.payrollv as
      select *
         from payrollmaster;
quit;
```

Note: If you are creating a view that is stored in a different library from that of the tables that are referenced in the FROM clause, you must specify a two-level name for the tables.

Using an Embedded LIBNAME Statement

As an alternative to omitting the libref in the FROM clause, you can embed a LIBNAME statement in a USING clause to store a SAS libref in a view. Embedding a LIBNAME statement is a more flexible approach for these reasons:

- It can be used regardless of whether the view and the underlying tables reside in the same library.
- It avoids the confusion that might arise if a libref is omitted from a table name in the FROM clause.

An embedded LIBNAME statement can be used only with a PROC SQL view. A libref that is created with an embedded LIBNAME statement will not conflict with an identically named libref in the SAS session.

Syntax, USING clause:

USING *libname-clause-1<,... libname-clause-n>*;

libname-clause
   is one of the following:

   - a valid LIBNAME statement
   - a valid SAS/ACCESS LIBNAME statement

TIP   The USING clause must be the last clause in the CREATE VIEW statement.

Example: Using an Embedded LIBNAME Statement

In the following example, while the view Certadv.Payrollv is executing in the PROC PRINT step, the libref Airline is dynamically assigned in the USING clause.

```
proc sql;
   create view certadv.payrollv as
      select*
         from airline.payrollmaster
         using libname airline 'SAS-library-one';
quit;
proc print data=certadv.payrollv;
run;
```

If an earlier assignment of the libref AIRLINE exists, the EMBEDDED LIBNAME statement overrides the assignment for the duration of the view's execution. After the view executes, the original libref assignment is re-established and the embedded assignment is cleared.

Creating a View to Enhance Table Security

One advantage of PROC SQL views is that they can bring data together from separate sources. This enables views to be used to shield sensitive or confidential columns from some users while enabling the same users to view other columns in the same table.

Note: Although PROC SQL views can be used to enhance table security, it is strongly recommended that you use the security features that are available in your operating environment to maintain table security.

The following PROC SQL step creates the view Certadv.Infoview. The view accesses data about flight attendants that is stored in three SAS libraries: Fa1, Fa2, and Fa3. The Fa1, Fa2, and Fa3 libraries can be assigned access privileges at the operating system level to ensure the following results:

- Level-1 flight attendants cannot read the data stored in the Fa2 and Fa3 libraries.
- Level-2 flight attendants cannot read the data stored in the Fa1 and Fa3 libraries.
- Level-3 flight attendants cannot read the data stored in the Fa1 and Fa2 libraries.

Access privileges can also be assigned to permit managers (who are authorized to access all SAS libraries) to view all of the information.

```
proc sql;
   create view certadv.infoview as
      select *
         from fa1.info
      outer union corr
      select *
         from fa2.info
      outer union corr
      select *
         from fa3.info;
quit;
```

Updating PROC SQL Views

A Brief Overview

You can update the data underlying a PROC SQL view using the INSERT, DELETE, and UPDATE statements under the following conditions:

- You can update only a single table through a view. The table cannot be joined or linked to another table, nor can it contain a subquery.
- You can update a column using the column's alias, but you cannot update a derived column. A derived column is a column that is produced by an expression.
- You can update a view that contains a WHERE clause. The WHERE clause can be specified in the UPDATE clause or in the view. You cannot update a view that contains any other clause such as an ORDER BY or a HAVING clause.
- You cannot update a summary view, which is a view that contains a GROUP BY clause.

Updating a view does not change the stored instructions for the view. Only the data in the underlying tables is updated.

Example: Updating PROC SQL Views

The following PROC SQL step creates the view Certadv.Raisev, which includes the columns Salary and MonthlySalary. A subsequent query that references the view shows the columns.

```
proc sql;
   create view certadv.raisev as
      select empid, jobcode,
             salary format=dollar12.,
             salary/12 as MonthlySalary
             format=dollar12.
         from certadv.payrollmaster;
quit;
proc sql;
   select *
      from certadv.raisev
      where jobcode in ('PT2','PT3');
quit;
```

Output 5.8 *PROC SQL Query Result: Certadv.Raisev*

EmpID	JobCode	Salary	MonthlySalary
1333	PT2	$124,048	$10,337
1404	PT2	$127,926	$10,661
1118	PT3	$155,931	$12,994
1410	PT2	$118,559	$9,880
1777	PT3	$153,482	$12,790
1106	PT2	$125,485	$10,457
1442	PT2	$118,350	$9,863
1478	PT2	$117,884	$9,824
1890	PT2	$120,254	$10,021
1107	PT2	$125,968	$10,497
1830	PT2	$118,259	$9,855
1928	PT2	$125,801	$10,483

Suppose you want to update the view to show a salary increase for employees whose job code is PT3. You can use an UPDATE statement to change the column Salary and a WHERE clause in the UPDATE clause to identify the rows where the value of JobCode equals **PT3**. Though MonthlySalary is a derived column and cannot be changed using an UPDATE statement, it will be updated because it is derived from Salary.

When the PROC SQL step is submitted, a note appears in the SAS log that indicates how many rows were updated.

```
proc sql;
   update certadv.raisev
      set salary=salary * 1.20
      where jobcode='PT3';
quit;
```

Log 5.3 SAS Log

```
NOTE: 2 rows were updated in CERTADV.RAISEV.
```

Note: Remember that the rows were updated in the table that underlies the view Certadv.Raisev.

When you resubmit the query, the updated values for Salary and MonthlySalary appear in the rows where JobCode equals **PT3**.

```
proc sql;
   select *
      from certadv.raisev
      where jobcode in ('PT2', 'PT3');
quit;
```

Output 5.9 PROC SQL Query Result: Certadv.Raisev View with Updated Values

EmpID	JobCode	Salary	MonthlySalary
1333	PT2	$124,048	$10,337
1404	PT2	$127,926	$10,661
1118	PT3	$187,117	$15,593
1410	PT2	$118,559	$9,880
1777	PT3	$184,178	$15,348
1106	PT2	$125,485	$10,457
1442	PT2	$118,350	$9,863
1478	PT2	$117,884	$9,824
1890	PT2	$120,254	$10,021
1107	PT2	$125,968	$10,497
1830	PT2	$118,259	$9,855
1928	PT2	$125,801	$10,483

The DROP VIEW Statement

DROP VIEW Statement Syntax

Use the DROP VIEW statement to drop or delete a view.

Syntax, DROP VIEW statement:

DROP VIEW *view-name-1* <,...*view-name-n*>;

view-name
   specifies a SAS data view of any type (PROC SQL view or DATA step view) and can be one of the following:

   - a one-level name
   - a two-level *libref.view* name
   - a physical pathname that is enclosed in single quotation marks

Example: Dropping a PROC SQL View

The following PROC SQL step drops the view Certadv.Raisev. After the step is submitted, a message appears in the SAS log to confirm that the view has been dropped.

```
proc sql;
   drop view certadv.raisev;
quit;
```

Log 5.4 SAS Log

```
NOTE: View CERTADV.RAISEV has been dropped.
```

Quiz

Select the best answer for each question. After completing the quiz, check your answers using the answer key in the appendix.

1. Which PROC SQL query removes duplicate values of MemberType from the query output, so that only the unique values are listed?

    a. ```
        proc sql nodup;
           select membertype
              from certadv.frequentflyers;
        quit;
        ```

    b.  ```
        proc sql;
           select distinct(membertype) as MemberType
              from certadv.frequentflyers;
        quit;
        ```

    c. ```
        proc sql;
           select unique membertype
              from certadv.frequentflyers
                group by membertype;
        quit;
        ```

    d.  ```
        proc sql;
           select distinct membertype
              from certadv.frequentflyers;
        quit;
        ```

2. Which of the following causes PROC SQL to list rows that have no data in the Address column?

    a. `WHERE address is missing`

    b. `WHERE address not exists`

    c. `WHERE address is null`

    d. Both a and c.

3. You are creating a PROC SQL query to list all employees who have spent (or overspent) their allotted 120 hours of vacation for the current year. The hours that each employee used are stored in the existing column Spent. Your query defines a new column, Balance, to calculate each employee's balance of vacation hours.

Which query produces the report that you want?

a.
```
proc sql;
    select name, spent, 120-spent as calculated Balance
        from certadv.absences
        where balance <= 0;
quit;
```

b.
```
proc sql;
    select name, spent, 120-spent as Balance
        from certadv.absences
        where calculated balance <= 0;
quit;
```

c.
```
proc sql;
    select name, spent, 120-spent as Balance
        from certadv.absences
        where balance <= 0;
quit;
```

d.
```
proc sql;
    select name, spent, 120-spent as calculated Balance
        from certadv.absences
        where calculated balance <= 0;
quit;
```

4. Consider this PROC SQL query:

```
proc sql;
    select flightnumber,
        count(*) as Flights,
        avg(boarded)
        label="Average Boarded"
        format=3.
    from certadv.internationalflights
    group by flightnumber
    having avg(boarded) > 150;
quit;
```

The table Certadv.Internationalflights contains 201 rows, 7 unique values of FlightNumber, 115 unique values of Boarded, and 4 different flight numbers that have an average value of Boarded that is greater than **150**. How many rows of output will the query generate?

a. 150

b. 7

c. 4

d. 1

5. You are writing a PROC SQL query to display the names of all library cardholders who work as volunteers for the library, and the number of books that each volunteer currently has checked out. Use one or both of the following tables:

- Certadv.Circulation lists the name and contact information for all library cardholders, and the number of books that each cardholder currently has checked out.

- Certadv.Volunteers lists the name and contact information for all library volunteers.

Assume that the values of Name are unique in both tables.

Which of the following PROC SQL queries will produce your report?

a.
```
proc sql;
    select name, checkedout
        from certadv.circulation
        where * in
            (select *
                from certadv.volunteers);
quit;
```

b.
```
proc sql;
    select name, checkedout
        from certadv.circulation
        where name in
            (select name
                from certadv.volunteers);
quit;
```

c.
```
proc sql;
    select name
        from certadv.volunteers
        where name, checkedout in
            (select name, checkedout
                from certadv.circulation);
quit;
```

d.
```
proc sql;
    select name, checkedout
        from certadv.circulation
        where name in
            (select name
                from certadv.volunteers);
quit;
```

6. By definition, a noncorrelated subquery is a nested query that does which of the following?

   a. returns a single value to the outer query

   b. contains at least one summary function

   c. executes independently of the outer query

   d. requires only a single value to be passed to it by the outer query

7. Which statement about the following PROC SQL query is false?

```
proc sql;
    validate
    select name label='Country',
           rate label='Literacy Rate'
        from certadv.literacy
        where 'Asia' =
            (select continent
                from certadv.continents
                where literacy.name =
                    continents.country)
        order by 2;
quit;
```

   a. The query syntax is not valid.

b. The outer query must pass values to the subquery before the subquery can return values to the outer query.

c. PROC SQL will not execute this query when it is submitted.

d. After the query is submitted, the SAS log indicates whether the query has valid syntax.

8. Consider the following PROC SQL query:

```
proc sql;
   select lastname, firstname, total, since
      from certadv.donors
      where not exists
         (select lastname
            from certadv.current
            where donors.lastname =
               current.lastname);
quit;
```

The query references two tables:

- Certadv.Donors lists name and contact information for all donors who have made contributions since the charity was founded. The table also contains these two columns: Total, which shows the total dollars given by each donor, and Since, which stores the first year in which each donor gave money.

- Certadv.Current lists the names of all donors who have made contributions in the current year, and the total dollars each has given this year (YearTotal).

Assume that the values of LastName are unique in both tables.

What will the output of this query display?

a. all donors whose rows do not contain any missing values

b. all donors who made a contribution in the current year

c. all donors who did not make a contribution in the current year

d. all donors whose current year's donation in Certadv.Current has not yet been added to Total in Certadv.Donors

9. Which statement about data remerging is true?

a. When PROC SQL remerges data, it combines data from two tables.

b. By using data remerging, PROC SQL can avoid making two passes through the data.

c. When PROC SQL remerges data, it displays a related message in the SAS log.

d. PROC SQL does not attempt to remerge data unless a subquery is used.

10. A public library has several categories of books. Each book in the library is assigned to only one category. The table Certadv.Inventory contains one row for each book in the library. The Checkouts column indicates the number of times that each book has been checked out.

You want to display only the categories that have an average circulation (number of checkouts) that is less than 2500. Does the following PROC SQL query produce the results that you want?

```
proc sql;
title 'Categories with Average Circulation';
title2 'Less than 2500';
```

```
       select category, avg(checkouts) as AvgCheckouts
          from certadv.inventory
          having avg(checkouts) < 2500
          order by 1;
quit;
```

a. No. This query will not run because a HAVING clause cannot contain a summary function.

b. No. This query will not run because the HAVING clause must include the CALCULATED keyword before the summary function.

c. No. Because there is no GROUP BY clause, the HAVING clause treats the entire table as one group.

d. Yes.

Chapter 6
Advanced SQL Techniques

Creating Data-Driven Macro Variables with PROC SQL **155**
    Creating Data-Driven Macro Variables with the INTO Clause 155
    Displaying Macro Variable Values 157
    Removing Leading and Trailing Blanks 157
    Concatenating Values in Macro Variables 158
    Applying a Format to Character and Numeric Variables 159

Accessing DBMS Data with SAS/ACCESS **161**
    A Brief Overview 161
    SQL Pass-Through Facility 162
    SAS/ACCESS LIBNAME Engine 164

The FedSQL Procedure **165**
    A Brief Overview 165
    Comparing PROC FedSQL and PROC SQL 166
    PROC FEDSQL Syntax 166
    The LIBNAME Statement 167
    The LIMIT Clause 168
    The PUT Function 169
    System Options in FedSQL 170

Quiz **171**

Creating Data-Driven Macro Variables with PROC SQL

A SAS macro variable stores text that is substituted in your code when SAS runs the program. Macro variable execution is similar to an automatic find-and-replace. Macro variables are temporary, and they are stored in-memory, so when you exit SAS, they are deleted. However, you can create data-driven macro variables with a PROC SQL query and then use those macro variables in your SAS program, procedure, and DATA step.

Creating Data-Driven Macro Variables with the INTO Clause

The INTO Clause
You can access the macro facility in a PROC SQL step by using the INTO clause in the SELECT statement. The various forms of the INTO clause can perform a variety of functions. For example, you can create a series of macro variables, a varying number of

macro variables, or a single macro variable that records a value that is the result of concatenating the unique values of an SQL variable.

The INTO clause in a SELECT statement enables you to create or update macro variables. You can create multiple macro variables from query results. If the macro variable does not exist, INTO creates it. The INTO clause in the SELECT statement can also assign the result of a query to a macro variable. However, the INTO clause can be used only in the outer query of a SELECT statement and not in a subquery. Note that the INTO clause cannot be used when you are creating a table or a view.

Syntax, INTO clause:

PROC SQL <*options*>;
    SELECT *column-1* <,...*column-n*>
        INTO: *macro-variable-specification-1* <..., :*macro-variable-specification-n*>
QUIT;

macro-variable-specification
    names one or more macro variables to create or update. Precede each macro variable name with a colon (:).

Note: When you create or update macro variables during execution of a PROC SQL step, you might not want any output to be displayed. The PRINT | NOPRINT option specifies whether a SELECT statement's results are displayed in output. PRINT is the default setting.

TIP Values that are assigned by the INTO clause use the BEST8. format.

Step 1: Create the Macro Variable

Suppose you are asked to find out which employees who were hired after 01JAN2015 are earning above the average salary for the company. First, create the macro variable AvgSal.

```
proc sql;
   select avg(Salary)
      into:avgSal
       from certadv.payrollmaster;
quit;
```

The average salary value is stored in the AvgSal macro variable. If the query produces more than one row of output, the macro variable contains only the value from the first row. If the query has no rows in its output, the macro variable is not modified. If the macro variable does not yet exist, it is not created.

Step 2: Use the Macro Variable

You can use the macro variable AvgSal in titles and queries.

```
title "Salaries above: &AvgSal";
proc sql;
   select EmpID, JobCode, Salary, DateofHire
      from certadv.payrollmaster
      where Salary>&avgSal and DateofHire>'01JAN2015'd;
quit;
```

The query above filters the data by the value of the AvgSal macro variable. The query returns rows for all employees earning above the average salary.

Output 6.1 PROC SQL Query Result

Salaries above 54079.62

EmpID	JobCode	Salary	DateOfHire
1499	ME3	$60,235	11JUN2018
1333	PT2	$124,048	14FEB2019
1404	PT2	$127,926	04JAN2018
1409	ME3	$58,171	26OCT2018
1107	PT2	$125,968	13FEB2017
1480	TA3	$55,416	29MAR2017

> **TIP** You can format the macro variable value in the title by using SAS functions and formats. Here is an example: `title "Salaries above: %left(%qsysfunc(putn(&AvgSal,dollar16.)))";`

Displaying Macro Variable Values

You can use the %PUT statement to display the resolved macro value in the SAS log. This is a good debugging technique to ensure that the value is what you expected.

Syntax, %PUT statement:

%PUT *text*;

text
  is any text string.

Suppose you want to view the macro variable's value after you have used the NOPRINT option. You can use the %PUT statement to view the value.

```
%put avgsal=&avgSal;
```

The value of the macro variable is printed in the SAS log.

Log 6.1 SAS Log

```
avgSal=54079.62
```

> **TIP** You can also enter the following code `%put &=AvgSal;` and receive the same value for the macro variable as above.

Removing Leading and Trailing Blanks

When storing a value in a single macro variable, PROC SQL preserves leading or trailing blanks. You can remove leading and trailing blanks by using the TRIMMED option in the INTO clause.

Syntax, INTO clause:

PROC SQL <*options*>;
   SELECT *column-1* <,...*column-n*>
      INTO: *macro-variable-specification-1* <..., :*macro-variable-specification-n*>
        TRIMMED
QUIT;

The following example illustrates the difference between using and not using the TRIMMED option to remove leading and trailing blanks.

```
proc sql;
   select min(PointsEarned)
       into:MinMiles
       from certadv.frequentflyers;
quit;
%put &=MinMiles;
```

The following is printed to the SAS log.

```
MINMILES=      146
```

In HTML output, the spaces are automatically removed, so extra spaces are not noticeable there. If your output is sent to the SAS log or is printed in a format other than HTML, you can still see the leading and trailing blanks.

Output 6.2 *PROC SQL Query Result*

146

If you included the TRIMMED option in the INTO clause, the macro variable is captured with no leading or trailing blanks.

```
proc sql;
   select min(PointsEarned)
       into:MinMiles trimmed
       from certadv.frequentflyers;
quit;
%put &=MinMiles;
```

The following is printed to the SAS log.

Log 6.2 *SAS Log*

```
MINMILES=146
```

Concatenating Values in Macro Variables

Sometimes, during execution of a PROC SQL step, you might want to create one macro variable that holds all values of a certain data set variable. You can use an alternate form of the INTO clause in order to take the values of a column and concatenate them into the value of one macro variable. Use the SEPARATED BY keyword to specify a character to delimit the values into a macro variable.

Syntax, INTO clause:

PROC SQL <*options*>;
   SELECT *column-1* <,...*column-n*>
      INTO: *macro-variable-1* <..., :*macro-variable-n*> **SEPARATED BY** "*delimiter*"
QUIT;

delimiter
   is enclosed in quotation marks and specifies the character that is used as a delimiter in the value of the macro variable.

Note: This form of the INTO clause removes leading and trailing blanks from each value before performing the concatenation of values.

Suppose you want to create a macro variable named Sites that contains the names of all the training centers in your Certadv.Schedule data set. The names are separated by blanks.

```
proc sql noprint;
   select distinct location into: sites separated by ' '
      from certadv.schedule;
quit;
```

Now, you can use the Sites macro variable in the title for your query or procedure result.

```
title1 "Total Revenue";
title2 "from Course Sites: &sites";
proc means data=certadv.all sum maxdec=0;
   var fee;
run;
```

Output 6.3   PROC MEANS Output

Total Revenue
from Course Sites: Boston Dallas Seattle

The MEANS Procedure

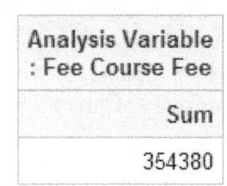

Analysis Variable : Fee Course Fee
Sum
354380

Applying a Format to Character and Numeric Variables

Suppose you have census data, Certadv.Census. You are asked to create a report that finds the states where the estimated population for 2018 is greater than the average census population in April 2010. You are also asked to find the difference between the census data and the population estimate for 2018 where the population estimate for 2018 is greater than 10 million.

The following example creates two different macro variables, CensusAvg2010 and CensusAvg2010_Format. The CensusAvg2010 macro variable has no format applied to the value of the macro variable. The CensusAvg2010_Format applies the COMMA16. format to the value of the macro variable.

```
proc sql noprint;
   select avg(Census_Apr2010) as No_Format,
          avg(Census_Apr2010) as Format format=comma16.
      into:CensusAvg2010,
          :CensusAvg2010_Format
      from certadv.census;
quit;
```

The following example creates one macro variable, StateList, with the UPCASE23. format applied to the value of the macro variable. The value of the macro variable is filtered based on criteria in the WHERE clause and is ordered by the state name.

```
proc sql noprint;
   select State format=$upcase23. as State
      into:StateList separated by ', '
      from certadv.census
      where PopEst_Apr2018>&CensusAvg2010 and PopEst_Apr2018>10000000
      order by State
;
quit;
%put &=StateList;
```

The following is printed to the SAS log.

Log 6.3 *SAS Log*

```
ARIZONA, CALIFORNIA, FLORIDA, GEORGIA, ILLINOIS, INDIANA, MARYLAND,
MASSACHUSETTS,
MICHIGAN, MISSOURI, NEW JERSEY, NEW YORK, NORTH CAROLINA, OHIO, PENNSYLVANIA,
TENNESSEE, TEXAS,
VIRGINIA, WASHINGTON
```

The following example produces a query result using the macro variables created above.

```
title "States with Population Estimates Above Census Avg: &CensusAvg2010_Format";
footnote "&StateList";
proc sql;
   select strip(State) format=$upcase23. as State,
          Census_Apr2010 format=comma12.,
          PopEst_Apr2010 format=comma12.,
          (PopEst_Apr2018-Census_Apr2010) format=comma12. as PopChange
      from certadv.census
      where PopEst_Apr2018>&CensusAvg2010 and PopEst_Apr2018>10000000
      order by State;
quit;
title;
footnote;
```

Output 6.4 PROC SQL Query Result

States with Population Estimates Above Census Avg: 6,009,064

State	Census_Apr2010	PopEst_Apr2018	PopChange
CALIFORNIA	37,253,956	39,557,045	2,303,089
FLORIDA	18,801,310	21,299,325	2,498,015
GEORGIA	9,687,653	10,519,475	831,822
ILLINOIS	12,830,632	12,741,080	-89,552
NEW YORK	19,378,102	19,542,209	164,107
NORTH CAROLINA	9,535,483	10,383,620	848,137
OHIO	11,536,504	11,689,442	152,938
PENNSYLVANIA	12,702,379	12,807,060	104,681
TEXAS	25,145,561	28,701,845	3,556,284

CALIFORNIA, FLORIDA, GEORGIA, ILLINOIS, NEW YORK, NORTH CAROLINA, OHIO, PENNSYLVANIA, TEXAS

Accessing DBMS Data with SAS/ACCESS

A Brief Overview

The SAS/ACCESS interface engine is a tool that enables you to transfer data between a database management system (DBMS) and SAS. SAS can access a variety of DBMS, such as Teradata, Oracle, SQL Server, Greenplum, and so on. This particular interface engine has transparent Read and Write access capabilities, so you might be reading Teradata data and not even realize it.

SAS/ACCESS offers interface engines that enable you to read third-party data. For example, if you need to read data in DB2, there is a SAS/ACCESS Interface engine to DB2. If you need to read Oracle, there is a SAS/ACCESS Interface to Oracle, and an Oracle engine.

Figure 6.1 SAS/ACCESS Technology

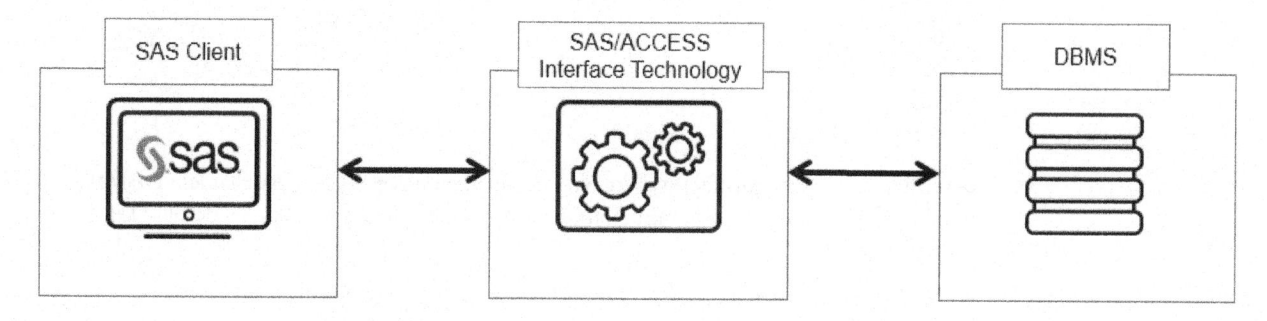

When using SAS and working with a DBMS, you must take into account the data transfer between the two systems.

The best way to have more efficient code is first to maximize the amount of processing that occurs on the DBMS. Then bring the data back to SAS for more advanced data manipulation, analytics, or visualizations.

There are two ways to connect to a database in SAS:

- SQL pass-through facility
- SAS/ACCESS LIBNAME statement

In the SQL pass-through facility, you can pass the SQL statements directly to the database.

In most instances, the SAS/ACCESS LIBNAME statement enables you to use a library reference that you assign to your relational database. It enables you to reference a database object directly within your SAS code. For example, where you would traditionally use a SAS data set name in your DATA step, you can use the name of your database table in the DATA step, as well as any of the SAS procedures. There are many options such as the SQL pass-through facility and the SAS/ACCESS LIBNAME engine that control how you connect directly to the database.

When you are reading data from a specific database, each SAS/ACCESS LIBNAME statement provides an engine name as part of the LIBNAME statement syntax.

SQL Pass-Through Facility

A Brief Overview

Suppose you are an Oracle SQL analyst, and you want to pull data from your Oracle database into SAS. You can use the SQL pass-through facility to send DBMS-specific SQL statements directly to Oracle for execution. The syntax executes as if you are coding inside Oracle, and processing occurs within Oracle. Once the Oracle query completes execution, the data is sent to SAS for processing.

Figure 6.2 SQL Pass-Through Facility

1 Establish a connection with the DBMS

2 Use native DBMS syntax to retrieve data in a PROC SQL query

3 Terminate the connection to the DBMS

With the pass-through facility, you can perform a native SQL query inside a DBMS using PROC SQL. To accomplish this, perform the following tasks inside the SQL procedure:

1. Establish a connection with the DBMS by using a CONNECT statement.
2. Retrieve data from the DBMS to be used in a PROC SQL query with the CONNECTION TO component in a SELECT statement's FROM clause.
3. Terminate the connection with the DISCONNECT statement.

CONNECT Statement Syntax

The CONNECT statement establishes a connection to send DBMS-specific SQL statements to the DBMS or to retrieve DBMS data. The connection remains in effect until you can issue a DISCONNECT statement or terminate the SQL procedure.

Syntax, CONNECT statement:

PROC SQL;

    CONNECT TO *DBMS-name* <AS *alias*> (*DBMS-connection-options*);

QUIT;

dbms-name
    identifies the database management system to which you want to connect. You must specify the DBMS name for your SAS/ACCESS interface. You can also specify an optional alias.

alias
    specifies for the connection an optional alias that has 1 to 32 characters. If you specify an alias, the keyword AS must appear before the alias. If an alias is not specified, the DBMS name is used as the name of the SQL pass-through connection.

DBMS-connection-options
    specifies values for DBMS-specific arguments that PROC SQL needs in order to connect to the DBMS. Though they are optional for most databases, you must enclose the values in parentheses if you include any.

The CONNECT statement establishes a connection with the DBMS. Depending on your DBMS setup, you might have to specify specific DBMS connection arguments.

Once you connect to the DBMS, you can submit SELECT or EXECUTE statements.

DISCONNECT Statement Syntax

The DISCONNECT statement ends the connection with the DBMS. If you do not include the DISCONNECT statement, SAS performs an implicit DISCONNECT when PROC SQL terminates. The SQL procedure continues to execute until you submit a QUIT statement, another SAS procedure, or a DATA step. Any return code or message that is generated by the DBMS is available in the macro variables SQLXRC and SQLXMSG after the statement executes.

Syntax, DISCONNECT statement:

PROC SQL;

    CONNECT TO *dbms-name* <AS *alias*> (*DBMS-connection-options*);

DISCONNECT FROM *dbms-name* | *alias*

QUIT;

dbms-name
    specifies the database management system from which you want to disconnect. You must either specify the DBMS name for your SAS/ACCESS interface or use an alias in the DISCONNECT statement.

    Note: If you used the CONNECT statement to connect to the DBMS, the DBMS name or alias in the DISCONNECT statement must match what you specified in the CONNECT statement.

alias
    specifies an alias that was defined in the CONNECT statement.

Example: Connecting to an Oracle Database

This example connects to Oracle and performs a simple query on the Customers table.

```
proc sql;
   connect to oracle (user=User password=Student827 path=localhost);
   select *
      from connection to oracle
      (select * from customers
        where customer like '1%');
   disconnect from oracle;
quit;
```

Additional Notes about the SQL Pass-Through Facility

When you are using the SQL pass-through facility, there are a few advantages and disadvantages to keep in mind. The DBMS optimizes data summarization, ordering tables, joining, and querying because DBMS SQL code is executed within the DBMS. Any DBMS-specific functions and features can be used. You can also combine SAS features with DBMS-specific features within your query. For example, you can use SAS labels and formats with DBMS-specific features. The results of your query can be saved as a SAS data file or SAS view.

Only the SQL code that is within the parentheses is passed to the DBMS. If you are returning results that contain an ORDER BY clause outside the DBMS-specific SQL query, the ordering of the table occurs in SAS. This also applies to labels and formats. If you specify WHERE processing or sorting within SAS step (for example, as an SQL view), the SQL view executes the instructions within the DBMS. However, the results that are returned are executed by SAS.

SAS/ACCESS LIBNAME Engine

A Brief Overview

If you are familiar with the LIBNAME statement, recall that it enables you to assign a library reference, or an alias, to a SAS library. The syntax for the LIBNAME statement is the keyword LIBNAME, followed by the library reference name, the location of your SAS data in quotation marks, and some options. When you name a library reference, the name can be between one and eight characters long. The name must begin with a letter or an underscore, and it can continue with any number of characters, letters, or numbers and underscores up to eight.

For example, suppose your company uses Teradata, and you need to connect to the database.

When you are using the SAS/ACCESS LIBNAME statement, it enables you to make a connection to Teradata. It establishes a library reference that acts as an alias, or a nickname, to Teradata. This enables you to use the Teradata tables with the SAS syntax, where you reference the table name as a two-level name. It also enables you to use the Teradata table in order to update the table, if you have the correct authority to do so. The SAS/ACCESS LIBNAME statement also enables you to use SAS/ACCESS LIBNAME options to specify how Teradata objects are processed by SAS. Last, it enables you to customize how to connect to Teradata.

When you are using PROC SQL with the SAS/ACCESS LIBNAME engine connection to a database, the engine converts PROC SQL syntax to the native SQL of the database wherever possible.

Figure 6.3 SAS/ACCESS LIBNAME Statement

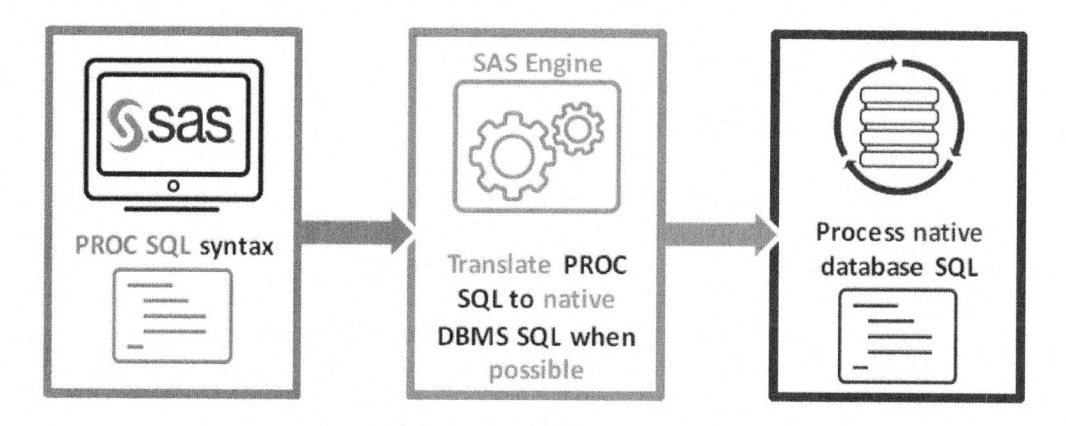

When you are reading data from a specific database, each SAS/ACCESS LIBNAME statement provides an engine name as part of the LIBNAME statement syntax.

The SAS/ACCESS LIBNAME Statement

The LIBNAME statement enables you to assign a library reference, or an alias, to a database. To use the SAS/ACCESS LIBNAME statement, specify a libref, engine-name, and necessary connection options to connect to the database.

Syntax, SAS/ACCESS LIBNAME statement:

LIBNAME *libref engine* <*SAS/ACCESS-engine-options*>;

- *libref* is the name of the SAS library.
- *engine* is the name of the SAS/ACCESS engine.
- *SAS/ACCESS-engine-options* depend on the SAS/ACCESS engine that you are using.

Closing the DBMS Connection

You can submit a LIBNAME statement with the CLEAR option to release the DBMS and associated resources. It is a good practice to close the DBMS connection when you end your session.

```
LIBNAME libref clear;
```

The FedSQL Procedure

A Brief Overview

SAS FedSQL is a SAS proprietary implementation of ANSI SQL:1999 core standard. It provides support for new data types and other ANSI 1999 core compliance features and proprietary extensions.

At the highest level, FedSQL provides a common ANSI SQL syntax across all data sources. FedSQL is a vendor-neutral SQL dialect that accesses data from various data sources without having to submit queries in the SQL dialect that is specific to the data source (or DBMS). An ANSI standard SQL allows for as much processing to be pushed into a DBMS as possible.

FedSQL is not a replacement for PROC SQL. On the contrary, both are tools that are used for specific scenarios. They offer different strengths for different situations. However, when you know one, you can easily transition to another.

Comparing PROC FedSQL and PROC SQL

Table 6.1 Comparing PROC FedSQL and PROC SQL

PROC FedSQL	PROC SQL
Complies with ANSI standard 3.	Follows ANSI standard 2.
Processes 17 ANSI data types.	Is limited to SAS data types (numeric or character).
Provides vendor-neutral ANSI SQL.	Provides SAS SQL implementation.
Is fully multi-threaded on the SAS Platform.	Is multi-threaded for sorting and indexing on the SAS Platform.
Includes very few non-ANSI SAS enhancements.	Includes many non-ANSI standard SAS enhancements.

- PROC FedSQL processes 17 ANSI data types including BIGINT, BINARY(*n*), CHAR( ), VARCHAR( ). PROC SQL is limited to only SAS data types: numeric or character.

- As noted, PROC FedSQL enables you to work with ANSI data types. Some ANSI data types allow for numbers larger than 15-16 digits, and FedSQL enables you to work with them accurately.

- PROC FedSQL provides a scalable, threaded, high-performance way to access, manage, and share relational data in multiple data sources. When possible, PROC FedSQL queries are optimized with multi-threaded algorithms in order to resolve large-scale operations. By contrast, PROC SQL is mostly a single-threaded procedure, and PROC SQL only sorts and indexes multi-threaded on the SAS Platform.

PROC FEDSQL Syntax

The foundation of the PROC FedSQL syntax is similar to PROC SQL. The only major change is the PROC name: Instead of PROC SQL, write PROC FedSQL.

Syntax, PROC FEDSQL step:

PROC FedSQL;
    SELECT *col-name*
        FROM *input-table*
        <WHERE *clause*>
        <GROUP BY *clause*>
        <HAVING *clause*>
        <ORDER BY *clause*>
;
QUIT;

The LIBNAME Statement

PROC FedSQL can process any data set that is accessible via libref with a supported engine. In order to connect to a data source, the FedSQL language requires that a connection string be submitted. The connection string defines how FedSQL can connect to a data source. The FedSQL procedure generates a connection string by using the attributes of currently assigned librefs. First, submit a LIBNAME statement for the data source that you want to access (for example, submit a Base SAS LIBNAME statement or a Hadoop LIBNAME statement). Then run PROC FedSQL.

Syntax, PROC FedSQL step:

LIBNAME *libref-engine* <*SAS/ACCESS-engine-options*>;
PROC FedSQL;
    SELECT *col-name*
        FROM *input-table*
        <WHERE *clause*>
        <GROUP BY *clause*>
        <HAVING *clause*>
        <ORDER BY *clause*>
;
QUIT;

To run PROC FedSQL, specify the LIBNAME statement with the correct SAS/ACCESS engine and connection options. Then reference the DBMS table like a SAS library.

```
libname market oracle user=cert password=student
                           path=localhost schema=Analyst;
proc fedsql;
   select State,
        count(*) as TotalCustomer format=comma14.
     from market.customer
     where CreditScore > 650
     group by State
     order by TotalCustomer desc;
quit;
```

The LIMIT Clause

Suppose you wanted to limit the number of rows that the SELECT statement displays in the query output. With PROC SQL you could use INOBS= or OUTOBS=, but those options are not available in PROC FedSQL. However, you can use the LIMIT clause to specify the number of rows that the SELECT statement returns. The LIMIT clause is similar to OUTOBS=, but is a much more common approach to limit SQL query output rows in ANSI systems.

Syntax, LIMIT clause:

LIBNAME *libref-engine* <*SAS/ACCESS-engine-options*>;
PROC FedSQL;
   SELECT *col-name*
      FROM *input-table*
      <LIMIT {*count*}>
;
QUIT;

count
   specifies the number of rows that the SELECT statement returns.

> **TIP** *count* can be an integer or any simple expression that resolves to an integer value.

Note: When you use the LIMIT clause, it is recommended that you use an ORDER BY clause to create an ordered sequence. Otherwise, you can get an unpredictable subset of a query's rows.

Suppose you want to create a FedSQL query that contains the variables State, Census_Apr2010, and PopEst_Apr2018. The query is ordered by the state name. However, you want to limit the result to the first ten rows only.

```
libname certadv v9 'C:\Users\Student\certadv\';
proc fedsql;
   select State, Census_Apr2010, PopEst_Apr2018
      from certadv.census
      order by State
      limit 10;
quit;
```

Output 6.5 PROC FedSQL Query Result

State	Census_Apr2010	PopEst_Apr2018
Alabama	4779736	4887871
Alaska	710231	737438
Arizona	6392017	7171646
Arkansas	2915918	3013825
California	37253956	39557045
Colorado	5029196	5695564
Connecticut	3574097	3572665
Delaware	897934	967171
District of Columbia	601723	702455
Florida	18801310	21299325

The PUT Function

Suppose you want to format the output of a FedSQL query. In PROC SQL, you would use the FORMAT statement in the SELECT clause to apply the format. However, in FedSQL, the FORMAT statement does not work in applying a format to the output.

Use the PUT function to apply a format to a value in the FedSQL list to change its appearance. It is not analogous to applying a format using FORMAT= in PROC SQL. Using PUT to format a value in FedSQL also modifies the column's data type in the result set.

Syntax, PUT function:

LIBNAME *libref-engine* <*SAS/ACCESS-engine-options*>;
PROC FedSQL;
    SELECT *col-name* <PUT(*col-name*, *format*) as *col-name*>
        FROM *input-table*
;
QUIT;

col-name
    identifies the variable or constant whose value you want to reformat.

format
    contains the SAS or FedSQL format that you want applied to the variable or constant that is specified in the source.

Formats can be associated with any of the data types that are supported by FedSQL. However, the data types are converted. Any value that is passed to the PUT function with a numeric format is converted to NVARCHAR, VARBINARY, or BINARY. The type conversions are carried out based on the format name. Any value that is passed with a character format to the PUT function is converted to NVARCHAR.

If the result set is saved using a CREATE TABLE statement, columns that are formatted with a PUT function have a new data type (NVARCHAR, VARBINARY, or BINARY) instead of the data type that is found in the source table. Column values and data types in the source table are not affected.

Suppose you need to format your query output. There are two ways to use the PUT function to do that.

The first way is to use the PUT function with no AS keyword. This method replaces the column names with a generic column name such as Column.

```
libname certadv v9 'C:\Users\Student\certadv\';
proc fedsql;
   select SalesRep,
          put(Sales1, dollar10.2),
          put(Sales2, dollar10.2),
          put(Sales3, dollar10.2),
          put(Sales4, dollar10.2)
      from certadv.qsales;
quit;
```

Output 6.6   PROC FedSQL Query Result

SalesRep	column	column	column	column
Britt	$8,400.00	$8,800.00	$9,300.00	$9,800.00
Fruchten	$9,500.00	$9,300.00	$9,800.00	$8,900.00
Goodyear	$9,150.00	$9,200.00	$9,650.00	$11,000.00

The second method is to use the AS keyword and include either the current or new variable name for each time a format is associated using the PUT function.

```
libname certadv v9 'C:\Users\Student\certadv\';
proc fedsql;
   select SalesRep,
          put(Sales1, dollar10.2) as Sales1,
          put(Sales2, dollar10.2) as Sales2,
          put(Sales3, dollar10.2) as Sales3,
          put(Sales4, dollar10.2) as Sales4
      from certadv.qsales;
quit;
```

Output 6.7   PROC FedSQL Query Result

SalesRep	SALES1	SALES2	SALES3	SALES4
Britt	$8,400.00	$8,800.00	$9,300.00	$9,800.00
Fruchten	$9,500.00	$9,300.00	$9,800.00	$8,900.00
Goodyear	$9,150.00	$9,200.00	$9,650.00	$11,000.00

System Options in FedSQL

FedSQL does not provide any options that affect the processing of an entire SAS program or interactive SAS session from the time the option is specified until it is changed. Nor does FedSQL support SAS system options, with the exception of certain SAS invocation options such as NOPRINT and NUMBER.

Quiz

Select the best answer for each question. After completing the quiz, check your answers using the answer key in the appendix.

1. Which of the following correctly creates a macro variable in a PROC SQL step?

    a.
    ```
    proc sql noprint;
        select avg(Days)
            into:NumDays
            from certadv.all;
    quit;
    %put &=NumDays;
    ```

    b.
    ```
    proc sql noprint;
        select avg(Days)
            into NumDays
            from certadv.all;
    quit;
    %put &=NumDays;
    ```

    c.
    ```
    proc sql noprint;
        select avg(Days) as NumDays
            from certadv.all;
    quit;
    %put &=NumDays;
    ```

    d.
    ```
    proc sql noprint;
        select Days
            into avg(Days) as NumDays
            from certadv.all;
    quit;
    %put &=NumDays;
    ```

2. Suppose you are asked to create a report of the courses that are offered in all three available locations. The report should not contain any duplicate items. Which program correctly displays the following query result?

    Courses Offered in BOSTON, DALLAS, SEATTLE

Course Code	Description	Course Fee
C001	Basic Telecommunications	$795
C002	Structured Query Language	$1150
C003	Local Area Networks	$650
C004	Database Design	$375
C005	Artificial Intelligence	$400
C006	Computer Aided Design	$1600

    a.
    ```
    proc sql noprint;
        select distinct strip(Location) format=$upcase8.
                    as LocalList separated by ', '
            from certadv.schedule
    ```

```
            order by Location
        ;
        quit;

        %put &=LocalList;
        footnote;
        title "Courses Offered in &LocalList";
        proc sql;
            select distinct Course_Code, Course_Title, Fee
                from certadv.all
                order by Course_Code;
        quit;

b.      proc sql noprint;
            select distinct strip(Location) format=$upcase8. as Location
                into LocalList separatedby ', '
                from certadv.schedule
                order by Location
        ;
        quit;

        %put &=LocalList;
        footnote;
        title "Courses Offered in &LocalList";
        proc sql;
            select distinct Course_Code, Course_Title, Fee
                from certadv.all
                order by Course_Code;
        quit;

c.      proc sql noprint;
            select distinct strip(Location) format=$upcase8. as Location
                into:LocalList separated by ', '
                from certadv.schedule
                order by Location
        ;
        quit;

        %put &=LocalList;
        footnote;
        title "Courses Offered in &LocalList";
        proc sql;
            select distinct Course_Code, Course_Title, Fee
                from certadv.all
                order by Course_Code;
        quit;

d.      proc sql noprint;
            select distinct strip(Location) format=$upcase8. as Location
                into:LocalList separated by ', '
                from certadv.schedule
                order by Location
        ;
        quit;

        %put &=LocalList;
        footnote;
        title "Courses Offered in &LocalList";
```

```
proc sql;
    select distinct strip(Location) format=$upcase8. as Location,
                Course_Code, Course_Title, Fee
        into:LocalList separated by ', '
        from certadv.all
        order by Course_Code;
quit;
```

3. Complete the following SQL code to remove leading and trailing blanks when storing the value of the macro variable CensusAvg2010.

    ```
    proc sql noprint;
        select avg(Census_Apr2010),
        _____
            from certadv.census
        ;
    quit;
    %put &=CensusAvg2010;
    ```

    a. `into:CensusAvg2010 separated by ''`

    b. `into CensusAvg2010 separated by ''`

    c. `intoCensusAvg2010 trimmed`

    d. `into:CensusAvg2010 trimmed`

4. Suppose you are asked to concatenate the list of instructors who teach at the Dallas location and suppose also that the begin date for the course is after 01JAN2020. The list of instructors should be stored in a macro variable and should be separated by a comma with no leading or trailing blanks. Which SQL program would correctly accomplish the task?

    a.
    ```
    proc sql noprint;
        select distinct Teacher format=$upcase21.
            into:NameListDallas separated by ','
            from certadv.schedule
            where Location='Dallas' and Begin_Date>'01JAN2020'd;
    quit;
    %put &=NameListDallas;
    ```

    b.
    ```
    proc sql noprint;
        select distinct Teacher format=$upcase21.
            into:NameListDallas separated by ',' trimmed
            from certadv.schedule
            where Location='Dallas' and Begin_Date>'01JAN2020'd;
    quit;
    %put &=NameListDallas;
    ```

    c.
    ```
    proc sql noprint;
        select distinct Teacher format=$upcase21.,
            into NameListDallas separated by ','
            from certadv.schedule
            where Location='Dallas' and Begin_Date>'01JAN2020'd;
    quit;
    %put &=NameListDallas;
    ```

    d.
    ```
    proc sql noprint;
        select distinct Teacher format=$upcase21. as NameListDallas
            separated by ',' trimmed
            from certadv.schedule
            where Location='Dallas' and Begin_Date>'01JAN2020'd;
    ```

```
          quit;
          %put &=NameListDallas;
```

5. What is the FedSQL equivalent of the following PROC SQL query?

```
    proc sql;
       select State,
              Census_Apr2010 format=comma12.,
              PopEst_Apr2018 format=comma12.,
              (PopEst_Apr2018-Census_Apr2010) format=comma12. as PopChange
          from certadv.census
          where Census_Apr2010>PopEst_Apr2018
          order by State;
    quit;
```

   a.
```
       libname certadv v9 'C:\Users\Student\certadv\';
       proc fedsql;
          select State,
                 Census_Apr2010 format=comma12.,
                 PopEst_Apr2018 format=comma12.,
                 (PopEst_Apr2018-Census_Apr2010) format=comma12. as PopChange
             from certadv.census
             where Census_Apr2010>PopEst_Apr2018
             order by State;
       quit;
```

   b.
```
       libname certadv v9 'C:\Users\Student\certadv\';
       proc fedsql;
          select   State,
                   put(Census_Apr2010, comma12.) as Census_Apr2010,
                   put(PopEst_Apr2018, comma12.) as PopEst_Apr2018,
                   put(PopEst_Apr2018-Census_Apr2010, comma12.) as PopChange
             from certadv.census
             where Census_Apr2010>PopEst_Apr2018
             order by state;
       quit;
```

   c.
```
       libname certadv v9 'C:\Users\Student\certadv\';
       proc fedsql;
          select State,
                 Census_Apr2010,
                 PopEst_Apr2018,
                 (PopEst_Apr2018-Census_Apr2010) as PopChange
             from certadv.census
             where Census_Apr2010>PopEst_Apr2018
             order by State;
       quit;
```

   d.
```
       libname certadv v9 'C:\Users\Student\certadv\';
       proc fedsql;
          select State,
                 Census_Apr2010,
                 PopEst_Apr2018,
                 (PopEst_Apr2018-Census_Apr2010) as PopChange
             from certadv.census
             where Census_Apr2010>PopEst_Apr2018
             order by State;
             format Census_Apr2010 PopEst_Apr2018 PopChange comma8.
       quit;
```

6. What is the FedSQL equivalent of the following PROC SQL query?

```
proc sql inobs=5;
   select *
      from certadv.airports
      order by ID;
quit;
```

a.
```
libname certadv v9 'C:\Users\Student\certadv\';
proc fedsql inobs=5;
   select *
      from certadv.airports
      order by ID;
quit;
```

b.
```
libname certadv v9 'C:\Users\Student\certadv\';
proc fedsql limit 10;
   select *
      from certadv.airports
      order by ID;
quit;
```

c.
```
libname certadv v9 'C:\Users\Student\certadv\';
proc fedsql;
   select *
      from certadv.airports
      order by ID
      limit=5;
quit;
```

d.
```
libname certadv v9 'C:\Users\Student\certadv\';
proc fedsql;
   select*
      from certadv.airports
      order by ID
      limit=5;
quit;
```

Part 2

SAS Macro Language Processing

Chapter 7
Creating and Using Macro Variables *179*

Chapter 8
Storing and Processing Text *197*

Chapter 9
Working with Macro Programs *231*

Chapter 10
Advanced Macro Techniques *259*

Chapter 7
Creating and Using Macro Variables

Introducing Macro Variables	**179**
A Brief Overview	179
Example: Using Macro Variables	180
The SAS Macro Facility	**181**
SAS Processing of Macros	181
Tokenization	182
Macro Triggers	187
Using Macro Variables	**188**
Using User-Defined Macro Variables	188
Using Automatic Macro Variables	188
Troubleshooting Macro Variable References	**190**
SYMBOLGEN Option Syntax	190
Example: Using the SYMBOLGEN Option	191
%PUT Statement Syntax	191
Example: Using the %PUT Statement	191
The %SYMDEL Statement	192
Delimiting Macro Variable References	**193**
A Brief Overview	193
Example: Using a Delimiter to Reference Macro Variables	193
Quiz	**194**

Introducing Macro Variables

A Brief Overview

The SAS macro facility is a tool for extending and customizing SAS. It also reduces the amount of program code that you enter to perform common tasks. The macro facility has its own language, which enables you to package small or large amounts of text into units that are assigned names called *macro variables*. After a macro variable is created, you can insert the text into your code simply by referencing the macro variable by its name.

SAS macro variables enable you to substitute text in your SAS programs. Macro variables can also provide the following information:

- operating system

- SAS session
- text strings

When you reference a macro variable in a SAS program, SAS replaces the reference with the text value that has been assigned to that macro variable. By substituting text into the program, SAS macro variables make your programs more reusable and dynamic.

There are two types of macro variables:

- automatic macro variables, which are provided by SAS
- user-defined macro variables, whose values you create and define

Whether automatic or user-defined, a macro variable is independent of a SAS data set and contains one text string value that remains constant until you change it. The value of a macro variable is substituted into your program wherever the macro variable is referenced.

Macro variables are stored in the global symbol table that makes the values available in your SAS session.

Macro variables can be defined and referenced anywhere in a SAS program except within the data lines of a DATALINES statement.

Example: Using Macro Variables

In a SAS program, you might need to reference the same variable, data set, or text string multiple times.

```
title "Employees Hired in 2012";
data work.emp2012;
   set certadv.empdata;
   if year(HireDate)=2012;
run;
proc print data=work.emp2012;
run;
```

Later, you might need to reference a different variable, data set, or text string. Especially if your programs are lengthy, scanning for specific references and updating them manually can take a lot of time. It is also easy to overlook a reference that needs to be updated.

```
title "Employees Hired in 2011";
data work.emp2011;
   set certadv.empdata;
   if year(HireDate)=2011;
run;
proc print data=work.emp2011;
run;
```

If you need to change your program, macro variables make these updates quick and easy because you make the change in only one place. To change the value of the macro variable in the code below, change the value of the %LET statement from 2012 to 2011.

```
%let year=2012;
title "Employees Hired in &year";
data work.emp&year;
   set certadv.empdata;
   if year(HireDate)=&year;
run;
proc print data=work.emp&year;
```

```
run;
```

The SAS Macro Facility

SAS Processing of Macros

A SAS program can be any combination of the following elements:

- DATA steps or PROC steps
- global statements
- Structured Query Language (SQL) code
- SAS macro language code

When you submit a SAS program, the code is copied to a memory location called the *input stack*. The presence of text in the input stack triggers a component called the *word scanner* to begin its work.

Figure 7.1 SAS Processing with an Input Stack

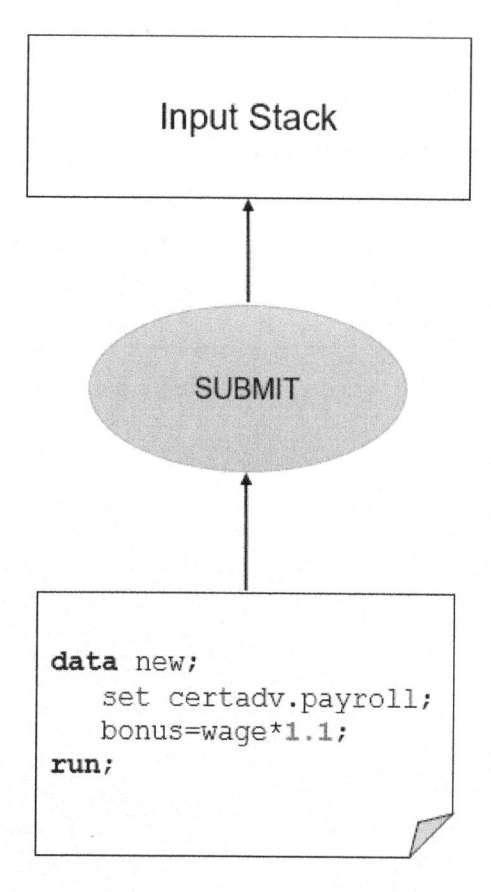

```
data new;
    set certadv.payroll;
    bonus=wage*1.1;
run;
```

The word scanner has two major functions. First, it pulls the raw text from the input stack character by character and transforms it into tokens. Second, it sends tokens for processing to the compiler and macro processor. A program is then separated into components called *tokens*. There are four types of tokens: name, number, special, and literal.

To build a token, the word scanner extracts characters until it reaches a delimiter, or until the next character does not meet the rules of the current token. A delimiter is any whitespace character such as a space, tab, or end-of-line character.

Name tokens consist of a maximum of 32 characters, must begin with a letter or underscore, and can include only letter, digit, and underscore characters.

Number tokens define a SAS floating-point numeric value. They can consist of a digit, decimal point, leading sign, and exponent indicator (e or E). Date, time, and datetime specifications also become number tokens (for example: '29APR2019'd, '14:05:32.1't, '29APR2019 14:05:32.1'dt).

Literal tokens consist of a string of any characters enclosed in single or double quotation marks. They can contain up to 32,767 characters and are handled as a single unit.

Special tokens are made up of any character or group of characters that have special meaning in the SAS language. Examples include * / + - ; ( ) . & %

Knowing how tokenization works helps you understand how the various parts of SAS and the macro processor work together. Understanding differences in timing between macro processing and SAS code compilation and execution is especially important.

Tokenization

Between the input stack and the compiler, SAS programs are tokenized into smaller pieces.

1. Tokens are passed on demand to the compiler.
2. The compiler requests tokens until it receives a semicolon.
3. The compiler performs a syntax check on the statement.

The following example illustrates how the input stack, word scanner, and compiler work together.

```
title "MPG City Over 25";
proc print data=sashelp.cars noobs;
   var Make Model Type MPG_City MPG_Highway MSRP;
   where MPG_City>25;
run;
```

Figure 7.2 *The First Step in the Tokenization Process*

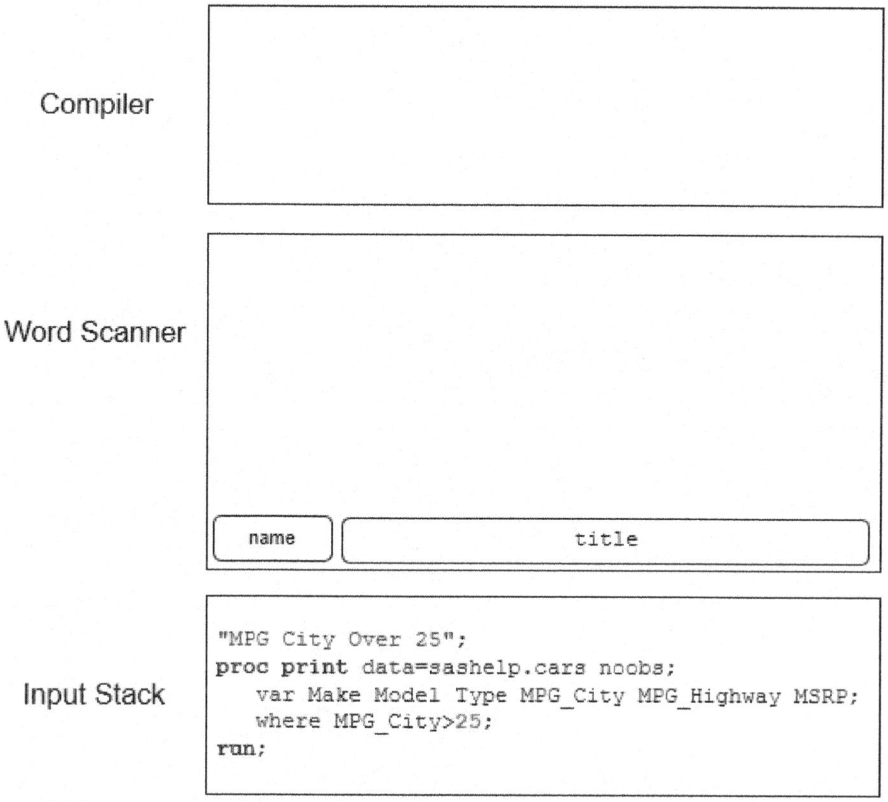

Compiler

Word Scanner

| name | title |

Input Stack

```
"MPG City Over 25";
proc print data=sashelp.cars noobs;
   var Make Model Type MPG_City MPG_Highway MSRP;
   where MPG_City>25;
run;
```

When the code is copied to the input stack, the word scanner retrieves one character at a time until it reaches the first delimiter, a blank. When TITLE is recognized as a name token, the word scanner tags it and passes it to the compiler.

Figure 7.3 *The Tokenization Process, continued*

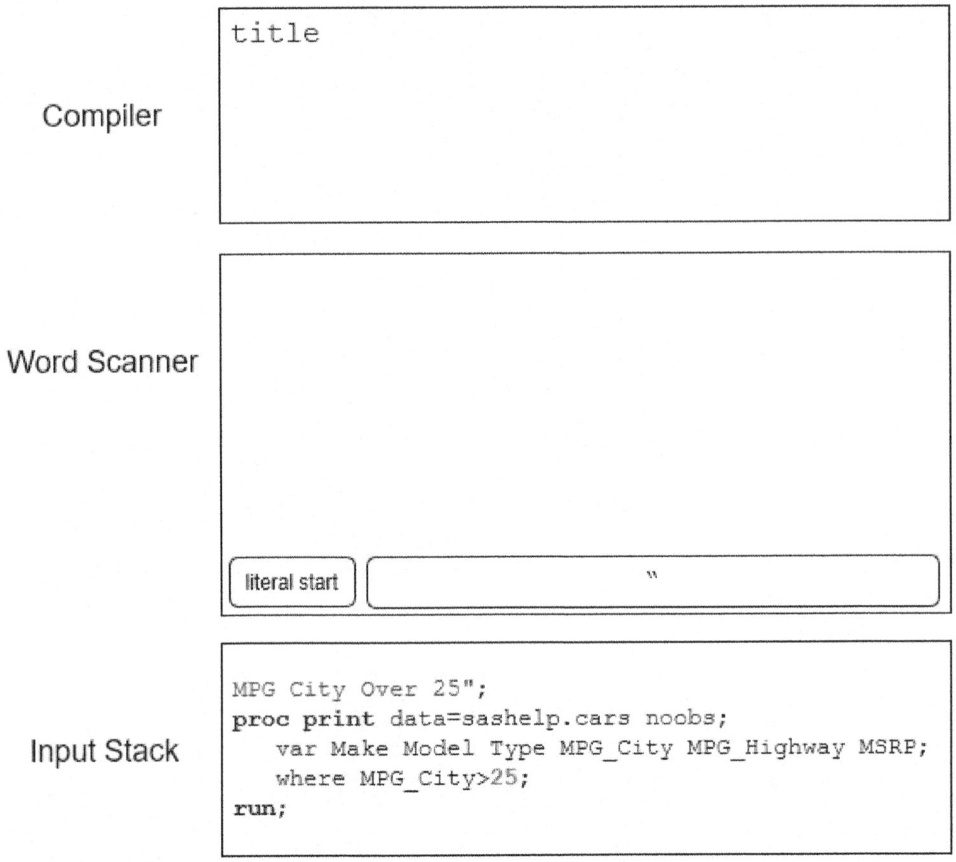

Compiler

```
title
```

Word Scanner

| literal start | " |

Input Stack

```
MPG City Over 25";
proc print data=sashelp.cars noobs;
   var Make Model Type MPG_City MPG_Highway MSRP;
   where MPG_City>25;
run;
```

The word scanner tags the double quotation mark as the start of a literal token.

Figure 7.4 *The Tokenization Process, continued*

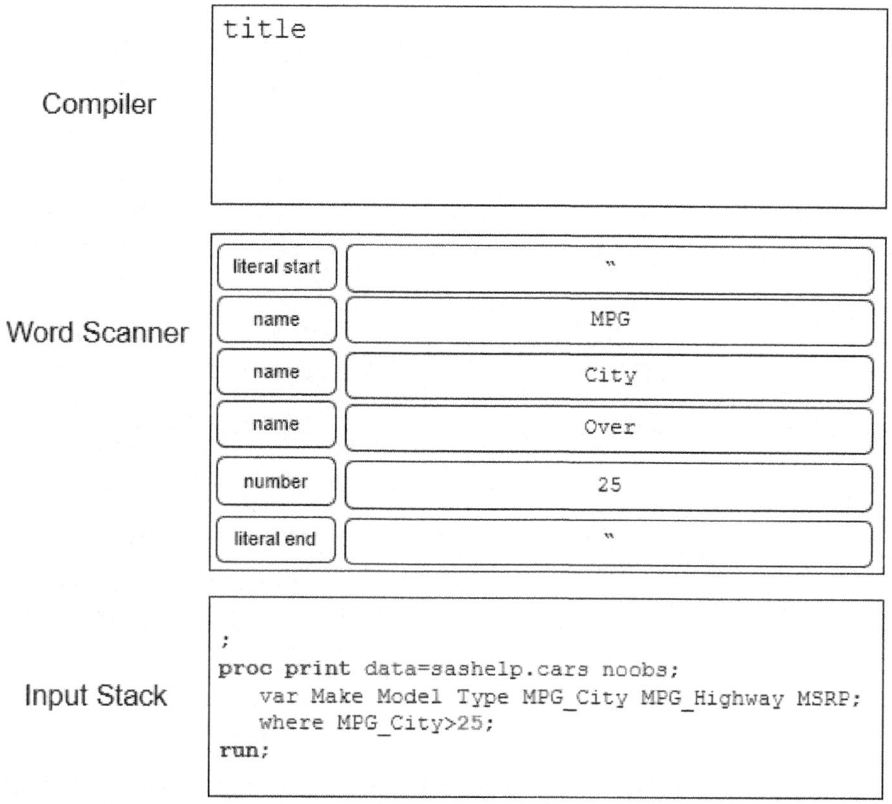

Compiler	title

Word Scanner	literal start	"
	name	MPG
	name	City
	name	Over
	number	25
	literal end	"

Input Stack	`;`
	`proc print data=sashelp.cars noobs;`
	`   var Make Model Type MPG_City MPG_Highway MSRP;`
	`   where MPG_City>25;`
	`run;`

It then retrieves, tokenizes, and holds additional text until it retrieves another double quotation mark. It passes the text as a single literal token to the compiler, and then tokenization continues. The semicolon is a special token, and the end-of-line character is a delimiter.

Figure 7.5 The Tokenization Process, continued

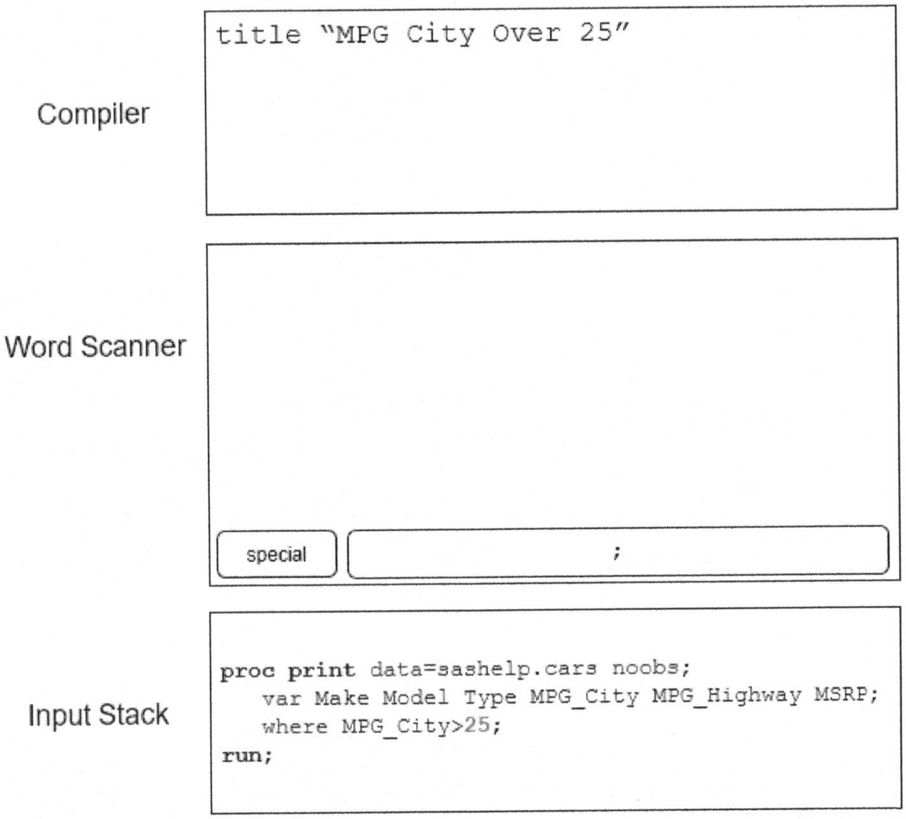

Compiler:
```
title "MPG City Over 25"
```

Word Scanner: special `;`

Input Stack:
```
proc print data=sashelp.cars noobs;
   var Make Model Type MPG_City MPG_Highway MSRP;
   where MPG_City>25;
run;
```

The semicolon is sent to the compiler, ending the TITLE statement. The compiler checks the syntax, and because TITLE is a global statement, it is executed immediately. The tokenization process continues with the PROC PRINT step. The compiler performs a syntax check at the end of each statement.

Figure 7.6 The Tokenization Process, concluded

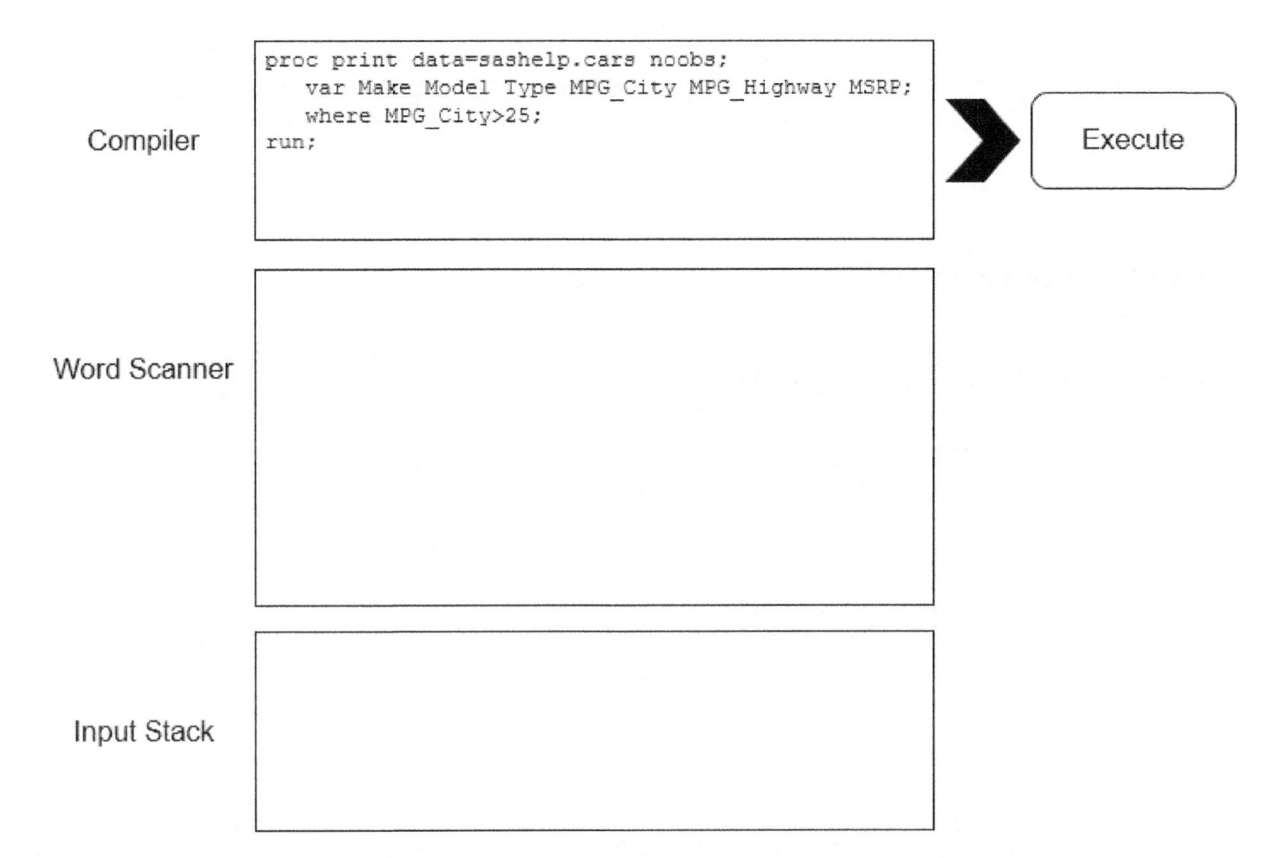

Compiler:
```
proc print data=sashelp.cars noobs;
   var Make Model Type MPG_City MPG_Highway MSRP;
   where MPG_City>25;
run;
```
→ Execute

Word Scanner:

Input Stack:

The code executes when it encounters a step boundary, in this case the RUN statement.

Macro Triggers

The macro facility includes a macro processor that is responsible for handling all macro language elements. Certain token sequences, known as *macro triggers*, alert the word scanner that the subsequent code should be sent to the macro processor.

The word scanner recognizes the following token sequences as macro triggers:

- % followed immediately by a name token (such as %LET)
- & followed immediately by a name token (such as &AMT)

When a macro trigger is detected, the word scanner passes it to the macro processor for evaluation. Here is the sequence that the macro processor follows:

- It examines these tokens.
- It requests additional tokens as necessary.
- It performs the action indicated.

For macro variables, the processor does one of the following:

- It creates a macro variable in the global symbol table and assigns a value to the variable.
- It changes the value of an existing macro variable in the global symbol table.
- It looks up an existing macro variable in the global symbol table and returns the variable's value to the input stack in place of the original reference.

The word scanner then resumes processing tokens from the input stack.

Note: The word scanner does not recognize macro triggers that are enclosed in single quotation marks. Remember that if you need to reference a macro variable within a literal token, such as the title text in a TITLE statement, you must enclose the text string in double quotation marks or else the macro variable reference is not resolved.

Using Macro Variables

Using User-Defined Macro Variables

%LET Statement Syntax

Use the %LET statement to define your macro variable and assign a value to it.

Syntax, %LET statement:

%LET *variable=value*;

variable
 is any name that follows the SAS naming convention.

value
 can be any string from 0 to 65,534 characters long.

Note: If the variable already exists, then the value replaces the current value. If either variable or value contains a reference to another macro variable (such as `&macvar`), the reference is evaluated before the assignment is made.

Using Automatic Macro Variables

What Are Automatic Macro Variables?

SAS creates and defines several automatic macro variables for you. Automatic macro variables contain information about your computing environment, such as the date and time of the session, and the version of SAS that you are running. Keep the following facts in mind about these automatic macro variables:

- They are created when SAS starts.
- They are global (always available).
- They are usually assigned values by SAS.
- They can be assigned values by the user in some cases.

Some automatic macro variables have fixed values that are set when SAS starts.

Name	Value
SYSDATE	the date of the SAS invocation (DATE7.)
SYSDATE9	the date of the SAS invocation (DATE9.)

Name	Value
SYSDAY	the day of the week of the SAS invocation
SYSTIME	the time of the SAS invocation
SYSENV	FORE (interactive execution) or BACK (noninteractive or batch execution)
SYSSCP	an abbreviation for the operating system that is being used, such as WIN or LINUX
SYSVER	the release of SAS that is being used
SYSJOBID	an identifier for the current SAS session or for the current batch job (the user ID or job name for mainframe systems, the process ID (PID) for other systems)

Some automatic macro variables have values that automatically change based on submitted SAS statements.

Name	Value
SYSLAST	the name of the most recently created SAS data set, in the form **LIBREF.NAME**. This value is always stored in all capital letters. If no data set has been created, the value is _NULL_.
SYSPARM	text that is specified when SAS starts.
SYSERR	contains a return code status that is set by the DATA step and some SAS procedures to indicate whether the step or procedure executed successfully.

Example: Using Automatic Macro Variables

You can substitute system information such as the time, day, and date on which your SAS session started in footnotes for a report.

```
footnote1 "Created &systime &sysday, &sysdate9";
title "MPG City Over 25";
proc print data=sashelp.cars;
   var Make Model Type MPG_City MPG_Highway MSRP;
   where MPG_City>25;
run;
```

Output 7.1 *PROC PRINT Output of Automatic Macro Variables*

MPG City Over 25

Obs	Make	Model	Type	MPG_City	MPG_Highway	MSRP
68	Chevrolet	Aveo 4dr	Sedan	28	34	$11,690
69	Chevrolet	Aveo LS 4dr hatch	Sedan	28	34	$12,585
70	Chevrolet	Cavalier 2dr	Sedan	26	37	$14,610

...more observations...

397	Toyota	MR2 Spyder convertible 2dr	Sports	26	32	$25,130
401	Toyota	Matrix XR	Wagon	29	36	$16,695
405	Volkswagen	Jetta GLS TDI 4dr	Sedan	38	46	$21,055

Created 13:01 Wednesday, 12JUN2019 ① ② ③

1. time of day (SYSTIME)
2. day of the week (SYSDAY)
3. date (day, month, and year) (SYSDATE9)

Troubleshooting Macro Variable References

When you submit a macro variable reference, the macro processor resolves the reference and passes the value directly back to the input stack. You will not see the value that the compiler receives. To debug your programs, use the SYMBOLGEN option or the %PUT statement to see what value replaces your macro variable references. You can use the %SYMDEL statement to remove macro variables from the global symbol table.

SYMBOLGEN Option Syntax

Use the SYMBOLGEN system option to monitor the value that is substituted for a macro variable reference.

Syntax, OPTIONS statement with the SYMBOLGEN option:

OPTIONS NOSYMBOLGEN | SYMBOLGEN ;

NOSYMBOLGEN
  specifies that log messages about macro variable references will not be displayed. This is the default.

SYMBOLGEN
  specifies that log messages about macro variable references will be displayed.

When the SYMBOLGEN option is turned on, SAS writes a message to the log for each macro variable that is referenced in your program. The message states the macro variable name and the resolved value.

Example: Using the SYMBOLGEN Option

Use the SYMBOLGEN option to view the results of the resolving macro variable references in the SAS log.

```
options symbolgen;
%let CarType=Wagon;
proc print data=sashelp.cars;
   var Make Model Type MSRP;
   where Type="&CarType";
run;
options nosymbolgen;
```

The SAS log shows the messages that are generated by the SYMBOLGEN option.

Log 7.1 SAS Log

```
SYMBOLGEN:  Macro variable CARTYPE resolves to Wagon
```

%PUT Statement Syntax

Use the %PUT statement to write your own messages to the SAS log.

Syntax, %PUT statement:

%PUT *text*;

text
   is any text string.

Here is a quick description of the %PUT statement:

- writes only to the SAS log
- always writes to a new log line, starting in column one
- writes a blank line if text is not specified
- does not require quotation marks around text
- resolves macro triggers in text before text is written
- removes leading and trailing blanks from text unless a macro quoting function is used
- wraps lines when the length of text is greater than the current line size setting
- can be used either inside or outside a macro definition

Example: Using the %PUT Statement

Suppose you want to verify the value of the macro variable CarType. Since the %PUT statement resolves macro references in text before writing text to the SAS log, you can use it to show the stored value of CarType.

```
%put The value of the macro variable CarType is: &CarType
```

Log 7.2 SAS Log

```
119  %put The value of the macro variable CarType is: &CarType
The value of the macro variable CarType is: Wagon
```

You can also submit the statement `%put &=cartype;` This writes the macro variable name and its value in the log as follows:

Log 7.3 SAS Log

```
CARTYPE=SEDAN
```

The %PUT statement has several optional arguments.

Argument	Result in the SAS Log
ALL	lists the values of all macro variables
AUTOMATIC	lists the values of all automatic macro variables
GLOBAL	lists user-generated global macro variables
LOCAL	lists user-generated local macro variables
USER	lists the values of all user-defined macro variables

Note: When you use optional arguments such as _ALL_, each macro variable name is also written to the SAS log, along with a label of either AUTOMATIC or GLOBAL.

The %SYMDEL Statement

A Brief Overview

The %SYMDEL statement deletes the specified variables from the macro global symbol table. It also issues a warning when an attempt is made to delete a non-existent macro variable. To suppress this message, use the NOWARN option.

%SYMDEL Syntax

Syntax, %SYMDEL statement:

%SYMDEL *macro-variable-1<...macro-variable-n></option>*;

macro-variable
> is the name of one or more macro variables or a text expression that generates one or more macro variable names. You cannot use a SAS variable list or a macro expression that generates a SAS variable list in a %SYMDEL statement.

option
> NOWARN
>> suppresses the warning message when an attempt is made to delete a non-existent macro variable.

Example: Using the %SYMDEL Statement

The following example illustrates how the %SYMDEL statement deletes the listed variables from the global symbol table and releases memory back to the system.

```
%symdel CarType;
```

Nothing is written to the SAS log when the statement is executed.

Output 7.2 *Global Symbol Table*

Name	Value
~~CarType~~	~~Wagon~~
a	one
b	two

Delimiting Macro Variable References

A Brief Overview

Tokens are delimited by spaces or special tokens by default. Sometimes when you use a macro variable reference in combination with other text, the reference does not resolve as you expect if you simply concatenate it. Instead, you might need to delimit the reference by adding a period to the end of it.

A period immediately following a macro variable reference acts as a delimiter. That is, a period at the end of a reference forces the macro processor to recognize the end of the reference. The period does not appear in the resulting text.

Example: Using a Delimiter to Reference Macro Variables

The following example illustrates using a delimiter, a period (.), between the libref and the table name to reference the macro variable.

```
%let CarType=Wagon;
%let lib=sashelp;
title "&CarType.s from the &lib..CARS Table";
```

```
proc freq data=&lib..cars;
   tables Origin/nocum;
   where Type="&CarType";
run;
proc print data=&lib..cars;
   var Make Model Type MSRP;
   where Type="&CarType";
run;
```

Note: When the character following a macro variable reference is a period, use two periods. The first is the delimiter for the macro reference, and the second is part of the text.

Output 7.3 PROC FREQ Output

Wagons from the sashelp.CARS Table

The FREQ Procedure

Origin	Frequency	Percent
Asia	11	36.67
Europe	12	40.00
USA	7	23.33

Output 7.4 PROC PRINT Output

Wagons from the sashelp.CARS Table

Obs	Make	Model	Type	MSRP
25	Audi	A6 3.0 Avant Quattro	Wagon	$40,840
26	Audi	S4 Avant Quattro	Wagon	$49,090
46	BMW	325xi Sport	Wagon	$32,845

...*more observations*...

416	Volkswagen	Passat W8	Wagon	$40,235
427	Volvo	V40	Wagon	$26,135
428	Volvo	XC70	Wagon	$35,145

Quiz

Select the best answer for each question. After completing the quiz, check your answers using the answer key in the appendix.

1. Which of the following statements is false?

    a. A macro variable can be defined and referenced anywhere in a SAS program except within data lines.

b. Macro variables are always user-defined, and their values remain constant until they are changed by the user.

c. Macro variables are text strings that are independent of SAS data sets.

d. The values of macro variables can be up to 65,534 characters long.

2. Which of the following TITLE statements correctly references the macro variable Month?

   a. `title "Total Sales for '&month' ";`

   b. `title "Total Sales for 'month'";`

   c. `title "Total Sales for &month";`

   d. `title Total Sales for "&month";`

3. Which of the following statements generates an error message while trying to display the value of the macro variable Month in the SAS log?

   a. `options &month;`

   b. `%PUT &=month;`

   c. `options symbolgen;`

   d. `%PUT the macro variable MONTH has the value &month.;`

4. Which statement creates a macro variable named Location that has the value **storage**?

   a. `&let location = storage;`

   b. `let &location = storage;`

   c. `%let location = "storage";`

   d. `%let location = storage;`

5. What value will these statements assign to the macro variable Reptile?

   ```
   %let area = "Southeast";
   %let reptitle = *  Sales Report for &area Area  *;
   ```

   a. `Sales Report for Southeast Area`

   b. `Sales Report for "Southeast" Area`

   c. `*Sales Report for "Southeast" Area*`

   d. `*  Sales Report for "Southeast" Area  *`

6. If a macro trigger is embedded in a literal token and you want the trigger to resolve, then the literal string must be enclosed in double quotation marks.

   a. True

   b. False

7. What are the four types of tokens that SAS recognizes?

   a. expressions, literals, names, and special characters

   b. literals, names, numbers, and special characters

   c. expressions, names, numbers, and special characters

   d. expressions, literals, numbers, and special characters

8. Which statement about the macro processor is false?
    a. It compiles and executes macro statements.
    b. It breaks SAS programs into tokens.
    c. It writes macro variables and values to the global symbol table.
    d. It reads values from the global symbol table and writes them to the input stack.
9. How does the word scanner detect the end of a token?
    a. It encounters a new token, or encountering a blank delimiter.
    b. It encounters the end-of-file character.
    c. It encounters an error.
    d. It encounters a statement such as RUN or QUIT.

Chapter 8
Storing and Processing Text

Processing Text with Macro Functions **198**
Using SAS Macro Functions to Manipulate Character Strings **198**
    Macro Character Functions 198
    The %UPCASE Function 198
    The %SUBSTR Function 200
    The %INDEX Function 201
    The %SCAN Function 202

Using SAS Functions with Macro Variables **203**
    The %SYSFUNC Function 203
    The %EVAL Function 204
    The %SYSEVALF Function 206

Using SAS Macro Functions to Mask Special Characters **207**
    Macro Quoting Functions 207
    The %STR Function 208
    The %NRSTR Function 209
    The %SUPERQ Function 210
    The %BQUOTE Function 211
    Macro Q Functions 212

Creating Macro Variables during PROC SQL Step Execution **214**
    INTO Clause and the NOPRINT Option Syntax 214
    Example: Using the INTO Clause and the NOPRINT Option 214
    Example: Creating Variables with the INTO Clause 215
    Example: Creating a Delimited List of Values 216

Creating Macro Variables during DATA Step Execution **217**
    The CALL SYMPUTX Routine 217
    The PUT Function 225

Referencing Macro Variables Indirectly **226**
    Indirect References 226
    Example: Referencing Macro Variables Indirectly 226
    Example: Creating a Series of Macro Variables 227

Quiz **228**

Processing Text with Macro Functions

Macro functions can be used to manipulate text in a SAS program. Macro functions accept one or more arguments, process the argument text, and return the result as text. The text that is read in during the processing is returned to the top of the input stack.

Using SAS Macro Functions to Manipulate Character Strings

Macro Character Functions

Often when working with macro variables, you need to manipulate character strings. Here are ways you can do this by using macro character functions:

- change lowercase letters to uppercase
- produce a substring of a character string
- extract a word from a character string
- determine the length of a character string

Macro character functions have the same basic syntax as the corresponding DATA step functions, and they yield similar results. However, it is important to remember that although they might be similar, macro character functions are distinct from DATA step functions. As part of the macro language, macro functions enable you to communicate with the macro processor in order to manipulate text strings that you insert into your SAS programs.

Note: You cannot use SAS data set variables in macro functions.

The %UPCASE Function

A Brief Overview

The %UPCASE function converts lowercase characters in the argument to uppercase. %UPCASE does not mask special characters or mnemonic operators in its result, even when the argument was previously masked by a macro quoting function.

%UPCASE is useful in the comparison of values because the macro facility does not automatically convert lowercase characters to uppercase before comparing values.

%UPCASE Syntax

Syntax, %UPCASE function:

%UPCASE(*character-string|text-expression*)

To convert characters to lowercase, use the %LOWCASE or %QLOWCASE autocall macro.

Example: Using the %UPCASE Function

The Certadv.All data set contains student information and registration information for computer training courses. Suppose, you want to create a summary of the uncollected course fees. This example shows how to do that.

```
%let paidval=n;
title "Uncollected Fees for Each Course";
proc means data=certadv.all sum maxdec=0;
   where paid="&paidval";
   var fee;
   class course_title;
run;
```

The following is written to the SAS log.

Log 8.1 SAS Log

```
163  %let paidval=n;
164  title "Uncollected Fees for Each Course"
165  proc means data=certadv.all sum maxdec=0;
166       where paid="&paidval";
167       var fee;
168       class course_title;
169  run;
NOTE: No observations were selected from data set CERT.ALL.
```

Because the value of the macro variable Paidval was specified in lowercase, the WHERE expression finds no matching observations. All the values of the data set variable Paid are stored in uppercase. Use the %UPCASE function in the WHERE statement.

```
%let paidval=n;
title "Uncollected Fees for Each Course";
proc means data=certadv.all sum maxdec=0;
   where paid="%upcase(&paidval)";
   var fee;
   class course_title;
run;
```

Output 8.1 PROC MEANS Output of Certadv.All

Uncollected Fees for Each Course

The MEANS Procedure

Analysis Variable : Fee Course Fee		
Description	N Obs	Sum
Artificial Intelligence	24	9600
Basic Telecommunications	14	11130
Computer Aided Design	13	20800
Database Design	17	6375
Local Area Networks	19	12350
Structured Query Language	20	23000

The %SUBSTR Function

A Brief Overview

The %SUBSTR function produces a substring of character string (*argument*) by extracting the specified number of characters (*length*) beginning at the specified starting position. %SUBSTR does not mask special characters or mnemonic operators in its result, even when the argument was previously masked by a macro quoting function.

Note: If *length* is not specified, %SUBSTR returns a substring containing the characters from *position* to the end of *argument*. If *length* is greater than the number of characters following *position*, %SUBSTR issues a warning message and returns a substring that contains the characters from *position* to the end of *argument*.

%SUBSTR Syntax

Syntax, %SUBSTR function:

%SUBSTR(*argument, position, <,length>*)

argument
> is a character string or a text expression. If *argument* might contain a special character or mnemonic operator, use %QSUBSTR.

position
> is an integer or an expression (text, logical, or arithmetic) that yields an integer, That integer specifies the position of the first character in the substring. If *position* is greater than the number of characters in the string, %SUBSTR issues a warning message and returns a null value. An automatic call to %EVAL causes *n* to be treated as a numeric value.

length
> is an optional integer or an expression (text, logical, or arithmetic) that yields an integer. That integer specifies the number of characters in the substring. If *length* is greater than the number of characters following *position* in an argument, %SUBSTR issues a warning message and returns a substring containing the characters from *position* to the end of the string. By default, %SUBSTR produces a string containing the characters from *position* to the end of the character string.

Example: Using the %SUBSTR Function

Suppose you want to print a report on all courses that have been taught since the start of the current month. You can use the %SUBSTR function and the SYSDATE9 automatic macro variable to determine the month and year.

```
proc print data=certadv.schedule;
    where begin_date between
        "30%substr(&sysdate9,3)"d and
        "&sysdate9"d;
    title "All Courses Held So Far This Month";
    title2 "(as of &sysdate9)";
run;
```

Output 8.2   PROC PRINT Output

**All Courses Held So Far This Month
(as of 03JUN2019)**

Obs	Course_Number	Course_Code	Location	Begin_Date	Teacher
8	8	C002	Boston	11JUN2019	Wickam, Dr. Alice

Assume that the macro variable Date has the value `05JAN2017`.

- The code `%substr(&date,3)` returns the value `JAN2017`.
- The code `%substr(&date,3,3)` returns the value `JAN`.
- The code `%substr(&date,3,9)` returns the value `JAN2017` and produces a warning message.

The values of *position* and *length* can also be the result of a mathematical expression that yields an integer. For example, `%substr(&var,%length(&var)-1)` returns the last two characters of the value of the macro variable Var.

Note: The %LENGTH function accepts an argument that is either a character string or a text expression. If the argument is a character string, %LENGTH returns the length of the string. If the argument is a text expression, %LENGTH returns the length of the resolved value. If the argument has a null value, %LENGTH returns 0.

The %INDEX Function

%INDEX Syntax

The %INDEX function enables you to determine the position of the first character of a string within another string.

Syntax, %INDEX function:

%INDEX (*source, string*)

source and *string*
   both are character strings or text expressions that can include any of the following elements:
   - constant text
   - macro variable references
   - macro functions
   - macro calls

Here is what the %INDEX function does:

- searches source for the first occurrence of string
- returns a number representing the position in source of the first character of string when there is an exact pattern match
- returns 0 when there is no pattern match

Example: Using the %INDEX Function

The following statements find the first character v in a string:

Note: %INDEX function is case sensitive.

```
%let a=a very long value;
%let b=%index(&a,v);
%put The character v appears at position &b;
```

Executing these statements writes the following line to the SAS log.

Log 8.2 SAS Log

```
The character v appears at position 3
```

The %SCAN Function

A Brief Overview

The %SCAN function searches the argument and returns the *n*th word. A *word* is one or more characters separated by one or more delimiters.

%SCAN does not mask special characters or mnemonic operators in its result, even when the argument was previously masked by a macro quoting function.

The %SCAN function allows character arguments to be null. Null arguments are treated as character strings with a length of zero. Numeric arguments cannot be null.

CAUTION:
If *argument* contains a comma, you must enclose it in a quoting function. Similarly, in order to use a single blank or a single comma as the only delimiter, you must enclose the character in the %STR function.

You can specify the characters to be used as delimiters (*charlist*). If you do not specify delimiters, %SCAN uses a default set of delimiters. These delimiters differ slightly between ASCII and EBCDIC systems. SAS treats the following characters as default delimiters:

- ASCII systems: `blank . < ( + & ! $ * ) ; / , % | ^`
- EBCDIC systems: `blank . < ( + & ! $ * ) ; / , % | ¬ | ¢`

If you specify delimiters, all other characters, including default any delimiters not included in *charlist*, are treated as text.

%SCAN Syntax

Syntax, %SCAN function:

%SCAN (*argument, n<,charlist<,modifiers>>*)

argument
> consists of constant text, macro variable references, macro functions, or macro calls.

n
> is an integer or a text expression that yields an integer. That integer specifies the position of the word to return. If *n* is greater than the number of words in *argument*, the functions return a null string.

charlist
> specifies an optional character expression that initializes a list of characters. This list determines which characters are used as the delimiters that separate words. The following rules apply:
> - By default, all characters in *charlist* are used as delimiters.
> - If you specify the K modifier in the modifier argument, then all characters that are not in *charlist* are used as delimiters.
>
> *TIP* You can add more characters to *charlist* by using other modifiers.

modifier
> specifies a character constant, a variable, or an expression in which each non-blank character modifies the action of the %SCAN function. Blanks are ignored.

Example: Using the %SCAN Function

The following example illustrates using the %SCAN function to search *argument* and return the *n*th word.

```
%let a=one:two-three four;

%put First word is %scan(&a,1);
%put Second word is %scan(&a,2,:-);
%put Last word is %scan(&a,-1);
```

The following is written to the SAS log.

Log 8.3 *SAS Log*

```
First word is one:two
Second word is two
Last word is four
```

Using SAS Functions with Macro Variables

The %SYSFUNC Function

A Brief Overview

The %SYSFUNC function executes SAS functions or user-written functions in the macro facility. All arguments in DATA step functions within %SYSFUNC must be separated by commas. You cannot use argument lists preceded by the word OF.

Note: The arguments in %SYSFUNC are evaluated according to the rules of the SAS macro language. This includes both the function name and the argument list in the function. In particular, an empty argument position will not generate a NULL argument, but a zero-length argument.

%SYSFUNC does not mask special characters or mnemonic operators in its result.

When a function called by %SYSFUNC requires a numeric argument, the macro facility converts the argument to a numeric value. %SYSFUNC can return a floating-point number when the function that is executed supports floating-point numbers.

Note: Instead of INPUT and PUT, use INPUTN, INPUTC, PUTN, and PUTC.

CAUTION:
> **Values returned by SAS functions might be truncated.** Although values returned by macro functions are not limited to the length imposed by the DATA step, values returned by SAS functions do have that limitation.

%SYSFUNC Syntax

Syntax, %SYSFUNC function:

%SYSFUNC(*function*(*argument-1*<...*argument-n*>)<,*format*>)

function
> is the name of the function to execute. This function can be a SAS function, a function written with SAS/TOOLKIT software, or a function created using the FCMP procedure. The function cannot be a macro function.

argument
> is one or more arguments used by *function*. An argument can be a macro variable reference or a text expression that produces arguments for a function.

format
> is an optional format to apply to the result of function. There is no default value for format. If you do not specify a format, the SAS macro facility does not perform a format operation on the result and uses the default of the function.

Example: Using the %SYSFUNC Function

Use the %SYSFUNC function to execute the PROPCASE function to convert all uppercase letters to lowercase, and convert the first character of a word to uppercase.

```
%let string=william SMITH;
%put %sysfunc(propcase(&string));
```

The following is written to the SAS log.

Log 8.4 *SAS Log*

```
William Smith
```

The %EVAL Function

A Brief Overview

The %EVAL function evaluates arithmetic and logical expressions using integer arithmetic.

The %EVAL function evaluates integer arithmetic or logical expressions. %EVAL converts its argument from a character value to a numeric or logical expression and performs the evaluation. Finally, %EVAL converts the result back to a character value and returns that value.

If all operands can be interpreted as integers, the expression is treated as arithmetic. If at least one operand cannot be interpreted as numeric, the expression is treated as logical. If a division operation results in a fraction, the fraction is truncated to an integer.

Logical, or Boolean, expressions return a value that is evaluated as true or false. In the macro language, any numeric value other than 0 is true, and a value of 0 is false.

%EVAL accepts only operands in arithmetic expressions that represent integers (in standard or hexadecimal form). Operands that contain a period character cause an error when they are part of an integer arithmetic expression. The following examples show correct and incorrect usage, respectively:

```
%let d=%eval(10+20);      /* Correct usage   */
%let d=%eval(10.0+20.0);  /* Incorrect usage */
```

Because %EVAL does not convert a value containing a period to a number, the operands are evaluated as character operands. When %EVAL encounters a value containing a period, it displays an error message about finding a character operand where a numeric operand is required. An expression that compares character values in the %EVAL function uses the sort sequence of the operating environment for the comparison.

Note: %EVAL performs integer evaluations, but %SYSEVALF performs floating-point evaluations.

%EVAL Syntax

Syntax, %EVAL function:

%EVAL(*arithmetic or logical expression*)

Example: Using the %EVAL Function

The following example illustrates different types of integer arithmetic evaluation.

```
%let a=1+2;
%let b=10*3;
%let c=5/3;
%let eval_a=%eval(&a);
%let eval_b=%eval(&b);
%let eval_c=%eval(&c);

%put &a is &eval_a;
%put &b is &eval_b;
%put &c is &eval_c;
```

The following is written to the SAS log.

Log 8.5 *SAS Log*

```
1+2 is 3
10*3 is 30
5/3 is 1
```

The third %PUT statement shows that %EVAL discards the fractional part of the result when it performs division on integers that would produce a fraction:

The %SYSEVALF Function

A Brief Overview

The %SYSEVALF function evaluates arithmetic and logical expressions using floating-point arithmetic.

The %SYSEVALF function performs floating-point arithmetic and returns a value that is formatted using the BEST32. format. The result of the evaluation is always text. %SYSEVALF is the only macro function that can evaluate logical expressions that contain floating-point or missing values. Specify a conversion type to prevent problems when %SYSEVALF returns one of the following:

- missing or floating-point values in macro expressions
- macro variables that are used in other macro expressions that require an integer value

If the argument in the %SYSEVALF function contains no operator and no conversion type is specified, then the argument is returned unchanged.

Note: %SYSEVALF supports floating-point numbers. However, %EVAL performs only integer arithmetic. You must use the %SYSEVALF macro function in macros to evaluate floating-point expressions. However, %EVAL is used automatically by the macro processor to evaluate macro expressions.

%SYSEVALF Syntax

Syntax, %SYSEVALF function:

%SYSEVALF(*expression*<,*conversion-type*>)

expression
is an arithmetic or logical expression to evaluate.

conversion-type
converts the value returned by %SYSEVALF to the type of value specified. The value can then be used in other expressions that require a value of that type. Conversion-type can be one of the following:

BOOLEAN
returns **0** if the result of the expression is 0 or missing. It returns **1** if the result is any other value.

CEIL
returns a character value representing the smallest integer that is greater than or equal to the result of the expression. If the result is within 10^{-12} of an integer, the function returns a character value representing that integer.

FLOOR
returns a character value representing the largest integer that is less than or equal to the result of the expression. If the result is within 10^{-12} of an integer, the function returns that integer.

INTEGER
returns a character value representing the integer portion of the result (truncates the decimal portion). If the result of the expression is within 10^{-12} of an integer, the function produces a character value representing that integer. If the result of the expression is positive, INTEGER returns the same result as FLOOR. If the result of the expression is negative, INTEGER returns the same result as CEIL.

Example: Using the %SYSEVALF Function

The macro FIGUREIT performs all types of conversions for %SYSEVALF values.

```
%macro figureit(a,b);
   %let y=%sysevalf(&a+&b);
   %put The result with SYSEVALF is: &y;
   %put   The BOOLEAN value is: %sysevalf(&a +&b, boolean);
   %put   The CEIL value is: %sysevalf(&a+&b, ceil);
   %put   The FLOOR value is: %sysevalf(&a+&b, floor);
   %put   The INTEGER value is: %sysevalf(&a+&b, int);
%mend figureit;

%figureit(100,1.597)
```

The following is written to the SAS log.

Log 8.6 *SAS Log*

```
The result with SYSEVALF is: 101.597
  The BOOLEAN value is: 1
  The CEIL value is: 102
  The FLOOR value is: 101
  The INTEGER value is: 101
```

Using SAS Macro Functions to Mask Special Characters

Macro Quoting Functions

The SAS programming language uses matched pairs of either double or single quotation marks to distinguish character constants from names. The quotation marks are not stored as part of the token that they define. For example, in the following program, Var is stored as a 4-byte variable that has the value **text**. If **text** were not enclosed in quotation marks, it would be treated as a variable name. Var2 is stored as a 7-byte variable that has the value **example**.

```
data one;
   var='text';
   text='example';
   var2=text;
run;
```

Similarly, the title text in the following example is Joan's Report. Although the TITLE statement contains a matched pair of double quotation marks, the title itself does not include these outer quotation marks. However, the outer quotation marks cause the unmatched single quotation mark within the text to be interpreted as an apostrophe that is part of the title text.

```
proc print;
   title "Joan's Report";
run;
```

The %STR Function

A Brief Overview

The %STR function is used to mask tokens during compilation so that the macro processor does not interpret them as macro-level syntax. That is, the %STR function hides the usual meaning of a semicolon (and other special tokens and mnemonic equivalents of comparison or logical operators) so that they appear as constant text. Special tokens and mnemonic equivalents include the following:

```
; + - * / , < > = blank ^ ~ # |
LT EQ GT AND OR NOT LE GE NE IN
```

The %STR function also has these capabilities:

- enables macro triggers to work normally
- preserves leading and trailing blanks in its argument

%STR Syntax

Syntax, %STR function:

%STR (*argument*)

argument
    is any combination of text and macro triggers.

The %STR function can also be used to mask tokens that typically occur in pairs:

```
' " ) (
```

Example: Using %STR Function

Suppose you have text that contains an apostrophe (') and you want to assign that text to a macro variable. Without any quoting, this produces errors.

```
options symbolgen;
%let text=Joan's Report;
proc print data=certadvadv.courses;
   where days > 3;
title "&text";
run;
```

The following is written to the SAS log.

Log 8.7 *SAS Log*

```
75 %let text=Joan's Report;
             ---------
             32
WARNING 32-169: The quoted string currently being processed has
                become more than 262 characters long. You may
                have unbalanced quotation marks.
```

The word scanner interprets the apostrophe as the beginning of a literal that is defined by a pair of single quotation marks. You can use the %STR function to avoid this error. The previous section covered several methods of using the %STR function to mask the usual meaning of a semicolon. None of the methods shown correctly masks the apostrophe in the current example.

When you mask tokens that typically appear in pairs, such as quotation marks or parentheses, you must take one additional step. To perform this masking, you precede the token that you want to mask with a percent sign (%) within the %STR function argument.

```
%let text=%str(Joan%'s Report);
%let text=Joan%str(%')s Report;
```

The value of Text is **Joan's Report** in both cases.

The %NRSTR Function

A Brief Overview

To hide the normal meaning of an ampersand or a percent sign, use the %NRSTR function. The %NRSTR performs in the same way as %STR, except that it also masks macro triggers (& and %). The NR in the name %NRSTR stands for No Resolution. %NRSTR has the same syntax as %STR.

%NRSTR Syntax

Syntax, %NRSTR function:

%NRSTR (*character-string*)

Note: The maximum level of nesting for the macro quoting functions is 10.

Example: Using %NRSTR Function

Suppose you want to create a macro variable named Period and assign a value of **May&Jun** to it. If you use the %STR function in the assignment statement, SAS interprets the ampersand as a macro trigger and generates a warning message. You must use the %NRSTR function instead.

```
%let Period=%str(May&Jun);
%put Period resolves to: &period;
%let Period=%nrstr(May&Jun);
%put Period resolves to: &period;
```

The following portion of a SAS log shows the results of both the %STR and the %NRSTR functions for this example.

Log 8.8 *SAS Log*

```
1    %let Period=%str(May&Jun);
WARNING: Apparent symbolic reference JUN not resolved.
2    %put Period resolves to &period:
WARNING: Apparent symbolic reference JUN not resolved.
Period resolves to: May&Jun
3
4    %let Period=%nrstr(May&Jun);
5    %put Period resolves to &period;
Period resolves to: May&Jun
```

The %SUPERQ Function

A Brief Overview

The %SUPERQ macro quoting function locates the macro variable named in its argument and retrieves the masked value of that macro variable without permitting any resolution to occur. It masks all items that might require macro quoting at macro execution. This ensures that the macro processor will never attempt to resolve macro triggers in the text resolved with %SUPERQ.

%SUPERQ is the only quoting function that prevents the resolution of macro variables and macro references in the value of the specified macro variable.

%SUPERQ accepts only the name of a macro variable as its argument, without an ampersand, but the other quoting functions accept any text expression, including constant text, as an argument.

The %SUPERQ function returns the value of a macro variable without attempting to resolve any macros or macro variable references in the value. %SUPERQ masks the following special characters and mnemonic operators:

&, %, ', ", ( ), + ,- ,* ,/ ,< >, =, ¬, ^, ~, ; , #, blank,

AND, OR, NOT, EQ, NE, LE, LT, GE, GT, IN

Note:

- The argument for %SUPERQ is just the macro variable name. There is no ampersand.
- The maximum level of nesting for the macro quoting functions is 10.

%SUPERQ Syntax

Syntax, %SUPERQ function:

%SUPERQ (*argument*)

argument
   is the name of either a macro variable with no leading ampersand or an expression that produces the name of a macro variable with no leading ampersand.

Example: Using the %SUPERQ Function

In this example, %SUPERQ prevents the macro processor from attempting to resolve macro references in the values of MV1 and MV2 before assigning them to macro variables TESTMV1 and TESTMV2.

```
data _null_;
   call symputx('mv1','Smith&Jones');
   call symputx('mv2','%macro abc;');
run;
%let testmv1=%superq(mv1);
%let testmv2=%superq(mv2);
%put Macro variable TESTMV1 is &testmv1;
%put Macro variable TESTMV2 is &testmv2;
```

The following is written to the SAS log.

Log 8.9 SAS Log

```
102  %let testmv1=%superq(mv1);
103  %let testmv2=%superq(mv2);
104  %put Macro variable TESTMV1 is &testmv1;
Macro variable TESTMV1 is Smith&Jones
105  %put Macro variable TESTMV2 is &testmv2;
Macro variable TESTMV2 is %macro abc;
```

You might think of the values of TESTMV1 and TESTMV2 as "pictures" of the original values of MV1 and MV2. The %PUT statement then writes the pictures in its text. The macro processor does not attempt resolution. It does not issue a warning message for the unresolved reference &JONES or an error message for beginning a macro definition inside a %LET statement.

The %BQUOTE Function

A Brief Overview

The %BQUOTE macro quoting function allows the macro processor to resolve all macro expressions before quoting the resulting text. It masks the characters that %STR masks without the requirement to mark unmatched quotation marks or parentheses with a % sign. The %BQUOTE function treats all parentheses and quotation marks produced by resolving macro variable references or macro calls as special characters to be masked at execution time. (It does not mask parentheses or quotation marks that are in the argument at compile time.) Therefore, it does not matter whether quotation marks and parentheses in the resolved value are matched. Each one is masked individually.

The %BQUOTE function masks a character string or resolved value of a text expression during execution of a macro or macro language statement. It masks the following special characters and mnemonic operators:

&, %, ', ", ( ), + ,- ,* ,/ ,< >, =, ¬, ^, ~, ; , #, blank,

AND, OR, NOT, EQ, NE, LE, LT, GE, GT, IN

%BQUOTE Syntax

Syntax, %BQUOTE function:

%BQUOTE (*character string | text expression*)

character string | text expression
  accepts any text including macro triggers.

Example: Using the %BQUOTE Function

```
data _null_;
   call symputx('text',"Sally's Seashell Store at Old Towne's Beach");
run;
data _null_;
   put "%bquote(&text)";
run;
```

Log 8.10 SAS Log

```
Sally's Seashell Store at Old Towne's Beach
```

Macro Q Functions

A Brief Overview

The macro Q functions process text in the macro facility just like the non-Q versions, but the Q functions return their results as quoted text. This means that the text produced by a Q function will never be mistaken for macro code. Unless you intend the function output to execute as macro code, it is a best practice to always use the Q function instead of the non-Q version.

Table 8.1 Macro Q Functions

Function Name	Description
%QUPCASE	converts values to uppercase
%QSUBSTR	extracts a substring from a character string
%QSCAN	extracts a word from a character string
%QSYSFUNC	executes a DATA step function and returns formatted results

The functions listed above work just like the non-Q version, but return the quoted text.

Example: Using the %QUPCASE Function

This example illustrates using the %PUT statement and %QUPCASE function to convert the lowercase values to uppercase.

```
%let a=%nrstr(Address&name);
%put QUPCASE produces: %qupcase(&a);
```

The following is written to the SAS log.

Log 8.11 SAS Log

```
QUPCASE produces: ADDRESS&NAME
```

Example: Using the %QSUBSTR Function

These statements show the results produced by %SUBSTR and %QSUBSTR:

```
%let a=one;
%let b=two;
%let c=%nrstr(&a &b);

%put C: &c;
%put With SUBSTR: %substr(&c,1,2);
%put With QSUBSTR: %qsubstr(&c,1,2);
```

Executing these statements produces the following messages in the SAS log. As you can see, the first %PUT statement shows that &c resolves to the value &a &b. In the second %PUT statement, the %SUBSTR function extracts the value &a from the resolved value of the macro variable reference &c, and resolves &a to 1. The third %PUT statement shows that the %QSUBSTR function prevents the value &a from being resolved further.

Log 8.12 *SAS Log*

```
11   %let a=one;
12   %let b=two;
13   %let c=%nrstr(&a &b);
14
15   %put C: &c;
C: &a &b
16   %put With SUBSTR: %substr(&c,1,2);
With SUBSTR: one
17   %put With QSUBSTR: %qsubstr(&c,1,2);
With QSUBSTR: &a
```

Example: Using the %QSCAN Function

These statements show the results produced by %SUBSTR and %QSUBSTR.

```
%macro a;
    aaaaaa
%mend a;
%macro b;
    bbbbbb
%mend b;
%macro c;
    cccccc
%mend c;

%let x=%nrstr(%a*%b*%c);
%put X: &x
%put The third word in X, with SCAN: %scan(&x,3,*);
%put The third word in X, with QSCAN: %qscan(&x,3,*);
```

Log 8.13 *SAS Log*

```
The third word in X, with SCAN: cccccc
The third word in X, with QSCAN: %c
```

Example: Using the %QSYSFUNC Function

Use the %QSYSFUNC function to mask the comma and execute the LEFT function. The LEFT function expects only one argument, but this example passes "June 4, 2019" to it. It interprets the comma as the delimiter between two arguments. You can mask the comma by using the %QSYSFUNC function.

```
title "Report Produced on %sysfunc(left(%qsysfunc(today(),worddate.)))";
```

The modified statement generates the following title:

```
Report Produced on June 4, 2019
```

Creating Macro Variables during PROC SQL Step Execution

INTO Clause and the NOPRINT Option Syntax

You can create or update macro variables during the execution of a PROC SQL step. Remember that the SELECT statement in a PROC SQL step retrieves and displays data. The INTO clause in a SELECT statement enables you to create or update macro variables.

When you create or update macro variables during execution of a PROC SQL step, you might not want any output to be displayed. The PRINT and NOPRINT options specify whether a SELECT statement's results are displayed in output. PRINT is the default setting.

Syntax, PROC SQL with the NOPRINT option and the INTO clause:

PROC SQL NOPRINT;
    SELECT *column1<,column2,...>*
        INTO *:macro-variable-1<,:macro-variable-2,...>* <TRIMMED>
        FROM *table-1 | view-1*
        <WHERE *expression*>
        <*other clauses*>;
QUIT;

column1, column2,...
    specifies one or more columns of the SQL table specified by *table-1 | view-1*.

:macro-variable-1, :macro-variable-2,...
    names the macro variables to create.

expression
    produces a value that is used to subset the data.

other clauses
    are other valid clauses that group, subset, or order the data.

Note: Macro variable names are preceded by a colon.

This form of the INTO clause does not automatically trim leading or trailing blanks. Use the TRIMMED modifier to explicitly remove leading and trailing blanks before storing the results in your macro variable. Also, the INTO clause cannot be used when you create a table or a view.

Example: Using the INTO Clause and the NOPRINT Option

You can create a macro variable named TotalFee that contains the total of all course fees. In addition, you can use the NOPRINT option to suppress the output from the PROC SQL step.

```
proc sql noprint;
    select sum(fee) format=dollar10.
        into :totalfee trimmed
        from certadv.all;
```

```
    quit;

    proc means data=certadv.all sum maxdec=0;
       class course_title;
       var fee;
       title "Grand Total for All Courses Is &totalfee";
    run;
```

The title in the output from the PROC MEANS step shows the sum of all course fees in the DOLLAR10. format.

Output 8.3   PROC MEANS Output of Certadv.All

Grand Total for All Courses Is $354,380

The MEANS Procedure

Analysis Variable : Fee Course Fee		
Description	N Obs	Sum
Artificial Intelligence	71	28400
Basic Telecommunications	69	54855
Computer Aided Design	66	105600
Database Design	77	28875
Local Area Networks	74	48100
Structured Query Language	77	88550

Example: Creating Variables with the INTO Clause

Suppose you want to create a series of macro variables that contain the course code, location, and starting date of all courses that are scheduled in 2019. You do not know the number of courses. If you name a numbered macro variable to begin the series followed by a hyphen, SQL determines the number of macro variables that are required based on the number of rows in the query results set. A macro variable named SQLOBS is automatically created to store the number of rows that were read.

```
proc sql noprint;
   select course_code, location, begin_date format=mmddyy10.
      into :crsid1- ,
         :place1- ,
         :date1-
      from certadv.schedule
      where year(begin_date)=2019
      order by begin_date;
quit;

%put There are &sqlobs courses in 2019;
%put _user_;
```

The SAS log shows that SQLOBS is assigned a value of **12**. The %PUT statement at the end of the program shows the names and values of all the macro variables that are created in the SELECT statement.

Log 8.14   SAS Log

```
There are 12 courses in 2019
GLOBAL CRSID1 C003
GLOBAL CRSID10 C006
GLOBAL CRSID11 C001
GLOBAL CRSID12 C002
GLOBAL CRSID2 C004
GLOBAL CRSID3 C005
GLOBAL CRSID4 C006
GLOBAL CRSID5 C001
GLOBAL CRSID6 C002
GLOBAL CRSID7 C003
GLOBAL CRSID8 C004
GLOBAL CRSID9 C005
GLOBAL DATE1 01/08/2019
GLOBAL DATE10 10/01/2019
GLOBAL DATE11 11/12/2019
GLOBAL DATE12 12/03/2019
GLOBAL DATE2 01/22/2019
GLOBAL DATE3 02/26/2019
GLOBAL DATE4 04/02/2019
GLOBAL DATE5 05/21/2019
GLOBAL DATE6 06/11/2019
GLOBAL DATE7 07/16/2019
GLOBAL DATE8 08/13/2019
GLOBAL DATE9 09/17/2019
GLOBAL NUMROWS 12
GLOBAL PLACE1 Boston
GLOBAL PLACE10 Seattle
GLOBAL PLACE11 Boston
GLOBAL PLACE12 Seattle
GLOBAL PLACE2 Seattle
GLOBAL PLACE3 Dallas
GLOBAL PLACE4 Boston
GLOBAL PLACE5 Dallas
GLOBAL PLACE6 Boston
GLOBAL PLACE7 Seattle
GLOBAL PLACE8 Dallas
GLOBAL PLACE9 Boston
GLOBAL SQLEXITCODE 0
GLOBAL SQLOBS 12
GLOBAL SQLOOPS 28
GLOBAL SQLRC 0
GLOBAL SQLXOBS 0
GLOBAL SQLXOPENERRS 0
GLOBAL SYS_SQL_IP_ALL -1
GLOBAL SYS_SQL_IP_STMT
```

There is a NOPRINT option in the code. Therefore, a report is not generated.

Example: Creating a Delimited List of Values

You can use the SQL procedure to create one macro variable named Sites that contains the names of all training centers that appear in the Certadv.Schedule data set. The names will be separated by blanks.

```
proc sql noprint;
    select distinct location
```

```
            into :sites separated by ' '
         from certadv.schedule;
   quit;

   title1 'Total Revenue from Course Sites:';
   title2 &sites;
   proc means data=certadv.all sum maxdec=0;
      var fee;
   run;
```

Output 8.4 PROC MEANS Output of Certadv.All

Total Revenue from Course Sites:
Boston Dallas Seattle

The MEANS Procedure

Analysis Variable : Fee Course Fee
Sum
354380

Creating Macro Variables during DATA Step Execution

The CALL SYMPUTX Routine

A Brief Overview
The CALL SYMPUTX routine does the following:

- assigns a value produced in a DATA step to a macro variable
- if a macro variable does not exist, the CALL SYMPUTX routine creates the variable
- creates a macro variable assignment when the program is executed
- removes both leading and trailing blanks from both arguments

Note: The CALL SYMPUT routine is an older version of CALL SYMPUTX. CALL SYMPUT has fewer features.

CALL SYMPUTX Routine Syntax

Syntax, CALL SYMPUTX routine:

CALL SYMPUTX(*macro-variable-name, value* <,*symbol-table*>);

macro-variable-name
is assigned the character value of *expression*, and any leading or trailing blanks are removed from both *macro variable* and *expression*.

macro-variable and *expression*
can each be specified as one of the following items:

- a literal, enclosed in quotation marks
- a DATA step variable
- a DATA step expression

value
is the value to be assigned, which can be any of these items:

- a string enclosed in quotation marks.
- the name of a numeric or character variable. The current value of the variable is assigned as the value of the macro variable. If the variable is numeric, SAS performs an automatic numeric-to-character conversion and writes a message in the log.

  Note: This form is most useful when macro-variable is also the name of a SAS variable or a character expression that contains a SAS variable. A unique macro variable name and value can be created from each observation.

- a DATA step expression. The value returned by the expression in the current observation is assigned as the value of *macro-variable*. If the expression is numeric, SAS performs an automatic numeric-to-character conversion and writes a message in the log.

symbol-table
specifies a character constant, variable, or expression. The value of *symbol-table* is not case sensitive. The first non-blank character in *symbol-table* specifies the symbol table in which to store the macro variable. The following values are valid as the first non-blank character in *symbol-table*:

G
specifies that the macro variable is stored in the global symbol table, even if the local symbol table exists.

L
specifies that the macro variable is stored in the most local symbol table that exists. That is the global symbol table, if it is used outside a macro.

F
specifies that if the macro variable exists in any symbol table, CALL SYMPUTX uses the version in the most local symbol table in which it exists. If the macro variable does not exist, CALL SYMPUTX stores the variable in the most local symbol table.

Using SYMPUTX with a Literal

In the SYMPUTX routine, you use a literal string in the following places:

- the first argument, to specify an exact name for the name of the macro variable
- the second argument, to specify the exact character value to assign to the macro variable

To use a literal with the SYMPUTX routine, you enclose the literal string in quotation marks.

CALL SYMPUTX('*macro-variable*', '*text*');

Using CALL SYMPUTX Routine with a DATA Step Variable

You can assign the value of a DATA step variable as the value for a macro variable by using the DATA step variable's name as the second argument in a CALL SYMPUTX routine.

To use a DATA step variable as the value for a macro variable in a CALL SYMPUTX routine, place the name of the DATA step variable after the name of the macro variable, separated by a comma. You do not enclose the name of the DATA step variable in quotation marks.

CALL SYMPUTX('*macro-variable*',*DATA-step-variable*)**;**

This form of the CALL SYMPUTX routine creates a macro variable named *macro-variable* and assigns to it the current value of *DATA-step-variable*.

Using a DATA step variable as the second argument has these results:

- A maximum of 32,767 characters can be assigned to the receiving macro variable.

- Any leading or trailing blanks that are part of the DATA step variable's value are stored in the macro variable.

- Values of numeric variables are automatically converted to character values, using the BEST12. format.

CAUTION:
  If you enclose the DATA step variable name in quotation marks, SAS interprets the name as a literal value rather than as a variable name, and the DATA step variable's value is not resolved.

Example: Using the CALL SYMPUTX Routine

Suppose you want the title to contain the course name and the course number, as well as the date on which the course was held. You also want the footnote to list the current amount of unpaid fees for the course.

This example creates three macro variables. The macro variable Csrname records the value of the DATA step variable Course_title. The macro variable date records the value of the DATA step variable Begin_date in MMDDYY10. format. Finally, the macro variable Due uses the values of the DATA step variables Paidup, Total, and Fee to record the current amount of unpaid fees in DOLLAR8. format. These macro variables are referenced later in the program in the TITLE and FOOTNOTE statements.

```
%let crsnum=3;
data revenue;
   set certadv.all end=final;
   where course_number=&crsnum;
   total+1;
   if paid='Y' then paidup+1;
   if final then do;
      call symputx('crsname',course_title);
      call symputx('date',put(begin_date,mmddyy10.));
      call symputx('due',put(fee*(total-paidup),dollar8.));
   end;
run;
proc print data=revenue;
   var student_name student_company paid;
   title "Fee Status for &crsname (#&crsnum) Held &date";
   footnote "Note: &due in Unpaid Fees";
run;
```

Output 8.5 *PROC PRINT Output of Work.Revenue*

Fee Status for Local Area Networks (#3) Held 01/08/2019

Obs	Student_Name	Student_Company	Paid
1	Bills, Ms. Paulette	Reston Railway	Y
2	Chevarley, Ms. Arlene	Motor Communications	N
3	Clough, Ms. Patti	Reston Railway	N
4	Crace, Mr. Ron	Von Crump Seafood	Y
5	Davis, Mr. Bruce	Semi;Conductor	Y
6	Elsins, Ms. Marisa F.	SSS Inc.	N
7	Gandy, Dr. David	Paralegal Assoc.	Y
8	Gash, Ms. Hedy	QA Information Systems Center	Y
9	Haubold, Ms. Ann	Reston Railway	Y
10	Hudock, Ms. Cathy	So. Cal. Medical Center	Y
11	Kimble, Mr. John	Alforone Chemical	N
12	Kochen, Mr. Dennis	Reston Railway	Y
13	Larocque, Mr. Bret	Physicians IPA	Y
14	Licht, Mr. Bryan	SII	Y
15	McKnight, Ms. Maureen E.	Federated Bank	Y
16	Scannell, Ms. Robin	Amberly Corp.	N
17	Seitz, Mr. Adam	Lomax Services	Y
18	Smith, Ms. Jan	Reston Railway	N
19	Sulzbach, Mr. Bill	Sailbest Ships	Y
20	Williams, Mr. Gene	Snowing Petroleum	Y

Note: $3,900 in Unpaid Fees

Example: Using the CALL SYMPUTX Routine with Literal Strings

Use the CALL SYMPUTX routine with literal strings as both arguments in order to conditionally assign a value to the macro variable Foot based on values that are generated during DATA step execution.

```
options symbolgen pagesize=30;
%let crsnum=3;
data revenue;
   set certadv.all end=final;
   where course_number=&crsnum;
   total+1;
   if paid='Y' then paidup+1;
   if final then do;
   if paidup<total then do;
      call symputx('foot','Some Fees Are Unpaid');
   end;
   else do;
```

```
         call symputx('foot','All Students Have Paid');
      end;
   end;
run;

proc print data=work.revenue;
   var student_name student_company paid;
   title "Payment Status for Course &crsnum";
   footnote "&foot";
run;
```

This time, the value that is assigned to Foot is either **Some Fees Are Unpaid** or **All Students Have Paid**, depending on the value of the DATA step variable Paidup, because the value is assigned during the execution of the DATA step. When you submit this code, you get the following output.

Output 8.6 PROC PRINT Output for Work.Revenue

Payment Status for Course 3

Obs	Student_Name	Student_Company	Paid
1	Bills, Ms. Paulette	Reston Railway	Y
2	Chevarley, Ms. Arlene	Motor Communications	N
3	Clough, Ms. Patti	Reston Railway	N
4	Crace, Mr. Ron	Von Crump Seafood	Y
5	Davis, Mr. Bruce	Semi;Conductor	Y
6	Elsins, Ms. Marisa F.	SSS Inc.	N
7	Gandy, Dr. David	Paralegal Assoc.	Y
8	Gash, Ms. Hedy	QA Information Systems Center	Y
9	Haubold, Ms. Ann	Reston Railway	Y
10	Hudock, Ms. Cathy	So. Cal. Medical Center	Y
11	Kimble, Mr. John	Alforone Chemical	N
12	Kochen, Mr. Dennis	Reston Railway	Y
13	Larocque, Mr. Bret	Physicians IPA	Y
14	Licht, Mr. Bryan	SII	Y
15	McKnight, Ms. Maureen E.	Federated Bank	Y
16	Scannell, Ms. Robin	Amberly Corp.	N
17	Seitz, Mr. Adam	Lomax Services	Y
18	Smith, Ms. Jan	Reston Railway	N
19	Sulzbach, Mr. Bill	Sailbest Ships	Y
20	Williams, Mr. Gene	Snowing Petroleum	Y

Some Fees Are Unpaid

Example: Using the CALL SYMPUTX Routine with a DATA Step Variable

Once again, suppose you want to create a report about students who are enrolled in a particular course. This time, suppose you want to add a title that contains the course title and the course number, and you want to include a footnote that summarizes how many students have paid their fees.

In this example, a DATA step variable named Paidup records the number of students who have paid, and a DATA step variable named Total records the total number of students who are registered for the class. Macro variables are created to record the values of Paidup, the value of Total, and the value of Course_title. These macro variables are referenced later in the program.

```
%let crsnum=3;
data revenue;
   set certadv.all end=final;
   where course_number=&crsnum;
   total+1;
   if paid='Y' then paidup+1;
   if final then do;
      call symputx('numpaid',paidup);
      call symputx('numstu',total);
      call symputx('crsname',course_title);
   end;
run;
proc print data=revenue noobs;
   var student_name student_company paid;
   title "Fee Status for &crsname (#&crsnum)";
   footnote "Note: &numpaid Paid out of &numstu Students";
run;
```

This time, the footnote shows the correct information for how many students have paid.

Output 8.7 PROC PRINT Output for Work.Revenue with Correct Footnote

Fee Status for Local Area Networks (#3)

Student_Name	Student_Company	Paid
Bills, Ms. Paulette	Reston Railway	Y
Chevarley, Ms. Arlene	Motor Communications	N
Clough, Ms. Patti	Reston Railway	N
Crace, Mr. Ron	Von Crump Seafood	Y
Davis, Mr. Bruce	Semi;Conductor	Y
Elsins, Ms. Marisa F.	SSS Inc.	N
Gandy, Dr. David	Paralegal Assoc.	Y
Gash, Ms. Hedy	QA Information Systems Center	Y
Haubold, Ms. Ann	Reston Railway	Y
Hudock, Ms. Cathy	So. Cal. Medical Center	Y
Kimble, Mr. John	Alforone Chemical	N
Kochen, Mr. Dennis	Reston Railway	Y
Larocque, Mr. Bret	Physicians IPA	Y
Licht, Mr. Bryan	SII	Y
McKnight, Ms. Maureen E.	Federated Bank	Y
Scannell, Ms. Robin	Amberly Corp.	N
Seitz, Mr. Adam	Lomax Services	Y
Smith, Ms. Jan	Reston Railway	N
Sulzbach, Mr. Bill	Sailbest Ships	Y
Williams, Mr. Gene	Snowing Petroleum	Y

Note: 14 Paid out of 20 Students

Example: Creating Multiple Macro Variables with CALL SYMPUTX

Suppose you want to write a program that lists all of the scheduled dates for a particular course, using a macro variable to record the title of the course. You can use one call to the SYMPUTX routine to create a macro variable for each value of the DATA step variable Course_code and assign the corresponding value of Course_title to each macro variable. The macro processor creates a new macro variable for each observation. The new macro variable has the same name as the value of the data set variable Course_code for that observation. The value of the new macro variable is the value of the data set variable Course_title for that observation.

```
data _null_;
   set certadv.courses;
   call symputx(course_code,course_title);
run;
%put _user_;
```

The following is written to the SAS log.

Log 8.15 *SAS Log*

```
GLOBAL A one:two-three four
GLOBAL C001 Basic Telecommunications
GLOBAL C002 Structured Query Language
GLOBAL C003 Local Area Networks
GLOBAL C004 Database Design
GLOBAL C005 Artificial Intelligence
GLOBAL C006 Computer Aided Design
GLOBAL CRSNAME Local Area Networks
GLOBAL CRSNUM 3
GLOBAL DELIM \
GLOBAL NUMPAID              14
GLOBAL NUMSTU               20
GLOBAL PATH C:\Users\certadv\
GLOBAL STRING william SMITH
```

```
%let crsid=C005;
proc print data=certadv.schedule noobs label;
   where course_code="&crsid";
   var location begin_date teacher;
   title1 "Schedule for &c005";
run;
```

Output 8.8 *PROC PRINT Output for Schedule for Artificial Intelligence*

Schedule for Artificial Intelligence

Location	Begin	Instructor
Dallas	26FEB2019	Hallis, Dr. George
Boston	17SEP2019	Tally, Ms. Julia
Seattle	05FEB2020	Hallis, Dr. George

```
%let crsid=C002;
proc print data=certadv.schedule noobs label;
   where course_code="&crsid";
   var location begin_date teacher;
   title1 "Schedule for &c002";
run;
```

Output 8.9 *PROC PRINT Output of Schedule for Structured Query Language*

Schedule for Structured Query Language

Location	Begin	Instructor
Dallas	04DEC2018	Wickam, Dr. Alice
Boston	11JUN2019	Wickam, Dr. Alice
Seattle	03DEC2019	Wickam, Dr. Alice

The PUT Function

A Brief Overview

Messages are written to the SAS log to alert you that automatic conversion has occurred. Remember that the CALL SYMPUTX routine automatically uses the BEST12. format for the conversion.

You might want to have explicit control over the numeric-to-character conversion. The PUT function returns a character string that is formed by writing a value with a specified format.

You can use the PUT function in the following ways:

- perform explicit numeric-to-character conversions
- format the result of a numeric expression

PUT Function Syntax

Syntax, PUT function:

PUT(*source,format.*)

source
    is a constant, a variable, or an expression (numeric or character).

format.
    is any SAS format or user-defined format that determines these details:

    - the length of the resulting string
    - whether the string is right- or left-aligned

source and *format.*
    must be the same type (numeric or character).

Example: Using the PUT Function

Suppose you want to create a report that shows the amount of fees that are unpaid for a specific course. In the following example, you use the SYMPUTX routine to format the value of the numeric variable Begin_date with the MMDDYY10. format and assign that value to the macro variable Date. Then you also use another call to the SYMPUTX routine to format the result of an expression involving Fee, Total, and Paidup as a dollar amount and assign that value to the macro variable Due.

```
%let crsnum=3;
data revenue;
   set certadv.all end=final;
   where course_number=&crsnum;
   total+1;
   if paid='Y' then paidup+1;
   if final then do;
      call symputx('crsname',trim(course_title));
      call symputx('date',put(begin_date,mmddyy10.));
      call symputx('due',strip(put(fee*(total-paidup),dollar8.)));
   end;
run;
```

You can use the macro variables Date and Due in a PROC PRINT step to create your report. The values of these macro variables appear in the report with the formatting that you assigned to them when you created them.

```
proc print data=revenue;
   var student_name student_company paid;
   title "Fee Status for &crsname (#&crsnum) Held &date";
   footnote "Note: &due in Unpaid Fees";
run;
```

Referencing Macro Variables Indirectly

Indirect References

The rules for indirect references for macro variables rules are as follows:

- When multiple ampersands or percent signs precede a name token, the macro processor resolves two ampersands (&&) to one ampersand (&), and re-scans the reference.
- To reference macro variables indirectly, the macro processor scans and resolves tokens from left to right from the point where multiple ampersands or percent signs are coded, until no more triggers can be resolved.

Example: Referencing Macro Variables Indirectly

Suppose you want to write a PROC PRINT step that you can reuse without any modification to print information about each course. You can do this by using an indirect reference in the TITLE statement.

```
data _null_;
   set certadv.courses;
   call symputx(course_code,(course_title));
run;

%let crsid=C002;
proc print data=certadv.schedule noobs label;
   where course_code="&crsid";
   var location begin_date teacher;
   title1 "Schedule for ???";
run;
```

In the example above, the macro variable C002 (as created by the SYMPUTX routine) has a value of **Structured Query Language**. Therefore, the TITLE statement should reference a macro variable that resolves to **Structured Query Language**. Remember that you want this reference to be flexible enough to apply to any of the macro variables that the SYMPUTX routine creates, such as C003 or C004, by changing only the %LET statement.

To obtain the value that you want, you must indirectly reference the macro variable C002 through a reference to the macro variable Crsid. If the value of the macro variable Crsid is **C002**, the following process might seem to be correct:

1. Resolve the macro variable Crsid to the value **C002**.

2. Attach an ampersand (**&**) to the front of the resolved value in order to create a new reference (&C002).

3. Resolve the resulting macro variable reference to the value `Structured Query Language`.

This sequence seems to imply that you should use the reference &&crsid to convert the value of the macro variable Crsid to the corresponding course description. However, the indirect reference rules indicate that this is not the correct solution.

Here is the correct solution:

```
title1 "Schedule for &&&crsid";
```

Example: Creating a Series of Macro Variables

You can create a series of macro variables, Teach1 to Teach*n*, each containing the name of the instructor who is assigned to a specific course.

```
options symbolgen;
data _null_;
   set certadv.schedule;
   call symputx(cats('teach',course_number),teacher);
run;
```

The CATS function converts numeric values to character strings and removes leading and trailing blanks before concatenation. The SYMPUTX call routine eliminates leading and trailing blanks from the macro variables and values.

Then, you can reference one of these variables when a course number is designated. If you designate a course number in a %LET statement, you can use multiple ampersands in order to create a reference to the Teach*n* macro variable that corresponds to the current course number.

```
%let crs=3;
proc print data=certadv.register noobs;
   where course_number=&crs;
   var student_name paid;
   title1 "Roster for Course &crs";
   title2 "Taught by &&teach&crs";
run;
```

The following is written to the SAS log, which shows the steps that lead to the resolution of the reference &&teach&crs.

Log 8.16 SAS Log

```
SYMBOLGEN:   Macro variable CRS resolves to 3
SYMBOLGEN:   Macro variable CRS resolves to 3
SYMBOLGEN:   && resolves to &.
SYMBOLGEN:   Macro variable CRS resolves to 3
SYMBOLGEN:   Macro variable TEACH3 resolves to Forest, Mr. Peter
```

Figure 8.1 PROC PRINT Output of Roster for Course 3 Taught by Forest, Mr. Peter

Roster for Course 3
Taught by Forest, Mr. Peter

Student_Name	Paid
Bills, Ms. Paulette	Y
Chevarley, Ms. Arlene	N
Clough, Ms. Patti	N
... more observations ...	
Sulzbach, Mr. Bill	Y
Williams, Mr. Gene	Y

Quiz

Select the best answer for each question. After completing the quiz, check your answers using the answer key in the appendix.

1. Which of the following is false?

    a. A %LET statement causes the macro processor to create a macro variable before the program is compiled.

    b. To create a macro variable that is based on data calculated by the DATA step, you use the SYMPUTX routine.

    c. Macro functions are always processed during the execution of the DATA step.

    d. Macro variable references in a DATA step are always resolved before DATA step execution.

2. The SYMPUTX routine cannot do which of the following things?

    a. be used to assign a data set variable as a value to a macro variable

    b. create a series of macro variables in one DATA step

    c. automatically convert a numeric value to a character value when used to assign a value to a macro variable in a DATA step

    d. be used in a procedure to store a calculated value

3. Which of the following programs correctly creates a series of macro variables whose names are values of the data set variable Course_code, and then indirectly references one of those macro variables in a later step?

    a.
    ```
    data _null_;
       set certadv.courses;
       call symputx(course_code,(course_title));
    %let crsid=C005;
    proc print data=certadv.schedule noobs label;
       where course_code="&crsid";
       var location begin_date teacher;
       title1 "Schedule for &c005";
    run;
    ```

    b.
    ```
    data _null_;
       set certadv.courses;
    ```

```
        call symputx(course_code, trim(course_title));
    run;
    %let crsid=C005;
    proc print data=certadv.schedule noobs label;
        where course_code="&crsid";
        var location begin_date teacher;
        title1 "Schedule for &&&crsid";
    run;
```

c.
```
    data _null_;
        set certadv.courses;
        call symputx('course_code', trim(course_title));
    run;
    %let crsid=C005;
    proc print data=certadv.schedule noobs label;
        where course_code="&crsid";
        var location begin_date teacher;
        title1 "Schedule for &&&crsid";
    run;
```

d.
```
    data _null_;
        set certadv.courses;
        put(course_code, trim(course_title));
    run;

    %let crsid=C005;
    proc print data=certadv.schedule noobs label;
        where course_code="&crsid";
        var location begin_date teacher;
        title1 "Schedule for &&&crsid";
    run;
```

4. Which of the following statements about the resolution of macro variable references is false?

   a. Two ampersands resolve to one ampersand.

   b. If more than four consecutive ampersands precede a name token, the macro processor generates an error message.

   c. Re-scanning continues until there are no remaining macro triggers that the macro processor can resolve.

   d. The macro processor always re-scans a name token that is preceded by multiple ampersands or by multiple percent signs.

5. Which of the following correctly creates a macro variable in a PROC SQL step?

   a. `call symputx(daily_fee, put(fee/days, dollar8.);`

   b. `%let daily_fee=put(fee/days, dollar8.)`

   c. `select fee/days format=dollar8.`
      `into :daily_fee from certadv.all;`

   d. `select fee/days format=dollar8.`
      `into daily_fee from certadv.all;`

6. According to the global symbol table shown here, what value will a reference to &&teach&crs resolve to?

Global Symbol Table	
TEACH1	Hallis, Dr. George
TEACH2	Wickam, Dr. Alice
TEACH3	Forest, Mr. Peter
CRS	3

   a. `&TEACH3`

   b. `TEACH3`

   c. `Forest, Mr. Peter`

   d. None of the above.

7. Which of the following is false?

   a. The SYMPUTX routine can be used to create a macro variable during execution of the DATA step.

   b. The SYMPUTX routine can be used to create a macro variable during execution of a PROC SQL query.

   c. In the DATA step, the SYMPUTX routine automatically converts numeric values to character strings before assigning values to macro variables.

   d. By default, the INTO clause in PROC SQL does not remove leading and training blanks before assigning macro variable values.

Chapter 9
Working with Macro Programs

Defining and Calling a Macro 232
   Defining a Macro 232
   Compiling a Macro 233
   Calling a Macro 234
   Macro Execution 235

Passing Information into a Macro Using Parameters 237
   Macros That Include Positional Parameters 237
   Example: Using Positional Parameters to Create Macro Variables 238
   Macros That Include Keyword Parameters 238
   Example: Using Keyword Parameters to Create Macro Variables 239
   Macros That Include Mixed Parameter Lists 239
   Example: Using Mixed Parameters to Create Macro Variables 240

Controlling Variable Scope 240
   Scope of Macro Variables 240
   The %GLOBAL Statement 241
   The %LOCAL Statement 243
   Nested Scope 245

Debugging Macros 245
   The MPRINT System Option 245
   Comments in Macro Programs 246

Conditional Processing 247
   The %IF-%THEN Statement and %ELSE Statement 247
   The %DO-%END Statement with the %IF-%THEN Statement 248
   Example: Using %IF-%THEN, %DO-%END with IF-THEN Statements 249
   Example: Controlling Text Copied to the Input Stack 249
   The MLOGIC System Option 251

Iterative Processing 252
   The %DO Statement 252
   Example: Using the %DO Statement 253
   Example: Generating Complete Steps 254

Quiz 254

Defining and Calling a Macro

A macro definition stores text. This might include macro language statements or expressions as well as complete or partial SAS program statements or program steps. The macro definition begins with a %MACRO statement and ends with a %MEND statement.

Defining a Macro

%MACRO and %MEND Statements Syntax

In order to create a macro program, you must first define it. You begin a macro definition with a %MACRO statement, and you end the definition with a %MEND statement.

Syntax, %MACRO statement and %MEND statement:

%MACRO *macro-name*;

   text

%MEND <*macro-name*>;

macro-name
   names the macro. The value of *macro-name* can be any valid SAS name that is not a reserved word in the SAS macro facility.

text
   can be any of the following elements:

   - constant text, possibly including SAS data set names, SAS variable names, or SAS statements
   - macro variables, macro functions, or macro program statements
   - any combination of the above

TIP You might want to include the optional *macro-name* in the %MEND statement in order to make your program more readable.

Example: Defining a Macro

In the following example, the macro Printit generates a PROC PRINT step.

```
%macro printit;
proc print data=&syslast (obs=5);
   title "Listing of &syslast data set";
run;
%mend printit;
%printit;
```

Note: Your output might differ, depending on the value of the &SYSLAST automatic macro variable at the time.

Output 9.1 Printit Macro Output

Listing of WORK.CARS_MSRP data set

Obs	Make	Model	Type	Origin	DriveTrain	MSRP	Invoice	EngineSize	Cylinders	Horsepower	MPG_City	MPG_Highway	Weight	Wheelbase	Length
1	Kia	Rio 4dr manual	Sedan	Asia	Front	$10,280	$9,875	1.6	4	104	26	33	2403	95	167
2	Hyundai	Accent 2dr hatch	Sedan	Asia	Front	$10,539	$10,107	1.6	4	103	29	33	2255	96	167
3	Toyota	Echo 2dr manual	Sedan	Asia	Front	$10,760	$10,144	1.5	4	108	35	43	2035	93	163
4	Saturn	Ion1 4dr	Sedan	USA	Front	$10,995	$10,319	2.2	4	140	26	35	2692	103	185
5	Kia	Rio 4dr auto	Sedan	Asia	Front	$11,155	$10,705	1.6	4	104	25	32	2458	95	167

Compiling a Macro

A Brief Overview

In order to use the Printit macro later in your SAS programs, you must first compile it by submitting the macro definition, as follows:

```
%macro printit;
proc print data=&syslast (obs=5);
   title "Listing of &syslast data set";
   run;
%mend;
```

When you submit this code, the word scanner divides the macro into tokens and sends the tokens to the macro processor for compilation. Here is what the macro processor does:

- checks all macro language statements for syntax errors (non-macro language statements are not checked until the macro is executed).

- writes error messages to the SAS log if any syntax errors are found in the macro language statements.

- stores all compiled macro language statements and constant text in a SAS catalog entry if no syntax errors are found in the macro language statements. By default, a catalog named Work.Sasmacr is opened, and a catalog entry named Macro-Name.Macro is created.

That is, if there are no syntax errors in the macro language statements within the macro, the text between the %MACRO statement and the %MEND statement is stored under the name Printit for execution at a later time.

The MCOMPILENOTE= Option

By default, no note is written to the log if a macro program compiles successfully. The MCOMPILENOTE= system option writes a note to the SAS log when a macro has completed compilation.

Syntax, MCOMPILENOTE= system option:

OPTIONS MCOMPILENOTE= NONE | NOAUTOCALL | ALL;

NONE
> is the default value, which specifies that no notes are issued to the log.

NOAUTOCALL
> specifies that a note is issued to the log for completed macro compilations for all macros except autocall macros.

ALL
> specifies that a note is issued to the log for all completed macro compilations.

Example: Using the MCOMPILENOTE Option

A macro might compile but still contain non-macro syntax errors. If there are any macro statement errors, an error message is written to the SAS log, in addition to the note. Here is an example of the note that is written to the log when a macro compiles without errors:

```
options mcompilenote=all;
%macro printit;
   proc print data=&syslast(obs=5);
      title "Listing of &syslast data set";
   run;
%mend printit;
```

The following is written to the SAS log.

Log 9.1 SAS Log

```
NOTE: The macro PRINTIT completed compilation without errors.
      3 instructions 20 bytes
```

Calling a Macro

A Brief Overview

After the macro is successfully compiled, you can use it in your SAS programs for the duration of your SAS session without resubmitting the macro definition. Just as you must reference macro variables in order to access them in your code, you must call a macro program in order to execute it within your SAS program.

Here are the requirements for using a macro call:

- It is specified by placing a percent sign (%) before the name of the macro.
- It can be made anywhere in a program except within the data lines of a DATALINES statement (similar to a macro variable reference).
- It requires no semicolon because it is not a SAS statement.

To execute the macro Printit you call the macro as follows:

```
%printit
```

CAUTION:
> A semicolon after a macro call might insert an inappropriate semicolon into the resulting program, leading to errors during compilation or execution.

Example: Calling a Macro

Suppose you have a SAS program that consists of several program steps that create SAS data sets. After each of these program steps, you want to print out the data set that has been created. Remember that the macro Printit prints the most recently created data set. If Printit has been compiled, you can call it after each step in order to print each data set.

```
proc sort data=sashelp.cars out=cars_mpg;
   by MPG_City;
run;
%printit
proc sort data=sashelp.cars out=cars_msrp;
   by MSRP;
run;
%printit
```

Output 9.2 %PRINTIT Output 1: Sorted by MPG_City

Listing of WORK.CARS data set

Obs	Make	Model	Type	Origin	DriveTrain	MSRP	Invoice	EngineSize	Cylinders	Horsepower	MPG_City	MPG_Highway	Weight	Wheelbase	Length
1	Ford	Excursion 6.8 XLT	SUV	USA	All	$41,475	$36,494	6.8	10	310	10	13	7190	137	227
2	Hummer	H2	SUV	USA	All	$49,995	$45,815	6.0	8	316	10	12	6400	123	190
3	Dodge	Viper SRT-10 convertible 2dr	Sports	USA	Rear	$81,795	$74,451	8.3	10	500	12	20	3410	99	176
4	Land Rover	Range Rover HSE	SUV	Europe	All	$72,250	$65,807	4.4	8	282	12	16	5379	113	195
5	Land Rover	Discovery SE	SUV	Europe	All	$39,250	$35,777	4.6	8	217	12	16	4576	100	185

Output 9.3 %PRINTIT Output 2: Sorted by MSRP

Listing of WORK.CARS_MSRP data set

Obs	Make	Model	Type	Origin	DriveTrain	MSRP	Invoice	EngineSize	Cylinders	Horsepower	MPG_City	MPG_Highway	Weight	Wheelbase	Length
1	Kia	Rio 4dr manual	Sedan	Asia	Front	$10,280	$9,875	1.6	4	104	26	33	2403	95	167
2	Hyundai	Accent 2dr hatch	Sedan	Asia	Front	$10,539	$10,107	1.6	4	103	29	33	2255	96	167
3	Toyota	Echo 2dr manual	Sedan	Asia	Front	$10,760	$10,144	1.5	4	108	35	43	2035	93	163
4	Saturn	Ion1 4dr	Sedan	USA	Front	$10,995	$10,319	2.2	4	140	26	35	2692	103	185
5	Kia	Rio 4dr auto	Sedan	Asia	Front	$11,155	$10,705	1.6	4	104	25	32	2458	95	167

Macro Execution

A Brief Overview

When you call a macro in your SAS program, the word scanner passes the macro call to the macro processor, because the percent sign that precedes the macro name is a macro trigger. Here is what the macro processor does when it receives %*macro-name*:

1. It searches the designated SAS catalog (Work.Sasmacr by default) for an entry named *macro-name.macro*.

2. It executes compiled macro language statements within *macro-name*.

3. It sends any remaining text in *macro-name* to the input stack for word scanning.

4. It suspends macro execution when the SAS compiler receives a global SAS statement or when it encounters a SAS step boundary.

5. It resumes execution of macro language statements after the SAS code executes.

The macro call is processed by the macro processor before any SAS language statements such as DATA steps are compiled or executed. During macro execution, the macro processor can communicate directly with the following elements:

- both global and local symbol tables. For example, the macro processor can store macro variable values with a %LET statement and can resolve macro variable references.

- the input stack. For example, the macro processor can generate SAS code for tokenization by the word scanner.

Example: Executing a Macro

This example demonstrates macro execution. Assume that the Printit macro has been compiled and that it has been stored in the Work.Sasmacr catalog.

1. First, you submit the macro call, as follows:

   ```
   %printit
   ```

2. When the word scanner encounters this call, it passes the call to the macro processor. The macro processor searches for the compiled macro in the catalog entry Work.Sasmacr.Printit.Macro.

   ```
   %macro printit;
      proc print data=&syslast;
      title "Listing of &syslast data set";
      run;
   %mend printit;
   ```

3. The macro processor begins executing compiled macro language statements. However, in this example, no compiled macro statements are included in the macro.

4. The macro processor places non-compiled items (SAS language statements) on the input stack, and pauses as the word scanner tokenizes the inserted text. In this example, the macro processor places the PROC PRINT step on the input stack.

   ```
   proc print data=&syslast;
      title "Listing of &syslast data set";
   run;
   ```

5. The word scanner passes these tokens to the compiler. When the word scanner encounters a macro variable reference such as &SYSLAST, it passes the reference to the macro processor for resolution. The macro processor returns the macro variable value to the input stack, and word scanning continues.

6. After all of the statements in the PROC PRINT step have been compiled, the PROC PRINT step is executed, and SAS creates output of the most recently created data set.

7. Once the PROC PRINT step has been executed, the macro processor resumes execution of any remaining macro language statements in the macro (there are none in this example). The macro processor ends execution when it reaches the %MEND statement.

Assume that the most recently created data set is Work.Update_Schedule from an earlier example. Here is the output that is generated by calling the Printit macro.

Figure 9.1 *Partial Output: Printit Macro Output: &SYSLAST*

Listing of WORK.UPDATE_SCHEDULE data set

Obs	Course_Number	Course_Code	Location	Begin_Date	Teacher
1	1	C001	Seattle	26JUL2018	Hallis, Dr. George
2	2	C002	Dallas	06SEP2018	Wickam, Dr. Alice
3	3	C003	Boston	11OCT2018	Forest, Mr. Peter
4	4	C004	Seattle	25OCT2018	Tally, Ms. Julia
5	5	C005	Dallas	29NOV2018	Hallis, Dr. George

The following is written to the SAS log when %printit is submitted, assuming that the most recently data set is Work.Update_Schedule.

Log 9.2 *SAS Log*

```
NOTE: There were 5 observations read from the data set WORK.UPDATE_SCHEDULE.
NOTE: PROCEDURE PRINT used (Total process time):
      real time           0.02 seconds
      cpu time            0.00 seconds
```

Notice that in this SAS log message you see a note from PROC PRINT, but not the PROC PRINT code itself since the call to the macro does not display the text that is sent to the compiler.

Passing Information into a Macro Using Parameters

You have seen the basic form for a macro definition. Your macros will often contain macro variables. To make your macros more dynamic, you could use the %LET statement to update the values of the macro variables that are used within the macros. However, parameter lists in your macro definitions enable you to update the macro variables within your macro programs more conveniently. A *parameter list* is an optional part of the %MACRO statement that names one or more macro variables whose values you specify when you create or call the macro.

Macros That Include Positional Parameters

When you include positional parameters in a macro definition, a macro variable is automatically created for each parameter when you call the macro. To define macros that include positional parameters, you list the names of macro variables in the %MACRO statement of the macro definition. Positional parameters are so named because the order in which you specify them in a macro definition determines the order in which they are assigned values from the macro call. That is, when you call a macro that includes positional parameters, you specify the values of the macro variables that are defined in the parameters in the same order in which they are defined.

Syntax, macro definition that includes positional parameters:

%MACRO *macro-name(parameter-1<,...,parameter-n>)*;

  text

%MEND *<macro-name>*;

parameter-1<,...,parameter-n>
  specifies one or more positional parameters, separated by commas. You must supply each parameter with a name: you cannot use a text expression to generate it.

To call a macro that includes positional parameters, precede the name of the macro with a percent sign, and enclose the parameter values in parentheses. List the values in the same order in which the parameters are listed in the macro definition, and separate them with commas, as follows:

%macro-name(value-1<,...,value-n>)

The following statements are true about the values listed in a macro call:

- They can be null values, text, macro variable references, or macro calls.
- They are assigned to the parameter variables using a one-to-one correspondence.

Example: Using Positional Parameters to Create Macro Variables

You can use positional parameters to create the macro variables Dsn and Vars in the Printdsn macro definition, as follows:

```
%macro printdsn(dsn,vars);
   proc print data=&dsn;
      var &vars;
      title "Listing of %upcase(&dsn) data set";
   run;
%mend;
```

In this case, when you call the Printdsn macro you assign values to the macro variables that are created in the parameters. In the following example, the value `Certadv.Courses` is assigned to the macro variable Dsn, and the value `course_code course_title days` is assigned to the macro variable Vars. Notice that the value for Dsn is listed first and the value for Vars is listed second, since this is the order in which they are listed in the macro definition.

```
%printdsn(certadv.courses,course_code course_title days)
```

Note: To substitute a null value for one or more positional parameters, use commas as placeholders for the omitted values, as follows:

```
%printdsn(,course_code course_title days)
```

Macros That Include Keyword Parameters

You can also include keyword parameters in a macro definition. Like positional parameters, keyword parameters create macro variables. However, when you use keyword parameters to create macro variables, you specify the name, followed by the equal sign, and the value of each macro variable in the macro definition.

Keyword parameters can be listed in any order. Whatever value you assign to each parameter (or variable) in the %MACRO statement becomes its default value. Null values are allowed.

Syntax, macro definition that includes keyword parameters:

%MACRO *macro-name(keyword-1=<value-1><,...,keyword-n=<value-n>>);*
   text
%MEND *<macro-name>*;

keyword-1=<value-1><,...,keyword-n=<value-n>>
   names one or more macro parameters followed by equal signs. You can specify default values after the equal signs. If you omit a default value, the keyword parameter has a null value.

When you call a macro whose definition includes keyword parameters, you specify the keyword, followed by the equal sign, and the value for each parameter, in any order. If you omit a keyword parameter from the macro call, the keyword variable retains its default value, as follows:

```
%macro-name(keyword-1=value-1<,...,keyword-n=value-n>)
```

Example: Using Keyword Parameters to Create Macro Variables

You can use keyword parameters to create the macro variables Dsn and Vars in the Printdsn macro. This example assigns a default value of `Certadv.Courses` to the macro variable Dsn and assigns a default value of `course_codecourse_title days` to the macro variable Vars:

```
%macro printdsn(dsn=certadv.courses,
            vars=
course_code course_title days);
   proc print data=&dsn;
      var &vars;
   title "Listing of %upcase(&dsn) data set";
   run;
%mend;
```

To call the Printdsn macro with a value of `Certadv.Schedule` for Dsn and a value of `teacher course_codebegin_date` for Vars, issue the following call:

```
%printdsn(vars=teacher course_code begin_date, dsn=certadv.schedule)
```

To call the Printdsn macro with default values for the parameters (`Certadv.Courses` as the value for Dsn and `course_codecourse_title days` as the value for Vars), you could issue the following call:

```
%printdsn()
```

Note: To call the macro Printdsn with default values for the parameters, you could also issue a macro call that specified these values explicitly, as follows:

```
%printdsn(dsn=certadv.courses,vars=course_code course_title days)
```

Macros That Include Mixed Parameter Lists

You can also include a parameter list that contains both positional and keyword parameters in your macro definitions. All positional parameter variables in the %MACRO statement must be listed before any keyword parameter variable is listed.

Syntax, macro definition that includes mixed parameters:

%MACRO *macro-name(parameter-1<,...,parameter-n>,*
  keyword-1=<value-1><,...,keyword-n=<value-n>>);
  text
%MEND *macro-name;*

parameter-1<,...,parameter-n>
  is listed before *keyword-1=<value-1><,...,keyword-n=<value-n>>.*

Similarly, when you call a macro that includes a mixed parameter list, you must list the positional values before any keyword values, as follows:

```
%macro-name(value-1<,...,value-n>,
            keyword-1=value-1<,...,keyword-n=value-n>)
```

Example: Using Mixed Parameters to Create Macro Variables

You can use a combination of positional and keyword parameters to create the macro variables in the Printdsn macro definition. This code uses a positional parameter to create the macro variable Dsn, and a keyword parameter to create the macro variable Vars:

```
%macro printdsn(dsn, vars=course_title course_code days);
   proc print data=&dsn;
      var &vars;
      title "Listing of %upcase(&dsn) data set";
   run;
%mend;
```

The following call to the Printdsn macro assigns the value `Certadv.Schedule` to the macro variable Dsn and assigns the value `teacher location begin_date` to the macro variable Vars. Notice that the value for Dsn is listed first, since Dsn is the positional parameter.

```
%printdsn(certadv.schedule, vars=teacher location begin_date)
```

Now, suppose you want to execute the Printdsn macro, assigning the default value `course_titlecourse_code days` to the macro variable Vars and assigning the value `Certadv.Courses` to the macro variable Dsn. You could issue the following call:

```
%printdsn(certadv.courses)
```

Because this call omits the keyword parameter (Vars), the default value for that parameter is used.

Controlling Variable Scope

Scope of Macro Variables

Every macro variable has a scope.

Macro variable scope can either be global or local. Global macro variables can be created at any time during a SAS session, can persist for the duration of the SAS session, and can be referenced anywhere in the SAS session except for the DATALINES statement. To remove a global macro variable from memory within a SAS session, you must explicitly delete it using a %SYMDEL statement.

Local macro variables are created only during execution of a macro program, persist only as long as the macro is executing, and therefore can be referenced only while the macro is executing. When a macro terminates execution, its local symbol table is automatically deleted.

The %GLOBAL Statement

Global Symbol Table

Macro variables are stored in symbol tables, which list the macro variable name and its value. There is a global symbol table, which stores all global macro variables. Local macro variables are stored in a local symbol table that is created at the beginning of the execution of a macro.

Figure 9.2 Global Symbol Table

Global Symbol Table	
SYSDATE	04APR11
SYSDAY	Monday
SYSVER	9.2
uservar1	value1
uservar2	value2

The global symbol table is created during the initialization of a SAS session and is deleted at the end of the session. The following statements describe macro variables in the global symbol table:

- They are available anytime during the session.
- They can be created by a user.
- They have values that can be changed during the session (except for some automatic macro variables).

A Brief Overview of %GLOBAL Statement

Here is what the %GLOBAL statement does:

- It creates one or more macro variables in the global symbol table and assigns null values to them.
- It can be used either inside or outside a macro definition.
- It can create a READONLY macro variable with an initial value that cannot be changed.
- It has no effect on variables that are already in the global symbol table.

You can create global macro variables anytime during a SAS session or job. Except for some automatic macro variables, you can change the values of global macro variables anytime during a SAS session or job.

In most cases, once you define a global macro variable, its value is available to you anywhere in the SAS session or job and can be changed anywhere. So, a macro variable referenced inside a macro definition is global if a global macro variable already exists by the same name (assuming that the variable is not specifically defined as local with the %LOCAL statement or in a parameter list). The new macro variable definition simply updates the existing global one. The following are exceptions that prevent you from referencing the value of a global macro variable:

- When a macro variable exists both in the global symbol table and in the local symbol table, you cannot reference the global value from within the macro that contains the local macro variable. In this case, the macro processor finds the local value first and uses it instead of the global value.
- If you create a macro variable in the DATA step with the SYMPUT routine, you cannot reference the value with an ampersand until the program reaches a step boundary.

You can create a global macro variable with any of these elements:

- a %LET statement (used outside a macro definition)
- a DATA step that contains a SYMPUT routine
- a DATA step that contains a SYMPUTX routine
- a SELECT statement that contains an INTO clause in PROC SQL
- a %GLOBAL statement

%GLOBAL Statement Syntax

Syntax, %GLOBAL statement:

%GLOBAL *macro-variable-1* <*...macro-variable-n*>;

macro-variable
   is either the name of a macro variable or a text expression that generates a macro variable name.

Example: Using %GLOBAL Statement

To create a global macro variable inside a macro definition, you can use the %GLOBAL statement. The %GLOBAL statement in the following example creates two global macro variables, Dsn and Vars. The %LET statements assign values to the new global macro variables, as follows:

```
%macro printdsn;
   %global dsn vars;
   %let dsn=certadv.courses;
   %let vars=course_title course_code days;
   proc print data=&dsn;
      var &vars;
   title "Listing of &dsn data set";
   run;
%mend printdsn;

%printdsn
```

Note: You use the %SYMDEL statement to delete a macro variable from the global symbol table during a SAS session. To remove the macro variable dsn from the global symbol table, you submit the following statement:

```
%symdel dsn;
```

The %LOCAL Statement

Local Symbol Table

A local symbol table is created when a macro that includes a parameter list is called or when a request is made to create a local variable during macro execution. The local symbol table is deleted when the macro finishes execution. That is, the local symbol table exists only while the macro executes.

Figure 9.3 Local Symbol Table

Local Symbol Table	
parameter1	*value1*
parameter2	*value2*
uservar1	*value1*
uservar2	*value2*

The local symbol table contains macro variables.

- These variables can be created and initialized at macro invocation (that is, by parameters).
- They can be created or updated during macro execution.
- They can be referenced anywhere within the macro.

A local symbol table is not created until a request is made to create a local variable. Macros that do not create local variables do not have a local table. Remember, the SYMPUT routine can create local variables only if the local table already exists.

Since local symbol tables exist separately from the global symbol table, it is possible to have a local macro variable and a global macro variable that have the same name and different values.

A Brief Overview

The following is true of the %LOCAL statement:

- It can appear only inside a macro definition.
- It creates one or more macro variables in the local symbol table and assigns null values to them.
- It has no effect on variables that are already in the local symbol table.

You can create local macro variables with any of these elements:

- parameters in a macro definition
- a %LET statement within a macro definition
- a DATA step that contains a SYMPUT routine within a macro definition

- a DATA step that contains a SYMPUTX routine within a macro definition
- a SELECT statement that contains an INTO clause in PROC SQL within a macro definition
- a %LOCAL statement

Note: The SYMPUT routine can create a local macro variable only if a local symbol table already exists and no variable of the same name exists in the global symbol table. If no local symbol table exists when SYMPUT executes, the value is assigned to a global macro variable. The SYMPUTX call routine provides a third argument (*symbol-table*) that allows you to explicitly create a variable in a local symbol table while the macro that generated the DATA step is executing. If no local symbol table exists when a call to SYMPUTX with a local specification executes, a local symbol table is created, and then the macro variable is created in the local symbol table.

%LOCAL Statement Syntax

Syntax, %LOCAL statement:

%LOCAL *macro-variable-1* <*...macro-variable-n*>;

macro-variable
: is either the name of a macro variable or a text expression that generates a macro variable name.

Example: Using the %LOCAL Statement

In this example, the first %LET statement creates a global macro variable named Dsn and assigns a value of `CertAdv.Courses` to it.

The %LOCAL statement within the macro definition creates a local macro variable named Dsn, and the %LET statement within the macro definition assigns a value of `Certadv.Register` to the local variable Dsn.

The %PUT statement within the macro definition writes the value of the local variable Dsn to the SAS log, whereas the %PUT statement that follows the macro definition writes the value of the global variable Dsn to the SAS log:

```
%let dsn=certadv.courses;

%macro printdsn;
    %local dsn;
    %let dsn=certadv.register;
    %put The value of DSN inside Printdsn is &dsn;
%mend;

%printdsn
%put The value of DSN outside Printdsn is &dsn;
```

When you submit this code, the following statements are written to the SAS log.

Log 9.3 SAS Log

```
199  %let dsn=certadv.courses;
200
201  %macro printdsn;
202     %local dsn;
203     %let dsn=certadv.register;
204     %put The value of DSN inside Printdsn is &dsn;
205  %mend;
206
207  %printdsn
The value of DSN inside Printdsn is certadv.register
208  %put The value of DSN outside Printdsn is &dsn;
The value of DSN outside Printdsn is certadv.courses
```

Nested Scope

The scope of a macro variable can be nested, like boxes within boxes. The following example illustrates nesting variable scope.

```
%macro test;
   %local x;        /*❶*/
   %let x=FALSE;    /*❷*/
%macro test;
%test;
```

1. The macro variable, X, is defined with a %LOCAL statement. When the %LOCAL statement executes, a local symbol table is created for the test macro, and the macro variable, X, is created in this local table.

2. When the macro processor executes the %LET statement, it searches the test macro's local table for a macro variable named X. It finds X in this local table and sets its value to False.

The local table is deleted when the test macro ends.

Debugging Macros

The MPRINT System Option

A Brief Overview

The MPRINT system option displays the text generated by macro execution. Each SAS statement begins a new line. Each line of MPRINT output is identified with the prefix MPRINT(*macro-name*), to identify the macro that generates the statement.

You can direct MPRINT output to an external file by also using the MFILE option and assigning the fileref MPRINT to that file.

You might want to specify the MPRINT system option under these conditions:

- You have a SAS syntax error or execution error.
- You want to see the generated SAS code.

The MPRINT system option is often synchronized with the SOURCE system option to show, or hide, executed SAS code.

The MPRINT Option Syntax

Syntax, MPRINT system option:

MPRINT | NOMPRINT;

MPRINT
  displays the SAS statements that are generated by macro execution. The SAS statements are useful for debugging macros.

NOMPRINT
  does not display SAS statements that are generated by macro execution.

Example: Using the MPRINT Option

Suppose you want to call the Prtlast macro and use the MPRINT system option to show the SAS code that results from the macro execution.

Catalog Entry

```
%macro prtlast;
   proc print data=&syslast (obs=5);
      title "Listing of &syslast data set";
   run;
%mend prtlast;
```

The following sample code creates a data set named Sales, specifies the MPRINT system option, and references the Prtlast macro:

```
data sales;
   price_code=1;
run;
options mprint;
%prtlast
```

The messages that are written to the SAS log show the text that is sent to the compiler. Notice that the macro variable reference (&SYSLAST) is resolved to the value **Work.Sales** in the MPRINT messages that are written to the SAS log.

Log 9.4 SAS Log

```
101   %prtlast
MPRINT(PRTLAST): proc print data=WORK.SALES (obs=5);
MPRINT(PRTLAST): title "Listing of WORK.SALES";
MPRINT(PRTLAST): run;
NOTE: There were 1 observations read from the dataset WORK.SALES.
NOTE: PROCEDURE PRINT used:
      real time           0.04 seconds
      cpu time            0.04 seconds
```

Comments in Macro Programs

A Brief Overview

The macro comment statement is useful for describing macro code. Text from a macro comment statement is not constant text and is not stored in a compiled macro. Because a semicolon ends the comment statement, the comment cannot contain internal semicolons unless the internal semicolons are enclosed in quotation marks or a macro quoting function. Macro comments are not recognized when they are enclosed in quotation marks.

Quotation marks within a macro comment must match.

Comment Statement Syntax

Syntax, macro comment statement:

/*comment*/;

comment
>   can be any message. Like other SAS statements, each macro comment statement ends with a semicolon.

Example: Use Macro Comments

The following code uses macro comments to describe the functionality of the macro:

```
%macro printit;
   /*The value of &syslast will be substituted appropriately*/
   /* as long as a data set has been created during this session.*/
   proc print data=&syslast(obs=5);
/* Print only the first 5 observations */
   title "Last Created Data Set Is &syslast";
   run;
%mend;
```

Conditional Processing

The %IF-%THEN Statement and %ELSE Statement

A Brief Overview
You can perform conditional execution at the macro level with %IF-%THEN and %ELSE statements.

Although they look similar, the %IF-%THEN/%ELSE statement and the IF-THEN/ELSE statement belong to two different languages. Most of the same rules that apply to the DATA step IF-THEN/ELSE statement also apply to the %IF-%THEN/%ELSE statement. However, there are several important differences between the macro %IF-%THEN statement and the DATA step IF-THEN statement.

%IF-%THEN Rules	IF-THEN Rules
Can be used both inside or outside a macro program.	Is used only in a DATA step program.
Executes during macro execution.	Executes during DATA step execution.

%IF-%THEN Rules	IF-THEN Rules
Uses macro variables in logical expressions and cannot refer to DATA step variables in logical expressions.	Uses DATA step variables in logical expressions.
Determines what text should be copied to the input stack.	Determines what DATA step statement(s) should be executed. When inside a macro definition, it is copied to the input stack as text.

The %IF-%THEN and %ELSE Statement Syntax

Syntax, %IF-%THEN and %ELSE statements:

%IF *expression* **%THEN** *text*;

<%ELSE *text*;>

expression
    can be any valid macro expression that resolves to an integer.

text
    can be specified in any of these forms:

- constant text
- a text expression
- a macro variable reference, a macro call, or a macro program statement

If *expression* resolves to 0, then it is false and the %THEN text is not processed (the optional %ELSE text is processed instead). If it resolves to any integer other than 0, then the expression is true and the %THEN text is processed. If it resolves to null or to any noninteger value, an error message is issued.

The %ELSE statement is optional. However, the macro language does not contain a subsetting %IF statement. Thus, you cannot use %IF without %THEN.

The %DO-%END Statement with the %IF-%THEN Statement

A Brief Overview

Simple %DO and %END statements often appear in conjunction with %IF-%THEN/%ELSE statements in order to designate a section of the macro to be processed depending on whether the %IF condition is true or false. Use %DO and %END statements following %THEN or %ELSE in order to conditionally place text that contains multiple statements onto the input stack. Each %DO statement must be paired with an %END statement.

The %DO statement designates the beginning of a section of a macro definition that is treated as a unit until a matching %END statement is encountered. This macro section is called a %DO group. %DO groups can be nested. A simple %DO statement often appears in conjunction with %IF-%THEN/%ELSE statements to designate a section of the macro to be processed depending on whether the %IF condition is true or false.

%DO-%END Statement with %IF-%THEN Statement Syntax

Syntax, %DO-%END with %IF-%THEN and %ELSE statements:

%IF *expression* **%THEN %DO;**
> *text and/or macro language statements*

%END;

%ELSE %DO;
> *text and/or macro language statements*

%END;

text and/or macro language statements
> is either constant text, a text expression, and/or a macro statement.

Example: Using %IF-%THEN, %DO-%END with IF-THEN Statements

The following example illustrates using %IF-%THEN and %DO statements with IF-THEN/ELSE statements to define and call a macro. SYSERR is an automatic macro variable that is assigned a value of 0 if the previous step executes without error. If there is an error, SYSERR is assigned another value. In this program, the PROC PRINT step executes only if the DATA step runs without errors.

```
data work.sports;
   set sashelp.cars;
   where Type="Sports";
   AvgMPG=mean(MPG_City, MPG_Highway);
run;

%if &syserr ne 0 %then %do;
   %put ERROR: The rest of the program will not execute;
%end;
%else %do;
title "Sports Cars";
proc print data=work.sports noobs;
   var Make Model AvgMPG MSRP;
run;
%end;
```

Output 9.4 Work Sports (partial output)

Sports Cars

Make	Model	AvgMPG	MSRP
Acura	NSX coupe 2dr manual S	20.5	$89,765
Audi	RS 6 4dr	18.5	$84,600
Audi	TT 1.8 convertible 2dr (coupe)	24.0	$35,940
Audi	TT 1.8 Quattro 2dr (convertible)	24.0	$37,390

... *more observations* ...

Example: Controlling Text Copied to the Input Stack

You can control text that is copied to the input stack with the %IF-%THEN while controlling DATA step logic with IF-THEN. In this example, the value of the macro variable Status determines which variables and observations are included in the new data set. The value of the data set variable Location determines the value of the new data set variable Totalfee.

```
%macro choice(status);
   data fees;
      set certadv.all;
      %if &status=PAID %then %do;
         where paid='Y';
         keep student_name course_code begin_date totalfee;
      %end;
      %else %do;
         where paid='N';
         keep student_name course_code
              begin_date totalfee latechg;
         latechg=fee*.10;
      %end;
      if location='Boston' then totalfee=fee*1.06;
      else if location='Seattle' then totalfee=fee*1.025;
      else if location='Dallas'  then totalfee=fee*1.05;
   run;
%mend choice;
```

If the MPRINT and MLOGIC system options are both set, the SAS log displays messages showing the text that is sent to the compiler. For example, suppose you submit the following macro call:

```
options mprint mlogic;
%choice(PAID)
```

The following messages are written to the log. Notice that the MLOGIC option shows the evaluation of the expression in the %IF statement, but it does not show the evaluation of the expression in the IF statement.

Log 9.5 SAS Log

```
160  %choice(PAID)
MLOGIC(CHOICE): Beginning execution.
MLOGIC(CHOICE): Parameter STATUS has value PAID
MPRINT(CHOICE): data fees;
MPRINT(CHOICE): set certadv.all;
MLOGIC(CHOICE): %IF condition &status=PAID is TRUE
MPRINT(CHOICE): where paid='Y';
MPRINT(CHOICE): keep student_name course_code begin_date totalfee;
MPRINT(CHOICE): if location='Boston' then totalfee=fee*1.06;
MPRINT(CHOICE): else if location='Seattle' then totalfee=fee*1.025;
MPRINT(CHOICE): else if location='Dallas' then totalfee=fee*1.05;
MPRINT(CHOICE): run;
```

Suppose you submit the following macro call:

```
options mprint mlogic;
%choice(OWED)
```

The following messages are written to the SAS log. Notice that the text that is written to the input stack is different this time.

Log 9.6 SAS Log

```
161  %choice(OWED)
MLOGIC(CHOICE): Beginning execution.
MLOGIC(CHOICE): Parameter STATUS has value OWED
MPRINT(CHOICE): data fees;
MPRINT(CHOICE): set certadv.all;
MLOGIC(CHOICE): %IF condition &status=PAID is FALSE
MPRINT(CHOICE): where paid='N';
MPRINT(CHOICE): keep student_name course_code begin_date totalfee
                latechg;
MPRINT(CHOICE): latechg=fee*.10;
MPRINT(CHOICE): if location='Boston' then totalfee=fee*1.06;
MPRINT(CHOICE): else if location='Seattle' then totalfee=fee*1.025;
MPRINT(CHOICE): else if location='Dallas' then totalfee=fee*1.05;
MPRINT(CHOICE): run;
```

During macro compilation, macro statements are checked for syntax errors. If a macro definition contains macro statement syntax errors, error messages are written to the SAS log, and a non-executable (dummy) macro is created.

The MLOGIC System Option

A Brief Overview

Use the MLOGIC system option to debug macros. Each line that is generated by the MLOGIC option is identified with the prefix MLOGIC(*macro-name*). If MLOGIC is in effect and the macro processor encounters a macro invocation, the macro processor displays messages that identify the following:

- the beginning of macro execution
- values of macro parameters at invocation
- execution of each macro program statement
- whether each %IF condition is true or false
- the ending of macro execution

Note: Using MLOGIC can produce a great deal of output in the SAS log.

MLOGIC System Option Syntax

Syntax, MLOGIC system option:

MLOGIC | NOMLOGIC;

MLOGIC
  causes the macro processor to trace its execution and to write the trace information to the SAS log. This option is a useful debugging tool.

NOMLOGIC
  does not trace execution. Use this option unless you are debugging macros.

Example: Using MLOGIC System Option

Suppose you want to repeat the previous example with only the MLOGIC system option in effect. This sample code creates a data set named Sales, sets the MLOGIC system option, and calls the Prtlast macro.

```
data sales;
   price_code=1;
run;
options nomprint mlogic;
%prtlast
```

When this code is submitted, the messages that are written to the SAS log show the beginning and the end of macro processing.

Log 9.7 *SAS Log*

```
107    %prtlast
MLOGIC(PRTLAST): Beginning execution.
NOTE: There were 1 observations read from the dataset WORK.SALES.
NOTE: PROCEDURE PRINT used:
      real time           0.02 seconds
      cpu time            0.02 seconds
MLOGIC(PRTLAST): Ending execution.
```

The MLOGIC system option, along with the SYMBOLGEN option, is typically set as follows:

- turned *on* for development and debugging purposes
- turned *off* when the application is in production mode

Iterative Processing

The %DO Statement

A Brief Overview

Many macro applications require iterative processing. With the iterative %DO statement you can do the following repeatedly:

- execute macro programming code
- generate SAS code

The iterative %DO and %END statements are valid only inside a macro definition. The index variable is created in the local symbol table if it does not appear in any existing symbol table.

The iterative %DO statement evaluates the value of the index variable at the beginning of each loop iteration. The loop stops processing when the index variable has a value that is outside the range of the start and stop values.

%DO Syntax

Syntax, iterative %DO statement with %END statement:

%DO *index-variable=start* **%TO** *stop* <**%BY** *increment*>;
    text
%END;

index-variable
> is either the name of a macro variable or a text expression that generates a macro variable name.

start and *stop*
> specify either integers or macro expressions that generate integers to control how many times the portion of the macro between the iterative %DO and %END statements is processed.

increment
> specifies either an integer (other than 0) or a macro expression that generates an integer to be added to the value of the index variable in each iteration of the loop. By default, *increment* is 1.

text
> can be any of these elements:
> - constant text, possibly including SAS data set names, SAS variable names, or SAS statements
> - macro variables, macro functions, or macro program statements
> - any combination of the above

Example: Using the %DO Statement

You can use a macro loop to create and display a series of macro variables.

This example creates a series of macro variables named Teach1-Teach*n*, one for each observation in the Certadv.Schedule data set, and assigns teacher names to them as values. Then the Putloop macro uses a %DO statement and a %END statement to create a loop that writes these macro variables and their values to the SAS log.

```
proc sql noprint;
   select teacher
      into :teach1-
      from certadv.schedule;
run;

%macro putloop;
   %local i;
   %do i=1 %to &sqlobs
      %put TEACH&i is &teach&i
   %end;
%mend;

%putloop
```

TIP SQLOBS macro variable stores the number of rows in the previous SQL query.

TIP It is a good idea to specifically declare the index variable of a macro loop as a local variable to avoid accidentally changing the value of a macro variable that has the same name in other symbol tables.

When the Putloop macro is executed, no code is sent to the compiler because the %PUT statements are executed by the macro processor.

The following messages are written to the SAS log.

Log 9.8 SAS Log

```
TEACH1 is Hallis, Dr. George
TEACH2 is Wickam, Dr. Alice
TEACH3 is Forest, Mr. Peter
TEACH4 is Tally, Ms. Julia
TEACH5 is Hallis, Dr. George
TEACH6 is Berthan, Ms. Judy
TEACH7 is Hallis, Dr. George
TEACH8 is Wickam, Dr. Alice
TEACH9 is Forest, Mr. Peter
TEACH10 is Tally, Ms. Julia
TEACH11 is Tally, Ms. Julia
TEACH12 is Berthan, Ms. Judy
TEACH13 is Hallis, Dr. George
TEACH14 is Wickam, Dr. Alice
TEACH15 is Forest, Mr. Peter
TEACH16 is Tally, Ms. Julia
TEACH17 is Hallis, Dr. George
TEACH18 is Berthan, Ms. Judy
```

You can also use a macro loop to generate statements that can be placed inside a SAS program step.

Example: Generating Complete Steps

You can use the iterative %DO statement to build macro loops that create complete SAS steps. Suppose you want to generate a roster for each of the 18 classes that you have. You can use a %DO statement to create a loop that creates a roster for each class.

```
%macro rosters;
   %do class=1 %to 18;
      title "Roster for Class #&class";
      proc print data=certadv.all;
         where Course_Number=&class
      run;
   %end;
%mend;

%rosters
```

The macro prints 18 rosters for each course titles.

Quiz

Select the best answer for each question. After completing the quiz, check your answers using the answer key in the appendix.

1. Which of the following is false?

    a. A %MACRO statement must always be paired with a %MEND statement.

b. A macro definition can include macro variable references, but it cannot include SAS language statements.

c. Only macro language statements are checked for syntax errors when the macro is compiled.

d. Compiled macros are stored in a temporary SAS catalog by default.

2. Which of the following examples correctly defines a macro named Print that defines and resolves parameters named vars and total?

a.
```
%macro print(vars, total);
    proc print data=classes;
        var vars;
        sum total;
    run;
%mend print;
```

b.
```
%macro print('vars', 'total');
    proc print data=classes;
        var &vars;
        sum &total;
    run;
%mend print;
```

c.
```
%macro print(vars, total);
    proc print data=classes;
        var &vars;
        sum &total;
    run;
%mend print;
```

d.
```
%macro print(vars, total);
    proc print data=classes;
        var :vars;
        sum :total;
    run;
%mend print;
```

3. Which of the following correctly references the macro named Printdsn as shown here:

```
%macro printdsn(dsn,vars);
    %if &vars= %then %do;
        proc print data=&dsn;
        title "Full Listing of %upcase(&dsn) data set";
        run;
    %end;
    %else %do;
        proc print data=&dsn;
            var &vars;
        title "Listing of %upcase(&dsn) data set";
        run;
    %end;
%mend;
```

a. `%printdsn(certadv.courses, course_title days);`

b. `%printdsn(dsn=certadv.courses, vars=course_title days)`

c. `%printdsn(certadv.courses, course_title days)`

d. `%printdsn(certadv.courses, course_title, days)`

4. If you use a mixed parameter list in your macro program definition, which of the following is false?

    a. You must list positional parameters before any keyword parameters.

    b. Values for both positional and keyword parameters are stored in a local symbol table.

    c. Default values for keyword parameters are the values that are assigned in the macro definition, whereas positional parameters have a default value of null.

    d. You can assign a null value to a keyword parameter in a call to the macro by omitting the parameter from the call.

5. Which of the following is false?

    a. A macro program is compiled when you submit the macro definition.

    b. A macro program is executed when you call it (for example, `%macro-name`).

    c. A macro program is stored in a SAS catalog entry only after it is executed.

    d. A macro program is available for execution throughout the SAS session in which it is compiled.

6. When you use an %IF-%THEN statement in your macro program, which of the following is true?

    a. You must place %DO and %END statements around code that describes the conditional action, if that code contains multiple statements.

    b. The %ELSE statement is optional.

    c. You cannot refer to DATA step variables in the logical expression of the %IF statement.

    d. All of the above.

7. Which of the following can be used for debugging macros?

    a. MPRINT

    b. MLOGIC

    c. comments in macro programs

    d. All of the above.

8. Which of the following creates a macro variable named Class in a local symbol table?

    a.
    ```
    data _null_;
        set certadv.courses;
        %let class=course_title;
    run;
    ```

    b.
    ```
    data _null_;
        set certadv.courses;
        call symputx('class', course_title);
    run;
    ```

    c.
    ```
    %macro sample(dsn);
        %local class;
        %let class=course_title;
        data _null_;
            set &dsn;
    ```

```
        run;
    %mend;
```

d.
```
%global class;
%macro sample(dsn);
    %let class=course_title;
    data _null_;
        set &dsn;
    run;
%mend;
```

Chapter 10
Advanced Macro Techniques

Storing Macro Definitions in External Files **259**
    The %INCLUDE Statement 259
    Example: Using the %INCLUDE Statement 260

Understanding Session Compiled Macros **261**

Using the Autocall Facility **262**
    A Brief Overview 262
    Creating an Autocall Library 262
    Example: Saving a Macro 262
    Default Autocall Library 263
    Example: Using the LOWCASE Macro 263
    Accessing Autocall Macros 264

Data-Driven Macro Calls **266**
    A Brief Overview 266
    The DOSUBL Function 266
    Example: Using the DOSUBL Function 266

Quiz **268**

Storing Macro Definitions in External Files

The %INCLUDE Statement

One way to store macro programs permanently is to save them to an external file. You can then use the %INCLUDE statement to insert the statements that are stored in the external file into a program. If the external file contains a macro definition, the macro is compiled when the %INCLUDE statement is submitted. Then the macro can be called again later in the same program, or anytime later in the current SAS session.

Note: %INCLUDE is a global SAS statement, not a macro statement.

Syntax, %INCLUDE statement:

%INCLUDE *file-specification* </SOURCE2>;

file-specification
> describes the location of the file that contains the SAS code to be inserted.

SOURCE2
> causes the SAS statements that are inserted into the program to be displayed in the SAS log. If SOURCE2 is not specified in the %INCLUDE statement, then the setting of the SAS system option SOURCE2 controls whether the inserted code is displayed.

By storing your macro program externally and using the %INCLUDE statement, you gain several advantages over using session compiled macros.

- The source code for the macro definition does not need to be part of your program.
- A single copy of a macro definition can be shared by many programs.
- Macro definitions in external files are easily viewed and edited with any text editor.
- No special SAS system options are required in order to access a macro definition that is stored in an external file.

Example: Using the %INCLUDE Statement

You can compile a macro by using the %INCLUDE statement to insert its definition into a program. Then you can call the macro in order to execute it.

Suppose the following macro definition is stored in the external file `C:\Users\certadv\prtlast.sas`:

```
%macro prtlast;
   %if &syslast ne _NULL_ %then %do;
      proc print data=&syslast (obs=5);
         title "Listing of &syslast data set";
      run;
   %end;
   %else
      %put No data set has been created yet.;
%mend;
```

You could submit the following code to access, compile, and execute the Prtlast macro. The PROC SORT step is included in this example in order to create a data set that the Prtlast macro can print.

```
%include 'C:\Users\certadv\prtlast.sas' /source2;
proc sort data=certadv.courses out=work.bydays;
   by days;
run;
%prtlast
```

Note: The location and names of external files are specific to your operating environment.

The following messages are written to the SAS log when this code is submitted. Notice that the macro definition is written to the log because SOURCE2 was specified in the %INCLUDE statement.

Log 10.1 SAS Log

```
NOTE: %INCLUDE (level 1) file prtlast.sas is file
         C:\Users\certadv\prtlast.sas.
31   +%macro prtlast;
32   +   %if &syslast ne _NULL_ %then %do;
33   +      proc print data=&syslast(obs=5);
34   +      title "Listing of &syslast data set";
35   +      run;
36   +   %end;
37   +   %else
38   +      %put No data set has been created yet.;
39   +%mend;
NOTE: %INCLUDE (level 1) ending.
40
41   proc sort data=certadv.courses out=work.bydays;
42      by days;
43   run;

NOTE: There were 6 observations read from the dataset
      CERTADV.COURSES.
NOTE: The data set WORK.BYDAYS has 6 observations and
      4 variables.
NOTE: PROCEDURE SORT used:
      real time         0.04 seconds
      cpu time          0.04 seconds

44
45   %prtlast
NOTE: There were 5 observations read from the dataset
      WORK.BYDAYS.
NOTE: PROCEDURE PRINT used:
      real time         1.07 seconds
      cpu time          0.26 seconds
```

Output 10.1 PROC PRINT Result of Work.Bydays

Listing of WORK.BYDAYS data set

Obs	Course_Code	Course_Title	Days	Fee
1	C004	Database Design	2	$375
2	C005	Artificial Intelligence	2	$400
3	C001	Basic Telecommunications	3	$795
4	C003	Local Area Networks	3	$650
5	C002	Structured Query Language	4	$1150

Understanding Session Compiled Macros

By default, when a macro definition is submitted, the macro is compiled and stored in a temporary SAS catalog as Work.Sasmacr. Macros that are stored in this temporary SAS catalog are known as *session compiled macros*. Once a macro has been compiled, it can be invoked from a SAS program.

Session compiled macros are available for execution during the SAS session in which they are compiled. They are deleted at the end of the session. But suppose you want to save your macros so that they are easily reused in another SAS session.

Using the Autocall Facility

A Brief Overview

You can make macros accessible to your SAS session or program by using the autocall facility to search predefined source libraries for macro definitions. These predefined source libraries are known as *autocall libraries*. You can store your macro definitions permanently in an autocall library, and you can set up multiple autocall libraries.

When you store macro definitions in an autocall library, you do not need to compile the macro definition ahead of time to make it available for execution. That is, if the macro definition is stored in an autocall library, then you do not need to submit or include the macro definition before you submit a call to the macro.

Suppose you have stored a file that contains a macro definition in your autocall library. Here is what happens when you submit a call to that macro:

- The macro processor searches the autocall library for the macro.
- The macro is compiled and stored as it would be if you had submitted it (that is, the compiled macro is stored in the default location of Work.Sasmacr).
- The macro is executed.

Once it has been compiled, the macro can be executed as needed throughout the same SAS session. At the end of the SAS session, the compiled macro is deleted from the Work.Sasmacr catalog, but the source code remains in the autocall library.

Creating an Autocall Library

An autocall library can be in either of these forms:

- a directory that contains source files
- a SAS catalog

To create an autocall library in a directory-based operating system, create a directory in which to store macro definitions. Each macro definition in this directory will be a separate file that has the extension .sas and that has the same name as the macro that it contains.

Note: On UNIX the file name containing the macro definition must be in all lowercase letters. It is considered a best practice to use all lowercase letters for macro definition program files on all operating systems.

Example: Saving a Macro

To save the definition for the macro PrintLast in an autocall library, first determine where you want to save your autocall macro file. You can either use an existing folder containing other autocall macro programs (if you have Write access) or you can create a new folder to store your autocall macros. Then, save your macro definition program in a file named printlast.sas in the designated folder.

Default Autocall Library

SAS provides several macros in a default autocall library for you. Some of the macros in the autocall library that SAS provides are listed here.

Macro Syntax	Purpose
%LOWCASE(*argument*)	converts letters in its argument from uppercase to lowercase
%QLOWCASE(*argument*)	converts letters in its argument from uppercase to lowercase, and returns a result that masks special characters and mnemonic operators
%LEFT(*argument*)	removes leading blanks from the argument
%TRIM(*argument*)	removes trailing blanks from the argument
%CMPRES(*argument*)	removes multiple blanks from the argument
%DATATYP(*argument*)	returns the string NUMERIC or CHAR, depending on whether the argument is an integer or a character string

You might be familiar with SAS functions such as TRIM and LEFT. The macros that SAS supplies look like macro functions, but they are in fact macros. One of the useful things about these macros is that in addition to using them in your SAS programs, you can see their source code.

Example: Using the LOWCASE Macro

The macro definition for the LOWCASE macro is shown below. Notice that the comments that are included in this macro provide information about using the macro. All of the macros that SAS provides in the autocall library include explanatory comments, making them easy for you to understand and use.

Log 10.2 SAS Log

```
%macro lowcase(string);
%*********************************************************;
%*                                                        *;
%* MACRO: LOWCASE                                         *;
%*                                                        *;
%* USAGE: 1) %lowcase(argument)                           *;
%*                                                        *;
%* DESCRIPTION:                                           *;
%*   This macro returns the argument passed to           *;
%*   it unchanged except that all upper-case             *;
%*   alphabetic characters are changed to their          *;
%*   lower-case equivalents.                             *;
%*                                                        *;
%* E.g.: %let macvar=%lowcase(SAS Institute Inc.);       *;
%* The variable macvar gets the value                    *;
%*   "sas institute inc."                                *;
%* NOTES:                                                 *;
%*   Although the argument to the %UPCASE macro          *;
%*   function may contain commas, the argument to        *;
%*   %LOWCASE may not, unless they are quoted.           *;
%*   Because %LOWCASE is a macro, not a function,        *;
%*   it interprets a comma as the end of a parameter.   *;
%*********************************************************;
%sysfunc(lowcase(%nrbquote(&string)))
%mend;
```

Accessing Autocall Macros

Overview

Remember that an autocall library is either a SAS catalog, an external directory, or a partitioned data set. This is true both for the default autocall library that SAS supplies and for autocall libraries that you create.

In order to access a macro definition that is stored in an autocall library, you must use two SAS system options, as follows:

- The MAUTOSOURCE system option must be specified.
- The SASAUTOS= system option must be set to identify the location of the autocall library or libraries.

Both the MAUTOSOURCE and SASAUTOS= system options can be set either at SAS invocation or with an OPTIONS statement during program execution.

The MAUTOSOURCE System Option

The MAUTOSOURCE system option controls whether the autocall facility is available.

Syntax, MAUTOSOURCE system option:

OPTIONS MAUTOSOURCE | NOMAUTOSOURCE;

MAUTOSOURCE
   is the default setting, and specifies that the autocall facility is available.

NOMAUTOSOURCE
   specifies that the autocall facility is not available.

The SASAUTOS System Option

The SASAUTOS= system option controls where the macro facility looks for autocall macros.

Syntax, SASAUTOS= system option:

OPTIONS SASAUTOS=*library-1*;

OPTIONS SASAUTOS=(*library-1,...,library-n***)**;

the values of *library-1* through *library-n*
: are references to source libraries that contain macro definitions. To specify a source library:

- Use a fileref to refer to its location.
- Specify the pathname (enclosed in quotation marks) for the library.

Unless your system administrator has changed the default value for the SASAUTOS= system option, its value is the fileref Sasautos, and that fileref points to the location where the default autocall library was created during installation. The Sasautos fileref can refer to multiple locations that are concatenated.

TIP Remember to concatenate any autocall libraries that you create yourself with the default autocall library supplied by SAS. Otherwise, the new autocall library will replace the default or existing libraries in the value of SASAUTOS=, and the autocall facility will have access to only the new autocall library.

Example: Accessing Autocall Macros

Suppose you want to access the Prtlast macro, which is stored in the autocall library `C:\Mysasfiles`. You also want to make sure that the default autocall library (which the fileref Sasautos points to) is still available to the autocall facility. You would submit the following code:

```
options mautosource sasautos=('c:\mysasfiles',sasautos);
%prtlast
```

When the autocall facility is in effect, if you invoke a macro that has not been previously compiled, here is what the macro facility automatically does:

1. It searches the autocall library (or each autocall library in turn if multiple libraries are identified in the SASAUTOS= system option) for a library member that has the same name as the invoked macro.
2. It brings the source statements into the current SAS session if the library member is found.
3. It issues an error message if the library member is not found.
4. It submits all statements in the library member in order to compile the macro.
5. It stores the compiled macro in the temporary catalog Work.Sasmacr.
6. It calls the macro.

The autocall facility does not search for a macro in the autocall library if the macro has already been compiled during the current SAS session. In that case, the session compiled macro is executed.

Note: To see what SASAUTOS is set to, run the following statements:

```
%put %sysfunc(getoption(sasautos));
%put %sysfunc(pathname(sasautos));
```

Data-Driven Macro Calls

You can create data-driven macro calls using the DOSUBL DATA step function.

A Brief Overview

The DOSUBL function enables the immediate execution of SAS code after a text string is passed. Macro variables that are created or updated during the execution of the submitted code are exported back to the calling environment.

DOSUBL returns a value of 0 if SAS code was able to execute, and returns a nonzero value if SAS code was not able to execute.

DOSUBL should be used in a DATA step. It can also be used with %SYSFUNC outside a step boundary.

The DOSUBL Function

The DOSUBL function imports macro variables from the calling environment, and exports macro variables back to the calling environment.

Syntax, DOSUBL function:

DOSUBL(*text-string*)

text string
    specifies the SAS code to run within the DOSUBL function.

Note: In older macro programs, you might see CALL EXECUTE used in a similar manner to generate macro calls. CALL EXECUTE can encounter timing errors if the DATA step using CALL EXECUTE was itself generated by a macro program. DOSUBL avoids this issue.

Example: Using the DOSUBL Function

Suppose you create a macro called DelayReport that executes a PROC SQL query that joins two tables together.

```
%macro DelayReport(empid);
title "Flight Delays for Employee &Empid";
proc sql;
   select DelayCategory, Count(*) as Count
      from
         certadv.flightdelays d
         inner join
         certadv.flightschedule s
      on s.date=d.date and s.flightnumber=d.flightnumber
      where empid="&Empid"
      group by DelayCategory
   ;
quit;
title;
```

```
%mend;
```

Suppose you want to pull the report for each EmpId in Certadv.FlightCrewNew. Without a data-driven program you would manually call the macro for each EmpId.

```
%Delayreport(1928)
%Delayreport(1407)
%Delayreport(1574)
%Delayreport(1777)
```

Certadv.FlightCrewNew has only four observations, so manually calling the macro is not too tedious. However, if your data set had hundreds of observations, manually calling the macro for each EmpId would be time consuming. Instead, you can create a data-driven program that uses the DOSUBL function to call the DelayReport macro and generate results for each EmpId.

The DOSUBL function uses the value found in EmpID concatenated between '%DelayReport (' and ')' to generate a valid macro call.

```
data _null_;
   set certadv.FlightCrewNew;
   rc=dosubl(cats('%DelayReport(',empid,')'));
run;
```

Output 10.2 Data-Driven Macro Call Result

Flight Delays for Employee 1928

DelayCategory	Count
1-10 Minutes	4
No Delay	3

Flight Delays for Employee 1407

DelayCategory	Count
1-10 Minutes	2
11+ Minutes	3
No Delay	1

Flight Delays for Employee 1574

DelayCategory	Count
1-10 Minutes	4
11+ Minutes	1

Flight Delays for Employee 1777

DelayCategory	Count
1-10 Minutes	3
11+ Minutes	1

Quiz

Select the best answer for each question. After completing the quiz, check your answers using the answer key in the appendix.

1. Which of the following statements about the %INCLUDE statement is correct?

    a. It can be used to insert the contents of an external file into a program.

    b. It causes a macro definition that is stored in an external file to be compiled when the contents of that file are inserted into a program and submitted.

    c. It can be specified with the SOURCE2 option in order to write to the SAS log the contents of the external file that is inserted into a program.

d. All of the above.

2. What happens if you store a macro definition in a SAS catalog SOURCE entry?

    a. The macro definition can be submitted for compilation by using the FILENAME and %INCLUDE statements.

    b. The SOURCE entry will be deleted at the end of the session.

    c. You do not need to compile the macro before you invoke it in a program.

    d. All of the above.

3. Which of the following programs correctly sets the appropriate system options and calls the macro Prtlast? Assume that Prtlast is stored in an autocall library as a text file and that it has not been compiled during the current SAS session.

    a.
    ```
    libname mylib 'c:\mylib';
    filename macsrc 'mylib.macsrc';
    options mautosource sasautos=(macsrc, sasautos);
    %prtlast
    ```

    b.
    ```
    libname mylib 'c:\mylib';
    filename macsrc catalog 'mylib.macsrc';
    %prtlast
    ```

    c.
    ```
    filename mylib 'c:\mylib';
    options mautosource sasautos=(sasautos,mylib);
    %prtlast
    ```

    d.
    ```
    libname mylib 'c:\mylib';
    options mautosource sasautos=mylib;
    %prtlast
    ```

4. When you submit the following code, what happens?

    ```
    %macro prtlast;
        proc print data=&syslast (obs=5);
            title "Listing of &syslast data set";
        run;
    %mend;
    ```

    a. A session compiled macro named Prtlast is stored in Work.Sasmacr.

    b. A macro named Prtlast is stored in the autocall library.

    c. The Prtlast macro is stored as a stored compiled macro.

    d. The Prtlast macro is stored as a SOURCE entry in a permanent SAS catalog.

5. Why would you want to store your macros in external files?

    a. You could easily share your macros with others.

    b. You could edit your macros with any text editor.

    c. Your macros would be available for use in later SAS sessions.

    d. All of the above.

6. Which of the following is not true?

    a. The autocall macro facility stores compiled SAS macros in a collection of external files called an autocall library.

    b. Autocall libraries can be concatenated together.

c. One disadvantage of the autocall facility is that the first time you call an autocall macro in a SAS session, the macro processor must use system resources to compile it.

d. The autocall facility can be used with the stored compiled macro facility.

7. Suppose you had the program below, and you wanted to concatenate the values from the libname and memname columns to create a call to %Report3 for each row of data read. Which option would correctly run the program below and generate a result?

```
data _null_;
   set sashelp.vtable;
   where libname='MC1' and memtype='DATA';
   rc=_____;
run;
```

a. `rc=dosubl(cats('%Report3(',catx(',',libname,memname),')'));`

b. `rc=dosubl(catx(%Report3(',catx(',',libname,memname),')'));`

c. `rc=dosubl(catx(%Report3,',libname,memname),')');`

d. `rc=dosubl(cats(%Report3,',libname,memname),')');`

8. When does the DOSUBL function execute the text string?

a. The function executes the text string during the compilation phase.

b. The function executes the text string immediately.

c. The function does not execute the text string. The text string is stored as a macro.

d. The function executes the text string, but does not return any values.

Part 3

Advanced SAS Programming Techniques

Chapter 11
Defining and Processing Arrays *273*

Chapter 12
Processing Data Using Hash Objects *297*

Chapter 13
Using SAS Utility Procedures *317*

Chapter 14
Using Advanced Functions *337*

Chapter 11
Defining and Processing Arrays

Defining and Referencing One-Dimensional Arrays **273**
    A Brief Overview 273
    ARRAY Statement Syntax 274
    Defining the Number of Elements 275
    Specifying the Array Elements 275
    Using Column Lists as Array Elements 276
    Referencing a One-Dimensional Array 277
    DO Statement Syntax 277
    Example: Processing Repetitive Code 277
    Handling an Unknown Number of Array Elements 278
    Using the DIM Function 278
    Compilation and Execution Phases for Array Processing 279

Expanding Your Use of One-Dimensional Arrays **283**
    Creating Character Columns with an Array 283
    Specifying Lower and Upper Bounds 284
    Assigning Initial Values to Arrays 284
    Example: Assigning Initial Values to Arrays 285
    Specifying Temporary Array Elements 285
    Example: Rotating Data 286

Defining and Referencing Two-Dimensional Arrays **288**
    A Brief Overview 288
    Example: Creating a Two-Dimensional Array with Initial Values 288
    Example: Creating a Two-Dimensional Array to Perform Table Lookup 290

Quiz **293**

Defining and Referencing One-Dimensional Arrays

A Brief Overview

Suppose you have a table that contains patient names and five health indicators for each patient. You want to keep a running total of the count of high values for each patient. You can do this by using five IF-THEN statements or DO-loops. The only syntax that differs in each statement is the name of the health indicator column. However, this creates a program that contains repetitive code and is less efficient. Suppose your data set had fifty health indicators instead of five. With fifty indicators, you would need fifty assignment statements. Instead of writing repetitive code, you can use an array.

A SAS array provides a way to reference a group of columns for processing in the DATA step. By grouping columns into an array, you can process the variables in a DO loop. Each column that is grouped together in an array is referred to as an *element*. You can reference an element in the array by using the *array-name* and a numeric subscript as shown in the figure below.

Figure 11.1   Referencing a One-Dimensional Array

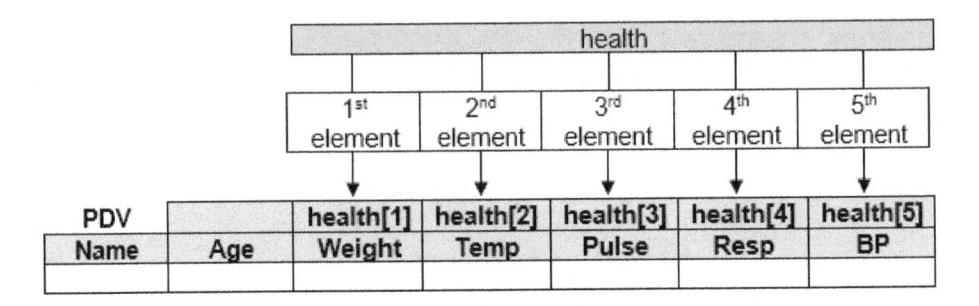

		health[1]	health[2]	health[3]	health[4]	health[5]
PDV		Weight	Temp	Pulse	Resp	BP
Name	Age					

(1st element, 2nd element, 3rd element, 4th element, 5th element — all under "health")

Arrays are often referenced in DO loops because more than one element in an array must be processed. By using fewer statements in your program, the DATA step program can be more easily modified or corrected. The array name distinguishes it from any other arrays in the same DATA step. The array name is not a variable.

Arrays are used when you want to perform the same task on multiple columns. For example, you can use arrays to process repetitive code, rotate data, and perform table lookups. The array is created at compile time, and it is referenced during execution.

ARRAY Statement Syntax

Using arrays is a two-part process. First you define the array with the ARRAY statement. Second, you reference the array specifying the column that is desired. When you are defining the array, the ARRAY statement includes the ARRAY keyword, the array name, and the number of elements, which are also known as *columns*. Typically, you list the variables that make up the array. A semicolon is used at the end of the statement.

Syntax, ARRAY statement:

ARRAY *array-name* [*number-of-elements*] <*array-elements*>;

- *array-name* specifies the name of the array. The name must be a SAS name that is not the name of a SAS variable in the same DATA step.
- *number-of-elements* specifies the number of elements included in the array.
- *array-elements* specifies the variables to be included in the array, which must be either be all numeric or all character.

Note: The number of elements must be enclosed in either parentheses ( ), braces { }, or brackets [ ].

CAUTION:
  Avoid using the name of a SAS function for an array. The array will work, but you will not be able to use the function in the same DATA step, and a note appears in the SAS log.

Defining the Number of Elements

The Certadv.Patdata table contains the patient data with health indicators. Suppose you need to define an array named Health and specify the correct number of elements.

Figure 11.2 Referencing One-Dimensional Array

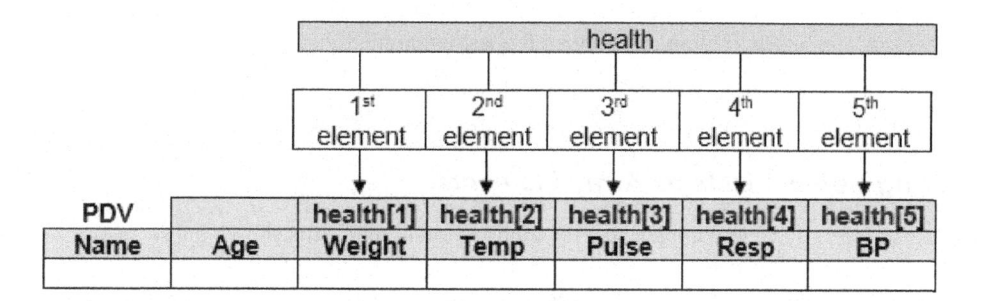

PDV		health[1]	health[2]	health[3]	health[4]	health[5]
Name	Age	Weight	Temp	Pulse	Resp	BP

The following example illustrates a one-dimensional array named Health. It contains five elements. The columns are defined as Weight, Temp, Pulse, Resp, and BP.

```
array health[5] Weight Temp Pulse Resp BP;
```

The number 5 indicates a one-dimensional array with 5 elements and an implied subscript range of 1 to 5. The elements 1 through 5 in the Health array can be referenced by the array name and subscript.

There are several ways to define the number of array elements:

- You can specify a range of values for the array elements when you define an array. In the following example, the lower bound is 2 and upper bound is 4. Explicitly specifying lower and upper bounds is beneficial if you want to start the lower bound at a value other than 1.

    ```
    array health[2:4] Temp Pulse Resp;
    ```

- You can use an asterisk [*] to determine the subscript by counting the variables in the array. When you specify the asterisk, you must include the elements in the ARRAY statement. Using an asterisk enables SAS to determine the size of the array based on the number of elements provided.

    ```
    array health[*] Weight Temp Pulse Resp BP;
    ```

- The array elements can be enclosed in parentheses, braces, or brackets. The following three statements are equivalent:

    ```
    array health(5) Weight Temp Pulse Resp BP;

    array health{5} Weight Temp Pulse Resp BP;

    array health[5] Weight Temp Pulse Resp BP;
    ```

Specifying the Array Elements

Elements in the ARRAY statement are optional unless you are using an asterisk[*] to determine the size of an array. However, if the elements are not specified and they do not exist in the PDV, then variables are created with default names. The default names are created by concatenating the array name that has the subscript.

You can specify the five columns—Weight, Temp, Pulse, Resp, and BP—as your array elements. The array elements can be specified in any order and do not have to be positioned consecutively in the PDV. Weight corresponds with the first element, Temp is the second element, and so on.

```
array health[5] Weight Temp Pulse Resp BP;
```

Array elements can be specified using column lists. The double hyphen specifies that all columns will be ordered as they are in the PDV. Since these columns are located consecutively in the PDV, you can refer to the first column, followed by a double hyphen, and then the last column.

```
array health[5] Weight--BP;
```

Using Column Lists as Array Elements

You can specify column lists in the forms shown below.

Column	Description	Form
Numbered range list	Specifies all columns from x1 to x*n* inclusive. You can begin with any number and end with any number as long as you do not violate the rules for user-supplied column names and the numbers are consecutive.	x1–x*n*
Name range list	Specifies all columns ordered as they are in the program data vector, from x to b, inclusive.	x- - b
	Specifies all numeric columns from x to b, inclusive.	x-numeric-b
	Specifies all character columns from x to b, inclusive.	x-character-b
Name prefix list	Specifies all the columns that begin with REV, such as REVJAN, REVFEB, and REVMAR.	REV:
Special SAS name lists	Specifies all numeric columns that are already defined in the current DATA step.	_NUMERIC_
	Specifies all character columns that are already defined in the current DATA step.	_CHARACTER_
	Specifies all columns that are already defined in the current DATA step. *Note:* Variables must be either all numeric or character.	_ALL_

Referencing a One-Dimensional Array

Once an array has been defined, elements within the array can be referenced. To reference an element, specify the name of the array followed by the number of the desired element. The value of *element-number* is the number of the element desired. The array reference is in the following form:

```
array-name[element-number]
```

An *array reference* enables you to reference a column in a DATA step. For example, if you wanted to reference the third element in the Health array, you would be referencing the Pulse column. The following example references the third element in the Health array.

```
health[3]
```

What gives arrays their power is their ability to reference the elements of an array by subscripts. Typically, arrays are used with DO loops to process multiple variables and to perform repetitive calculations.

DO Statement Syntax

An array is typically referenced within a DO loop. You can use the index column to specify which element to reference. The index column changes for each iteration of the DO loop from a start value to a stop value, which can be the number of array elements.

Syntax, DO statement:

DO *index-column* = 1 **TO** *number-of-elements*;

　...*array-name*[*index-column*]...

- *index-column* is used to reference the element number.
- *number-of-elements* refers to the number of elements included in the array.
- *array-name* specifies the name of the array. The name must be a SAS name that is not the name of a SAS variable in the same DATA step.

Example: Processing Repetitive Code

Suppose you want to keep a running total of the count of high values for each patient. You can use the Health array in your IF-THEN statement within a DO loop.

```
data work.highcount;
   set certadv.patdata;
   array health[5] Weight--BP;
   do i = 1 to 5;
      if health[i]='High' then HighCount+1;
   end;
run;
```

When *i* is equal to 1, SAS looks at the value of the first element, which is the Weight column. When *i* is equal to 2, it looks at the second element, which is the Temp column, and so on. SAS iterates over the DO loop five times to reference the five health indicator columns to calculate the HighCount column.

Output 11.1 *Work.HighCount Data Set*

	Name	Age	Weight	Temp	Pulse	Resp	BP	i	HighCount
1	Luka Poisson	30	High	Normal	High	Normal	High	6	3
2	Grant Farrell	40	Avg	Normal	High	High	Normal	6	5
3	Knight Cross	29	High	Normal	Normal	High	Normal	6	7
4	Rik Hooper	38	Normal	Normal	High	Normal	High	6	9
5	Mae Hagraves	58	Normal	High	High	Normal	High	6	12
6	Lauri Knowles	44	Normal	Normal	High	Normal	High	6	14
7	Geovanni Gallego	37	High	Normal	Normal	High	High	6	17
8	Paolo Vives	25	High	Normal	High	Normal	High	6	20
9	Amargo Leclercq	47	Normal	High	High	Normal	High	6	23
10	Morvyn Merle	24	High	Normal	High	High	Normal	6	26

Handling an Unknown Number of Array Elements

Suppose that you are asked to create a data set where there are a varying number of observations for a variable in the original data set. When you have an unknown number of array elements, use an asterisk (*) within your brackets when defining an array. SAS determines the number of elements by counting the number of columns referenced in the ARRAY statement.

The following example specifies that all columns starting with Ordt will be in the Ordt array, Deldt will be in the Deldt array, and Q will be in the Q array. The colon after the words Ordt, Deldt, and Q specifies that all columns that start with that specific string.

```
array Ordt[*] Ordt:;
array Deldt[*] Deldt:;
array Q[*] Q:;
```

Using the DIM Function

DIM Function Syntax

If the number of array elements is unknown, the DIM function can be used to return the number of elements in the array. When using DO loops to process arrays, you can also use the DIM function to specify the value for the TO clause of the iterative DO statement. For an array, specify the array name as the argument for the DIM function.

Syntax, DIM function:

DIM(*array-name*)

- *array-name* specifies the name of the array.

Example: Using the DIM Function in an Iterative DO Statement

When you specify the array name as the single argument for the DIM function, the function returns the number of elements in the array.

```
data work.sysbp2 (drop=i);
   set work.sysbp;
   array sbparray[*] sbp:;
   do i=1 to dim(sbparray);
      if sbparray[i]=999 then sbparray[i]=.;
   end;
```

Compilation and Execution Phases for Array Processing

Suppose you have survey data Certadv.Salary from Silicon Valley. The data set contains four salary variables identifying the four different people who took the survey at one time. You are asked to create a running total of the number of people whose salaries are less than or equal to the average salary of 51,000.

Compilation Phase

The following program is submitted.

```
data work.survsalary (drop=i);
   set certadv.salary;
   array BelowAvgS[4] Salary1-Salary4;
   do i=1 to 4;
      if BelowAvgS[i] <=51000 then BelowAvg+1;
   end;
run;
```

During the compilation phase, the PDV is created. The ARRAY statement is a compile-time statement only. At compile time, SAS reads the ARRAY statement and associates the four salary variables, Salary1 through Salary4, with the BelowAvgS array. The variables Salary1 through Salary4 are already in the PDV because they are existing variables in the input file being read by the SET statement, Certadv.Salary. If the variables were not already in the PDV, then SAS would add the variables to the PDV as new variables.

Program Data Vector

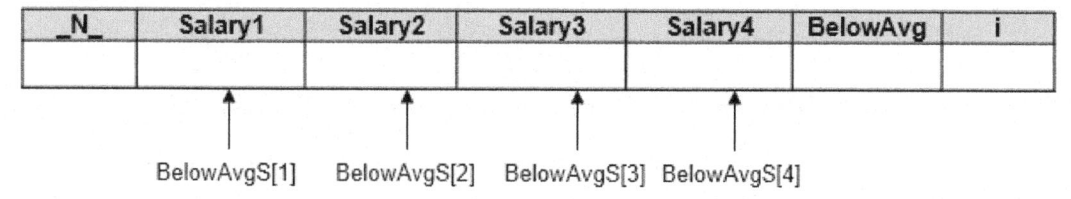

_N_	Salary1	Salary2	Salary3	Salary4	BelowAvg	i

        BelowAvgS[1]   BelowAvgS[2] BelowAvgS[3] BelowAvgS[4]

The array name BelowAvgS and array references are not included in the PDV. Syntax errors in the ARRAY statement are detected during the compilation phase.

Note: The array name is not included in the PDV because it is not a variable. It is a name that is used to reference a collection of variables. The array exists only for the duration of the DATA step.

Execution Phase

1. At the beginning of the execution phase, _N_ is set to 1 in the PDV. BelowAge is initialized to 0 because it is created using the SUM statement.

```
data work.survsalary (drop=i);
   set certadv.salary;
   array BelowAvgS[4] Salary1-Salary4;
   do i=1 to 4;
      if BelowAvgS[i] <=51000 then BelowAvg+1;
   end;
run;
```

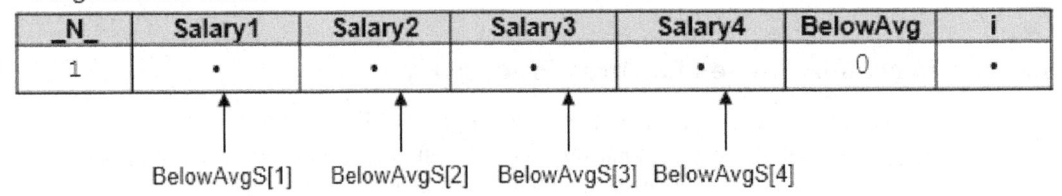

Program Data Vector

_N_	Salary1	Salary2	Salary3	Salary4	BelowAvg	i
1	.	.	.	.	0	.

   ↑   ↑   ↑   ↑

BelowAvgS[1] BelowAvgS[2] BelowAvgS[3] BelowAvgS[4]

The remaining variables are set to missing.

2. The SET statement copies the first observation from Certadv.Salary to the PDV.

   ```
   data work.survsalary (drop=i);
      set certadv.salary;
      array BelowAvgS[4] Salary1-Salary4;
      do i=1 to 4;
         if BelowAvgS[i] <=51000 then BelowAvg+1;
      end;
   run;
   ```

Program Data Vector

_N_	Salary1	Salary2	Salary3	Salary4	BelowAvg	i
1	$110,664	$98,011	$154,767	$144,845	0	.

   ↑   ↑   ↑   ↑

BelowAvgS[1] BelowAvgS[2] BelowAvgS[3] BelowAvgS[4]

3. The ARRAY statement is a compile-time statement. Therefore, it is ignored in the execution phase.

   ```
   data work.survsalary (drop=i);
      set certadv.salary;
      array BelowAvgS[4] Salary1-Salary4;
      do i=1 to 4;
         if BelowAvgS[i] <=51000 then BelowAvg+1;
      end;
   run;
   ```

4. In the first iteration of the DO loop, the index variable *i* is to set to 1.

   ```
   data work.survsalary (drop=i);
      set certadv.salary;
      array BelowAvgS[4] Salary1-Salary4;
      do i=1 to 4;
         if BelowAvgS[i] <=51000 then BelowAvg+1;
      end;
   run;
   ```

Program Data Vector

_N_	Salary1	Salary2	Salary3	Salary4	BelowAvg	i
1	$110,664	$98,011	$154,767	$144,845	0	1

BelowAvgS[1]   BelowAvgS[2]   BelowAvgS[3]   BelowAvgS[4]

Work.SurvSalary

	Salary1	Salary2	Salary3	Salary4	BelowAvg
1	$110,664	$98,011	$154,767	$144,845	0

The array reference BelowAvgS[i] becomes BelowAvgS[1]. BelowAvgS[1] refers to the first array element, Salary1. Since Salary1 through Salary4 are higher than 51,000, the BelowAvg column does not update its count to 1. Since all Salary values for this observation are above 51,000, the BelowAvg column remains 0.

```
data work.survsalary (drop=i);
   set certadv.salary;
   array BelowAvgS[4] Salary1-Salary4;
   do i=1 to 4;
      if BelowAvgS[i] <=51000 then BelowAvg+1;
   end;
run;
```

SAS reaches the end of the DO loop. SAS reaches the end of the first iteration of the DATA step, and the implicit OUTPUT statement writes the contents from the PDV to the data set Work.SurvSalary. SAS returns to the beginning of the DATA step.

5. At the beginning of the second iteration, _N_ increments to 2, and the variables Salary1 through Salary4 retain their values because they are being read from an existing SAS data set. BelowAvg remains 0 because its value is automatically retained.

Program Data Vector

_N_	Salary1	Salary2	Salary3	Salary4	BelowAvg	i
2	$110,664	$98,011	$154,767	$144,845	0	.

BelowAvgS[1]   BelowAvgS[2]   BelowAvgS[3]   BelowAvgS[4]

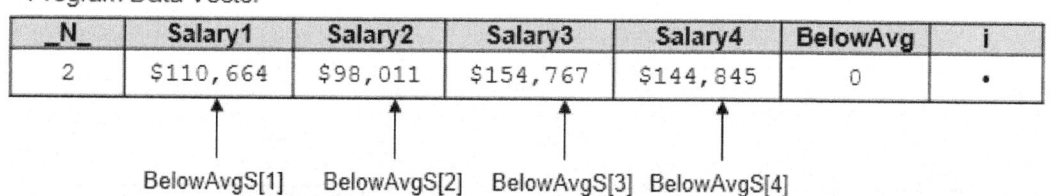

6. The SET statement reads the second observation from Certadv.Salary into the PDV.

```
data work.survsalary (drop=i);
   set certadv.salary;
   array BelowAvgS[4] Salary1-Salary4;
   do i=1 to 4;
      if BelowAvgS[i] <=51000 then BelowAvg+1;
   end;
run;
```

Program Data Vector

_N_	Salary1	Salary2	Salary3	Salary4	BelowAvg	i
2	$140,662	$155,235	$148,867	$46,229	0	.

BelowAvgS[1]   BelowAvgS[2]   BelowAvgS[3]   BelowAvgS[4]

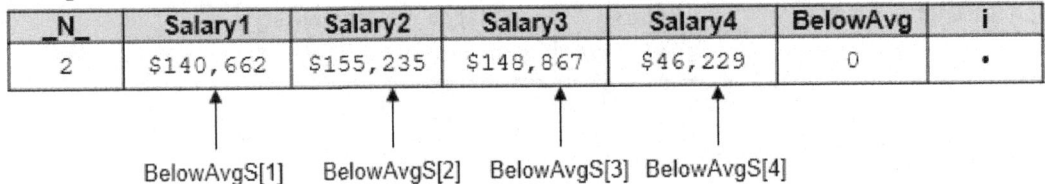

7. On the first iteration of the DO loop, the index variable *i* is set to 1. The array reference BelowAvgS[*i*] becomes BelowAvgS[1]. BelowAvgS[1] refers to the first array element, Salary1. Since Salary1 is not less than or equal to 51,000, the BelowAvg column remains 0.

```
data work.survsalary (drop=i);
   set certadv.salary;
   array BelowAvgS[4] Salary1-Salary4;
   do i=1 to 4;
      if BelowAvgS[i] <=51000 then BelowAvg+1;
   end;
run;
```

Program Data Vector

_N_	Salary1	Salary2	Salary3	Salary4	BelowAvg	i
2	$140,662	$155,235	$148,867	$46,229	0	1

BelowAvgS[1]   BelowAvgS[2]   BelowAvgS[3]   BelowAvgS[4]

8. The DO loop iterates through to the fourth iteration when the index variable *i* is set to 4. The array reference BelowAvgS[4] refers to the fourth array element, Salary4. Because Salary4 is less than 51,000, the BelowAvg column increments to 1.

```
data work.survsalary (drop=i);
   set certadv.salary;
   array BelowAvgS[4] Salary1-Salary4;
   do i=1 to 4;
      if BelowAvgS[i] <=51000 then BelowAvg+1;
   end;
run;
```

Program Data Vector

_N_	Salary1	Salary2	Salary3	Salary4	BelowAvg	i
2	$140,662	$155,235	$148,867	$46,229	1	4

BelowAvgS[1]   BelowAvgS[2]   BelowAvgS[3]   BelowAvgS[4]

Work.SurvSalary

	Salary1	Salary2	Salary3	Salary4	BelowAvg
1	$110,664	$98,011	$154,767	$144,845	0
2	$140,662	$155,235	$148,867	$46,229	1

Expanding Your Use of One-Dimensional Arrays 283

SAS reaches the end of the second iteration of the DATA step and the implicit OUTPUT statement writes the contents from the PDV to the data set Work.SurvSalary. SAS returns to the beginning of the DATA step.

The rest of the iterations of the DATA step are processed the same as above.

Graphical Displaying of Array Processing

As the DATA step continues processing, new observations are loaded into the PDV. The DO loop iterates over the four salary variables for each observation, checking to see whether any of those values are below $51,000. When a value below $51,000 is encountered, the BelowAvg variable is incremented by 1.

```
data work.survsalary (drop=i);
   set certadv.salary;
   array BelowAvgS[4] Salary1-Salary4;
   do i=1 to 4;
      if BelowAvgS[i] <=51000 then BelowAvg+1;
   end;
run;
```

Output 11.2 PROC PRINT Output of Work.SurvSalary

Obs	Salary1	Salary2	Salary3	Salary4	BelowAvg
1	$110,664	$98,011	$154,767	$144,845	0
2	$140,662	$155,235	$148,867	$46,229	1
3	$114,546	$102,034	$67,834	$75,416	1
4	$53,177	$167,071	$33,134	$174,879	2
5	$30,344	$57,672	$162,500	$43,597	4
6	$141,042	$148,845	$52,136	$46,566	5
7	$147,819	$58,913	$142,018	$158,280	5
8	$60,733	$131,744	$130,969	$141,397	5
9	$199,755	$85,736	$86,241	$140,417	5
10	$40,970	$35,107	$156,646	$125,516	7

... *more observations* ...

46	$139,043	$191,888	$131,246	$75,587	22
47	$111,887	$47,380	$97,918	$35,496	24
48	$72,914	$61,107	$136,612	$97,772	24
49	$85,520	$169,144	$174,758	$75,950	24

Expanding Your Use of One-Dimensional Arrays

Creating Character Columns with an Array

Suppose you need to create an array named States with 50 character columns.

By default, array columns are created as numeric and with the length of each column as 8. For character columns, you can specify a length other than 8 following the dollar sign ($).

The following example creates the States array with 50 character elements named State1-State50, each with a length of 12.

```
array States[50] $12 State1-State50;
```

If you do not specify a length, the default length of 8 is assigned to State1-State50.

```
array States[50] $ State1-State50;
```

Specifying Lower and Upper Bounds

When you specify an array with an asterisk (*), by default, the lower bound is 1, and the upper bound is the number of elements in the array. For example, both the following ARRAY statements have a lower bound of 1 and an upper bound of 6. The first element is referred to as element 1, and the second element as 2, and so on.

```
array years[6] yr2011-yr2016;
array years[*] yr2011-yr2016;
```

However, for some DATA step code it might be more efficient if the element number is referenced by another value. For example, it might be useful to reference the following element **yr2011** as element 2011, the second as 2012, and so on. To do so, you can specify the lower and upper bounds using a colon between the two values.

```
array years[2011:2016] yr2011-yr2016;
do i=2011 to 2016;
```

When lower and upper bounds are specified, but the names of the variables are omitted, SAS does not create variable names with the bound values as the suffix. The following example creates the variables Years1, Years2, and so on, with the array. It does not create the variables Years2011, Years2012, and so on.

```
array years[2011:2016];
```

Assigning Initial Values to Arrays

It can be useful to assign initial values to elements of an array when you define the array.

```
array goal[4] g1 g2 g3 g4 (initial values);
```

To assign initial values in an ARRAY statement:

1. Place the values after the array elements.
2. Specify one initial value for each corresponding array element.
3. Separate each value with a comma or blank.
4. Enclose the initial values in parentheses.
5. Enclose each character value in quotation marks.

It is also possible to assign initial values to an array without specifying each array element. The following statement creates the variables Var1, Var2, Var3, and Var4, and assigns them initial values of 1, 2, 3, and 4:

```
array Var[4] (1 2 3 4);
```

Example: Assigning Initial Values to Arrays

Suppose you want to compare the actual sales figures in the Certadv.Qsales data set to the sales goals for each sales representative at the beginning of the year. The sales goals are not recorded in Certadv.Qsales.

```
data work.report (drop=i);                        /* 1 */
   set certadv.qsales;
   array sale[4] sales1-sales4;                   /* 2 */
   array Goal[4] (9000 9300 9600 9900);           /* 3 */
   array Achieved[4];                             /* 4 */
   do i=1 to 4;                                   /* 5 */
      achieved[i]=100*sale[i]/goal[i];
   end;
run;
proc print data=work.report noobs;
run;
```

1. The DATA step reads the Certadv.Qsales data set to create the Work.Report data set. You can drop the index variable from the new data set by adding a DROP= option to the DATA statement.

2. The first ARRAY statement creates an array, Sale. The four sales variables, Sales1 through Sales4, are being read from the input table Certadv.Qsales.

3. The second ARRAY statement creates the array, Goal, along with four variables Goal1 through Goal4, to provide the Sales goals for each quarter. The Goal array is assigned initial values of 9000, 9300, 9600, and 9900.

4. The third ARRAY statement creates the variables Achieved1 through Achieved4 to store the comparison of actual sales versus sales goals.

5. A DO loop executes four times to calculate the value of each element of the Achieved array (expressed as a percentage).

The output data set shows the variables that were read from Certadv.Qsales and the eight variables that were created with ARRAY statements.

Figure 11.3 PROC PRINT Results of SAS Data Work.Report

SalesRep	Sales1	Sales2	Sales3	Sales4	Goal1	Goal2	Goal3	Goal4	Achieved1	Achieved2	Achieved3	Achieved4
Britt	8400	8800	9300	9800	9000	9300	9600	9900	93.333	94.624	96.875	98.990
Fruchten	9500	9300	9800	8900	9000	9300	9600	9900	105.556	100.000	102.083	89.899
Goodyear	9150	9200	9650	11000	9000	9300	9600	9900	101.667	98.925	100.521	111.111

Note: Variables to which initial values are assigned in an ARRAY statement are automatically retained.

Specifying Temporary Array Elements

Suppose you need to create an array with initial values. However, you know that you do not need to keep the values in the final table. You can specify the _TEMPORARY_ keyword in place of the array elements.

Temporary data elements do not have column names and can be referenced with the array reference. The temporary data elements do not appear in the output table and are also automatically retained. When you use the word _TEMPORARY_ there is no need to use a DROP statement to eliminate the unneeded columns in the final table.

When defining a temporary array, you must explicitly specify the number of elements within the array using a constant value within the array brackets. You cannot use an asterisk (*).

```
array salesquota[5] _temporary_;
```

Temporary arrays can either be numeric or character. You can create a temporary character array by including the dollar sign ($) after the array brackets.

```
array Names[20] $ _temporary_;
```

Temporary array elements are retained automatically between the iterations of the DATA step. You do not need to use the RETAIN statement. Temporary values within the array elements are never written to the output data set.

When referencing elements of a temporary array, use the array name and the number of elements (for example, SalesQuota[1] or Names[1]). Since there are no variables associated with the array, a reference to the columns SalesQuota1 or Names1 would not refer to the first element of the array.

Example: Rotating Data

Suppose you have the Certadv.QtrSales data set, which contains 25 rows of data. It contains sales data for the past five years for five different countries. For each country and year there are corresponding SalesQ columns. However, you are asked to create a new data set with the quarter sales values in one column.

Figure 11.4 *Original Data versus Desired Output*

Certadv.QtrSales

Obs	Country	Year	SalesQ1	SalesQ2	SalesQ3	SalesQ4
1	United States	2014	237865.86	366939.54	423585.04	475681.25
2	United States	2015	285906.41	177346.51	242372.76	252514.29
3	United States	2016	100795.73	229364.58	158368.65	465188.32
4	United States	2017	120795.73	158368.65	191173.86	117554.75
5	United States	2018	147361.33	248934.40	177593.31	227396.62

...more observations...

⇩

Desired Output

Obs	Country	Year	Quarter	Sales
1	United States	2014	1	237865.86
2	United States	2014	2	366939.54
3	United States	2014	3	423585.04
4	United States	2014	4	475681.25

...more observations...

To rotate the data, use an array pointing to the four quarterly sales variables. Then use a DO loop to assign the appropriate quarter value to the new Sales column.

```
data work.yrsales;
   set certadv.qtrsales;
   array Yr[4] SalesQ1-SalesQ4;
   do Quarter=1 to 4;
      Sales=Yr[Quarter];
      output;
   end;
run;
```

Your output data contains the following variables: Country, Year, SalesQ1, SalesQ2, SalesQ3, SalesQ4, Quarter, and Sales. To limit the number of variables displayed in the output, use the VAR statement with PROC PRINT to display only Country, Year, Quarter, and Sales.

```
proc print data=work.yrsales;
   var Country Year Quarter Sales;
run;
```

The output data set contains 100 observations.

Output 11.3   PROC PRINT of Work.YrSales (partial output)

Obs	Country	Year	Quarter	Sales
1	United States	2014	1	237865.86
2	United States	2014	2	366939.54
3	United States	2014	3	423585.04
4	United States	2014	4	475681.25
5	United States	2015	1	285906.41

... more observations ...

97	Saudi Arabia	2018	1	136508.93
98	Saudi Arabia	2018	2	116172.14
99	Saudi Arabia	2018	3	137075.27
100	Saudi Arabia	2018	4	156682.59

Defining and Referencing Two-Dimensional Arrays

A Brief Overview

Multidimensional arrays can also be created.

With a two-dimensional array, two numbers separated by a comma are used to specify the array size. Think of a two-dimensional array as consisting of rows and columns. The first number corresponds to a row, and the second number corresponds to a column. However, in the PDV, the values are still just specified as columns. A two-dimensional array is useful because you can take data from a table and load it into an array. The following figure is an example of a two-dimensional array. The array has two rows and two columns.

Figure 11.5   Two-Dimensional Array

Month	Year	
	2017	2018
1	1,1	1,2
2	2,1	2,2

Example: Creating a Two-Dimensional Array with Initial Values

Suppose you have the Certadv.StCoup data set, which contains unique data about a store's most recent customer order. You are asked to create a coupon value for each of the store's customers. Customers will receive coupons ranging from 10% to 40% off their next purchase based on the type and size of their last order.

Figure 11.6 Creating a Two-Dimensional Array

Certadv.Stcoup Data Set

CustomerID	OrderDate	DeliveryDate	OrderID	OrderType	ProductID	Quantity	TotalRetailPrice	CostPricePerUnit
4	09MAR2008	09MAR2008	1232455720	1	240600100017	1	$53.00	$23.25
5	30OCT2007	30OCT2007	1231663230	1	240100100433	1	$3.00	$1.15
9	15APR2008	20APR2008	1232698281	3	230100600035	1	$29.40	$14.15
10	09JUN2009	09JUN2009	1236055696	1	240800100041	1	$292.50	$121.75
11	29OCT2007	03NOV2007	1231653765	3	230100200047	1	$72.70	$35.20

⇩

Coupons for October 2019

Obs	CustomerID	OrderType	Quantity	CouponValue
1	4	1	1	10%
2	5	1	1	10%
3	9	3	1	20%
4	10	1	1	10%
5	11	3	1	20%

The ARRAY statement creates a two-dimensional array containing coupon values. The array named CpnValue has three rows and four columns. The initial values are a range from 0.10 to 0.40. Once this array is defined, you can refer to any of the columns by using array referencing.

Figure 11.7 Two-Dimensional Array with Initial Values

Order Type	Quantity (Previously Ordered)			
	1	2	3	4
1	.10	.15	.20	.25
2	.30	.40	.10	.15
3	.20	.25	.15	.10

```
array cpnval[3,4]  _temporary_ (.10, .15, .20, .25,
                                .30, .40, .10, .15,
                                .20, .25, .15, .10);
```

However, this example references the initial value columns by using OrderType as the row and Quantity as the column. If OrderType=1 and Quantity=1, then CouponValue=.10. If OrderType=3 and Quantity=1, then CouponValue=0.20, and so on.

```
data work.customercoupons;
    array cpnvalue[3,4] _temporary_ (.10, .15, .20, .25,
                                     .30, .40, .10, .15,
```

```
                                              .20, .25, .15, .10);
    set certadv.stcoup (keep=CustomerID OrderType Quantity);
    CouponValue=cpnvalue[OrderType,Quantity];
    format CouponValue percent10.;
run;
title 'Coupons for October 2019';
proc print data=work.customercoupons;
run;
```

Output 11.4 Partial Output of Work.CustomerCoupons

Coupons for October 2019

Obs	CustomerID	OrderType	Quantity	CouponValue
1	4	1	1	10%
2	5	1	1	10%
3	9	3	1	20%
4	10	1	1	10%
5	11	3	1	20%
6	12	1	3	20%
7	13	2	1	15%
8	16	2	2	20%
9	17	1	1	10%
10	18	1	2	15%

... *more observations* ...

Example: Creating a Two-Dimensional Array to Perform Table Lookup

Suppose you are asked to combine two SAS data sets, Certadv.US_Goals and Certadv.US_Sales, and find the difference between the quarterly sales amount and the quarterly goal.

Figure 11.8 Performing Table Lookup Using an Array (Illustration)

Certadv.US_Goals Data Set

Year	QtrNum	Goal
2014	1	$150,000.00
2014	2	$155,000.00
2014	3	$160,000.00
2014	4	$165,000.00
2015	1	$155,000.00

...more observations...

Certadv.US_Sales Data Set

Year	SalesQ1	SalesQ2	SalesQ3	SalesQ4
2014	$167,865.86	$156,939.54	$153,585.04	$160,681.25
2015	$165,906.41	$170,346.51	$172,372.76	$172,514.29
2016	$160,795.73	$169,364.58	$168,368.65	$175,188.32
2017	$160,795.73	$168,368.65	$171,173.86	$177,554.75
2018	$167,361.33	$168,934.40	$177,593.31	$184,396.62

Work.DiffSales Output Data Set

Obs	Year	QtrNum	Goal	Sales	Difference
1	2014	1	$150,000.00	$167,865.86	$17,865.86
2	2014	2	$155,000.00	$156,939.54	$1,939.54
3	2014	3	$160,000.00	$153,585.04	$-6,414.96
4	2014	4	$165,000.00	$160,681.25	$-4,318.75
5	2015	1	$155,000.00	$165,906.41	$10,906.41
6	2015	2	$160,000.00	$170,346.51	$10,346.51
7	2015	3	$165,000.00	$172,372.76	$7,372.76
8	2015	4	$170,000.00	$172,514.29	$2,514.29

...more observations...

You could use a DATA step with MERGE statement. However, that solution takes several steps because the two data sets are not laid out with a common column. You would need to use the TRANSPOSE procedure to rotate the Certadv.US_Goals data set, sort the data, and then merge the data sets. Instead, you can use a two-dimensional array in a single DATA step to accomplish the same task. The two-dimensional array solution is more efficient and requires less coding.

```
data work.diffsales;
   array yrsales[2014:2018,4] _temporary_;      /* 1 */
   if _N_=1 then do Yr=2014 to 2018;            /* 2 */
      set certadv.us_sales;                     /* 3 */
      array qtrsal[4] SalesQ1-SalesQ4;          /* 4 */
      do Qtr=1 to 4;                            /* 5 */
         yrsales[Yr,Qtr]=qtrsal[Qtr];
      end;
   end;
   set certadv.us_goals;                        /* 6 */
   Sales=yrsales[Year,QtrNum];                  /* 7 */
   Difference=Sales-Goal;                       /* 8 */
   drop Yr Qtr SalesQ1-SalesQ4;                 /* 9 */
```

```
run;
proc print data=work.diffsales;
   format Goal Sales Difference dollar14.2;
run;
```

1. The ARRAY statement defines a two-dimensional array named YrSales. The YrSales array contains five rows starting with 2014 and ending with 2018, and four columns that correspond to quarterly sales values. There are 20 elements in the YrSales array. Since the array is temporary, the elements do not appear in the output table.

2. The IF-THEN statement loads the YrSales array only the first time through the DATA step. The DO statement loops through enough times to read in every row of input data.

3. The SET statement reads in the four quarterly values from Certadv.US_Sales into the PDV.

4. The ARRAY statement defines a one-dimensional array named QtrSal with four elements, SalesQ1–SalesQ4.

    Note: The result is two ARRAY statements. The first one contains 20 values, and the second one is used to read in the quarterly sales values from the input table.

5. The DO loop reads in the four quarterly sales values for each year, loading the YrSales array.

6. The SET statement reads in the values from Certadv.US_Goals.

7. A new variable named Sales is created and assigns the YrSales array to the variable. The Sales variable looks up the Sales value based on the values of Year and QtrNum.

8. A new variable named Difference is created. The difference between the variable Sales and Goal is calculated to determine whether the sales team met their goals each quarter for the past five years.

9. The DROP statement is used to drop the index variables and any other nonessential variable.

Output 11.5   PROC PRINT Output of Work.DiffSales

Obs	Year	QtrNum	Goal	Sales	Difference
1	2014	1	$150,000.00	$167,865.86	$17,865.86
2	2014	2	$155,000.00	$156,939.54	$1,939.54
3	2014	3	$160,000.00	$153,585.04	$-6,414.96
4	2014	4	$165,000.00	$160,681.25	$-4,318.75
5	2015	1	$155,000.00	$165,906.41	$10,906.41
6	2015	2	$160,000.00	$170,346.51	$10,346.51
7	2015	3	$165,000.00	$172,372.76	$7,372.76
8	2015	4	$170,000.00	$172,514.29	$2,514.29
9	2016	1	$160,000.00	$160,795.73	$795.73
10	2016	2	$165,000.00	$169,364.58	$4,364.58
11	2016	3	$170,000.00	$168,368.65	$-1,631.35
12	2016	4	$180,000.00	$175,188.32	$-4,811.68
13	2017	1	$160,000.00	$160,795.73	$795.73
14	2017	2	$165,000.00	$168,368.65	$3,368.65
15	2017	3	$170,000.00	$171,173.86	$1,173.86
16	2017	4	$180,000.00	$177,554.75	$-2,445.25
17	2018	1	$165,000.00	$167,361.33	$2,361.33
18	2018	2	$170,000.00	$168,934.40	$-1,065.60
19	2018	3	$175,000.00	$177,593.31	$2,593.31
20	2018	4	$180,000.00	$184,396.62	$4,396.62

Quiz

Select the best answer for each question. After completing the quiz, check your answers using the answer key in the appendix.

1. Which statement is false regarding an ARRAY statement?

   a. It is an executable statement.

   b. It can be used to create variables.

   c. It must contain either all numeric or all character elements.

   d. It must be used to define an array before the array name can be referenced.

2. Which statement contains the incorrect syntax for a one-dimensional array?

   a.   `array coupon[3] (.10, .20, .25);`

   b.   `array year[2014:2018) Year2014-Year2018;`

   c.   `array student[4] Student1-Student4;`

   d.   `array student[4] _temporary_ $16`

('Anna Johnson', 'Ramesh Pinto', 'Ela Minsur', 'David Michaelsen');

3. For the program below, select an iterative DO statement to process all elements in the Contrib array.

```
data work.contrib;
    array contrib[4] qtr1-qtr4;
    ...
        contrib[i]=contrib[i]*1.25;
    end;
run;
```

   a. `do i=4;`

   b. `do i=1 to 4;`

   c. `do until i=4;`

   d. `do while i le 4;`

4. Complete the ARRAY statement to create temporary array elements that have the following initial values: 100, 85, 70, and 60.

```
array quizscore[4] _____;
```

   a. `temporary (100 85 70 60)`

   b. `_temporary_ 100 85 70 60`

   c. `(temporary) 100, 85, 70, 60`

   d. `_temporary_ (100, 85, 70, 60)`

5. What is the value of `diff[i]` at the end of the second iteration of the DO loop for the first iteration of the DATA step?

Weight1	Weight2	Weight3	Weight4	Weight5	Weight6	Weight7	Weight8	Weight9	Weight10
192	200	215	145	172	168	188	190	201	245
137	130	125	165	170	164	181	188	204	234
220	120	213	160	167	167	184	170	192	225

```
array wt[*] weight1-weight10;
array diff[9];
do i=1 to 9;
    diff[i]=wt[i+1]-wt[i];
end;
```

   a. 15

   b. 10

   c. 8

   d. -7

6. Which ARRAY statement correctly loads the following values into the array DataSurv?

3	3	2	1
4	4	2	4
5	4	1	2

a.   array datasurv [3,4] (3, 3, 2, 1,
                                      4, 4, 2, 4,
                                      5, 4, 1, 2);

b.   array datasurv [3:4] (3, 3, 2, 1,
                                      4, 4, 2, 4,
                                      5, 4, 1, 2);

c.   array datasurv [4,2] (3, 3, 2, 1,
                                      4, 4, 2, 4,
                                      5, 4, 1, 2);

d.   array datasurv [4:2] (3, 3, 2, 1,
                                            4, 4, 2, 4,
                                          5, 4, 1, 2);

7. Which DO statement processes all of the elements in the Yearx array?

   ```
   array Yearx[12] Jan--Dec;
   ```

   a. `do i=1 to dim(yearx);`

   b. `do i=1 to 12;`

   c. `do i=Jan to Dec;`

   d. a and b only.

8. Given the following program, which statement is not true?

   ```
   data work.lookup1;
      array Targets[2016:2018,12] _temporary_;
      if _n_=1 then do i=1 to 3;
         set certadv.ctargets;
         array mnth[*] Jan--Dec;
         do j=1 to dim(mnth);
            targets[year,j]=mnth[j];
         end;
      end;
      set certadv.monthsum(keep=salemon revcargo monthno);
      year=input(substr(salemon,4),4.);
      Ctarget=targets[year,monthno];
   run;
   ```

   a. The IF-THEN statement specifies that the Targets array is loaded once.

   b. During the first iteration of the DATA step, the outer DO loop executes three times.

   c. After the first iteration of the DO loop, the pointer drops down to the second SET statement.

   d. During the second iteration of the DATA step, the condition _N_=1 is false. So, the DO loop does not execute.

Chapter 12
Processing Data Using Hash Objects

Declaring Hash Objects **297**
    A Brief Overview 297
    Key Components 298
    Data Components 299
    Declaring a Hash Object 299
    Hash Object Process 300

Defining Hash Objects **300**
    Hash Object Methods 300
    Defining a Hash Object 301
    Example: Defining a Hash Object 301

Finding Key Values in a Hash Object **302**
    The FIND Method 302
    Retrieving Matching Data 303

Writing a Hash Object to a Table **304**
    The ADD Method 304
    Example: Adding Key and Data Values 305
    The OUTPUT Method 305
    Controlling Output with the OUTPUT Method 305
    Avoiding Messages in the SAS Log 306

Hash Object Processing **306**

Using Hash Iterator Objects **311**
    What Is a Hash Iterator Object? 311
    Declaring and Defining a Hash Object and a Hash Iterator Object 312
    Retrieving Hash Object Data with the Hash Iterator Object 312
    Example: Using the Hash Iterator Object 313

Quiz **314**

Declaring Hash Objects

A Brief Overview

Hash objects are helpful when performing table lookups. A *hash object* is an in-memory table that contains key and data components. In the following example, the hash object contains two key columns, col_A and col_B, and three data columns, col_C, col_D, and col_E.

Figure 12.1 Hash Object with Key and Data Components

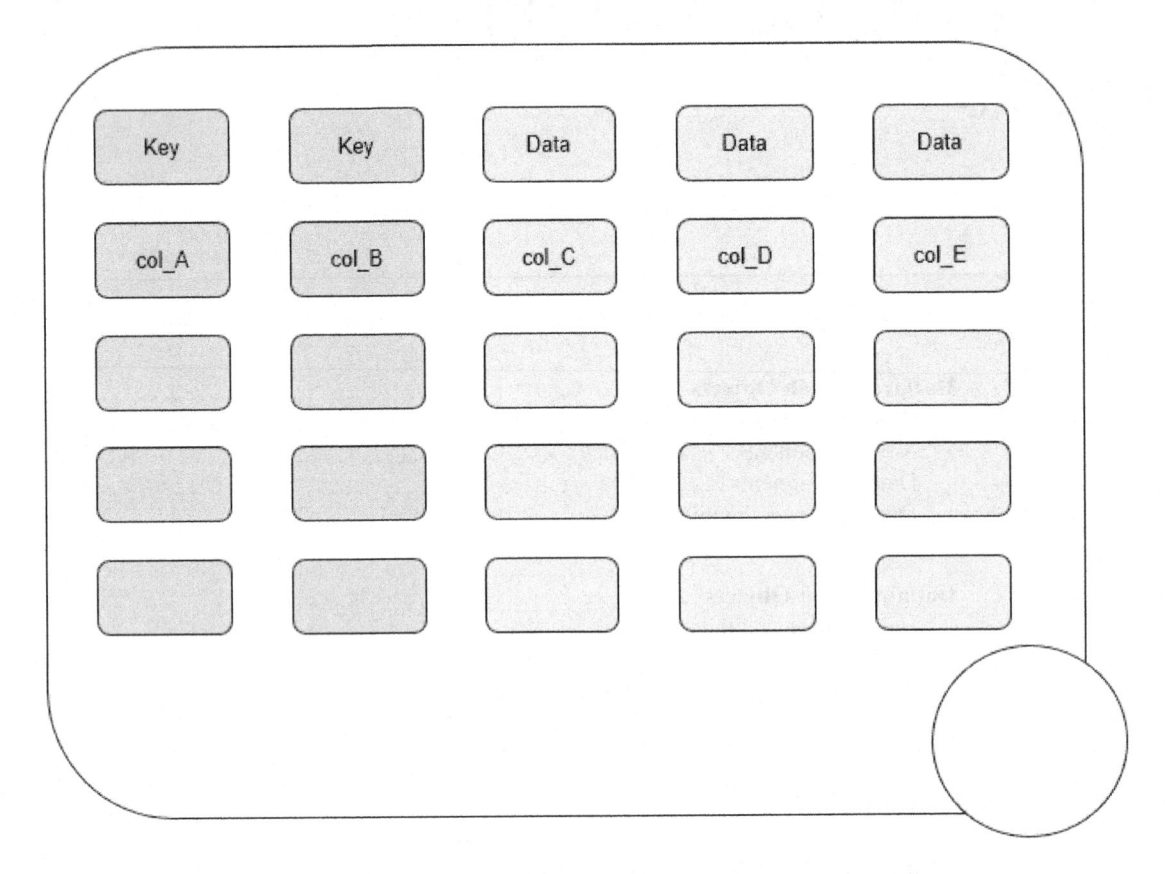

Key	Key	Data	Data	Data
col_A	col_B	col_C	col_D	col_E

You can quickly and efficiently store, search, and retrieve data based on the key components. When the key component values are found, the data values are copied to the program data vector (PDV).

The use of hash objects is specific to the DATA step. A hash object is available only to the DATA step that creates it. When the DATA step is over, the hash object is deleted. Whereas an array is defined at compile time, a hash object is defined at execution. This makes the size of a hash object dynamic, and that means that the object can expand and shrink as data is added or deleted.

A hash object resembles a table with rows and columns and contains key and data components.

Key Components

- Key components can consist of one or more key columns.
- Key components can be numeric, character, or both.
- Key components must be defined as PDV columns, and your hash object does not have to be sorted by the keys.
- Be default, each row of keys must be unique.

Data Components

- You can have multiple data components per each row of key components.
- Data components can be numeric, character, or both.
- Data components must be defined as PDV columns.

Declaring a Hash Object

The DECLARE statement creates an instance of data, and initializes data for an object. Use the DECLARE statement to name your hash object and specify information such as the name of the table that should be used to load the hash object.

Syntax, DECLARE statement:

DECLARE *object object-name(<argument_tag-1:value-1, ...>)*;

object
  specifies the component object. An object can be one of the following values:

  hash
    indicates a hash object.

  hiter
    indicates a hash iterator object.

object-name
  specifies the name of the hash object.

argument_tag-1
  specifies the information that is used to create an instance of the component object.

  DATASET: '*data-set-name <(data-set-option)>*'

value
  specifies the value for an argument tag. Valid values depend on the component object.

In the following example, you are creating a hash object named States. The example does not contain any arguments or tag values. The parentheses are still required.

```
declare hash States();
```

In the following example, you are reading the data for the hash object from a table. In the example, the DATASET argument loads the Work.Population_USStates table into the hash object. After the argument DATASET, place a colon and then the value of the argument. If you specify a literal value for the table, enclose the value in single or double quotation marks. Within those quotation marks and after the table name, specify data set options such as WHERE=, DROP=, KEEP=, RENAME=, or OBS=.

```
declare hash States(dataset:'work.population_usstates
                 (where=(StatePop2017>20000000))');
```

If you have duplicate key values, use the MULTIDATA argument in the DECLARE statement. If you want to allow duplicate key components, then set MULTIDATA to 'YES'. The default value is 'NO'.

```
declare hash ContName(MULTIDATA:'YES');
```

Hash Object Process

Besides declaring the hash object, you must also provide key and data components by using the three DEFINE methods. Once the hash object is declared and defined, the hash object can be used. Finding values in a hash object is only one of the ways that you can use hash objects. Other ways include adding data to the hash object and writing data from the hash object to an output table.

Table 12.1 Hash Object Process

Steps	Syntax	Example
Declare the hash object.	`DECLARE object object-name (<argument_tag-1:value-1, ...>);`	`declare hash ContName();`
Define the hash object.	`object-name.DEFINEKEY('key-1' <, ...'key-n'>);`	`ContName.definekey('ContinentID');`
	`object-name.DEFINEDATA('data-1' <, ...'data-n'>);`	`ContName.definedata('ContinentName');`
	`object-name.DEFINEDONE( );`	`ContName.definedone();`
Use the hash object.	`object-name.FIND(<KEY:value-1, ... KEY:value-n>);`	`rc=ContName.find();`

Defining Hash Objects

Hash Object Methods

Hash object methods are operations that are performed on a hash object using dot notation. With dot notation, specify the name of the hash object to the left of the dot and specify the method to the right of the dot. All methods include a set of parentheses. Within the parentheses, arguments can be specified.

Table 12.2 Hash Object Methods

Method	Description	Syntax
ADD	Adds the specified data that is associated with the given key to the hash object.	*object-name*.**ADD( )**
DEFINEDATA	Defines data to be stored in the hash object.	*object-name*.**DEFINEDATA( )**
DEFINEDONE	Specifies that all key and data definitions are complete.	*object-name*.**DEFINEDONE( )**

Method	Description	Syntax
DEFINEKEY	Defines key components to the hash object.	*object-name*.**DEFINEKEY( )**
FIND	Determines whether the key is stored in the hash object.	*object-name*.**FIND( )**
OUTPUT	Creates one or more data sets containing the data in the hash object.	*object-name*.**OUTPUT( )**

Defining a Hash Object

To define a hash object, three DEFINE methods are required.

object-name.**DEFINEKEY(**'*key-1*' <, ...'*key-n*'>**)**

object-name.**DEFINEDATA(**'*data-1*' <, ...'*data-n*'>**)**

object-name.**DEFINEDONE( );**

- The DEFINEKEY method defines the columns that make up the key component. A column can be specified as numeric or character. A character column can be literal in quotation marks, a character column, or a character expression.

- The DEFINEDATA method defines the columns that make up the data component. A column can be specified as a character literal in quotation marks, a character column, or a character expression.

- The DEFINEDONE method indicates that all key and data components are complete. This method also loads the hash object if a table is specified in the DECLARE statement.

TIP Multiple DEFINEKEY and DEFINEDATA statements can be used for one hash object.

Example: Defining a Hash Object

The following example defines the hash object Airports.

```
data work.report;
    if 0 then
        set certadv.ctcities (keep=Code City Name);
    if _N_=1 then do;                                       /* 1 */
        declare hash airports (dataset: "certadv.ctcities"); /* 2 */
        airports.definekey ("Code");                         /* 3 */
        airports.definedata ("City", "Name");                /* 4 */
        airports.definedone ();                              /* 5 */
    end;
```

1. When _N_ is equal to 1, the code declares and defines the hash object only for the first DATA step iteration. This statement is never executed, but it makes a place in the PDV for every column that is in the table. Without this logic, the statements that are associated with the hash object are all executable. Hash object memory is not released and reused each time. You can potentially run out of memory if you have a lot of data to load into the hash object.

2. The DECLARE statement declares a hash object named Airports. The DATASET argument refers to the Certadv.CtCities data set that contains the values to be loaded.
3. The DEFINEKEY method defines Code as the key component.
4. The DEFINEDATA method defines City and Name as the data components.
5. The DEFINEDONE method loads the Certadv.CtCities data set into the hash object.

Table 12.3 Hash Object Airports

Key: Code	Data: City	Data: Name
ANC	Anchorage, AK	Anchorage International Airport
BNA	Nashville, TN	Nashville International Airport
CDG	Paris	Charles de Gaulle
LAX	Los Angeles, CA	Los Angeles International Airport
RDU	Raleigh-Durham, NC	Raleigh-Durham International Airport

Note: The hash object can store multiple key variables as well as multiple data variables.

Finding Key Values in a Hash Object

The FIND Method

The FIND method searches the hash object for the current key values. The method returns a code of 0 if the key value is found, or matched. If the value is not found, then a nonzero value is returned. If the value is found, the FIND method copies the data component values to the PDV.

Syntax, FIND method:

object-name.**FIND**(<KEY: *value-1*, ... KEY: *value-n*>)

object-name
    specifies the name of the component object.

value
    specifies the key value whose type must match the corresponding key variable that is specified in a DEFINEKEY method call.

    The number of "KEY:*value*" pairs depends on the number of key variables that you define by using the DEFINEKEY method.

Retrieving Matching Data

The following example retrieves the value of ContinentName from the hash object, ContName, based on the value of ContinentID. The KEY argument is not needed if the PDV column has the same name as the key component.

```
rc=ContName.find();
```

Figure 12.2 *Retrieving Matching Data - Find Matching Value*

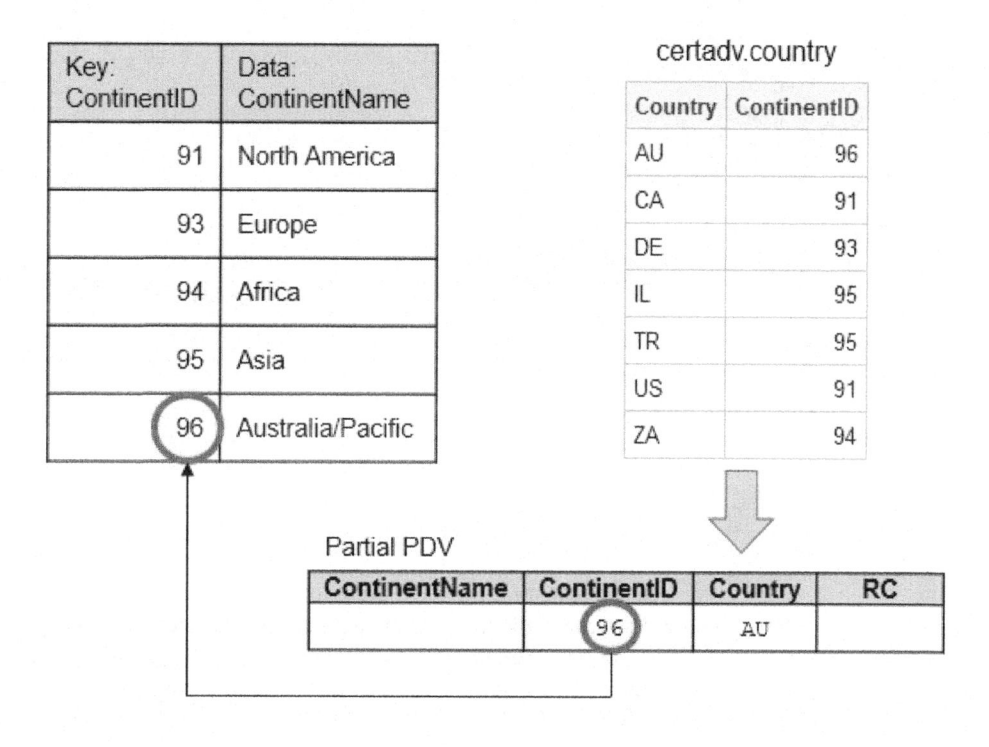

Key: ContinentID	Data: ContinentName
91	North America
93	Europe
94	Africa
95	Asia
96	Australia/Pacific

certadv.country

Country	ContinentID
AU	96
CA	91
DE	93
IL	95
TR	95
US	91
ZA	94

Partial PDV

ContinentName	ContinentID	Country	RC
	96	AU	

```
rc=ContName.find();
```

The FIND method returns Austrialia/Pacific as the continent name. A return value of 0 indicates success. If the value is not found, then the RC value is equal to a nonzero value. If the method does not find a match, no data is returned to the PDV.

Figure 12.3 *Retrieving Matching Data - Find Matching Value*

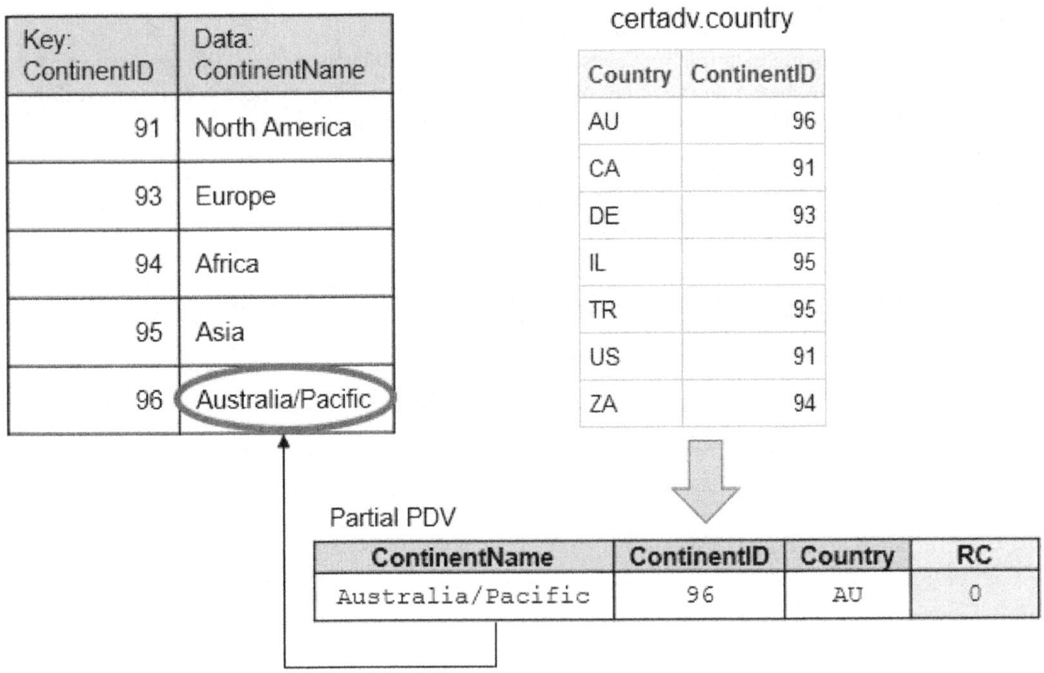

Key: ContinentID	Data: ContinentName
91	North America
93	Europe
94	Africa
95	Asia
96	Australia/Pacific

certadv.country

Country	ContinentID
AU	96
CA	91
DE	93
IL	95
TR	95
US	91
ZA	94

Partial PDV

ContinentName	ContinentID	Country	RC
Australia/Pacific	96	AU	0

The KEY argument is required if the PDV column has a different name from the key component.

```
rc-ContName.find(key:ID)
```

You can also use multiple KEY arguments. If your hash object has multiple key components, then the key arguments must be specified in the order in which the key components are defined in the DEFINEKEY method. In this example, the value for the CITY key component must be specified first, followed by values for the MONTH key component.

```
Monthly.definekey('City','Month');
Monthly.find(key:CityName,key:MonthName);
```

Writing a Hash Object to a Table

The ADD Method

The ADD method adds data in the PDV columns to the corresponding key and data components within a hash object. This method returns a zero if adding is successful and a nonzero if adding is not successful.

Syntax, ADD method:

object-name.**ADD( )**

object-name
   specifies the name of the component object.

Tip: A zero value indicates success, and a nonzero value indicates failure.

Example: Adding Key and Data Values

The ADD method adds the key and data values to the hash object.

```
ContName.add(key:91, data:'North America');
ContName.add(key:93, data:'Europe');
ContName.add(key:94, data:'Africa');
ContName.add(key:95, data:'Asia');
ContName.add(key:96, data:'Australia/Pacific');
```

The OUTPUT Method

The OUTPUT method creates a table containing the data components of the hash object. The DATASET argument is used with the OUTPUT method to name the desired output table.

Syntax, OUTPUT method:

object-name.**OUTPUT**(**DATASET:**'*data-set-name<(data-set-option)>*');

object-name
   specifies the name of the component object.

DATASET:*data-set-name*
   names the desired output table.

Tip: A zero value indicates success, and a nonzero value indicates failure.

Controlling Output with the OUTPUT Method

When you write a hash object to a table, you can specify how the output table should be sorted. Use the ORDERED argument in the DECLARE statement for the hash object, along with the OUTPUT method. The ORDERED argument specifies an order of ascending or descending for the key components.

(ORDERED:'*option*'<, ...>)

In the following example, when the ContName hash object is written to a table, the rows will be in descending order of the key components.

```
declare hash ContName (ordered:'descending');
```

Once you have read in all of your input data and added data to the hash object, you can write the hash object to a table. To determine when you have read in the last row of data, use the END= option. This option is applied in the SET statement and is not specific to hash objects. This option is set equal to a new column that you are creating. Note that this column is temporary, exists in the PDV, but is not in the final output table. SAS supplies for the column a value based on whether it is the end of file of the input table. A value of 0 means that it is not the last row of the input table, and a value of 1 means that it is the last row of the input table.

END=*column*

The following example sets the END= option to a new column, LastRow. Then, in a conditional statement, it checks to see whether LastRow is equal to 1 or the end of the file. If so, it writes the ContName hash object to an output table named Work.ContName.

```
set certadv.country(keep=ContinentID Country CountryName) end=lastrow;
```

```
if lastrow=1 then ContName.output(dataset: 'work.contname');
```

Avoiding Messages in the SAS Log

The hash object does not assign values to key variables, and the SAS compiler cannot detect the implicit key and data variable assignments that are handled by the hash object. Therefore, if no explicit assignment to a key or data variable appears in the program, SAS writes a note to the SAS log stating that the variables are uninitialized.

To avoid receiving these notes, use the CALL MISSING routine with the key and data variables as parameters. The CALL MISSING routine assigns a missing value to the specified character or numeric variables.

```
call missing(ContinentName);
```

Note: Another way to avoid receiving notes stating that the variables are uninitialized is to provide an initial assignment statement that assigns a missing value to each key and data variable.

Hash Object Processing

At the beginning of the DATA step execution that follows, the hash object ContName is declared with a key component of ContinentID and data component of ContinentName. The Certadv.Country table is used to populate the hash object.

```
data work.countrycode;
   drop rc;
   length ContinentName $30;
   if _n_=1 then do;                                        /* 1 */
      call missing (ContinentName);                         /* 2 */
      declare hash ContName();                              /* 3 */
      ContName.definekey('ContinentID');                    /* 4 */
      ContName.definedata('ContinentName');                 /* 5 */
      ContName.definedone();                                /* 6 */
      ContName.add(key: 91, data: 'North America');         /* 7 */
      ContName.add(key: 93, data: 'Europe');
      ContName.add(key: 94, data: 'Africa');
      ContName.add(key: 95, data: 'Asia');
      ContName.add(key: 96, data: 'Australia/Pacific');
   end;                                                     /* 8 */
   set certadv.country                                      /* 9 */
         (keep=ContinentID Country CountryName);
   rc=ContName.find();                                      /* 10 */
run;                                                        /* 11 */
proc print data=work.countrycode noobs;
run;
```

1. `if _n_1= then do;`

   When the _N_ is equal to 1, it declares and defines the hash object only one time.

Partial **certadv.country**

Country	CountryName	ContinentID
AU	Australia	96
CA	Canada	91
DE	Germany	93

Program Data Vector

_N_	ContinentName	Country	CountryName	ContinentID	rc
①				.	.

2. `call missing (ContinentName);`

   CALL MISSING sets the key column, ContinentName, to missing.

3. `declare hash ContName();`

   The DECLARE statement declares a hash object named ContName with no arguments.

Partial **certadv.country**

Country	CountryName	ContinentID
AU	Australia	96
CA	Canada	91
DE	Germany	93

Hash Object ContName

Program Data Vector

_N_	ContinentName	Country	CountryName	ContinentID	rc
1				.	.

4. `ContName.definekey('ContinentID');`

   The DEFINEKEY method specifies the ContinentID column as the key component.

Partial **certadv.country**

Country	CountryName	ContinentID
AU	Australia	96
CA	Canada	91
DE	Germany	93

Hash Object ContName

KEY: ContinentID	

Program Data Vector

_N_	ContinentName	Country	CountryName	ContinentID	rc
1				.	.

5. `ContName.definedata('ContinentName');`

   The DEFINEDATA method specifies the ContinentName column as the data component.

Partial **certadv.country**

Country	CountryName	ContinentID
AU	Australia	96
CA	Canada	91
DE	Germany	93

Hash Object ContName

KEY: ContinentID	DATA: ContinentName

Program Data Vector

_N_	ContinentName	Country	CountryName	ContinentID	rc
1				.	.

6. `ContName.definedone();`

   The DEFINEDONE method indicates that the key and data components are complete.

Partial certadv.country

Country	CountryName	ContinentID
AU	Australia	96
CA	Canada	91
DE	Germany	93

Hash Object ContName

KEY: ContinentID	DATA: ContinentName

Program Data Vector

_N_	ContinentName	Country	CountryName	ContinentID	rc
1				.	.

7. `ContName.add(key: 91, data: 'North America');`
   `ContName.add(key: 93, data: 'Europe');`
   `ContName.add(key: 94, data: 'Africa');`
   `ContName.add(key: 95, data: 'Asia');`
   `ContName.add(key: 96, data: 'Australia/Pacific');`

   The ADD method adds the specified data that is associated with the given key to the hash object. This method returns a zero if adding is not successful.

Partial certadv.country

Country	CountryName	ContinentID
AU	Australia	96
CA	Canada	91
DE	Germany	93

Hash Object ContName

KEY: ContinentID	DATA: ContinentName
91	North America
93	Europe
94	Africa
95	Asia
96	Australia/Pacific

Program Data Vector

_N_	ContinentName	Country	CountryName	ContinentID	rc
1				.	.

8. `end;`

   The END statement ends the group processing.

9. `set certadv.country (keep=ContinentID Country CountryName);`

   The SET statement reads observations from Certadv.Country data set and the KEEP= data set option keeps only the specified variables.

Partial **certadv.country**

Country	CountryName	ContinentID
AU	Australia	96
CA	Canada	91
DE	Germany	93

Hash Object ContName

KEY: ContinentID	DATA: ContinentName
91	North America
93	Europe
94	Africa
95	Asia
96	Australia/Pacific

Program Data Vector

_N_	ContinentName	Country	CountryName	ContinentID	rc
1		AU	Australia	96	.

Partial **work.countrycode**

ContinentName	Country	CountryName	ContinentID
Australia/Pacific	AU	Australia	96

10. `rc=ContName.find();`

The FIND method searches the ContName hash object for the current key values. The function returns a 0 if the key is found. The key value is not returned to the PDV.

Partial **certadv.country**

Country	CountryName	ContinentID
AU	Australia	96
CA	Canada	91
DE	Germany	93

Hash Object ContName

KEY: ContinentID	DATA: ContinentName
91	North America
93	Europe
94	Africa
95	Asia
96	Australia/Pacific

Program Data Vector

_N_	ContinentName	Country	CountryName	ContinentID	rc
1	Australia/Pacific	AU	Australia	96	0

Partial **work.countrycode**

ContinentName	Country	CountryName	ContinentID
Australia/Pacific	AU	Australia	96

11. The RUN statement has an implicit OUTPUT statement and an implicit RETURN statement.

The DATA statement initializes the PDV again after the RUN statement. On the second iteration of the DATA step the IF statement does not execute again because _N_ is not equal to 1. This continues until the end-of-file marker is reached.

Output 12.1 PROC PRINT of Work.Countrycode

ContinentName	Country	CountryName	ContinentID
Australia/Pacific	AU	Australia	96
North America	CA	Canada	91
Europe	DE	Germany	93
Asia	IL	Israel	95
Asia	TR	Turkey	95
North America	US	United States	91
Africa	ZA	South Africa	94

Using Hash Iterator Objects

What Is a Hash Iterator Object?

A *hash iterator object* is associated with a hash object, enabling you to retrieve hash object data in either forward or reverse key order. Think of the hash iterator object, or hiter, as an ordered view of a hash object.

Figure 12.4 Hash Object Iterator

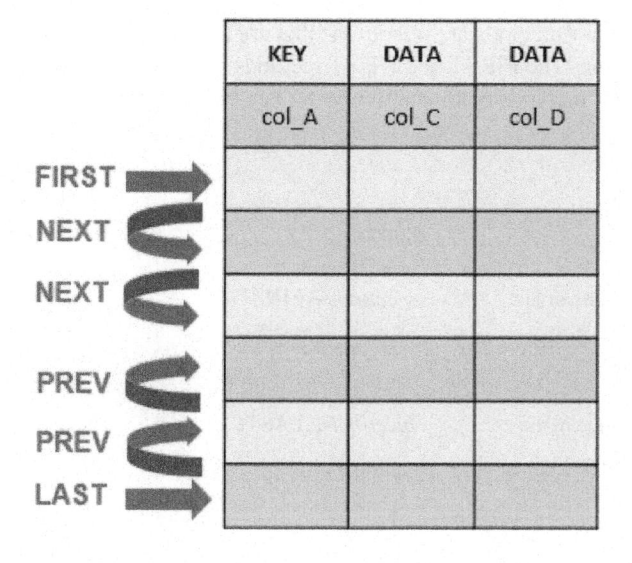

KEY	DATA	DATA
col_A	col_C	col_D

FIRST →
NEXT
NEXT
PREV
PREV
LAST →

Note: Declare the hash object before defining the hash iterator object.

In the following example, the Certadv.Orderfact table is loaded into the hash object Customer. The hash object Customer then feeds into the hash iterator object C. Notice that there is a DECLARE statement for the hash object Customer and a DECLARE statement for hiter (hash iterator) object C. The hash object name must be enclosed in quotation marks when it is referenced in the DECLARE statement for the hash iterator object.

```
declare hash Customer (dataset: 'certadv.orderfact', ordered: 'descending');
...statements..
declare hiter C('Customer');
```

The ORDERED argument in the hash object is not controlling the sort order of the hash object. The ORDERED argument controls the sort order of an output table only if an OUTPUT method is used in the hash object or the sort order of a hash iterator object that points to the hash object.

Declaring and Defining a Hash Object and a Hash Iterator Object

The hash object loads the data in the order in which it occurs in the data set. The ORDERED argument specifies retrieving data from the hash object by descending order of key values.

```
declare hash Customer(dataset: 'certadv.orderfact', ordered: 'descending');
```

The DEFINEKEY, DEFINEDATA, and DEFINEDONE methods execute. The key values are not returned to the PDV.

```
customer.definekey('TotalRetailPrice', 'CustomerID');
customer.definedata('TotalRetailPrice', 'CustomerID', 'ProductID');
customer.definedone();
```

The second DECLARE statement defines the hash iterator object, C. It points to the hash object, Customer, whose data is in descending order of key values.

```
declare hiter C('customer');
```

Retrieving Hash Object Data with the Hash Iterator Object

Hash iterator methods are operations that are performed on a hash iterator object using dot notation. The FIRST and NEXT methods read data in forward key order. The LAST and PREV methods read data in reverse key order.

Table 12.4 Hash Iterator Methods

Method	Description	Syntax	Example

FIRST	Returns the first data value in the underlying hash object.	*object-name*.**FIRST**( );	`declare hiter C('customer');`
			`<more SAS code>;`
			`C.first();`

LAST	Returns the last data value in the underlying hash object.	*object-name*.**LAST**( );	`declare hiter C('customer');`
			`<more SAS code>;`
			`C.last();`

Method	Description	Syntax	Example

NEXT	Returns the data components in key order.
	
	Note: If you use the NEXT method without the FIRST method, it returns the first item in the hash object.
		object-name.**NEXT( )**;	`C.first();`
			`<more SAS code>;`
			`C.next();`
			`C.next();`

PREV	Returns the data components in reverse key order.	*object-name*.**PREV( )**;	`C.prev();`

object-name
: specifies the name of the hash iterator object.

- The FIRST method returns the first data item in the hash object. The LAST method returns the last data component in the hash object.
- You can use the NEXT method to return the next data component in the hash object.
- Use the PREV method iteratively to traverse the hash object and return the data components in reverse key order.

Note: The PREV method sets the data variable to the value of the data component so that it is available for use after the method call.

Example: Using the Hash Iterator Object

Suppose you need to identify which two customers ordered the most and least expensive items. You can use the hash iterator object to retrieve the data in either ascending or descending key order to efficiently identify these four customers.

```
data work.topbottom;
   drop i;
   if _N_=1 then do;
      if 0 then set certadv.Orderfact (keep=CustomerID
                                      ProductID TotalRetailPrice);
      declare hash customer(dataset: 'certadv.Orderfact',
                            ordered: 'descending');
      customer.definekey('TotalRetailPrice', 'CustomerID');
      customer.definedata('TotalRetailPrice', 'CustomerID',
                          'ProductID');
      customer.definedone();
      declare hiter C('customer');
   end;
      C.first();
      do i=1 to 2;
         output work.topbottom;
         C.next();
      end;
      C.last();
      do i=1 to 2;
         output work.topbottom;
         C.prev();
      end;
      stop;
   run;
```

Output 12.2 PROC PRINT Output of Work.TopBottom

Obs	CustomerID	ProductID	TotalRetailPrice
1	70100	240200100173	$1,937.20
2	79	240200100076	$1,796.00
3	79	230100500045	$2.60
4	11171	240200100021	$2.70

Quiz

1. In which step does the SAS hash object exist?
   a. PROC step
   b. DATA step
   c. OPTIONS
   d. a and b only.

2. What does a component object consist of?
   a. Methods
   b. Attributes
   c. Both a and b.
   d. None of the above.

3. What are the DEFINE methods that are required to define a hash object?
   a. DEFINEKEY
   b. DEFINEDATA
   c. DEFINEDONE
   d. All of the above.

4. What does the FIND hash object method do?
   a. Adds data associated with a key to the hash object.
   b. Determines whether the key is stored in the hash object.
   c. Defines key variables to the hash object.
   d. Specifies that all key and data definitions are complete.

5. What does the PREV method do?
   a. Returns the first value in the underlying hash object.
   b. Returns the next value in the underlying hash object.
   c. Returns the last value in the underlying hash object.
   d. Returns the previous value in the underlying hash object.

6. What does the CALL MISSING routine do?
   a. Instantiates the hash object.

b. Assigns a missing value to the specified character or numeric variables.

c. Declares a hash object.

d. Calls to retrieve multiple data values.

7. You can define a hash iterator without defining a hash object.

   a. True

   b. False

8. Which of the following programs correctly associates more than one data value with one key?

   a.
   ```
   data work.sample1;
      if 0 then
         set certadv.acities(keep= Code City Name);
      if _N_=1 then do;
      declare hash airports (dataset:"certadv.acities");
      airports.defineKey ("Code");
      airports.defineData ("City", "Name");
      airports.defineDone();
      end;
   run;
   ```

   b.
   ```
   data work.sample2;
      if 0 then
         set certadv.acities(keep= Code City Name);
      if _N_=1 then do;
      declare hash airports (dataset:"certadv.acities");
      airports.defineKey ("City", "Name");
      airports.defineData ("Code");
      airports.defineDone();
      end;
   run;
   ```

   c.
   ```
   data work.sample3;
      if 0 then
         set certadv.acities(keep= Code City Name);
      if _N_=1 then do;
      declare hash airports (dataset:"certadv.acities");
      airports.defineKey ("Code", "City");
      airports.defineData ("City", "Name");
      airports.defineDone();
      end;
   run;
   ```

   d.
   ```
   data work.sample4;
      if 0 then
         set certadv.acities(keep= Code City Name);
      if _N_=1 then do;
      declare hash airports ();
      airports.defineKey ();
      airports.defineData ();
      airports.defineDone();
      end;
   run;
   ```

Chapter 13
Using SAS Utility Procedures

Creating Picture Formats with the FORMAT Procedure **317**
    A Brief Overview 317
    PICTURE Statement Syntax 318
    Example: Using the PICTURE Statement 318
    Creating Custom Date, Time, and Datetime Formats Using Directives 319
    Specifying Date and Time Directives 320
    Example: Using Directives 321
    Creating Custom Numeric Formats 322

Creating Functions with PROC FCMP **328**
    A Brief Overview 328
    PROC FCMP Syntax 328
    CMPLIB= Option Syntax 329
    Example: Creating a Custom Character Function with One Argument 329
    Example: Creating a Custom Numeric Function with One Argument 330
    Example: Creating a Custom Character Function with Multiple Arguments 332

Quiz **334**

Creating Picture Formats with the FORMAT Procedure

A Brief Overview

The FORMAT procedure enables you to define your own formats for variables. The VALUE statement is commonly used to create numeric or character formats by defining character strings to display in place of values. Suppose you have airline data and you want to create several custom formats that you can use for your report. You need to create three different types of formats to do these tasks:

- group airline routes into zones
- label airport codes as International or Domestic
- group cargo revenue figures into ranges

You can use PROC FORMAT with the VALUE statement to create two character formats, $ROUTES. and $DEST., and a numeric format, REVFMT.

318 Chapter 13 • *Using SAS Utility Procedures*

Suppose one of the variables in your data set has numeric values that you want to format a certain way. For example, you have an emergency phone number listed for each of the flight crew members in your data set. The number is listed as 5556874239 and you want to format it as (555) 687-4239.

Use the PICTURE statement to create a custom format that specifies a template for displaying a numeric value. Define a format that accepts special characters, such as leading zeros, commas, and negative numbers. Only numeric variables can have picture formats. For example, the following PICTURE statement tells SAS to print numbers in the specified format.

```
PICTURE phonepix OTHER= '(999)999-9999';
```

PICTURE Statement Syntax

The PICTURE statement creates a format that specifies a template for displaying numeric values.

Syntax, PROC FORMAT with the PICTURE statement:

PROC FORMAT;

  PICTURE *format-name* <(*format-options*)>

   <*value-range-set-1* = '*template-value*' (*template-options*)>

   <*value-range-set-n* = '*template-value*' (*template-options*)>;

RUN;

format-name
  is the name of the format that you are creating.

  Note: A user-defined format cannot be the name of a format supplied by SAS. The name must be a valid SAS name. A numeric format name can be up to 32 characters long.

value-range-set
  specifies one or more variable values and a template for printing those values. *value-range-set* has the following form: *value-or-range* = '*template-value*'.

value-or-range
  a single value, such as 12 or a range of values, such as 1-100.

template-value
  specifies a template for formatting values of numeric variables.

digit selectors
  are numeric characters (0 through 9) that define positions for numeric values.

directives
  are special characters that you can use in the template to format date, time, or datetime value.

template options
  are specific to the specified template.

format options
  are specific to the format as a whole, which includes all templates created by the PICTURE statement.

Example: Using the PICTURE Statement

The following example uses the PICTURE statement, which contains both digit selectors and message characters. Since the RAINAMT. format has nonzero digit selectors, values are printed with leading zeros. A numeric range is used to include or exclude values in a range using the less than symbol (<) preceded or followed by the value. For example, the 2<-4 range does not include 2, but includes 4. However, 4<-<10 excludes both 4 and 10. The keyword OTHER is used to print values and message characters for any values that do not fall into the specified range.

Note: Not all values are printed with leading zeros. Values that are printed with leading zeros might not have an available format to display.

```
proc format;
   picture rainamt
           0-2='9.99 slight'
           2<-4='9.99 moderate'
           4<-<10='9.99 heavy'
           other='999 check value';
run;
proc print data=certadv.rain;
   format amount rainamt.;
run;
```

The following output shows the values with the RAINAMT. format applied.

Figure 13.1 PROC PRINT Output with the RAINAMT. Format Applied

Obs	Amount
1	4.00 moderate
2	3.90 moderate
3	020 check value
4	0.50 slight
5	6.00 heavy

Creating Custom Date, Time, and Datetime Formats Using Directives

Suppose you have the date value July 1 2019 and the time value 8:30:10 a.m. You need to create three new columns with the date and time values, StartDate, StartTime, and StartDateTime columns. You are given specific requirements for displaying the date and time values in those columns. The data in the columns must look like the figure below.

Figure 13.2 Custom Date, Time, and Datetime Formats Illustration

StartDate	StartTime	StartDateTime
Mon-1-Jul-2019	H:08 M:30 S:10	2019.07.01 @8:30:10 AM

Currently, SAS does not supply formats that can create the columns that match the figure above. However, you can use directives to create the templates that you need. *Directives* are special characters that define a template to display date, time, or datetime values. If you use directives, you must specify the DATATYPE= option in the PICTURE statement after the template. This option specifies that the picture applies to a SAS date, SAS time, or SAS datetime value.

Syntax, PICTURE statement with the DATATYPE= option:

PICTURE *format-name* (**DEFAULT**=*length*)

    value-or-range-1='*directives*'

       (**DATATYPE=DATE|TIME|DATETIME**);

RUN;

(DEFAULT=*length*)
: specifies the default length of the formatted value. If the DEFAULT= option is not used, the length of the formatted value is based on the length of the longest template.

'*directives*'
: specifies special characters that define a template for the display of date, time, or datetime values. The special characters must be placed within quotation marks.

(DATATYPE=DATE | TIME | DATETIME)
: enables the use of directives in the template to format date, time, or datetime values. The DATATYPE= option must be specified for each value-range set. The DATATYPE= option must be placed within parentheses.

Specifying Date and Time Directives

The percent sign (%) followed by a letter indicates a directive. Directives that you can use to create a picture format are listed in the table below.

Table 13.1 Date Directives

Directive	Description	Result
%A	Weekday name in full	Wednesday
%a	Weekday name, the first three letters	Wed
%d	Day of the month in one or two digits	2 or 11
%0d	Day of month two digits	02
%B	Month name in full	January
%3B	Month name, the first three letters	Jan
%m	Month number in one or two digits	4 or 12
%0m	Month number in two digits	04
%Y	Year in four digits	2019
%0y	Year in two digits	19

For example, the SAS date value of 21731 is equivalent to Mon-1–Jul-2019. You would use the following directives to transform 21731 to Mon-1-Jul-2019: %a-%d-%3B-%Y.

Table 13.2 Time Directives

Directive	Description	Result
%H	Hour, 24-hour clock in one or two digits	21
%0H	Hour, 24-hour clock in two digits with a leading zero	021
%I	Hour, 12-hour clock in one or two digits	9
%0I	Hour, 12-hour clock in two digits with a leading zero	09
%M	Minute in one or two digits	13
%0M	Minute, in two digits with a leading zero	013
%S	Second in one or two digits	5
%0S	Second in two digits with a leading zero	05
%p	AM or PM	PM

The time value 30610 is equivalent to H:8 M:30 S:10. You would use the following directive to transform 30610 to 8:30:10: H:%H M:%M S:%S.

Or you can transform 30610 to H:08 M:30 S:10 using the following directive: H:%0H M:%0M S:%0S.

Note: To add a leading zero before a single digit, insert a 0 before the directive. When you add a leading zero, it is changing only the values of hour, minute, seconds, and so on, to display a leading zero. It is not changing any other part of the output.

When you create a template with a directive, the maximum length of the formatted value is the length of 8. Use DEFAULT= to set a length that is greater than the default length of 8.

Example: Using Directives

Suppose you want to display values for employee hire dates in the format dd-mmmyyyy (such as 25-JAN2017) for the Certadv.Empdata data set.

322 Chapter 13 • *Using SAS Utility Procedures*

Figure 13.3 Certadv.Empdata Data Set before Format Is Applied (partial output)

Division	HireDate	LastName	FirstName	Country	Location	Phone	EmpID	JobCode	Salary
FLIGHT OPERATIONS	19758	MILLS	DOROTHY E	USA	CARY	2380	E00001	FLTAT3	$25,000
FINANCE & IT	18753	BOWER	EILEEN A.	USA	CARY	1214	E00002	FINCLK	$27,000
HUMAN RESOURCES & FACILITIES	19202	READING	TONY R.	USA	CARY	1428	E00003	VICEPR	$120,000
HUMAN RESOURCES & FACILITIES	19881	JUDD	CAROL A.	USA	CARY	2061	E00004	FACMNT	$42,000
AIRPORT OPERATIONS	19023	WONSILD	HANNA	DENMARK	COPENHAGEN	1086	E00005	GRCREW	$19,000

... more observations ...

This format requires spaces for 10 characters.

- The keywords LOW and HIGH are used to include all values.
- The %0d directive indicates that if the day of the month is one digit, it should be preceded by a 0.
- Because there are only nine characters inside the single quotation marks, use DEFAULT= to increase the length to 10. If you omit DEFAULT=, the length is 8.

```
proc format;
   picture mydate (default=10)
          low-high='%0d-%3b%Y' (datatype=date);
run;

proc print data=certadv.empdata
    (keep=division hireDate lastName obs=5);
   format hiredate mydate.;
run;
```

The output below shows the values for HireDate formatted with the MYDATE. picture format.

Figure 13.4 PROC PRINT Result of MYDATE. Picture Format (partial output)

Obs	Division	HireDate	LastName
1	FLIGHT OPERATIONS	04-FEB2014	MILLS
2	FINANCE & IT	06-MAY2011	BOWER
3	HUMAN RESOURCES & FACILITIES	28-JUL2012	READING
4	HUMAN RESOURCES & FACILITIES	07-JUN2014	JUDD
5	AIRPORT OPERATIONS	31-JAN2012	WONSILD

... more observations ...

Creating Custom Numeric Formats

PICTURE Statement Syntax with Digit Selectors

The PICTURE statement can also use digit selectors with non-numeric characters. You can use the ROUND, MULTIPLIER=, and PREFIX= options for the template.

Syntax, PICTURE statement using digit selectors:

PICTURE *format-name* (**ROUND DEFAULT**=*length*)
> *value-or-range-1*='*digit selectors with non-numeric characters*'
>> (**MULT** | **MULTIPLIER**=*n* **PREFIX**='*prefix*');

RUN;

(ROUND)
> rounds the value to the nearest integer.

(MULT | MULTIPLIER=*n*)
> specifies a number to multiply the value by.

(PREFIX='*prefix*')
> specifies a character string to place in front of the formatted value.

Digit Selectors with Non-Numeric Characters

You can use digit selectors (0 through 9) to define positions for numeric values. Digit selectors of 0 do not print leading zeros. Nonzero digit selectors print leading zeros. The digit selector 9 is commonly used as the nonzero digit selector. Non-numeric characters are printed as specified. The following example specifies a digit selector with non-numeric characters.

```
picture Discount (round) low-high='009.9%' (multiplier=10);
```

If the template contains digit selectors, then a digit selector must be the first character in the template. Use the PREFIX= option to specify a character string to place in front of the formatted value.

The MULTIPLIER= Option

Use the MULTIPLER=*n* option to specify a number that the variable's value will be multiplied by before the variable is formatted. The value of the MULTIPLIER= option depends both on the result of the multiplication and on the digit selectors in the picture portion of *value-range-set*.

Suppose you have the data set Certadv.Grocery. You need to create a format that formats the CustomDiscount variable to a percentage. For example, if the value is 5, it should be 5.0%.

Figure 13.5 *Certadv.Grocery Data Set (partial output)*

Product	Price	CustomDiscount
Dehydrated Kelp Kombo	1.99	5
Chocolate - White	5.99	15
Sping Loaded Cup Dispenser	2.49	5
Cheese - Parmesan Grated	0.99	5
Chocolate Liqueur - Godet White	2.99	10

... *more observations* ...

⇩

Product	Price	CustomDiscount
Dehydrated Kelp Kombo	1.99	5.0%
Chocolate - White	5.99	15.0%
Sping Loaded Cup Dispenser	2.49	5.0%
Cheese - Parmesan Grated	0.99	5.0%
Chocolate Liqueur - Godet White	2.99	10.0%

... *more observations* ...

```
proc format;
   picture Discount low-high='009.0%' (multiplier=10);
run;
data work.customerdiscount;
   set certadv.grocery;
   format CustomDiscount Discount.;
run;
proc print data=work.customerdiscount noobs;
run;
```

The values for CustomDiscount are multiplied by 10.

Note: The default is 10^n, where *n* is the number of digits after the first decimal point in the picture. For example, suppose your data contains a value 123.456, and you want to print it using a picture of '999.999'. The format multiplies 123.456 by 10^3 to obtain a value of 123456, which results in a formatted value of 123.456.

The PREFIX= Option

You can create custom numeric formats with a character prefix using the PREFIX= option. The PREFIX= option specifies a character prefix to place in front of the formatted value. The prefix is placed in front of the value's first significant digit. You must use zero-digit selectors or the prefix is not used. Typical uses for PREFIX= are printing leading currency symbols and minus signs.

The following example uses the Work.CustomerDiscount created in the previous example. The PICTURE statement creates a new format named NewPrice that formats the values for the NewPrice column with a dollar sign. The NewPrice column is produced by multiplying CustomDiscount by the value in the Price column.

```
proc format;
   picture NewPrice low-high='000,009.99' (prefix='$');
```

```
run;
data work.newprice;
   set work.customerdiscount;
   NewPrice=Price-(Price*(CustomDiscount*0.01));
   format NewPrice NewPrice. CustomDiscount Discount.;
run;
proc print data=work.newprice;
run;
```

Output 13.1 PROC PRINT Result of Work.NewPrice (partial output)

Product	Price	CustomDiscount	NewPrice
Dehydrated Kelp Kombo	1.99	5.0%	$1.89
Chocolate - White	5.99	15.0%	$5.09
Sping Loaded Cup Dispenser	2.49	5.0%	$2.36
Cheese - Parmesan Grated	0.99	5.0%	$0.94
Chocolate Liqueur - Godet White	2.99	10.0%	$2.69

. . . more observations . . .

CAUTION:

Truncation of the prefix. If the picture is not wide enough to contain both the value and the prefix, then the format is truncated or the prefix is omitted, which results in inaccurate data.

The ROUND Option

The ROUND option rounds the value to the nearest integer before formatting. Without the ROUND option, the format multiplies the variable value by the multiplier, truncates the decimal portion (if any), and prints the result according to the template that you define. With the ROUND option, the format multiplies the variable value by the multiplier, rounds that result to the nearest integer, and then formats the value according to the template.

TIP The ROUND option rounds a value of .5 to the next highest integer.

CAUTION:

The picture must be wide enough for an additional digit if rounding a number adds a digit to the number. For example, the picture for the number .996 could be '99' (prefix '.' mult=100). After rounding the number and multiplying it by 100, the resulting number is 100. When the picture is applied, the result is .00, an inaccurate number. In order to ensure accuracy of numbers when you round numbers, make the picture wide enough to accommodate larger numbers.

Example: Creating a Custom Percent Format

In the previous examples, two new custom formats were created: Discount., which created a percent format, and NewPrice., which applied a prefix of a dollar sign ($). For this example, create a custom format that rounds your Difference column and applies a prefix of a dollar ($). First, the format applies the multiplier, if applicable. Then it rounds the values, and finally the format applies the numeric value to the template.

Figure 13.6 Certadv.Grocery Data Set (partial output)

Product	Price	CustomDiscount
Dehydrated Kelp Kombo	1.99	0.05
Chocolate - White	5.99	0.15
Sping Loaded Cup Dispenser	2.49	0.05
Cheese - Parmesan Grated	0.99	0.05
Chocolate Liqueur - Godet White	2.99	0.10
White Baguette	2.49	0.05
Cheese - Cream Cheese	0.99	0.05

⇩

Obs	Product	Price	CustomDiscount	NewPrice	Difference
1	Dehydrated Kelp Kombo	1.99	5.0%	$1.89	$0.10
2	Chocolate - White	5.99	15.0%	$5.09	$0.90
3	Sping Loaded Cup Dispenser	2.49	5.0%	$2.36	$0.12
4	Cheese - Parmesan Grated	0.99	5.0%	$0.94	$0.05
5	Chocolate Liqueur - Godet White	2.99	10.0%	$2.69	$0.30

... *more observations* ...

```
proc format;
   picture Discount low-high='009.0%' (multiplier=10);
   picture NewPrice low-high='000,009.99' (prefix='$');
   picture Diff (round) low-high='000,009.99' (prefix='$');
run;
data work.newPriceTot;
   set certadv.grocery;
   NewPrice=Price-(Price*(CustomDiscount*0.01));
   Difference=Price-NewPrice;
   format CustomDiscount Discount. NewPrice NewPrice. Difference Diff.;
run;
proc print data=work.newPriceTot;
run;
```

Example: Creating a Custom Numeric Format for Large Numbers

The following example illustrates how you can create a custom numeric format for large numbers. This example uses the ROUND, PREFIX, and MULTIPLIER= options.

Suppose you have the data set Certadv.Values, where the UnformattedValues column represents your original numbers with no formats applied. The Multiplier column displays the multiplier for each unformatted number, and the MultiValues column displays the values with the Multiplier applied. The MultiValuesRound column displays the values from the MultiValues column, but with the ROUND option applied.

The FormattedValues column below does not have any formats applied.

Creating Picture Formats with the FORMAT Procedure

Figure 13.7 Certadv.Values Data Set

UnformattedValues	Multiplier	MultiValues	MultiValuesRound	FormattedValues
34	1.00000	34.00	34	34
345	1.00000	345.00	345	345
3456	0.01000	34.56	35	3456
34567	0.01000	345.67	346	34567
345678	0.01000	3456.78	3457	345678
3456789	0.00001	34.57	35	3456789
34567890	0.00001	345.68	346	34567890
345678901	0.00001	3456.79	3457	345678901

Create a PICTURE format named dollar_KM that does the following:

- formats values less than 1000 with a dollar sign and with a multiplier of 1
- formats values between 1000 and 1000000 with a K, a dollar sign, and with a multiplier of 0.01
- formats values greater than 1000000 with an M, a dollar sign, and with a multiplier of 0.00001.

```
proc format;
   picture dollar_KM (round default=7)
            low-<1000='009' (prefix='$' multiplier=1)
            1000-<1000000='009.9K' (prefix='$' multiplier=.01)
            1000000-high='009.9M' (prefix='$' multiplier=.00001);
run;
```

When you apply this format to the FormattedValues column in a PROC PRINT step, the values are displayed as desired.

```
proc print data=certadv.values noobs;
   format MultiValues 12.5
          FormattedValues dollar_KM.;
run;
```

Output 13.2 PROC PRINT Output of Certadv.Values

Unformatted Values	Multiplier	Multiplied Values	Multiplied Values with Round	Formatted Values
34	1.00000	34.00000	34	$34
345	1.00000	345.00000	345	$345
3456	0.01000	34.56000	35	$3.5K
34567	0.01000	345.67000	346	$34.6K
345678	0.01000	3456.78000	3457	$345.7K
3456789	0.00001	34.56789	35	$3.5M
34567890	0.00001	345.67890	346	$34.6M
345678901	0.00001	3456.78901	3457	$345.7M

Creating Functions with PROC FCMP

A Brief Overview

Within SAS, you can create your own functions. Creating your own functions is useful when you have repetitive routines in your programs. The SAS Function Compiler (FCMP) procedure enables you to create custom functions using DATA step syntax. This feature enables programmers to more easily read, write, and maintain complex code with independent and reusable routines.

PROC FCMP Syntax

Use PROC FCMP to build user-defined functions and call routines with DATA step syntax.

Syntax, PROC FCMP step:

PROC FCMP OUTLIB=*libref.table.package*;

    FUNCTION *function-name(arguments)*<*$*> <*length*>;

    ... *programming statements*. . .

    RETURN(*expression*);

    ENDSUB;

QUIT;

OUTLIB=*libref.table.package*
    specifies the table and package that stores the compiled function. This is a required argument that must be specified in the PROC FCMP statement.

FUNCTION statement
    The FUNCTION statement specifies the *function-name* and the function arguments, as well as whether the function returns a character or numeric value.

    function-name(arguments)<*$*> <*length*>
        specifies a subroutine declaration for a routine that returns a value. The FUNCTION statement begins the definition of a function.

    <*$*>
        specifies that the function returns a character value. If $ is not specified, the function returns a numeric value.

    argument
        specifies one or more arguments for the function. You specify character arguments by placing a dollar sign ($) after the argument name.

    function-name
        specifies the name of the function.

    <*length*>
        specifies the length of a character value.

RETURN(*expression*)
    specifies the value that is returned by the function.

ENDSUB
    ends the function.

CMPLIB= Option Syntax

In order for SAS to find the custom function, the CMPLIB= option must be specified in the OPTIONS statement. This option names the table where the function is stored within a package. The CMPLIB option is a global option. Once you set this option it remains in effect until you cancel, change, or exit your SAS session.

OPTIONS CMPLIB=*libref.table* | (*libref.table-1...libref.table-n*)

libref.table
: specifies the table or tables that SAS searches for a package that contains the desired function.

Example: Creating a Custom Character Function with One Argument

Suppose you need to create a new data set with the names of baseball players and their teams. The names of the baseball players in the Certadv.Baseball data set is in the wrong order. The Certadv.Baseball data set currently lists the players by last name followed by first name, and names are separated by commas. You need to create a custom function to reverse the order of the name so that the players' first names are followed by their last names, separated by a space.

```
proc fcmp outlib=certadv.functions.dev;        /*1*/
   function ReverseName(lastfirst $) $ 40;     /*2*/
      First=scan(lastfirst,2,',');             /*3*/
      Last=scan(lastfirst,1,',');
   return(catx(' ',First,Last));               /*4*/
   endsub;                                     /*5*/
run;
```

1. The FCMP procedure enables you to create a custom function. The OUTLIB= option specifies Certadv.Functions as the table in which the Dev package is stored. The Dev package is a collection of routines that have unique names.

2. The FUNCTION statement specifies the function name as ReverseName. ReverseName is a custom function that has one character argument named LastFirst and it returns a character value with a length of 40. If a return value type and length are not specified, the default is numeric with a length of 8.

3. The body of the function consists of DATA step syntax. The assignment statement creates two new variables, First and Last, that are created using the SCAN function. The new variable First uses the SCAN function to return the second word from the LastFirst variable and the Last variable returns the first word from the LastFirst variable.

4. The RETURN statement specifies the value of ReverseName. The RETURN statement defines the value returned by the function. It uses the CATX function to concatenate the first and last variable values created within the function definition separated by a space.

5. The ENDSUB statement ends the function.

Now that you have created your custom function, you can use it in a DATA step just like any other SAS function.

```
options cmplib=certadv.functions;      /*1*/
data work.baseball;                    /*2*/
   set certadv.baseball;
   Player=reversename(Name);           /*3*/
   keep Name Team Player;
run;
proc print data=work.baseball;
run;
```

1. The CMPLIB= option specifies the Certadv.Functions table for SAS to search for a package that contains the desired function.
2. The DATA step reads Certadv.Baseball to create Work.Baseball.
3. The DATA step creates a new variable named Player by referencing the custom function, ReverseName. The function reverses the order of FirstName and LastName values within Name and returns the string to the Player variable.

Output 13.3 PROC PRINT Result of Work.Baseball (partial output)

Obs	Name	Team	Player
1	Allanson, Andy	Cleveland	Andy Allanson
2	Ashby, Alan	Houston	Alan Ashby
3	Davis, Alan	Seattle	Alan Davis
4	Dawson, Andre	Montreal	Andre Dawson
5	Galarraga, Andres	Montreal	Andres Galarraga
6	Griffin, Alfredo	Oakland	Alfredo Griffin
7	Newman, Al	Montreal	Al Newman
8	Salazar, Argenis	Kansas City	Argenis Salazar
9	Thomas, Andres	Atlanta	Andres Thomas
10	Thornton, Andre	Cleveland	Andre Thornton

... *more observations* ...

Example: Creating a Custom Numeric Function with One Argument

Suppose you need to create a custom function to generate fiscal quarter buckets based on the value of Dates in your data set. The following example uses one numeric argument and returns a numeric value for the function.

```
proc fcmp outlib=certadv.functions.dat;        /*1*/
   function MyQuarter(month);                  /*2*/
      if month in(2,3,4) then myqtr=1;         /*3*/
         else if month in(5,6,7) then myqtr=2;
         else if month in (8,9,10) then myqtr=3;
         else myqtr=4;
      return(myqtr);                           /*4*/
   endsub;                                     /*5*/
run;

options cmplib=certadv.functions;              /*6*/
data work.dates;                               /*7*/
```

```
      do Dates='15JAN2019'd to '31DEC2019'd by 30;
         MonNum=month(Dates);
         FiscalQuarter=MyQuarter(MonNum);              /*8*/
         output;
      end;
   run;

   proc print data=work.dates;                         /*9*/
      format Dates mmddyy10.;
   run;
```

1. The FCMP procedure enables you to create a custom function. The OUTLIB= option specifies Certadv.Functions as the table in which the Dat package is stored. The Dat package is a collection of routines that have unique names.

2. The FUNCTION statement specifies a new function named MyQuarter that accepts one numeric argument named Month.

3. The body of the function consists of DATA step IF-THEN/ELSE syntax. This conditional logic defines the value to assign to MyQtr based on the value of the input argument Month.

4. The RETURN statement is used to return a value to the MyQtr function.

5. The ENDSUB statement ends the function.

6. The CMPLIB= option specifies the Certadv.Functions table for SAS to search for a package that contains the desired function.

7. The DATA step creates a temporary data set named Work.Dates. The DATA step uses the DO loop to create a Dates column with values from January 15 2019 to December 31 2019.

    The assignment statement creates a new variable MonNum that uses the month function. SAS supplies the MONTH function to generate a value using the Dates variable.

8. The assignment statement creates the FiscalQuarter variable using the custom function MyQuarter and the value of MonNum as the argument.

9. The PRINT procedure prints the Work.Dates data set. The FORMAT statement, applied to the Dates column, displays the dates as mmddyy10.

Output 13.4 PROC PRINT Output of Work.Dates

Obs	Dates	MonNum	FiscalQuarter
1	01/15/2019	1	4
2	02/14/2019	2	1
3	03/16/2019	3	1
4	04/15/2019	4	1
5	05/15/2019	5	2
6	06/14/2019	6	2
7	07/14/2019	7	2
8	08/13/2019	8	3
9	09/12/2019	9	3
10	10/12/2019	10	3
11	11/11/2019	11	4
12	12/11/2019	12	4

Example: Creating a Custom Character Function with Multiple Arguments

Thus far, the examples in this chapter have focused on creating functions that contained one argument. You can specify multiple arguments for custom functions by separating the arguments with a comma (,). If the argument is a character value, then a dollar sign ($) is placed after the argument before the comma.

The following example creates a character function called ReverseName with two character arguments, LastFirst and Pos.

```
proc fcmp outlib=certadv.functions.dev;             /* 1 */
   function ReverseName(lastfirst $, pos $) $ 40;   /* 2 */
      First=scan(lastfirst,2,',');                  /* 3 */
      Last=scan(lastfirst,1,',');
      if substr(pos,2,1)='F' then
         return(catx(' ','Outfielder',First,Last));
      else if substr(pos,2,1)='B' then
         return(catx(' ','Baseman',First,Last));
      else return(catx(' ',pos,First,Last));
   endsub;                                          /* 4 */
quit;

options cmplib=work.functions;                      /* 5 */

data work.baseball;                                 /* 6 */
   set certadv.baseball;
   Player=reversename(Name,Position);               /* 7 */
   keep Name Team Position Player;
run;
proc print data=baseball;
run;
```

1. The FCMP procedure enables you to create a custom function. The OUTLIB= option specifies Certadv.Functions as the table in which the Dev package is stored. The Dev package is a collection of routines that have unique names.

2. The FUNCTION statement specifies the function name as ReverseName. ReverseName has two character arguments named LastFirst and Pos, and it returns character values with the length of 40. If a return value type and length are not specified, the default is numeric with a length of 8.

3. The body of the function consists of DATA step syntax. The assignment statement creates two new variables First and Last using the SCAN function. The new variable First uses the SCAN function to return the second word from the LastFirst variable value and the Last variable returns the first word from the LastFirst variable value.

    The IF-THEN/ELSE statements use the SUBSTR function to extract the second character of the Pos value. Based on the value returned by the SUBSTR function, the appropriate concatenation is made using CATX. For example, in the fourth observation the second character in the Pos value is F so the ReverseName function returns Outfielder Andre Dawson.

    If none of the criteria for the IF-THEN statements are met, then the ELSE statement returns by the value of Pos and the reversed order of the name.

4. The ENDSUB statement ends the function.

5. The CMPLIB= option specifies the Certadv.Functions table for SAS to search for a package that contains the desired function.

6. The DATA step creates a temporary data set named Work.Baseball by reading Certadv.Baseball.

7. The DATA step creates a new variable named Player and references the custom function, ReverseName. The function reverses the order of Name concatenated with the value of position and returns the string to the Player variable.

Output 13.5 *PROC PRINT Result of Work.Baseball (partial output)*

Obs	Name	Team	Position	Player
1	Allanson, Andy	Cleveland	C	C Andy Allanson
2	Ashby, Alan	Houston	C	C Alan Ashby
3	Davis, Alan	Seattle	1B	Baseman Alan Davis
4	Dawson, Andre	Montreal	RF	Outfielder Andre Dawson
5	Galarraga, Andres	Montreal	1B	Baseman Andres Galarraga
6	Griffin, Alfredo	Oakland	SS	SS Alfredo Griffin
7	Newman, Al	Montreal	2B	Baseman Al Newman
8	Salazar, Argenis	Kansas City	SS	SS Argenis Salazar
9	Thomas, Andres	Atlanta	SS	SS Andres Thomas
10	Thornton, Andre	Cleveland	DH	DH Andre Thornton
11	Trammell, Alan	Detroit	SS	SS Alan Trammell
12	Trevino, Alex	Los Angeles	C	C Alex Trevino
13	Van Slyke, Andy	St Louis	RF	Outfielder Andy Van Slyke
14	Wiggins, Alan	Baltimore	2B	Baseman Alan Wiggins
15	Almon, Bill	Pittsburgh	UT	UT Bill Almon

... *more observations* ...

Quiz

Select the best answer for each question. After completing the quiz, check your answers using the answer key in the appendix.

1. Which PICTURE statement displays a nine-digit account number with six leading asterisks followed by the last five digits, such as ******56789?

   a. `picture actfmt low-high='99999'(prefix='******');`

   b. `picture actfmt (prefix='******') low-high='99999';`

   c. `picture actfmt low-high='999999999' (prefix='******');`

   d. `picture actfmt (prefix='******') low-high='999999999';`

2. Which PICTURE statement generates a date format that produces the following results when used with the Date column?

Date
21793
21800
21807
21814
21821

   ⇒

Date
9/1/2019
9/8/2019
9/15/2019
9/22/2019
9/29/2019

a. `picture DateFmt low-high='%m/%d/%Y' (datatype=date);`
b. `picture DateFmt (default=10 )low-high='%m/%d/%Y'`
   `                (datatype=date);`
c. `picture DateFmt low-high='%m/%d/%Y'`
   `                (datatype=date default=10);`
d. `picture DateFmt (default=10) low-high='%m/%d/%Y'`
   `                (datatype=datetime);`

3. Which of the following are format options that can be placed after the format name?

    PICTURE *format-name<(format-options)>*
      <value-range-set-1 = 'template-value' (template-options)>
      <value-range-set-n = 'template-value' (template-options)>;

    a. DEFAULT=
    b. DATATYPE=
    c. MULTIPLIER=
    d. ROUND
    e. a and d only.
    f. b and c only.

4. What system option do you have to specify in order to use the new function that you created in a DATA step or a supported PROC step?

    a. FCMPLIB=
    b. LIBCMP=
    c. CMPLIB=
    d. OUTLIB=

5. Which directives create the following value?

    ```
    2019.03.19 @ 8:25:19 PM
    ```

    a. `%Y.%m.%d@%H:%M:%S%p`
    b. `%Y.%m.%d@%I:%0M:%0S%p`
    c. `%Y.%0m.%0d @ %I:%0M:%0S%p`
    d. `%0Y.%0m.%0d@%H:%0M:%0S%p`

6. Complete the FUNCTION statement to create a function named TitleName that consists of two character arguments.

    ```
    proc fcmp outlib=certadv.functions.samp;
      function TitleName _____ $50;
        if JobCode='S' then return(catx(' ','Software',',JobTitle'));
        else if JobCode='M' then return(catx(' ','Manager of ',',JobTitle'));
    ```

    a. `(JobTitle, JobCode)`
    b. `(JobTitle $, JobCode $)`
    c. `('JobTitle' $, 'JobCode' $)`
    d. `('JobTitle $', 'JobCode $')`

7. Which statement is true concerning the following PROC FCMP statement?

```
proc fcmp outlib=certadv.funcs.dev;
```

a. The custom function will be stored in the SAS table Funcs.Dev.

b. The custom function will be stored in the Certadv package within the SAS table Funcs.Dev.

c. The custom function will be stored in the Dev folder within the SAS package Certadv.Funcs.

d. The custom function will be stored in the Dev package within the SAS table Certadv.Funcs.

Chapter 14
Using Advanced Functions

Using a Variety of Advanced Functions **337**
    The LAG Function 337
    The COUNT/COUNTC/COUNTW Function 340
    The FIND/FINDC/FINDW Function 342

Performing Pattern Matching with Perl Regular Expressions **344**
    A Brief Overview 344
    Using Metacharacters 345
    Example: Using Metacharacters 346
    The PRXMATCH Function 347
    The PRXPARSE Function 349
    The PRXCHANGE Function 351

Quiz **355**

Using a Variety of Advanced Functions

The LAG Function

A Brief Overview
Suppose you have the Certadv.Stock6Mon data set that contains opening and closing stock prices for the past six months for two different companies. You are trying to determine which company has the bigger difference in the daily opening price between consecutive days.

To start, consider what you want the LAG function to return, as shown below.

338 Chapter 14 • *Using Advanced Functions*

Figure 14.1 Desired LAG Function Results for ABC Company, by Day

Obs	Stock	Date	Open	FirstPrevDay	SecondPrevDay	ThirdPrevDay
1	ABC Company	03/01/2019	54.37	.	.	.
2	ABC Company	03/04/2019	59.53	54.37	.	.
3	ABC Company	03/05/2019	59.45	59.53	54.37	.
4	ABC Company	03/06/2019	57.18	59.45	59.53	54.37
5	ABC Company	03/07/2019	57.55	57.18	59.45	59.53

Need to create

The LAG function enables you to compare the daily opening prices between consecutive days by retrieving the previous values of a column from the last time that the LAG function executed.

LAG Function Syntax

The LAG function retrieves a value from a previous observation. It is able to do so because the function maintains a queue of the previous values. If you use LAG or LAG1, you are looking for the previous value one row back. LAG2 gives you the previous value two rows back. LAG3 gives you the previous value three rows back, and so on. The LAG function is useful for computing differences between rows and computing moving averages.

Syntax, LAG function:

LAG<*n*>(*column*);

n
   specifies the number of lagged values.

column
   specifies a numeric or character constant, variable, or expression.

Example: Retrieving Previous Values

The following example uses the LAG function to retrieve previous values using assignment statements. The LAG function also creates new variables based on the previous values of Open. Using March 6 as an example, the first previous value is 59.45, the second previous value is 59.53, and the third previous value is 54.37. These values are highlighted in the table below.

Note: For the first observation, there are no previous values to look up, so the assignment statement returns a missing value. For the second observation, there is a first previous value but no second and third previous values, and so on.

```
data work.stockprev;
   set certadv.Stock6Mon(drop=Close);
   FirstPrevDay=lag1(Open);
   SecondPrevDay=lag2(Open);
   ThirdPrevDay=lag3(Open);
run;
proc print data=work.stockprev;
run;
```

Output 14.1 PROC PRINT Output of Work.StockPrev (partial output)

Obs	Stock	Date	Open	FirstPrevDay	SecondPrevDay	ThirdPrevDay
1	ABC Company	03/01/2019	54.37	.	.	.
2	ABC Company	03/04/2019	59.53	54.37	.	.
3	ABC Company	03/05/2019	59.45	59.53	54.37	.
4	ABC Company	03/06/2019	57.18	59.45	59.53	54.37
5	ABC Company	03/07/2019	57.55	57.18	59.45	59.53
6	ABC Company	03/08/2019	60.68	57.55	57.18	59.45
7	ABC Company	03/11/2019	62.50	60.68	57.55	57.18
8	ABC Company	03/12/2019	65.50	62.50	60.68	57.55
9	ABC Company	03/13/2019	65.26	65.50	62.50	60.68
10	ABC Company	03/14/2019	64.56	65.26	65.50	62.50

...*more observations*...

Example: Calculating a Moving Average

In addition to computing differences between rows, you can calculate a moving average using the LAG function.

Suppose you have stock prices for the Random Company. The data set contains the opening stock price for the first work day of each month. You need to calculate a moving three-month average. Again, consider what you want the LAG function to return, as shown below.

Figure 14.2 Desired LAG Function Results for Random Company, by Month

Obs	Stock	Date	Open	Open1Month	Open2Month	Open3MonthAvg
1	Random Company	03/01/2019	53.98	.	.	53.98
2	Random Company	04/01/2019	50.39	53.98	.	52.19
3	Random Company	05/01/2019	52.62	50.39	53.98	52.33
4	Random Company	06/03/2019	49.61	52.62	50.39	50.87
5	Random Company	07/01/2019	50.53	49.61	52.62	50.92
6	Random Company	08/01/2019	50.89	50.53	49.61	50.34
7	Random Company	09/03/2019	44.21	50.89	50.53	48.54

Need to create

You can use the LAG function to get the stock price for the past two months. The third row is the first row that calculates an average based on three values.

```
data work.stockavg;
   set certadv.stocks(drop=Close);
   Open1Month=lag1(Open);
   Open2Month=lag2(Open);
   Open3MonthAvg=mean(Open,Open1Month,Open2Month);
```

```
        format Open3MonthAvg 8.2;
run;
proc print data=work.stockavg;
run;
```

Output 14.2 PROC PRINT Output of Work.StockAvg

Obs	Stock	Date	Open	Open1Month	Open2Month	Open3MonthAvg
1	Random Company	03/01/2019	53.98	.	.	53.98
2	Random Company	04/01/2019	50.39	53.98	.	52.19
3	Random Company	05/01/2019	52.62	50.39	53.98	52.33
4	Random Company	06/03/2019	49.61	52.62	50.39	50.87
5	Random Company	07/01/2019	50.53	49.61	52.62	50.92
6	Random Company	08/01/2019	50.89	50.53	49.61	50.34
7	Random Company	09/03/2019	44.21	50.89	50.53	48.54

Note: The best practice is to create a lagged value in an assignment statement before using it in a conditional statement.

The COUNT/COUNTC/COUNTW Function

A Brief Overview

Suppose you have the Certadv.Slogans data set, which contains numerous slogans that a company can use for its business. You are asked to identify the number of times a specific word, 24/7, was used in a slogan and how many words were in a slogan. The slogans are separated by commas in a row.

You can use the COUNT function to count the number of times a specific word such as 24/7 appears in the slogan, or you can use the COUNTW function to count the number of words in a slogan. You could even use the COUNTC function to count the number of characters in a slogan.

Note: Word is defined as a character constant, variable, or expression.

COUNT/COUNTC/COUNTW Syntax

There are three variations of the COUNT function. Note the slight difference in syntax for the three functions.

Table 14.1 COUNT/COUNTC/COUNTW Syntax

Function Name	Syntax	Function Definition
COUNT	**COUNT**(*string, substring* <,*modifiers*>)	Counts the number of times that a specified substring appears within a character string.
COUNTC	**COUNTC**(*string, character-list* <,*modifiers*>)	Counts the number of characters in a string that appear or do not appear in a list of characters.

Function Name	Syntax	Function Definition
COUNTW	**COUNTW**(*string* <,*delimiters*><,*modifiers*>)	Counts the number of words in a character string.

character-list
    specifies a character constant, variable, or expression that initializes a list of characters. COUNTC counts characters in this list, provided that you do not specify the V modifier in the modifier argument. If you specify the V modifier, all characters that are not in this list are counted. You can add more characters to the list by using other modifiers.

delimiters
    can be any of several characters that are used to separate words. You can specify the delimiters by using the *chars* argument, the *modifier* argument, or both.

modifiers
    is a character constant, variable, or expression that specifies one or more modifiers. *modifiers* is an optional argument.

    i or I
        ignores the case of the characters. If this modifier is not specified, COUNT counts character substrings only with the same case as the characters in substring.

    t or T
        trims trailing blanks from string, substring, and chars arguments.

string
    specifies a character constant, variable, or expression in which substrings are to be counted.

    TIP Enclose a literal string of characters in quotation marks.

substring
    is a character constant, variable, or expression that specifies the substring of characters to search for in string.

    TIP Enclose a literal substring of characters in quotation marks.

Example: Counting the Number of Words

The following example uses the COUNT function to count the number of times 24/7 appears in the Slogans column. The COUNTW function counts the number of words in the Slogans column. The COUNTW function does not specify any delimiter. Therefore, a default list of `blank ! $ % & ( ) * + , - . / ; < ^ |` is used.

```
data work.sloganact;
   set certadv.slogans;
   Num24=count(Slogans,'24/7');
   NumWord=countw(Slogans);
run;
proc print data=work.sloganact;
run;
```

The COUNT function returns the number of times 24/7 appeared in the Slogan column and assigns the value to Num24. Notice that observation 5 contains 24/365. However, this was not counted as a part of the 24/7. If you change the string to search for to 24/, then 24/365 would appear in the Num24 column. The COUNTW function counts the number of words in each slogan and assigns the value to NumWord.

Output 14.3 PROC PRINT Output of Work.SloganAct

Obs	Slogans	Num24	NumWord
1	repurpose 24/7 markets,productize enterprise web services,brand efficient mindshare	1	11
2	revolutionize killer solutions,expedite e-business e-services,innovate back-end web services	0	13
3	harness 24/7 e-services,redefine visionary systems,exploit strategic schemas	1	11
4	reinvent clicks-and-mortar platforms,revolutionize B2B systems,target integrated models	0	11
5	reintermediate 24/365 systems,cultivate strategic functionalities,brand turn-key synergies	0	11
6	productize best-of-breed communities,benchmark out-of-the-box channels,generate seamless users	0	14
7	iterate killer functionalities,envisioneer user-centric supply-chains,extend end-to-end bandwidth	0	13
8	drive cross-platform portals,embrace clicks-and-mortar infrastructures,target dot-com content	0	13
9	seize holistic web services,harness best-of-breed mindshare,scale integrated synergies	0	12
10	incentivize global niches,generate impactful vortals,aggregate scalable deliverables	0	9

The FIND/FINDC/FINDW Function

A Brief Overview

Suppose you were asked to identify the starting position of the first occurrence of 24/7 in a string. The FIND function finds the starting position of the first occurrence of a substring in a string. Alternatives to the FIND function are the FINDC and FINDW functions, which are also based on finding the first occurrence. The FINDC function returns the starting position where a character from a list of characters is found in a string, and the FINDW function returns the starting position of a word in a string or the number of the word in a string.

FIND/FINDC/FINDW Function Syntax

There are three variations of the FIND function. Note the slight difference in syntax for the three functions.

Table 14.2 FIND/FINDC/FINDW Function Syntax

Function Name	Syntax	Function Definition
FIND	**FIND** (*string, substring* <, *modifiers*><, *start-position*>);	Searches for a specific substring of characters within a character string.
		Returns the starting position where a substring is found in a string.
FINDC	**FINDC** (*string, character-list* <, *modifiers*> <, *start-position*>);	Searches a string for any character in a list of characters.
		Returns the starting position where a character from a list of characters is found in a string.

Function Name	Syntax	Function Definition
FINDW	**FINDW** (*string, word<, delimiters><, modifiers> <, start-position>*);	Returns the character position of a word in a string, or returns the number of the word in a string.

character-list
> is a constant, variable, or character expression that initializes a list of characters. FINDC searches for the characters in this list, provided that you do not specify the K modifier in the *modifiers* argument. If you specify the K modifier, FINDC searches for all characters that are not in this list of characters. You can add more characters to the list by using other modifiers.

delimiters
> can be any of several characters that are used to separate words. You can specify the delimiters by using the *chars* argument, the *modifiers* argument, or both.

modifiers
> is a character constant, variable, or expression that specifies one or more modifiers.
>
> *i* or I
> > ignores the case of the characters. If this modifier is not specified, FIND searches only for character substrings with the same case as the characters in substring.
>
> *t* or T
> > trims trailing blanks from the *string*, *word*, and *chars* arguments.

start-position
> is a numeric constant, variable, or expression with an integer value that specifies the position at which the search should start and the direction of the search.

string
> specifies a character constant, variable, or expression that will be searched for substrings.
>
> **TIP** Enclose a literal string of characters in quotation marks.

substring
> is a character constant, variable, or expression that specifies the substring of characters to search for in string.
>
> **TIP** Enclose a literal substring of characters in quotation marks.

word
> is a character constant, variable, or expression that specifies the word to be searched for.

Example: Finding the Word Number

You can use the FINDW function to return the number of the word 24/7 in the Slogans string. The third argument uses a blank to specify the delimiter separating the words in the string. The E modifier tells SAS to count the number of words instead of returning the starting position. The *modifiers* argument must be positioned after the *delimiters* argument. The E modifier is just one of the modifiers that can be used.

```
data work.sloganact;
    set certadv.slogans;
    Num24=count(Slogans,'24/7');
    NumWord=countw(Slogans);
    FindWord24=findw(Slogans,'24/7',' ','e');
```

```
                        run;
                        proc print data=work.sloganact;
                        run;
```

Output 14.4 PROC PRINT Output of Work.SloganAct (partial output)

Obs	Slogans	Num24	NumWord	FindWord24
1	repurpose 24/7 markets,productize enterprise web services,brand efficient mindshare	1	11	2
2	revolutionize killer solutions,expedite e-business e-services,innovate back-end web services	0	13	0
3	harness 24/7 e-services,redefine visionary systems,exploit strategic schemas	1	11	2
4	reinvent clicks-and-mortar platforms,revolutionize B2B systems,target integrated models	0	11	0
5	reintermediate 24/365 systems,cultivate strategic functionalities,brand turn-key synergies	0	11	0
6	productize best-of-breed communities,benchmark out-of-the-box channels,generate seamless users	0	14	0
7	iterate killer functionalities,envisioneer user-centric supply-chains,extend end-to-end bandwidth	0	13	0
8	drive cross-platform portals,embrace clicks-and-mortar infrastructures,target dot-com content	0	13	0
9	seize holistic web services,harness best-of-breed mindshare,scale integrated synergies	0	12	0
10	incentivize global niches,generate impactful vortals,aggregate scalable deliverables	0	9	0

Performing Pattern Matching with Perl Regular Expressions

A Brief Overview

Perl regular expressions enable you to perform pattern matching by using functions. A *regular expression* is a sequence of strings that defines a search pattern.

For example, suppose you have the Certadv.NANumbr data set, which contains phone numbers for the United States, Canada, and Mexico.

Figure 14.3 Certadv.NaNumbr Data Set (partial output)

Obs	Name	PhoneNumber	Country
1	Alexander Mcknight	(738) 766-2114	Canada
2	Alison Campbell	943.519.8369	United States
3	Amador Alvaro Luna	3581599311	Mexico
4	Amanda Johnson	362-686-6286	Canada
5	Amy Williams	953-246-7733	United States
6	Ann Keith	(375) 862-7384	Canada
7	Anne Weaver	793-199-3925	United States
8	Arturo Longoria	203-752-8263	Mexico
9	Brandon Kerr	555-677-4102	United States
10	Camilo Indira Mojica Romero	718.690.4147	Mexico

By using a regular expression, you can find valid values for Phone. The advantage of using regular expressions is that you can often accomplish in only one Perl regular expression function something that would require a combination of traditional SAS functions to accomplish.

In SAS, you use Perl regular expressions within the functions and call routines that start with PRX. The PRX functions use a modified version of the Perl language (Perl 5.6.1) to perform regular expression compilation and matching.

Using Metacharacters

The Perl regular expressions within the PRX functions and call routines are based on using metacharacters. A metacharacter is a character that has a special meaning during pattern processing. You can use metacharacters in regular expressions to define the search criteria and any text manipulations. The following table lists the metacharacters that you can use to match patterns in Perl regular expressions.

Table 14.3 Basic Perl Metacharacters and Their Descriptions

Metacharacter	Description	Example
/.../	Provides the starting and ending delimiter.	`s/ ([a-z]) / X /` substitutes `X` in place of a space followed by a lowercase letter and then a space.
(...)	Enables grouping.	`f(u|boo)bar` matches `"fubar"` or `"foobar"`.
|	Denotes the OR situation.	
\d	Matches a digit (0–9).	`\d\d\d\d` matches any four-digit string (0-9) such as `"1234"` or `"6387"`
\D	Matches a non-digit such as a letter or special character.	`\D\D\D\D` matches any four non-digit string such as `"WxYz"` or `"AVG%"`
\s	Matches a whitespace character such as a space, tab, or newline.	`x\sx` matches `"x x"` (space between the letters x) or `"x x"` (tab between the letters x).
\w	Matches a group of one or more characters (a-z, A-Z, 0-9, or an underscore).	`\w\w\w` matches any three-word characters.
.	Matches any character.	`mi.e` matches `"mike"` and `"mice"`.
[...]	Matches a character in brackets.	`[dmn]ice` matches `"dice"` or `"mice"` or `"nice"`
		`\d[6789]\d` matches `"162"` or `"574"` or `"685"` or `"999"`
[^...]	Matches a character not in brackets.	[^] matches
		[^] matches " " but not " "

Metacharacter	Description	Example
^	Matches the beginning of the string.	`d[^a]me` matches "`dime`" or "`dome`" but not "`dame`".
$	Matches the end of the string.	`ter$` matches "`winter`" not "`winner`" or "`terminal`".
\b	Matches a word boundary (the last position before a space).	`bar\b` matches "`bar food`" but not "`barfood`" or "`barter`".
\B	Matches a non-word boundary.	`bar\B` matches "`foobar`" but not "`bar food`".
*	Matches the preceding character 0 or more times.	• `zo*` matches "`z`" and "`zoo`" • `*` is equivalent to {0,}
+	Matches the preceding character 1 or more times.	• `zo+` matches "`zo`" and "`zoo`". • `zo+` does not match "`z`" • `+` is equivalent to {1,}
?	Matches the preceding character 0 or 1 times.	• `do(es)?` matches the "`do`" in "`do`" or "`does`" • `?` is equivalent to {0,1}
{n}	Matches exactly *n* times.	`fo{2}bar` matches "`foobar`" but not "`fobar`" or "`fooobar`".
\	Overrides the next metacharacter such as a (or ?)	`final\.` matches "`final.`" "`final`" is followed by the character '.'

Example: Using Metacharacters

A valid United States, Canada, or Mexico phone number contains a three-digit area code, followed by a hyphen (-), a three-digit prefix, and then the remaining numbers. More specifically, the first digit of the area code and prefix cannot start with 0 or 1.

A Perl regular expression must start and end with a delimiter. The following example uses parentheses to represent a group of numbers that is required. The first two groups specify that first there must be a digit 2 through 9 followed by two more digits. In the last group, there must be four digits. The hyphens between the groups signify the hyphens between the numbers in the output.

```
/([2-9]\d\d)-([2-9]\d\d)-(\d{4})/
```

Output 14.5 *Certadv.NaNumbr Data Set (partial output)*

Obs	Name	PhoneNumber	Country
1	Alexander Mcknight	(738) 766-2114	Canada
2	Alison Campbell	943.519.8369	United States
3	Amador Alvaro Luna	3581599311	Mexico
4	Amanda Johnson	362-686-6286	Canada
5	Amy Williams	953-246-7733	United States
6	Ann Keith	(375) 862-7384	Canada
7	Anne Weaver	793-199-3925	United States
8	Arturo Longoria	203-752-8263	Mexico
9	Brandon Kerr	555-677-4102	United States
10	Camilo Indira Mojica Romero	718.690.4147	Mexico

The PRXMATCH Function

A Brief Overview

The Perl regular expression using metacharacters can be used with the PRX functions. The PRXMATCH function searches for a pattern match and returns the position at which the pattern is found. A value of zero is returned if no match is found. This function has two arguments. The first argument specifies the Perl regular expression that contains your pattern. The second argument is the character constant, column, or expression that you want to search.

PRXMATCH Syntax

Syntax, PRXMATCH function:

PRXMATCH (*Perl-regular-expression, source*);

Perl-regular-expression
    specifies a character value that is a Perl regular expression. The expression can be referenced using a constant, a column, or a pattern identifier number.

source
    specifies a character constant, variable, or expression that you want to search.

Example: PRXMATCH Function Using a Constant

The PRXMATCH function is commonly used for validating data. The following example uses the PRXMATCH function to validate whether a phone number pattern is present.

If the pattern is present, a numeric value is returned to the pattern's starting position. For this example, the pattern was found in 19 rows.

The example specifies the expression as a hard-coded constant as the first argument of the function. When a constant value is specified, the constant must be in quotation marks (either single or double). When you specify the expression as a constant, the expression is compiled once, and each use of the PRX function reuses the compiled expression.

Compiling the expression only once saves time. The compiled version is saved in memory.

```
data work.matchphn;
   set certadv.nanumbr;
   loc=prxmatch('/([2-9]\d\d)-([2-9]\d\d)-(\d{4})/',PhoneNumber);
run;
proc print data=work.matchphn;
   where loc>0;
run;
```

Output 14.6 *PROC PRINT Result of Work.MatchPhn*

Obs	Name	PhoneNumber	Country	loc
4	Amanda Johnson	362-686-6286	Canada	1
5	Amy Williams	953-246-7733	United States	1
8	Arturo Longoria	203-752-8263	Mexico	1
9	Brandon Kerr	555-677-4102	United States	1
16	Denise Todd	944-905-6288	United States	1
24	Francisco Javier Vanesa Espinoza Pajez	692-804-6430x771	Mexico	1
28	Jaime White	466-646-6557	United States	1
29	Jeffrey Archer	445-765-3784	United States	1
48	Leonor Cisneros	623-656-4441	Mexico	1
50	Lisa Evans PhD	244-697-6738	Canada	1
57	Marissa Hudson	814-917-4811	Canada	1
62	Melissa Gross	879-348-5158	United States	1
65	Minerva Baeza	542-214-2366	Mexico	1
66	Nancy Thomas	642-802-8384	United States	1
69	Pablo Montalvo	630-742-7059x89285	Mexico	1
71	Pedro Vallejo Salgado	875-613-3160	Mexico	1
77	Sarah Young	530-587-5777	United States	1
84	Timothy Christian	862-737-4712	Canada	1
87	William Small	480-398-3374	United States	1

Example: PRXMATCH Function Using a Column

Instead of using the first argument to specify a constant for the regular expression, you can refer to a column that contains the expression. This is a commonly used technique when you might need to manipulate the assignment statement that is specifying the expression.

When the first argument refers to a column instead of a constant, the expression is compiled for each execution of the function. To avoid compiling the expression each time, specify the option of a lower or uppercase O at the end of the expression. This makes SAS compile the expression only once. This is a useful approach when you have large data sets, as it decreases your processing time.

```
data work.phnumbr (drop=Exp);
```

```
      set certadv.nanumbr;
      Exp='/([2-9]\d\d)-([2-9]\d\d)-(\d{4})/o';
      Loc=prxmatch(Exp,PhoneNumber);
run;
proc print data=work.phnumbr;
   where loc>0;
run;
```

Output 14.7 PROC PRINT Result of Work.PhNumbr

Obs	Name	PhoneNumber	Country	loc
4	Amanda Johnson	362-686-6286	Canada	1
5	Amy Williams	953-246-7733	United States	1
8	Arturo Longoria	203-752-8263	Mexico	1
9	Brandon Kerr	555-677-4102	United States	1
16	Denise Todd	944-905-6288	United States	1
24	Francisco Javier Vanesa Espinoza Pajez	692-804-6430x771	Mexico	1
28	Jaime White	466-646-6557	United States	1
29	Jeffrey Archer	445-765-3784	United States	1
48	Leonor Cisneros	623-656-4441	Mexico	1
50	Lisa Evans PhD	244-697-6738	Canada	1
57	Marissa Hudson	814-917-4811	Canada	1
62	Melissa Gross	879-348-5158	United States	1
65	Minerva Baeza	542-214-2366	Mexico	1
66	Nancy Thomas	642-802-8384	United States	1
69	Pablo Montalvo	630-742-7059x89285	Mexico	1
71	Pedro Vallejo Salgado	875-613-3160	Mexico	1
77	Sarah Young	530-587-5777	United States	1
84	Timothy Christian	862-737-4712	Canada	1
87	William Small	480-398-3374	United States	1

The PRXPARSE Function

A Brief Overview

Another method for specifying the Perl regular expression is to specify a pattern identifier number. Before using PRXMATCH, you can use the PRXPARSE function to create the pattern identifier number. This function references the regular expression either as a constant or a column. The function returns a pattern identifier number. This number can then be passed to PRX functions and call routines to reference the regular expression. It is not required to use the pattern identifier number with the PRXMATCH function, but some of the other PRX functions and call routines do require the pattern identifier number.

PRXPARSE Function Syntax

The PRXPARSE function returns a pattern identifier number that is used by other PRX functions and call routines.

Syntax, PRXPARSE function:

pattern-ID-number=**PRXPARSE** (*Perl-regular-expression*);

pattern-ID-number
　is a numeric pattern identifier that is returned by the PRXPARSE function.

Perl-regular-expression
　specifies a character value that is a Perl regular expression. The expression can be referenced using a constant, a column, or a pattern identifier number.

Example: PRXPARSE and PRXMATCH Function Using a Pattern ID Number

In this example, the regular expression is being assigned to the column Exp. The PRXPARSE function is referencing this column. Because the expression ends with the O option, the function compiles the value only once. The PRXPARSE function returns a number that is associated with this expression. In this example, the number is a value of 1, and the value is being stored in the Pid column.

PRXMATCH then references this number in the Pid column as its first argument. If the O option had not used at the end of the Perl regular expression, the value of Pid would differ for each row.

```
data work.phnumbr (drop=Exp);
   set certadv.nanumbr;
   Exp='/([2-9]\d\d)-([2-9]\d\d)-(\d{4})/o';
   Pid=prxparse(Exp);
   Loc=prxmatch(Pid,PhoneNumber);
run;
proc print data=work.phnumbr;
run;
```

Output 14.8 PROC PRINT Output of Work.PhNumbr (partial output)

Obs	Name	PhoneNumber	Country	Pid	Loc
1	Alexander Mcknight	(738) 766-2114	Canada	1	0
2	Alison Campbell	943.519.8369	United States	1	0
3	Amador Alvaro Luna	3581599311	Mexico	1	0
4	Amanda Johnson	362-686-6286	Canada	1	1
5	Amy Williams	953-246-7733	United States	1	1
6	Ann Keith	(375) 862-7384	Canada	1	0
7	Anne Weaver	793-199-3925	United States	1	0
8	Arturo Longoria	203-752-8263	Mexico	1	1
9	Brandon Kerr	555-677-4102	United States	1	1
10	Camilo Indira Mojica Romero	718.690.4147	Mexico	1	0

The PRXCHANGE Function

A Brief Overview
The PRXCHANGE function performs a substitution for a pattern match. This function has three arguments. The first argument is the Perl regular expression, which can be specified as a constant, a column, or a pattern identifier number that comes from the PRXPARSE function. The second argument is a numeric value that specifies the number of times to search for a match and replace it with a matching pattern. If the value is -1, then the matching pattern continues to be replaced until the end of the source is reached. The third argument is the character constant, column, or expression that you want to search for.

PRXCHANGE Function Syntax
The PRXCHANGE function performs a substitution for a pattern match.

Syntax, PRXCHANGE function:

PRXCHANGE (*Perl-regular-expression, times, source*)

Perl-regular-expression
    specifies a character value that is a Perl regular expression. The expression can be referenced using a constant, a column, or a pattern identifier number.

times
    is a numeric constant, variable, or expression that specifies the number of times to search for a match and replace a matching pattern.

source
    specifies a character constant, variable, or expression that you want to search.

Example: Using the PRXCHANGE Function to Standardize Data
The PRXCHANGE function is commonly used to standardize data. For example, the Certadv.SocialAcct data set contains social media preference data for users between the ages of 18 and 50. The goal is to standardize the Certadv.SocialAcct data set by substituting Facebook for Fb and FB as well as Instagram for IG.

Figure 14.4 Certadv.SocialAcct (partial output)

Obs	Name	Age	Social_Media_Pref1	Social_Media_Pref2
1	Emily Stafford	23	IG	FB
2	Rachel Valenzuela	24	IG	FB
3	Roger Kelly	26	IG	FB
4	Laura Ramirez	27	IG	FB
5	Michael Williams	30	IG	FB
6	Danielle Middleton	31	IG	FB
7	Matthew Mcguire	32	IG	FB
8	Natalie Velasquez	33	IG	FB
9	Gary Andrews DVM	34	IG	FB
10	Jeremy Blake	37	IG	FB

When you are writing the Perl regular expression for substitution, start the expression with a lowercase *s*. The lowercase *s* signifies that substitution needs to happen instead of matching.

Following the lowercase *s*, place the beginning delimiter before the forward slash. Also, place the forward slash at the end of the expression. There is another forward slash between the starting and ending forward slashes.

Before the middle forward slash, specify the pattern that you are searching for, enclosed in parentheses. After the middle forward slash, specify the pattern that is to be used for substitution.

In this example, you are looking for the capital letters FB and IG in both Social_Media_Pref1 and Social_Media_Pref2 variables. If the pattern is found, then replace with Facebook and Instagram, respectively. The *i* modifier ignores the case of the pattern that you are searching for.

```
data work.prxsocial;
   set certadv.socialacct;
   Social_Media_Pref1=prxchange('s/(FB)/Facebook/i',-1,Social_Media_Pref1);
   Social_Media_Pref1=prxchange('s/(IG)/Instagram/i',-1,Social_Media_Pref1);
   Social_Media_Pref2=prxchange('s/(FB)/Facebook/i',-1,Social_Media_Pref2);
   Social_Media_Pref2=prxchange('s/(IG)/Instagram/i',-1,Social_Media_Pref2);
run;
proc print data=work.prxsocial;
run;
```

Output 14.9 PROC PRINT Output of Work.PrxSocial (partial output)

Obs	Name	Age	Social_Media_Pref1	Social_Media_Pref2
1	Emily Stafford	23	Instagram	Facebook
2	Rachel Valenzuela	24	Instagram	Facebook
3	Roger Kelly	26	Instagram	Facebook
4	Laura Ramirez	27	Instagram	Facebook
5	Michael Williams	30	Instagram	Facebook
6	Danielle Middleton	31	Instagram	Facebook
7	Matthew Mcguire	32	Instagram	Facebook
8	Natalie Velasquez	33	Instagram	Facebook
9	Gary Andrews DVM	34	Instagram	Facebook
10	Jeremy Blake	37	Instagram	Facebook

Example: Changing the Order Using the PRXCHANGE Function

Suppose you have the Certadv.SurvNames data set with names from the self-reported survey. Every 50th surveyor is given a gift card that is to be mailed to the surveyor's home. You are asked to quickly reverse the names of the survey takers. You can use the PRXCHANGE function to reverse the order of the names.

```
data work.revname;
    set certadv.survnames;
    ReverseName=prxchange('s/(\w+), (\w+)/$2 $1/', -1, name);
run;
proc print data=work.revname;
run;
```

Output 14.10   PROC PRINT Result of Work.RevName

Obs	Name	ReverseName
1	Rivera, Marilyn	Marilyn Rivera
2	Baker, Andrew	Andrew Baker
3	Wilson, Aaron	Aaron Wilson
4	Rush, Samantha	Samantha Rush
5	Hutchinson, Brittany	Brittany Hutchinson
6	Abbott, Angela	Angela Abbott
7	Lambert, Alyssa	Alyssa Lambert
8	Casey, James	James Casey
9	Owens, John	John Owens
10	Cross, Brandon	Brandon Cross
11	Hernandez, Maurice	Maurice Hernandez
12	Barajas, Katherine	Katherine Barajas
13	Maldonado, Wayne	Wayne Maldonado
14	Jones, Angela	Angela Jones
15	Larson, Christina	Christina Larson
16	Wu, Fong	Fong Wu
17	Patil, Sunish	Sunish Patil
18	Joram, Koko	Koko Joram

Example: Capture Buffers for Substitution Using the PRXCHANGE Function

Suppose you have the data set Certadv.Email with email addresses, longitude, and latitude of those who have visited the company website. You are asked to reorder the longitude and latitude values to latitude and longitude.

When specifying a substitution value, you might need to rearrange pieces of the found pattern. This is possible using capture buffers.

In an earlier section, parentheses were used to represent grouping. When you use parentheses for grouping, you are creating capture buffers. Each capture buffer is referenced with a sequential number starting at 1. The first set of parentheses is for capture buffer 1. The second set of parentheses is for capture buffer 2, and so on.

When referencing a capture buffer, use a dollar sign in front of the capture buffer number. In the following example, specify the third buffer first and the first buffer last.

```
data work.latlong;
   set certadv.email;
   LatLong=prxchange('s/(-?\d+\.\d*)(@)(-?\d+\.\d*)/$3$2$1/', -1, LongLat);
run;
proc print data=work.latlong;
run;
```

Output 14.11 PROC PRINT Output of Work.LatLong (partial output)

Obs	LongLat	Email	LatLong
1	65.2874@50.8984	nichole42@hotmail.com	50.8984@65.2874
2	3.5495@115.2165	fgomez@gmail.com	115.2165@3.5495
3	88.0188@95.1651	jennifer92@gmail.com	95.1651@88.0188
4	56.2354@76.1265	rdeleon@yahoo.com	76.1265@56.2354
5	72.8874@51.1568	blee@rojas.com	51.1568@72.8874
6	23.5249@64.1968	tross@clark.org	64.1968@23.5249
7	50.1589@129.1596	williamsaaron@gmail.com	129.1596@50.1589
8	26.2291@109.0581	tammymorrow@gmail.com	109.0581@26.2291
9	2.1916@13.0526	deannadavid@gmail.com	13.0526@2.1916
10	38.5944@170.5497	daniel79@young.com	170.5497@38.5944

Quiz

1. If a substring is not found in a string, the FIND function returns which value?

    a. 0

    b. 1

    c. 2

    d. Not found.

2. Given the following DATA step, what is the value of USNum and WordNum?

    ```
    data work.Count;
        Text='AUSTRALIA, ENGLAND, CANADA, AUSTRIA, ITALY, US, SPAIN';
        USNum=count(Text,'CANADA');
        WordNum=countw(Text);
    run;
    ```

    a. 0, 7

    b. 1, 7

    c. 3, 0

    d. 3, 0

3. Which program would correctly generate two separate lagged variables for each observation?

    a.
    ```
    data work.samp1;
        set work.lag0;
        y=lag1-lag2(item);
    run;
    proc print data=work.samp1;
    run;
    ```

    b.
    ```
    data work.samp2;
        set work.lag0;
    ```

```
                              y=lag2(item);
                        run;
                        proc print data=work.samp2;
                        run;
             c.         data work.samp3;
                              set work.lag0;
                              x=lag1(item);
                              y=lag2(item);
                        run;
                        proc print data=work.samp3;
                        run;
             d.         data work.samp4;
                              set work.lag0;
                              y=lag1(item);
                              y=lag2(item);
                        run;
                        proc print data=work.samp4;
                        run;
```

4. What is the value of the column Position?

   ```
   Position=prxmatch('/Dutch/','Sawyer Dutch Kenai');
   ```

   a. 2

   b. 7

   c. 8

   d. 12

5. Which program correctly searches a string for a substring and returns the position of a substring?

   a.
   ```
   data _null_;
      position=prxmatch('/mind/', 'Learning never exhausts the mind.');
      put position=;
   run;
   ```

   b.
   ```
   data _null_;
      position=prxchange('/mind/', 'Learning never exhausts the mind.');
      put position=;
   run;
   ```

   c.
   ```
   data _null_;
      position=prxparse('/mind/', 'Learning never exhausts the mind.');
      put position=;
   run;
   ```

   d.
   ```
   data _null_;
      position=findw('/mind/', 'Learning never exhausts the mind.');
      put position=;
   run;
   ```

6. Which program correctly changes the order of first and last names?

   a.
   ```
   data work.reverse;
      set certadv.reversedNames;
      name=prxmatch('/name/', name);
   run;
   ```

   b.   data work.reverse;

```
            set certadv.reversedNames;
            name=prxchange('s/(\w+),(\w+)/$2 $1/', -1, name);
         run;
```

   c.
```
         data work.reverse;
            if _N_=1 then do;
               pattern='/name';
               name=prxparse(pattern);
            end;
            set certadv.reversedNames;
         run;
```

   d. None of the above.

7. Perl regular expressions in the PRXMATCH function must start and end with a delimiter.

   a. True

   b. False

8. Which Perl regular expression replaces the string ABC with the string ABC87?

   a. `'r/ABC/ABC87/'`

   b. `'r/ABC87/ABC/'`

   c. `'s/ABC87/ABC/'`

   d. `'s/ABC/ABC87/'`

Part 4

Workbook

Chapter 15
Practice Programming Scenarios *361*

Chapter 15
Practice Programming Scenarios

Differences between the Workbook and Certification Exam 362
Scenario 1 362
    Directions 362
    Test Your Code 363
    Exam Objective 363
Scenario 2 363
    Directions 363
    Test Your Code 363
    Exam Objective 363
Scenario 3 363
    Directions 363
    Test Your Code 364
    Exam Objective 364
Scenario 4 364
    Directions 364
    Test Your Code 365
    Exam Objective 365
Scenario 5 365
    Directions 365
    Test Your Code 365
    Exam Objective 365
Scenario 6 366
    Directions 366
    Test Your Code 366
    Exam Objective 366
Scenario 7 366
    Directions 366
    Test Your Code 367
    Exam Objective 367
Scenario 8 367
    Directions 367
    Test Your Code 367
    Exam Objective 367
Scenario 9 368
    Directions 368
    Test Your Code 368

Exam Objective 368
Scenario 10 .... **368**
    Directions 368
    Test Your Code 369
    Exam Objective 369

Differences between the Workbook and Certification Exam

- The workbook scenarios ask you to answer questions about the results from your performance-based projects. You compare your answers with the answer key to determine whether you solved the problem correctly.

- By contrast, the certification exam requires you to use a scoring macro to assess your work. The macro investigates the results of your project to determine whether you solved the problem correctly. It looks at parameters and the content of any output data set, as well as values of macro variables that are stored in the symbol tables. The macro also investigates the code that you wrote.

    The scoring macro returns a 3-digit value to the SAS log. You record this 3-digit value as your answer to each project to determine your score. These are broad checks, so there is still a significant amount of freedom in your chosen coding solution. For example, in the SQL topic, the macro is checking to see whether an SQL procedure was used to create the output data set rather than a DATA step.

    Note: To prepare for the exam, you might want to take the practice exam. Practice exams are available for purchase through SAS and Pearson VUE. For more information about practice exams, see https://www.sas.com/certification/sas-practice-exams.html (https://www.sas.com/certification/sas-practice-exams.html). When working through the practice exam, be sure to use the techniques that are specified in the instructions. Otherwise, you will not get an accurate representation of the live certification exam.

Scenario 1

Directions

This scenario uses the Certadv.All data set. Write a SAS program that does the following:

- In a PROC FCMP step, create a temporary custom function called Adding with a numeric argument named Val. The function itself returns the value of `Final`, which is the value of `38` added to the value of Val. Store the function in the output library Work with the table name of Function and the package name of Add.

- In a global statement, add the appropriate option so that SAS knows where to search for the custom function.

- In a DATA step, create the temporary data set named Work.StudentCost by reading in the data set Certadv.All. Create a custom function for the Fee variable to create a variable named Final_Cost.

- In a PROC PRINT step, create a report based on Work.StudentCost with the following variables displayed: Student_Name, Course_Code, Fee, and Final_Cost.

Test Your Code

1. What is the value of Final_Cost for observation 144?
2. What is the value of Final_Cost for observation 282?

Exam Objective

Create custom functions with the FCMP procedure.

Scenario 2

Directions

This scenario uses the Certadv.Monsal data set. Write a SAS program that does the following:

- Use PROC FORMAT to create a numeric format that specifies a template for displaying month values.
    - If the value is 1 through 12, display the value as a two-digit number (month values 1 through 9 should contain a leading zero).
    - If the value is not a number between 1 and 12 inclusive, display the value 'Not a valid month'.
    - Name the custom format Monthfmt.
- Use a PROC PRINT step to create a report based on Certadv.Monsal. Apply the Monthfmt custom format to the Month variable.

Test Your Code

How many instances of 'Not a valid month' does your output contain?

Exam Objective

Specify a template using the PICTURE statement within the FORMAT procedure.

Scenario 3

Directions

This scenario uses the Certadv.Airports and Certadv.Continent data sets. Write a SAS program that does the following:

- Write a SAS DATA step that reads the Certadv.Airports data set and creates two temporary data sets named Work.Success and Work.Fail.
  - During the first iteration of the DATA step, load a hash object named C from the data set Certadv.Continent.
  - Use the numeric variable ID as the key component.
  - Use the character variable CtName as the data component.
  - Assign a length of 30 for the character variable CtName.
  - Set the initial value to missing to eliminate the uninitialized variable note.
- In the DATA step, look up the value of ID variable from Certadv.Airports in the C hash object.
  - Retrieve the value of CtName from the hash object.
  - Create a variable named RC that contains a numeric value representing whether a match is found.
  - Store the results of successful lookups in the Work.Success data set.
  - Store the results of the unsuccessful lookups in the Work.Fail data set.

Test Your Code

1. How many observations are in the Work.Success data set?
2. How many observations are in the Work.Fail data set?

Exam Objective

Process data using hash objects.

Scenario 4

Directions

This scenario uses the Certadv.All data set. Write a SAS program that does the following:

- Create a footnote that contains the text 'Printed on ' followed by the current date obtained using a SAS function, and formatted month, day, year (for example, 'Printed on July 30, 2019').
- Create a macro named Test that does the following:
  - accepts two keyword parameters, Vars and Dsn
  - produces a PROC PRINT report from the data set specified in the Dsn parameter, which contains only the columns specified in the Vars parameters and only the rows that have a Begin_Date of 21774
  - calls the Test macro, with the Dsn value of `Certadv.All` and a Vars value of `Course_Code and Fee`

Test Your Code

1. How many observations are in the output?
2. Are all the values for Course_Code c004?

Exam Objective

- Automate programs by defining and calling macros using the SAS macro language.
- Use macro functions.

Scenario 5

Directions

This scenario uses the Certadv.Schedule data set. Write a SAS program that does the following:

- Create a macro named CourseLoc with no parameters.
- Use the SQL procedure to create a series of macro variables named LOC1, LOC2, and so on, that store the distinct values of the Location column in the Certadv.Schedule table.
- Use the %DO loop to execute a PROC PRINT step once for each LOC*n* macro variable that is created. The PROC PRINT step should filter data based on the value of Location and the LOC*n* macro variable. Add a title with the text 'Courses Offered in' and substitute the value of the LOC*n* macro variable.
- Call the CourseLoc macro program.

Test Your Code

1. What is the value of Location for observation 18?
2. What is the observation number where the Course_Code is c001, and Location is Boston?

Exam Objective

- Automate programs by defining and calling macros using the SAS macro language.
- Create data-driven programs using the SAS macro language.

Scenario 6

Directions

This scenario uses the Certadv.Staff data set. Write a SAS program that does the following:

- Define a macro variable named Job with a value of **Analyst**.
- Use a DATA step to create a temporary data set Work.Staff from the data set Certadv.Staff. Within this DATA step, do the following:
  - Read in only those rows from the Certadv.Staff data set that contain the text specified in the macro variable Job.
  - Create a new column that keeps a running total of Salary. Code:**Total +Salary;**
  - Create a Count variable and increment its value by one for each observation. Code: **Count+1;**
  - Create a new macro variable named Avg. The value of Avg is the value of Total divided by the value of Count. Format Avg as DOLLAR9.
- Use PROC PRINT to print Work.Staff. The output should include these elements:
  - a title with the value of the macro variable Job followed by the constant text 'Staff'.
  - a footnote with the constant text 'Average Salary:' followed by the value of the macro variable Avg.

Test Your Code

1. What is the average salary?
2. How many observations are printed?

Exam Objective

Create and use user-defined and automatic macro variables within the SAS macro language.

Scenario 7

Directions

This scenario uses the Certadv.Empdata data set. Write an SQL query that does the following:

- Create a temporary table Work.Bonus.

- Include only the following variables in your report: EmpID, JobCode, and Salary.
- Create a new column named Bonus that contains an amount equal to 10% of the employee's salary.
- Order the query by the variable JobCode and then by Salary.

Test Your Code

1. What is the Bonus amount for EmpID `E00029`?
2. What is the value of Bonus for observation 4 in the Work.Bonus table?

Exam Objective

Generate detailed reports by working with a single table, joining tables, or using set operators in SQL.

Scenario 8

Directions

This scenario uses the Certadv.Empdata and Certadv.Newsals data sets. Write an SQL query that does the following:

- Create a temporary table Work.Raise.
- Include the following variables in your report: EmpID, LastName, Salary, NewSalary, and Raise.
- Join both Certadv.Empdata and Certadv.Newsals based on the EmpID column to display only matching rows of the data.
- Create a new column named Raise whose value is the difference between NewSalary and Salary. Format the column as DOLLAR10.2
- Display only the rows where the value of Raise is greater than 3000 and order the query by the EmpID.
- Include the row numbers in your report.

Test Your Code

1. What is the employee's last name where the value of Raise is `$5,141.86`?
2. What is the value of Raise for employee ID number `E0028` and last name of Lichtenstein?

Exam Objective

Generate detailed reports by working with a single, joining tables, or using set operators in SQL.

Scenario 9

Directions

This scenario uses the Certadv.Salesstaff data set. Write an SQL query that does the following:

- Create a report that displays the total salary and total count for each unique JobTitle.
  - Use a SAS function to concatenate a string that combines the constant text 'Total Paid to All' with the value of JobTitle and the constant text 'Staff'. For example, the string should be displayed in the output as 'Total Paid to All Sales Rep. I Staff'.
  - Find the total salary for each unique JobTitle. Use the DOLLAR14. format and a label of TotalSalary.
  - Use a function to count the total number of sales representatives in each unique JobTitle. Use the COMMA14. format and a label of Total.
  - Summarize the data in the Certadv.Salesstaff data set for those rows that have a unique JobTitle.

Test Your Code

1. What is the total number of Sales Rep. III staff?
2. What is the total paid to all Sales Rep. II staff?

Exam Objective

Generate summary reports by working with a single table, joining tables, or using set operators in SQL.

Scenario 10

Directions

This scenario uses the Certadv.EmpAdd, Certadv.EmpOrg, and Certadv.EmpPh data sets. Write an SQL query that does the following:

- Create a view named Work.PhoneList that contains the following columns:
  - Department with a format of $25.
  - EmployeeName with a format of $25.
  - PhoneNumber with a format of $16. and a label of Home Phone
- Use the data found in the following tables. Column names that you need from each data set are in parentheses.

- certadv.empadd (EmployeeID, EmployeeName)
- certadv.emporg (EmployeeID, Department)
- certadv.empph (EmployeeID, PhoneNumber, PhoneType)
- Use an alias for each table for simpler programming. Use 'a' for certadv.empadd, 'o' for certadv.emporg, and 'p' for certadv.empph.

• Include only those phone numbers in the view where the PhoneType was **Home** and where EmployeeID matches across all three tables.

• Use the Work.PhoneList view to create an SQL query:
  - The query must contain only the EmployeeName and PhoneNumber columns.
  - Subset the data to include only those employees who are in the Sales Management department.
  - Order the query by EmployeeName.
  - Add a title to the report: Sales Management Department Home Phone Numbers.
  - Display row numbers for the report.

Test Your Code

1. How many observations are displayed in the query result?
2. What is the value for Name in observation 6?

Exam Objective

Construct in-line views within an SQL procedure step.

Part 5

Solutions

Chapter 16
Chapter Quiz Answer Keys *373*

Chapter 17
Programming Scenario Solutions *387*

Chapter 16
Chapter Quiz Answer Keys

Chapter 1: PROC SQL Fundamentals 373
Chapter 2: Creating and Managing Tables 374
Chapter 3: Joining Tables Using PROC SQL 375
Chapter 4: Joining Tables Using Set Operators 376
Chapter 5: Using Subqueries 377
Chapter 6: Advanced SQL Techniques 378
Chapter 7: Creating and Using Macro Variables 379
Chapter 8: Storing and Processing Text 380
Chapter 9: Working with Macro Programs 381
Chapter 10: Advanced Macro Techniques 382
Chapter 11: Defining and Processing Arrays 383
Chapter 12: Processing Data Using Hash Objects 384
Chapter 13: Using SAS Utility Procedures 384
Chapter 14: Using Advanced Functions 385

Chapter 1: PROC SQL Fundamentals

1. Correct answer: a

   The SELECT clause in the program is written incorrectly. Columns that are listed in the clause must be separated by commas, not just blanks.

2. Correct answer: a

   There are two statements, the PROC SQL statement and the SELECT statement. The SELECT statement contains three clauses: the SELECT clause, the FROM clause, and the ORDER BY clause.

3. Correct answer: b

   The SELECT clause lists the columns from both tables to be queried. You must use a prefix with the Address column because it appears in both tables. The prefix specifies the table from which you want the column to be read.

4. Correct answer: b

   The ORDER BY clause specifies how the rows are to be sorted. You follow the keywords ORDER BY by one or more column names or numbers, separated by commas.

5. Correct answer: c

   In the FROM clause, you list the names of the tables to be queried, separated by commas.

6. Correct answer: b

   To create a new column and assign a column alias to the column, you specify the following in the SELECT clause, in the order shown here: an expression, (optional) the keyword AS, and a column alias. The case that you use when you create the column name is the one that will be displayed in the output.

7. Correct answer: a

   The GROUP BY clause is used in queries that include one or more summary functions. If you specify a GROUP BY clause in a query that does not contain a summary function, your clause is changed to an ORDER BY clause.

8. Correct answer: b

   The table names that are specified in the FROM clause must be separated by commas. Note that you can specify columns in the WHERE clause that are not specified in the SELECT clause.

Chapter 2: Creating and Managing Tables

1. Correct answer: c

   The CREATE TABLE statement enables you to store your results in a SAS table instead of displaying the query results as a report.

2. Correct answer: b

   The CREATE TABLE statement that includes a LIKE clause copies the column names and attributes from an existing table into a new table. No rows of data are inserted.

3. Correct answer: a

   The CREATE TABLE statement that includes the AS keyword and query clauses creates a table and loads the results of the query into the new table. The WHERE clause selects only the rows for the level-1 flight attendants.

4. Correct answer: a

   The INSERT statement is used to insert new rows into a new or existing table. There is no LOAD statement in PROC SQL, VALUES is a clause, and the CREATE TABLE statement is used to create a table.

5. Correct answer: b

   The DESCRIBE TABLE statement lists the column attributes for a specified table.

6. Correct answer: a

The CREATE TABLE statement can include column specifications to create an empty table. The entire group of column specifications must be enclosed in a single set of parentheses. You must list each column's name, data type, and (for character columns) length. The length is specified as an integer in parentheses. Multiple column specifications must be separated by commas.

Chapter 3: Joining Tables Using PROC SQL

1. Correct answer: a

   A Cartesian product is returned when join conditions are not specified in a PROC SQL join. In a Cartesian product, each row from the first table is combined with every row from the second table.

2. Correct answer: b

   This PROC SQL query is an inner join. It combines the rows from the first table that match rows from the second table, based on the matching criteria that are specified in the WHERE clause. Columns are not overlaid, so all columns from the referenced tables (including any columns with duplicate names) are displayed. Any unmatched rows from either table are not displayed.

3. Correct answer: a

   This PROC SQL query is a left outer join, which retrieves all rows that match across tables (based on the join conditions in the ON clause), plus nonmatching rows from the left (first) table. No columns are overlaid, so all columns from both tables are displayed.

4. Correct answer: c

   Inner joins combine the rows from the first table that match rows from the second table, based on one or more join conditions in the WHERE clause. The columns being matched must have the same data type, but they are not required to have the same name. For joins, the tables being joined can have different numbers of columns, and the rows do not need to be sorted.

5. Correct answer: c

   In order to generate the same output as the DATA step and PROC PRINT steps, the PROC SQL full outer join must use the COALESCE function with the duplicate columns specified as arguments.

6. Correct answer: d

   The use of summary functions does not require the use of table aliases. All of the other statements about table aliases that are shown here are true.

7. Correct answer: d

   If you are joining two tables that contain a same-named column, you must use a prefix to specify the table or tables from which you want the column to be read. Remember that if you join tables that do not contain columns that have matching data values, you can produce a huge amount of output. Be sure to specify a WHERE clause to select only the rows that you want.

Chapter 4: Joining Tables Using Set Operators

1. Correct answer: c

   In set operations that use the operators EXCEPT, INTERSECT, or UNION, and no keyword, columns are overlaid based on their position in the SELECT clause. It does not matter whether the overlaid columns have the same name. When columns are overlaid, the column name is taken from the first table that is specified in the SELECT clause.

2. Correct answer: d

   By default, when processing a set operation that contains the EXCEPT, INTERSECT, and UNION set operators, PROC SQL makes an extra pass through the data to eliminate duplicate rows. The keyword ALL is used to suppress that additional pass through the tables, allowing duplicate rows to appear in the result set. Because the OUTER UNION set operator displays all rows, the keyword ALL is invalid and cannot be used with OUTER UNION.

3. Correct answer: d

   The output contains all rows that are unique in the combined set of rows from both tables, and the columns have been overlaid by position. This output is generated by a set operation that uses the set operator UNION without keywords.

4. Correct answer: a

   The PROC SQL set operation that uses the set operator OUTER UNION without a keyword is the only code shown that does not overlay any columns in output.

5. Correct answer: a

   The keyword CORR (CORRESPONDING) can be used alone or together with the keyword ALL.

6. Correct answer: b

   This PROC SQL output includes all rows from the table Pets that do not appear in the table Dogs. No duplicates are displayed. A PROC SQL set operation that contains the set operator EXCEPT without keywords produces these results.

7. Correct answer: b

   The set operator EXCEPT returns all the rows in the first table that do not appear in the second table. The keyword ALL suppresses the extra pass that PROC SQL makes through the data to eliminate duplicate rows. The EXCEPT operator when used alone also produces the output that is specified in the question.

8. Correct answer: c

   The set operator UNION returns all rows that are unique in the combined set of rows from both tables.

9. Correct answer: c

   The set operator INTERSECT returns all rows that are common to both tables. Specifying the keyword ALL suppresses PROC SQL's additional pass through the data to eliminate duplicate rows.

Chapter 5: Using Subqueries

1. Correct answer: d

   To remove duplicate values from PROC SQL output, you specify the DISTINCT keyword before the column name in the SELECT clause.

2. Correct answer: d

   To list rows that have no data (that is, missing data), you can use either of these other conditional operators: IS MISSING or IS NULL. The NOT EXISTS operator is used specifically with a subquery, and resolves to true if the subquery returns no values to the outer query.

3. Correct answer: b

   When a WHERE clause references a new column that was defined in the SELECT clause, the WHERE clause must specify the keyword CALCULATED before the column name.

4. Correct answer: c

   To determine how PROC SQL calculates and displays output from summary functions, consider the key factors. This PROC SQL query has a GROUP BY clause, and it does not specify any columns that are outside summary functions. Therefore, PROC SQL calculates and displays the summary function for each group. There are 7 unique values of FlightNumber, but the HAVING clause specifies only the flights that have an average number of boarded passengers greater than 150. Because 4 of the 7 flight numbers meet this condition, the output will contain 4 rows.

5. Correct answer: b

   Your PROC SQL query needs to use data from both tables. The outer query reads the name and number of books checked out from Certadv.Circulation. The multiple-value noncorrelated subquery selects the names of volunteers from Certadv.Volunteers and passes these names back to the outer query. The outer query then selects data for only the volunteers whose names match the names that are returned by the subquery. The subquery is indented under the outer query's WHERE clause, is enclosed in parentheses, and does not require a semicolon inside the closing parenthesis.

6. Correct answer: c

   A noncorrelated subquery is a nested query that executes independently of the outer query. The outer query passes no values to the subquery.

7. Correct answer: a

   The syntax in this PROC SQL query is valid, so the first statement is false. The query contains a correlated subquery, so the second statement is true. The VALIDATE keyword is used after the PROC SQL statement, so the third statement is true. And the last statement correctly indicates that the VALIDATE keyword causes the SAS log to display a special message if the query syntax is valid, or standard error messages if the syntax is not valid.

8. Correct answer: c

   In this PROC SQL query, the outer query uses the operator NOT EXISTS with a correlated subquery. The outer query selects all rows from Certadv.Donors whose names do not appear in Certadv.Current. In other words, this PROC SQL query output lists all donors who did not make a contribution in the current year.

9. Correct answer: c

   The third statement about data remerging is correct.

10. Correct answer: c

    PROC SQL can execute this query, but the query will not produce the results that you want. If you omit the GROUP BY clause in a query that contains a HAVING clause, then the HAVING clause and any summary functions treat the entire table as one group. Without a GROUP BY clause, the HAVING clause in this example calculates the average circulation for the table as a whole (all books in the library), not for each group (each category of books). The output contains either all the rows in the table (if the average circulation for the entire table is less than 2500) or none of the rows in the table (if the average circulation for the entire table is greater than 2500).

Chapter 6: Advanced SQL Techniques

1. Correct answer: a

   You can use the INTO clause to create one or more macro variables in the SELECT clause. The INTO keyword is followed by a colon (:) and then the macro variable name.

2. Correct answer: c

   You cannot create a macro variable in the same SQL step in which you are calling the macro variable. To create a report that does not contain any duplicate items including the values in the macro variable, use the DISTINCT keyword in the SELECT clause.

3. Correct answer: d

   When storing a value in a single macro variable, PROC SQL preserves leading or trailing blanks. You can use the TRIMMED option in the INTO clause to remove the leading and trailing blanks. Use the INTO keyword followed by a colon (:), followed by the macro variable named, followed by the keyword TRIMMED.

4. Correct answer: a

   You can use the SEPARATED BY keyword in the INTO clause to specify a character to delimit the values into a macro variable. You do not need to use the TRIMMED keyword with the SEPARATED BY keyword because it removes leading and trailing blanks from each value before performing the concatenation of values.

5. Correct answer: b

   While the foundation of PROC FedSQL syntax is similar to PROC SQL, there are a few differences when it comes to specific SAS enhancements such as formats. In order to associate a format with a variable in the output, use the PUT function.

6. Correct answer: d

   In PROC FedSQL when you want to limit the number of rows, use the LIMIT clause in the SELECT statement. The LIMIT clause is the LIMIT keyword followed by the count or the number of rows you want to display in the output. You cannot use INOBS= in PROC FedSQL.

Chapter 7: Creating and Using Macro Variables

1. Correct answer: b

   Macro variables are always text strings that are independent of SAS data sets. The value of a macro variable can be up to 65,534 characters long, and the name of a macro variable can be up to 32 characters long. A macro variable can be defined or referenced anywhere in a SAS program except within data lines. There are two types of macro variables: automatic and user-defined.

2. Correct answer: c

   To reference a macro variable, you precede the name with an ampersand. You do not need to enclose the macro variable reference in quotation marks.

3. Correct answer: a

   There are two ways to display the value of a macro variable in the SAS log: you can turn on the SYMBOLGEN system option to list the values of all macro variables that are used, or you can use the %PUT statement to write specific text, including macro variable values, to the log. Therefore, answers b, c, and d are all valid ways to display the value of the macro variable in the SAS log.

4. Correct answer: d

   You use the %LET statement to define a macro variable. You do not need to enclose the value in quotation marks. If you do include quotation marks in the assigned value for a macro variable, the quotation marks will be stored as part of the value.

5. Correct answer: d

   Macro variables are stored as character strings. Quotation marks and most special characters are stored exactly as they are assigned, but leading blanks are stripped from assigned values. You can also include references to other macro variables within %LET statements.

6. Correct answer: a

   Macro triggers alert the word scanner that the subsequent code should be sent to the macro processor. When a macro trigger is embedded within a literal token and you want to resolve the trigger, enclose the literal string in double quotation marks. If you do not enclose the string in double quotation marks, the macro variable reference is not resolved.

7. Correct answer: b

   The word scanner recognizes four types of tokens. Expressions are not a type of token.

8. Correct answer: b

   The word scanner, not the macro processor, breaks SAS programs into tokens.

9. Correct answer: a

   The word scanner detects the end of a token when it encounters a new token or a blank delimiter. When the word scanner finds a blank or the beginning of a new token, it removes a token from the input stack and transfers it to the bottom of the queue.

Chapter 8: Storing and Processing Text

1. Correct answer: c

   Most macro functions are handled by the macro processor before any SAS language statements in the DATA step are executed. For example, the %LET statement and any macro variable references (&macvar) are passed to the macro processor before the program is compiled. In order to create or update macro variables during DATA step execution, you use the SYMPUT routine.

2. Correct answer: d

   The SYMPUTX routine enables you to assign a data set variable as the value of a macro variable. You can also use the SYMPUTX routine to create a series of related macro variables. Because all macro variable values are character strings, SYMPUTX automatically converts any numeric value that you attempt to assign as a value for a macro variable.

3. Correct answer: b

   You can use multiple ampersands to create an indirect reference when the value of one macro variable is the name of another. If you enclose the DATA step variable name in quotation marks in the SYMPUTX routine, the new macro variable will have the same name as the DATA step variable rather than having the DATA step variable's value as a name. Use the SYMGET function to obtain the value of a macro variable during the execution of a DATA step.

4. Correct answer: b

   If more than four consecutive ampersands precede a name token, re-scanning continues from left to right until no more triggers can be resolved. The Forward Re-scan rule describes how the macro processor resolves macro variable references that start with multiple ampersands or with multiple percent signs.

5. Correct answer: c

   To create a macro variable during the execution of a PROC SQL step, use the INTO clause of the SELECT statement. In the INTO clause, you precede the name of the macro variable with a colon.

6. Correct answer: c

   You can use multiple ampersands to delay the resolution of a macro variable reference. You can also combine macro variable references in order to create new tokens. In this example, the reference &&teach&crs resolves to `&teach3` on the first scan. On the next scan, &teach3 resolves to `Forest, Mr. Peter`.

7. Correct answer: b

   The SYMPUTX routine can be used in a DATA step. In the DATA step, the SYMPUTX routine performs automatic conversion on numeric values that you attempt to assign as values for macro variables, using the BEST12. format. However, you cannot use the SYMPUTX routine to create a macro variable during the execution of a PROC SQL query.

Chapter 9: Working with Macro Programs

1. Correct answer: b

   A macro definition must begin with a %MACRO statement and must end with a %MEND statement. The macro definition can include macro language statements as well as SAS language statements. When the macro is compiled, macro language statements are checked for syntax errors. The compiled macro is stored in a temporary SAS catalog by default.

2. Correct answer: c

   To include positional parameters in a macro definition, you list the parameters in parentheses and separate them with commas. When the macro is executed, macro variables are created in the local symbol table, and they have the same names as the parameters. You can then use these macro variables within the macro.

3. Correct answer: c

   To call a macro that includes positional parameters, you precede the macro name with a percent sign. You list the values for the macro variables that are defined by the parameters in parentheses. List values in the same order in which the parameters are listed, and separate them with commas. Remember that a macro call is not a SAS language statement and does not require a semicolon.

4. Correct answer: d

   In a mixed parameter list, positional parameters must be listed before any keyword parameters. Both positional and keyword parameters create macro variables in the local symbol table. To assign a null value to a keyword parameter, you list the parameter without a value in the macro call.

5. Correct answer: c

   When you submit a macro definition, the macro is compiled and is stored in a SAS catalog. Then when you call the macro, the macro is executed. The macro is available for execution anytime throughout the current SAS session.

6. Correct answer: d

   You can use %IF-%THEN statements to conditionally process code. Within a %IF-%THEN statement, you must use %DO and %END statements to enclose multiple statements. %IF-%THEN statements are similar to IF THEN statements in the DATA step, but they are part of the macro language.

7. Correct answer: d

   You can use MPRINT and MLOGIC options for debugging macros along with entering comments in macro programs. MPRINT displays the SAS statements that are generated by macro execution. MLOGIC causes the macro processor to trace its execution and to write the trace information to the SAS log.

8. Correct answer: c

   There are several ways to create macro variables in the local symbol table. Macro variables that are created by parameters in a macro definition or by a %LOCAL statement are always created in the local table. Macro variables that are created by a %LET statement or by the SYMPUT routine inside a macro definition might be created in the local table as well.

Chapter 10: Advanced Macro Techniques

1. Correct answer: d

   The %INCLUDE statement can be used to insert the contents of an external file into a SAS program. If a macro definition is stored in an external file, the %INCLUDE statement causes the macro definition to be compiled when it is inserted into the SAS program. The contents of the macro definition are written to the SAS log only if the SOURCE2 option is specified.

2. Correct answer: a

   When a macro definition is stored as a catalog SOURCE entry, you must compile it before you can call it from a SAS program. You compile a macro that is stored as a catalog SOURCE entry by using the CATALOG access method. This creates a session compiled macro that is deleted at the end of the SAS session. The PROC CATALOG statement enables you to view a list of the contents of a SAS catalog.

3. Correct answer: c

   To call a macro that is stored in an autocall library, you must specify both the MAUTOSOURCE system options and the SASAUTOS= system option. The SASAUTOS= system option can be set to include multiple pathnames or filerefs. Once these two system options are set, you can call the macro by preceding the macro name with a percent sign.

4. Correct answer: a

   When you submit a macro definition, SAS creates a session compiled macro and stores it in the temporary SAS catalog Work.Sasmacr. This macro is deleted at the end of the SAS session.

5. Correct answer: d

   If you store your macro definitions in external files, you can easily share these files with others. Also, you can edit a macro definition that is stored in an external file with any text editor, and you can reuse the macro in other SAS sessions.

6. Correct answer: a

   The autocall macro facility stores macro definitions — not compiled macros — permanently. The first time an autocall macro is called during a SAS session, the macro is compiled and a session compiled macro is created in Work.Sasmacr. You can have multiple autocall libraries that are concatenated, and you can use the autocall facility in conjunction with the Stored Compiled Macro Facility.

7. Correct answer: a

   The DOSUBL function uses the values that are found in the Libname and Memname columns concatenated between `%Report3` (' and ') to generate a valid macro call.

8. Correct answer: b

   The DOSUBL function enables the immediate execution of SAS code after a text string is passed. Macro variables that are created or updated during the execution of the submitted code are exported back to the calling environment.

Chapter 11: Defining and Processing Arrays

1. Correct answer: a

   An ARRAY statement is not an executable statement; it merely defines an array.

2. Correct answer: d

   The items in an ARRAY statement must be specified in the following order:

   ARRAY *array-name*[*number-of-array-elements*]<$ *length array-elements* _TEMPORARY_ (*initial-values*)>;

3. Correct answer: b

   In the DO statement, you specify the index variable that represents the values of the array elements. Then specify the start and stop positions of the array elements.

4. Correct answer: d

   To create a list of temporary array elements, use the _TEMPORARY_ keyword. The list of initial values must be enclosed in parentheses and separated by commas or blanks.

5. Correct answer: a

   At the end of the second iteration, `diff[i]` resolves as follows:

   ```
   diff[2]=wt[2+1]-wt[2];
   diff[2]=215-200
   ```

6. Correct answer: a

   In a two-dimensional array, elements are referenced using two numbers. The first number corresponds to the row and the second number corresponds to the column. The dimension values are separated with a comma. Initial values are loaded into a two-dimensional array by specifying the values one row at a time, left to right.

7. Correct answer: d

   To process all of the elements in an array, you can either use the DIM function with the array name as the argument or you can specify a stop value corresponding to the number of elements in the array.

8. Correct answer: c

   The IF-THEN statement specifies that the Targets array is loaded only once, during the first iteration of the DATA step. During the first iteration of the DATA step, the condition _N_=1 is true, so the outer DO loop executes three times—once for each observation in Cert.Ctargets. After the third iteration of the DO loop, the pointer drops down to the second SET statement, and the values from the first observation in Cert.Monthsum are read into the program data vector. During the second iteration of the DATA step, the condition _N_=1 is false. So, the DO loop does not execute again.

Chapter 12: Processing Data Using Hash Objects

1. Correct Answer: b

   A SAS hash object exists only within the DATA step in which it creates the hash objects. When the DATA step ends, SAS deletes the hash object.

2. Correct Answer: c

   Component objects are data elements that consist of attributes and methods. Attributes are the properties that specify the information while methods define the operations that an object can perform.

3. Correct Answer: d

   There are three DEFINE methods that are required to define a hash object. The DEFINEKEY method defines the columns that make up the key component. The DEFINEDATA method defines the columns that make up the data component. The DEFINEDONE method indicates that all key and data components are complete.

4. Correct Answer: b

   The FIND hash object method determines whether the key is stored in the hash object. The FIND method returns a value to indicate a found or not found key. You can use multiple FIND methods calls to retrieve multiple data values.

5. Correct Answer: d

   The PREV method returns the previous value in the underlying hash object. This method can be used to iteratively transverse the hash object and return the data items in reverse key order.

6. Correct Answer: b

   The CALL MISSING routine assigns a missing value to the specified character or numeric variables. Using the CALL MISSING routine helps you avoid receiving notes in the SAS log that your variables are uninitialized.

7. Correct Answer: b

   The statement is false. You cannot define an iterator without also defining a hash object. The hash iterator is designed to work with a hash object.

8. Correct Answer: a

   Answer a is correct because the code correctly associates two data values, City and Name, with one key, Code. The code also uses the three required methods correctly. Answer b defines two keys and one data value, while answer c defines two data and two keys. Answer d is invalid because it does not use the required methods properly.

Chapter 13: Using SAS Utility Procedures

1. Correct answer: a

   The five-digit digit selector truncates the leading digits, and the PREFIX= option specifies a character string to place in front of the formatted value. The PREFIX= option must be specified after the template.

2. Correct answer: b

   Without the DEFAULT= option, the length for the format is 8 characters, but 10 characters are needed. The DEFAULT= option is specified after the format name. The DATATYPE= value must match the data, which is Date in this example. %m displays a one- or two-digit month, %d displays a one- or two-digit day, and %Y displays a four-digit year.

3. Correct answer: e

   DEFAULT= and ROUND are format options that are specified after the format name. DEFAULT= specifies the default length of the formatted value. ROUND rounds the value to the nearest integer. DATATYPE= and MULTIPLIER= are template options that are specified after the template value.

4. Correct answer: c

   The CMPLIB= system option specifies where to look for previously compiled functions and subroutines.

5. Correct answer: c

   The correct directives are %Y, which produces a four-digit year, %0m, which produces a two-digit month, and %0d, which produces a two-digit day. Separate all date directives with a period. Following the date directives, use the @ symbol and use the time directives. The correct time directives are %I:%M:%S %p or %0I:%0M:%0S %p. You would use %I or %0I because the output shows 8 in the evening, which is in the 12-hour clock and not the 24-hour clock.

6. Correct answer: b

   Character arguments must be followed by a dollar sign and separated with a comma. No quotation marks are needed.

7. Correct answer: d

   Custom functions are stored in a package within a SAS table. The OUTLIB= option consists of a three-level name. The first two levels refer to the SAS table (*libref.table-name*), and the third level refers to the *package*.

Chapter 14: Using Advanced Functions

1. Correct answer: a

   The FIND function searches for a specific substring of characters within a character string. When the FIND function finds a substring, FIND returns the value of 1. When the substring is not found, FIND returns the value of 0.

2. Correct answer: b

   The COUNT function counts the number of times CANADA appeared within the Text string. The COUNTW function counts the number of words in the Text string. A default list of delimiters is used when there are no delimiters specified.

3. Correct answer: c

   The LAG function retrieves the previous value of a numeric or character column. You can use multiple LAG functions within a program. Answer c correctly assigns the variables and uses the LAG function to generate two lagged values.

4. Correct answer: c

PRXMATCH searches for a pattern match and returns the position at which the pattern is found. The string Dutch is found starting in the eighth position.

5. Correct answer: a

    Use the PRXMATCH function in a Perl regular expression to search a string for a substring and return the position of a substring.

6. Correct answer: b

    Use the PRXCHANGE function to change the order of first and last names. This PRXMATCH program uses metacharacters to define the search criteria and any text manipulation.

7. Correct answer: a

    A Perl regular expression within the PRXMATCH function must start and end with a delimiter such as the forward slash.

8. Correct answer: d

    The / (forward slash) is the beginning delimiter for a regular expression. The lowercase s specifies a substitution in a regular expression. ABC matches the letters ABC that you are attempting to replace. The / (forward slash) or middle delimiter separates the search pattern from the substitution pattern. ABC87 matches the letter ABC87 that are you attempting to substitute for ABC. The / (forward slash) is the ending delimiter for the regular expression.

Chapter 17
Programming Scenario Solutions

Scenario 1 .... **388**
    Code Solution 388
    Test Your Code Solution 389
Scenario 2 .... **389**
    Code Solution 389
    Test Your Code Solution 390
Scenario 3 .... **390**
    Code Solution 390
    Test Your Code Solution 392
Scenario 4 .... **392**
    Code Solution 392
    Test Your Code Solution 393
Scenario 5 .... **393**
    Code Solution 393
    Test Your Code Solution 395
Scenario 6 .... **395**
    Code Solution 395
    Test Your Code Solution 396
Scenario 7 .... **396**
    Code Solution 396
    Test Your Code Solution 397
Scenario 8 .... **398**
    Code Solution 398
    Test Your Code Solution 399
Scenario 9 .... **399**
    Code Solution 399
    Test Your Code Solution 400
Scenario 10 .... **400**
    Code Solution 400
    Test Your Code Solution 402

Scenario 1

Code Solution

Note: On the live exam, you will be evaluated both on the results of your code and the code itself. Your code should be similar to the following example code, but does not need to match exactly:

```
proc fcmp outlib=work.function.add;    /* 1 */
    function adding(val);              /* 2 */
        final=38+val;
        return(final);                 /* 3 */
    endsub;                            /* 4 */
run;

options cmplib=work.function;          /* 5 */

data work.studentcost;                 /* 6 */
    set certadv.all;
    Final_Cost=adding(fee);            /* 7 */
run;

proc print data=work.studentcost;      /* 8 */
    var Student_Name Course_Code Fee Final_Cost;
run;
```

1. The FCMP procedure enables you to create custom functions using DATA step syntax. The OUTLIB= option specifies Work.Function as the table in which the Add package is stored. The Add package is a collection of routines that have unique names.

2. The FUNCTION statement specifies the function name and the function arguments, as well as whether the function returns a character or numeric value. The Adding custom function has one numeric argument named Val, and it returns a numeric value. The variable Final is computed as 38 plus the value of the function's argument.

3. The RETURN statement specifies the value of Final to be returned from the function.

4. The ENDSUB statement ends the syntax for the function.

5. The CMPLIB= option specifies Work.Function table for SAS to search for a package that contains the desired function.

6. The DATA step creates a temporary data set named Work.StudentCost. SAS reads Certadv.All data set to create Work.StudentCost.

7. The DATA step creates a new variable named Final_Cost. The Final_Cost encompasses the fee for the course and an additional student fee. The new variable references the custom function Adding. The function adds a constant value of 38 to the value of Fee. The function returns the value of Final, which is then assigned to the value of Final_Cost.

8. The PROC PRINT step displays the output data with only the specified variables: Student_Name, Course_Code, Fee, and Final_Cost.

Output 17.1 PROC PRINT of Work.StudentCost (partial output)

Obs	Student_Name	Course_Code	Fee	Final_Cost
1	Abramson, Ms. Andrea	C004	$375	413
2	Abramson, Ms. Andrea	C006	$1600	1638
3	Alamutu, Ms. Julie	C002	$1150	1188
4	Albritton, Mr. Bryan	C001	$795	833
5	Albritton, Mr. Bryan	C005	$400	438

... more observations ...

Test Your Code Solution

1. Correct Answer: 438
2. Correct Answer: 688

Scenario 2

Code Solution

Note: On the live exam, you will be evaluated both on the results of your code and the code itself. Your code should be similar to the following example code, but does not need to match exactly:

```
proc format;
    picture monthfmt 1-12='99'              /*1*/
            other    ='Not a valid month';  /*2*/
run;
proc print data=certadv.monsal;
    format month monthfmt.;                 /*3*/
run;
```

1. The PICTURE statement creates a template called Monthfmt in which it specifies that characters in a range of **1** through **12** are numeric. Using digit selectors (99) specifies the positions for the numeric values. Using a digit selector of **1** through **9** guarantees a leading zero for the month values of **1** through **9**. If a digit selector of 0 is used, then there are no leading zeros.

2. The PICTURE statement also adds another definition to the template. It specifies that if the value is not between **1** through **12** inclusive, display the value **Not a valid month**.

3. The PROC PRINT step displays the data set Certadv.Monsal. You can use the FORMAT statement to apply the custom format Monthfmt to the Month variable.

Output 17.2 PROC PRINT Output of Certadv.Monsal with MonthFmt Template Applied (partial output)

Obs	id	month	salary
1	1007	01	$3,200
2	1007	02	$3,200
3	1007	03	$3,200
4	1007	04	$3,200
5	1007	05	$3,200
6	1007	06	$3,200
7	1007	07	$3,200
8	1007	08	$3,200
9	1007	09	$3,200
10	1007	Not a valid month	$3,200

...*more observations*...

Test Your Code Solution

Correct Answer: 7

Scenario 3

Code Solution

Note: On the live exam, you will be evaluated both on the results of your code and the code itself. Your code should be similar to the following example code, but does not need to match exactly:

```
data work.success work.fail;                              /*1*/
   drop rc;
   length CtName $30;                                     /*2*/
   if _N_=1 then do;                                      /*3*/
      call missing (CtName);
      declare hash C(dataset:'certadv.continent');        /*4*/
         c.definekey('ID');                               /*5*/
         c.definedata('CtName');                          /*6*/
         c.definedone();                                  /*7*/
   end;
   set certadv.airports;                                  /*8*/
   rc=c.find();                                           /*9*/
   if rc=0 then output work.success;                      /*10*/
      else output work.fail;
run;
proc print data=work.success;                             /*11*/
run;
proc print data=work.fail;
run;
```

1. The DATA step creates two temporary SAS data sets named Work.Success and Work.Fail by reading in Certadv.Airports.

2. The LENGTH statement assigns the length of 30 to the character variable CtName.

3. The IF-THEN/DO statement loads the hash object named C for the first iteration of the DATA step only. The CALL MISSING routine assigns missing values to the CtName character variable to eliminate the uninitialized variable note in the SAS log.

4. The DECLARE statement declares the hash object named C and loads the hash object with observations and variables from the data set Certadv.Continent.

5. The DEFINEKEY method defines the variable ID as the key component.

6. The DEFINEDATA method defines CtName as the data component.

7. The DEFINEDONE method completes the definition of the hash object.

8. The SET statement reads the data from the Certadv.Airports data set.

9. The FIND method retrieves the value of CtName from the hash object if the value of ID from Certadv.Airports is in the hash object C. The RC value is equal to 0 if a match is found. If a match is not found, the RC value is a nonzero value.

10. The IF-THEN/ELSE statement subsets the data to two separate data sets. If the value for RC is 0, then output to Work.Success. If the value for RC is a nonzero number, then write output to Work.Fail.

11. The PROC PRINT step displays the observations in the Work.Success and Work.Fail data sets with the value of RC.

Output 17.3   PROC PRINT Result of Work.Success (partial output)

Obs	CtName	ID	City	Code	AName	Country	rc
1	Australia/Pacific	96	Auckland	AKL	International	New Zealand	0
2	Europe	93	Amsterdam	AMS	Schiphol	Netherlands	0
3	North America	91	Anchorage, AK	ANC	Anchorage International Airport	USA	0
4	Europe	93	Stockholm	ARN	Arlanda	Sweden	0
5	Europe	93	Athens (Athinai)	ATH	Hellinikon International Airport	Greece	0
6	North America	91	Birmingham, AL	BHM	Birmingham International Airport	USA	0
7	Asia	95	Bangkok	BKK	Don Muang International Airport	Thailand	0
8	North America	91	Nashville, TN	BNA	Nashville International Airport	USA	0
9	North America	91	Boston, MA	BOS	General Edward Lawrence Logan Internatio	USA	0
10	Europe	93	Brussels (Bruxelles)	BRU	National/Zaventem	Belgium	0

. . . more observations . . .

Output 17.4   PROC PRINT Result of Work.Fail

Obs	CtName	ID	City	Code	AName	Country	rc
1		90	Dallas/Fort Worth, TX	DFW	Dallas/Fort Worth International Airport	USA	160038
2		90	Honolulu, HI	HNL	Honolulu International Airport	USA	160038
3		98	Singapore	SIN	Changi International Airport	Singapore	160038

Test Your Code Solution

1. Correct Answer: 46

2. Correct Answer: 3

Scenario 4

Code Solution

Note: On the live exam, you will be evaluated both on the results of your code and the code itself. Your code should be similar to the following example code, but does not need to match exactly :

```
footnote 'Printed on
                   %sysfunc(today(),worddate.)';   /*1*/
%macro test (dsn=, vars=);                         /*2*/
   proc print data=&dsn;
   where begin_date=21774;
   var &vars;
   run;
%mend test;                                        /*3*/
%test(dsn=certadv.all, vars=course_code fee);      /*4*/
```

1 The %SYSFUNC function executes the SAS function TODAY and formats the value Worddate. using the macro facility.

2 The %MACRO statement defines the macro Test, which accepts the keyword parameters Vars and Dsn. The macro generates a PROC PRINT step.

3 The %MEND statement ends the macro definition of Test.

4 The %test statement calls the macro Test with a Dsn parameter value of **Certadv.All** and Vars parameter values of **Course_Code** and **Fee**. When executed, it generates a PROC PRINT step that reads the Certadv.All data set and prints only the columns Course_Code and Fee.

Output 17.5 PROC PRINT of Certadv.All (partial output)

Obs	Course_Code	Fee
1	C004	$375
2	C004	$375
3	C004	$375
4	C004	$375
5	C004	$375
... more observations ...
20	C004	$375
21	C004	$375
22	C004	$375
23	C004	$375

Printed on July 31, 2019

Test Your Code Solution

1. Correct Answer: 23
2. Correct Answer: Yes

Scenario 5

Code Solution

Note: On the live exam, you will be evaluated both on the results of your code and the code itself. Your code should be similar to the following example code, but does not need to match exactly:

```
%macro CourseLoc;                           /*1*/
proc sql noprint;
   select distinct Location into:
      loc1-
      from certadv.schedule;
quit;
%do i=1 %to &sqlobs;                        /*2*/
title "Courses Offered in &&loc&i";
proc print data=certadv.schedule;
   where location="&&loc&i";
run;
%end;
%mend CourseLoc;                            /*3*/

%Courseloc                                  /*4*/
```

1. The %MACRO statement defines the macro CourseLoc. The macro itself executes a PROC SQL query where a series of macro variables are created. The macro variables store distinct values of the Location column from the Certadv.Schedule data set.

2. The %DO loop executes a PROC PRINT step for different Location values. The PROC PRINT step filters the data based on the value of Location. It also adds a TITLE statement where "Courses Offered in" is constant text while the value of the location changes.

3. The %MEND statement ends the macro definition of CourseLoc.

4. The CourseLoc macro is called to execute the macro program.

Output 17.6 PROC PRINT Output of Work.Sch1 (Boston)

Boston

Obs	Course_Number	Course_Code	Location	Begin_Date	Teacher
3	3	C003	Boston	08JAN2019	Forest, Mr. Peter
6	6	C006	Boston	02APR2019	Berthan, Ms. Judy
8	8	C002	Boston	11JUN2019	Wickam, Dr. Alice
11	11	C005	Boston	17SEP2019	Tally, Ms. Julia
13	13	C001	Boston	12NOV2019	Hallis, Dr. George
16	16	C004	Boston	21JAN2020	Tally, Ms. Julia

Output 17.7 PROC PRINT Output of Work.Sch1 (Dallas)

Dallas

Obs	Course_Number	Course_Code	Location	Begin_Date	Teacher
2	2	C002	Dallas	04DEC2018	Wickam, Dr. Alice
5	5	C005	Dallas	26FEB2019	Hallis, Dr. George
7	7	C001	Dallas	21MAY2019	Hallis, Dr. George
10	10	C004	Dallas	13AUG2019	Tally, Ms. Julia
15	15	C003	Dallas	07JAN2020	Forest, Mr. Peter
18	18	C006	Dallas	25FEB2020	Berthan, Ms. Judy

Output 17.8 *PROC PRINT Output of Work.Sch1 (Seattle)*

Seattle

Obs	Course_Number	Course_Code	Location	Begin_Date	Teacher
1	1	C001	Seattle	23OCT2018	Hallis, Dr. George
4	4	C004	Seattle	22JAN2019	Tally, Ms. Julia
9	9	C003	Seattle	16JUL2019	Forest, Mr. Peter
12	12	C006	Seattle	01OCT2019	Berthan, Ms. Judy
14	14	C002	Seattle	03DEC2019	Wickam, Dr. Alice
17	17	C005	Seattle	05FEB2020	Hallis, Dr. George

Test Your Code Solution

1. Correct Answer: Dallas
2. Correct Answer: 13

Scenario 6

Code Solution

Note: On the live exam, you will be evaluated both on the results of your code and the code itself. Your code should be similar to the following example code, but does not need to match exactly:

```
%let job=Analyst;                                          /*1*/
data work.staff;                                           /*2*/
   keep employeeID jobtitle salary;
   set certadv.staff;
   where jobtitle contains "&job";                         /*3*/
   total+salary;
   count+1;
   call symputx('avg',put(total/count,dollar9.));          /*4*/
run;
title "&job Staff";                                        /*5*/
footnote "Average Salary: &avg";                           /*6*/
proc print data=work.staff;
   sum salary;
run;
```

1. The %LET statement creates the macro variable Job and assigns the value of **Analyst**.

2. The DATA step creates a temporary SAS data set Work.Staff. Work.Staff that contains only the variables that are defined in the KEEP statement and reads in Certadv.Staff with only those variables.

3. The WHERE statement subsets the Work.Staff data set by the including those rows where the value of JobTitle equals the value of the macro variable Job.

4 The CALL SYMPUTX routine creates a new macro variable named Avg. The macro variable's value is the value of Total divided by the value of Count. It also formats the value of Avg to DOLLAR9.

5 The TITLE statement references the Job macro variable where the value is included in the title of the report.

6 The FOOTNOTE statement references the Avg macro variable where the value is included in the footnote of the report.

Output 17.9 PROC PRINT of Work.Staff

Analyst Staff

Obs	EmployeeID	JobTitle	Salary
1	120263	Financial Analyst III	$42,605
2	120264	Financial Analyst II	$37,510
3	120710	Business Analyst II	$54,840
4	120711	Business Analyst III	$59,130
5	120775	HR Analyst II	$41,580
6	120779	HR Analyst II	$43,690
7	121148	Business Analyst II	$52,930

Average Salary: $47,469

Test Your Code Solution

1. Correct Answer: $47,469
2. Correct Answer: 7

Scenario 7

Code Solution

Note: On the live exam, you will be evaluated both on the results of your code and the code itself. Your code should be similar to the following example code, but does not need to match exactly:

```
proc sql;                               /* 1 */
   create table work.bonus as           /* 2 */
   select EmpId, Jobcode, Salary,       /* 3 */
          Salary*.10 as Bonus           /* 4 */
   from certadv.empdata                 /* 5 */
   order by JobCode, Salary;            /* 6 */
quit;
```

1 The SQL procedure retrieves data from tables or views to generate a report.

2   The CREATE TABLE statement creates the temporary table Work.Bonus from the query result of the current PROC SQL query.

3   The SELECT statement retrieves the EmpId, Jobcode, and Salary columns and displays the column values in the query result.

4   The SELECT statement also creates a column alias by using the AS keyword followed by the column name of Bonus. The value of Bonus is 10% multiplied by the value of Salary.

5   The FROM clause specifies Certadv.Empdata as the source table to be queried.

6   The ORDER BY clause specifies to sort the rows by the values of the JobCode variable first and then Salary.

Output 17.10   SQL Query Result (partial output)

Employee Identification Number	Job Code	Employee Salary	Bonus
E00025	BAGCLK	$23,000	2300
E00042	BAGCLK	$32,000	3200
E00038	FACCLK	$20,000	2000
E00020	FACCLK	$21,000	2100
E00022	FACCLK	$27,000	2700
E00039	FACCLK	$38,000	3800
E00018	FACMNT	$33,000	3300
E00004	FACMNT	$42,000	4200
E00027	FINACT	$31,000	3100
E00002	FINCLK	$27,000	2700
E00045	FINMGR	$21,000	2100
E00029	FLSCHD	$17,000	1700
E00049	FLTAT1	$29,000	2900
E00040	FLTAT1	$32,000	3200

. . . *more observations* . . .

Test Your Code Solution

1. Correct Answer: 1700
2. Correct Answer: 2100

Scenario 8

Code Solution

Note: On the live exam, you will be evaluated both on the results of your code and the code itself. Your code should be similar to the following example code, but does not need to match exactly:

```
proc sql number;                                     /*1*/
    select empdata.empID,                            /*2*/
           empdata.LastName,
           empdata.Salary,
           newsals.NewSalary,
           (newsals.NewSalary-empdata.Salary)        /*3*/
               as Raise format=dollar10.2
        from certadv.empdata inner join              /*4*/
             certadv.newsals
             on empdata.EmpID= newsals.EmpID         /*5*/
        where calculated Raise>3000                  /*6*/
        order by EmpID;                              /*7*/
quit;
```

1. The SQL procedure retrieves data from tables or views to generate a report. The PROC SQL option NUMBER prints the row numbers in the query output.

2. The SELECT statement retrieves the columns EmpID, LastName, and Salary from Certadv.Empdata and NewSalary from Certadv.Newsals and displays the column values in the query result.

3. The SELECT statement also creates a column alias by using the AS keyword followed by the column name of Raise. The value of Raise is the difference between the column NewSalary from Certadv.Newsals and Salary from Certadv.Empdata. The DOLLAR 10.2 format is applied to the new column, Raise.

4. The FROM clause uses an INNER JOIN keyword to join Certadv.Empdata and Certadv.Newsals.

5. The ON clause specifies the column, EmpID, to be used when joining Certadv.Empdata and Certadv.Newsals.

6. The calculated keyword tells PROC SQL that the value is calculated within the query. The WHERE clause subsets the data to include only the observations where the value of Raise is greater than 3000.

7. The ORDER BY clause sorts the rows by EmpID.

Output 17.11 PROC SQL Query Result

Row	Employee Identification Number	Employee Last Name	Employee Salary	NewSalary	Raise
1	E00002	BOWER	$27,000	$31,153.98	$4,153.98
2	E00003	READING	$120,000	$143,789.80	$23,789.80
3	E00007	MASSENGILL	$29,000	$34,072.76	$5,072.76
. . . more observations . . .
21	E00047	ECKHAUSEN	$40,000	$44,104.09	$4,104.09
22	E00049	CHASE JR.	$29,000	$32,892.87	$3,892.87
23	E00050	DEXTER	$95,000	$109,644.45	$14,644.45

Test Your Code Solution

1. Correct Answer: Poole
2. Correct Answer: $7,588.61

Scenario 9

Code Solution

Note: On the live exam, you will be evaluated both on the results of your code and the code itself. Your code should be similar to the following example code, but does not need to match exactly:

```
proc sql;                                                    /*1*/
    select catx(" ",'Total Paid to All',JobTitle,'Staff'),   /*2*/
      sum(Salary) format=dollar14.,                          /*3*/
      count(*) as TotalCount format=comma16.                 /*4*
      from certadv.salesstaff                                /*5*/
      group by JobTitle;                                     /*6*/
quit;
```

1   The SQL procedure retrieves data from tables or views to generate a report.

2   The SELECT statement uses the CATX function to return a character string that combines **'Total Paid to All'**, the value of JobTitle, and **'Staff'**. For example, for rows where JobTitle is Sales Rep. I, the concatenated string is **'Total Paid to All Sales Rep. I Staff'**.

3   The SELECT statement uses the SUM function to calculate the total amount of salaries paid to each unique value for JobTitle. The FORMAT statement formats the value of the SUM function as DOLLAR14.

4   The SELECT statement uses the COUNT function to count the total number of sales representatives in each unique value for JobTitle. The COUNT function counts the number of rows and creates a column named TotalCount using the AS keyword.

5   The FROM clause specifies Certadv.Salesstaff as the source table to be queried.

6 The GROUP BY clause groups rows that have the same values into summary rows. The GROUP BY clause groups all unique values for JobTitle into one row. For example, Sales Rep. I is one row, Sales Rep. II is another, and so on.

Output 17.12 PROC SQL Query Result

	TotalSalary	TotalCount
Total Paid to All Sales Rep. I Staff	$1,669,395	63
Total Paid to All Sales Rep. II Staff	$1,377,442	50
Total Paid to All Sales Rep. III Staff	$1,001,175	34
Total Paid to All Sales Rep. IV Staff	$506,470	16

Test Your Code Solution

1. Correct Answer: 34
2. Correct Answer: $1,377,442

Scenario 10

Code Solution

Note: On the live exam, you will be evaluated both on the results of your code and the code itself. Your code should be similar to the following example code, but does not need to match exactly:

```
proc sql;
    create view work.phonelist as                          /*1*/
        select Department format=$25.,                     /*2*/
               EmployeeName as Name format=$25.,
               PhoneNumber 'Home Phone' format=$16.
        from certadv.empadd as a                           /*3*/
            inner join
            certadv.empph as p
            on a.EmployeeID = p.EmployeeID
            inner join
            certadv.emporg as o
            on o.EmployeeID = p.EmployeeID
        where PhoneType='Home';                            /*4*/
quit;

proc sql number;                                           /*5*/
title 'Sales Management Department Home Phone Numbers';
    select Name, PhoneNumber
        from work.phonelist                                /*6*/
        where Department='Sales Management'                /*7*/
        order by Name;                                     /*8*/
quit;
```

1. The CREATE VIEW statement creates the view that contains information about the employees' names, departments, and phone numbers. The view Work.PhoneList creates a virtual table from the accompanying SELECT statement. Although the underlying tables, Certadv.Empadd, Certadv.Empph, and Certadv.Org, can change, the instructions that comprise the view stay constant.

2. The SELECT statement selects three variables:

    - Department with a format of $25.

    - EmployeeName with a column alias of Name and a format of $25.

    - PhoneNumber with a label of Home Phone and a format of $16.

3. The FROM clause specifies Certadv.Empadd as the first source table with as alias of A. The INNER JOIN keyword is used to specify the type of join. Certadv.Empph is specified as the secondary source table with an alias of P. The ON keyword specifies the column on which the join occurs. The ON keyword specifies that from source table A, the values of EmployeeID must match the values of EmployeeID from source table P. Another INNER JOIN keyword is used to specify the type of join. Certadv.Emporg is specified as the third source table with an alias of O. The ON keyword specifies that from source table O, the value of EmployeeID must match the values of EmployeeID from source table P.

4. The WHERE clause subsets the data to include only those observations where the PhoneType is Home.

5. The SQL procedure retrieves data from tables or views to generate a report. The SQL option NUMBER prints the row numbers in the query output. The SQL procedure prints the title 'Sales Management Department Home Phone Numbers'. The SELECT statement includes Name and PhoneNumber in the result.

6. The FROM clause specifies Work.PhoneList as the view to be queried.

7. The WHERE clause specifies to subset the data based on the condition that only those in the Sales Management department are in the query result.

8. The ORDER BY clause orders the rows by EmployeeName.

Output 17.13 PROC SQL Query Result

Sales Management Department Home Phone Numbers

Row	Name	Home Phone
1	Bleu, Henri Le	+1(215)551-0417
2	Capachietti, Renee	+1(305)551-0420
3	Dawes, Wilson	+61(2)5555-3998
4	Favaron, Louis	+1(305)551-0419
5	Lansberry, Dennis	+1(305)551-0421
6	Lu, Patrick	+61(2)5555-1849
7	Sadig, Shane	+1(305)551-0424
8	Sangiorgio, Julieanne	+1(215)551-0422
9	Sneed, Christine	+1(305)551-0423
10	Steiber, Reginald	+1(215)551-0418
11	Zhou, Tom	+61(3)5555-9700

Test Your Code Solution

1. Correct Answer: 11
2. Correct Answer: Lu, Patrick

Recommended Reading

- *The Little SAS Book: A Primer, Sixth Edition*
- *Practical and Efficient SAS Programming: The Insider's Guide*
- *PROC SQL: Beyond the Basics Using SAS, Third Edition*
- *SAS Certified Specialist Prep Guide: Base Programming Using SAS 9.4*
- *SAS Macro Programming Made Easy, Third Edition*

For a complete list of SAS publications, go to sas.com/store/books. If you have questions about which titles you need, please contact a SAS Representative:

SAS Books
SAS Campus Drive
Cary, NC 27513-2414
Phone: 1-800-727-0025
Fax: 1-919-677-4444
Email: sasbook@sas.com
Web address: sas.com/store/books

Index

Special Characters
; (semicolon) 234
? conditional operator 13, 15
% (percent sign)
   macro programs and 234
   specifying directives 320
   tokens and 209
%a directive 320
%A directive 320
%b directive 320
%B directive 320
%CMPRES statement 263
%d directive 320
%DATATYP statement 263
%DO-%END statement 248, 252, 254
%EVAL function 204, 205
%GLOBAL statement 242
%H directive 320
%I directive 320
%IF-%THEN/%ELSE macro statement 247, 248
%INCLUDE statement 259
%INDEX function 201
%j directive 320
%LEFT statement 263
%LENGTH function 201
%LET statement
   macro parameter support 237
   user-defined macro variables and 188
%LOCAL statement 243, 244
%LOWCASE statement 263
%m directive 320
%M directive 320
%MACRO statement
   macro parameter support 237, 238, 239
   syntax 232
%MEND statement 232
%NRSTR function 209
%p directive 320
%PUT statement 191
%QLOWCASE statement 263
%S directive 320
%SCAN function 202
%STR function 208
%SUBSTR function 200
%SYMDEL statement 192, 193
%SYSEVALF function 206, 207
%SYSFUNC function 203, 204
%TRIM statement 263
%U directive 320
%UPCASE function 198, 199, 200
%w directive 320
%y directive 320
%Y directive 320
=* conditional operator
   description 13
   syntax 18

A
ADD method 304, 305
adding key and data values
   ADD method 304, 305
aliases
   column 8, 12, 71
   table 72
ALL conditional operator 13, 137
ALL keyword
   EXCEPT set operator and 106, 107
   INTERSECT set operator and 110, 112
   set operations and 102
   UNION set operator and 115, 117
ANY conditional operator
   comparison operator and 135
   description 13
arguments, summary functions and 21, 23, 24
array processing
   compilation phase 279
   execution phase 279
ARRAY statement
   syntax 274
arrays
   assigning initial values 284
   column lists 276
   creating character columns 283
   defining elements 275
   DIM function 278

one-dimensional 273, 274, 275, 276, 277, 278, 279, 283, 284, 285, 286
processing 279
referencing one-dimensional array 277
rotating data 286
specifying elements 275
specifying lower and upper bounds 284
table lookup 290
temporary elements 285
two-dimensional 288, 290
unknown number of array elements 278
AS keyword, CREATE TABLE statement (SQL) 49
autocall libraries
  accessing macros 264
  creating 262
  default 263
  defined 262
automatic macro variables
  functionality 188
  global symbol table and 240
AVG function 26

B

BETWEEN-AND conditional operator
  description 13
  syntax 14
BY variable
  joining tables 84, 85, 86

C

CALCULATED keyword 12
CALL MISSING routine 306
CALL SYMPUTX routine
  syntax 217
Cartesian product 66
character data types
  column widths and 47
  defined 46
character strings
  %INDEX function 201
  %LENGTH function 201
  %SCAN function 202
  %SUBSTR function 200
  macro character functions 198
CHART procedure 193
CMPLIB= option
  syntax 329
COALESCE function 86, 87
column alias
  CALCULATED keyword and 12
  defined 8
  renaming columns with 71
column modifiers 48

column widths 47
columns
  as multiple arguments for summary functions 24
  combining 101
  counting nonmissing values 28
  counting unique values 28
  creating new 8
  creating tables by defining 44, 45
  eliminating duplicate 70
  ordering by multiple 34
  ordering by position 34
  outside summary functions 24
  overlaying 101
  processing calculated 11
  renaming with column aliases 71
  rows numbers in output 38
  selecting 6
  summary functions and 23, 24
  viewing all 7
comments in macro programs 246, 247
comparison operators
  ALL conditional operator and 137
  ANY conditional operator and 135
  subqueries and 134
compiling macro programs 233
conditional operators 13
conditional processing
  for macro programs 247, 248
constants 207
CONTAINS conditional operator
  description 13
  syntax 15
controlling output
  OUTPUT method 305
conventional join 68
CORR keyword
  EXCEPT set operator and 106, 107
  INTERSECT operator and 111, 112
  OUTER UNION set operator and 122
  set operations and 102
  UNION set operator and 116, 117
correlated subqueries
  defined 132
  EXISTS conditional operator 139
  NOT EXISTS conditional operator 139
  subsetting data 138
COUNT function 26
COUNT/COUNTC/COUNTW function 340, 341
  counting words 341
  syntax 340
CREATE TABLE statement, SQL procedure 44, 45
  AS keyword 49
  creating empty tables 44, 45

creating like other tables 48
creating tables from query results 49
defining column structures 45
displaying table structure 59
FORMAT= option 48
INFORMAT= option 48
LABEL= option 48
LIKE clause 48
specifying column modifiers 48
specifying column widths 47
specifying data types 46
specifying empty tables like other tables 48
syntax with LIKE clause 48
syntax with query clauses 49
CREATE VIEW statement, SQL procedure
FROM clause 144
syntax 141
USING clause 145

D

data
  grouping 20, 29
DATA step
  CALL SYMPUTX routine and 217, 220
  comparing joins and 84, 85, 86
  IF-THEN/ELSE statement 247
  match-merges 84, 85, 86
  PUT function 204, 225
  SYMPUT routine and 219
  SYMPUTX routine and 217, 218
data types
  character 46, 47
  creating tables by defining columns 46
  numeric 46, 47
data-driven macro calls 266
  DOSUBL function 266
DATALINES statement 234
DATATYPE= option, PICTURE statement (FORMAT) 319
debugging
  FEEDBACK option, SQL procedure 7
  macro programs 245, 246, 247, 251
DECLARE statement 301
DEFINEDATA method 301
DEFINEKEY method 301
defining a hash object
  DEFINEDATA 301
  DEFINEONE 301
  DEFINEKEY 301
DELETE statement, SQL procedure
  updating views 146
deleting

views 148
delimiters
  in macro programs 234
  in macro variable names 193
DESCRIBE TABLE statement, SQL procedure
  displaying Dictionary table definitions 61
  displaying table structure 59
  syntax 59
DESCRIBE VIEW statement, SQL procedure 143
Dictionary tables
  functionality 60
  querying 61
DIM function 278
  syntax 278
directives, specifying pictures 319
DISTINCT keyword 9
DO statement
  processing repetitive code 277
DOSUBL function 266
DROP VIEW statement, SQL procedure 148
duplicate columns, eliminating 70
duplicate rows
  eliminating from output 9
  processing unique vs. 101

E

empty tables 48
EXCEPT set operator
  ALL keyword and 106, 107
  CORR keyword and 106, 107
  functionality 96, 103
EXISTS conditional operator
  correlated queries and 139
  description 13
external files
  storing macro definitions in 259

F

FCMP procedure
  CMPLIB= option 329
  syntax 328
FedSQL procedure
  LIBNAME statement 167
  LIMIT clause 168
  PUT function 169
  syntax 166
  system options 170
FEEDBACK option, SQL procedure 7
FIND method 302, 303
FIND/FINDC/FINDW function 342, 343

finding the word number 343
  syntax 342
finding key values
  FIND method 302
FORMAT procedure
  PICTURE statement 318, 319, 320, 322, 323, 324, 325
  VALUE statement 317
FORMAT= option
  CREATE TABLE statement (SQL) 48
formats
  creating with PICTURE statement 320
FROM clause
  CREATE VIEW statement (SQL) 144
  INSERT statement (SQL) 57
  SELECT statement (SQL) 9, 66
full outer join 78, 81
functions
  %EVAL function 204, 205
  %SYSEVALF function 206, 207
  %SYSFUNC function 203, 204
  macro variable support 203, 204, 205, 206, 207

G

GCHART procedure 193
global symbol table
  %GLOBAL statement 242
  macro variables and 240
GPLOT procedure 193
GROUP BY clause, SELECT statement (SQL)
  grouping 20
  selecting groups 30
  summarizing groups of data 19, 22
  summary functions and 25
groups, selecting 30

H

hash iterator object 311, 312
  DECLARE statement 312
  DEFINEDATA method 312
  DEFINEDONE method 312
  DEFINEKEY method 312
  FIRST method 312
  LAST method 312
  NEXT method 312
  PREV method 312
hash object processing 306
  ADD method 306
  CALL missing routine 306
  DECLARE statement 306
  DEFINEDATA method 306
  DEFINEDONE method 306
  DEFINEKEY method 306
  FIND method 306
hash objects
  ADD method 304, 305
  CALL MISSING routine 306
  declaring 299
  defining 300
  FIND method 302
  multiple data variables 301
  OUTPUT method 305
  retrieving matching data 303
  structure 297, 298, 299
HAVING clause, SELECT statement (SQL) 30
  grouping 29

I

IF-THEN/ELSE statement
  %IF-%THEN comparison 247
IN conditional operator
  description 13
  syntax 16
INFORMAT= option, CREATE TABLE statement (SQL) 48
inner joins
  defined 68
INOBS= option, SQL procedure 36
INPUT function 204
INPUTC function 204
INPUTN function 204
INSERT statement, SQL procedure
  FROM clause 57
  inserting rows from query results 57
  inserting rows of data in tables 51, 52, 54, 55
  SELECT clause 57
  SET clause 52
  syntax 52, 54, 55, 57
  updating views 146
  VALUES clause 54, 55
INTERSECT set operator
  ALL keyword and 110, 112
  CORR keyword and 111, 112
  functionality 96, 109
INTO clause, SELECT statement (SQL) 214
IS MISSING conditional operator 13, 16
IS NULL conditional operator 13, 16

J

joining data sets
  defined 66
joining tables
  advantages 88

COALESCE function 86, 87
comparing with DATA step match-
    merges 84, 85, 86
defined 66
EXCEPT set operator 103
for rows with matching values 72
inner joins 68
INTERSECT set operator 109
outer joins 78
OUTER UNION set operator 120
processes defined 69
set operations 97
UNION set operator 114

K

keyword parameters 238, 239
keywords, modifying set operations 102

L

LABEL= option
    CREATE TABLE statement (SQL) 48
LAG function 337, 338, 339
    calculating a moving average 339
    retrieving previous values 338
    syntax 337, 338
LEFT function 213
left outer join 78, 79
LIBNAME statement 145
    FedSQL procedure 167
librefs, views and 144
LIKE clause, CREATE TABLE statement (SQL) 48
LIKE conditional operator
    description 13
    specifying patterns 17
    syntax 17
LIMIT clause
    FedSQL procedure 168
local symbol table 243
    %LOCAL statement 244

M

macro character functions
    %INDEX function 201
    %LENGTH function 201
    %SCAN function 202
    %SUBSTR function 200
    %UPCASE function 198, 199, 200
    manipulating character strings 198
macro definitions 259
macro programs
    %DO-%END statement 248
    %GLOBAL statement 242

%IF-%THEN/%ELSE macro statement 247, 248
%LOCAL statement 243, 244
calling 234
comments in 246, 247
compiling 233
conditionally processing statements 247, 248
debugging 245, 246, 247, 251
defined 232
developing 245, 246, 247, 251
executing 235
iterative processing for 252, 254
log control 245, 246, 251
monitoring execution 245, 246, 247, 251
parameters and 237, 238, 239
storing in autocall libraries 262, 263, 264
storing macro in external files 259
storing session compiled macros 261
symbol tables 240, 242, 243, 244, 245, 246, 251
macro quoting functions
    %NRSTR function 209
    %STR function 208
    masking special characters 207
macro variable in PROC SQL
    displaying values in SAS log 157
macro variables
    %PUT statement 191
    automatic 188, 240
    CALL SYMPUTX routine 217, 220
    combining references with text 193
    creating during PROC SQL execution 214
    delimiters in names 193
    displaying values in SAS log 190, 191
    in symbol tables 240, 242, 243, 244, 245, 246, 251
    macro parameters and 237, 238, 239
    PUT function 204, 225
    referencing 193
    referencing macro variables indirectly 226
    SAS function support 203, 204, 205, 206, 207
    SAS statement support 192, 193
    SYMBOLGEN system option 190
    SYMPUT routine 219
    SYMPUTX routine 217, 218
    user-defined 188, 240
masking special characters
    %NRSTR function 209
    %STR function 208
    macro function support 207

MAUTOSOURCE system option 264
MCOMPILENOTE= system option 233
metadata 60
MLOGIC system option 251
MPRINT system option 245, 246

N

natural joins
   syntax 77
NMISS function 27
NOEXEC option, SQL procedure 38
noncorrelated subqueries
   defined 132
   multiple-value 133
   single-value 132
   subsetting data 132
NONUMBER option, SQL procedure 38
NOPRINT option
   SELECT statement (SQL) 214
NOT EXISTS conditional operator 139
NUMBER option, SQL procedure 38
numeric data types 46, 47

O

OPTIONS statement, SQL procedure
   MAUTOSOURCE option 264
   MCOMPILENOTE= option 233
   MLOGIC option 251
   MLOGIC system option 251
   SASAUTOS= option 264, 265
   SYMBOLGEN option 190
ORDER BY clause, SELECT statement (SQL)
   ordering by multiple columns 34
   ordering by position 34
   ordering rows 32, 33
outer joins
   functionality 78
   syntax 79
OUTER UNION set operator
   CORR keyword and 122
   functionality 96, 120, 121
OUTOBS= option, SQL procedure
   restricting row processing 36
   syntax 37
output
   controlling 38, 305
   eliminating duplicate rows from 9
   including row numbers 38
OUTPUT method 305

P

parameters
   in macro programs 237, 238, 239
   keyword 238, 239
   positional 237, 239
patterns 17
percent sign (%)
   macro programs and 234
   specifying directives 320
   tokens and 209
performing pattern matching
   metacharacters 345, 346
Perl regular expressions
   metacharacters 345, 346
   pattern matching 344, 345, 346
   PRXCHANGE function 351, 353, 354
   PRXMATCH function 347, 348
   PRXPARSE function 349, 350
PICTURE statement
   DATATYPE= option 319
   digit selectors 318, 322, 323, 324, 325
   directives 319
   MULTIPLIER= option 322, 323
   PREFIX= option 322, 324
   ROUND option 322, 325
   syntax 318
PICTURE statement, FORMAT procedure
   DATATYPE= option 319
   specifying directives 320
positional parameters 237, 239
procedures
   FCMP 328, 329
   FedSQL 165, 166, 167, 168, 169, 170
   FORMAT 317, 318, 319, 322, 323, 324, 325
   SQL 4, 166
process management
   CALL SYMPUTX routine 217, 220
   conditional processing for macro programs 247, 248
   controlling execution 36
   controlling output 38
   creating macro variables in PROC SQL 214
   Dictionary tables 60
   for macro programs 245, 246, 247, 251
   iterative processing for macro programs 252, 254
   PUT function 204, 225
   referencing macro variables indirectly 226
   specifying SQL options 35
   SYMPUT routine 219
   SYMPUTX routine 217, 218
PRXCHANGE function 351, 353, 354
   capture buffers 354
   changing order 353
   standardize data 351

syntax 351
PRXMATCH function 347, 348
  referring to columns 348
  syntax 347, 349, 350
  validating data 347
PRXPARSE function 349, 350
PUT function 204, 225
  FedSQL procedure 169
PUTC function 204
PUTN function 204

Q

queries
  creating tables from 49
  Dictionary tables and 61
  displaying all columns 7
  eliminating duplicate rows from output 9
  grouping 20, 29
  inserting rows from 57
  limiting number of rows displayed 37
  ordering rows 32, 33
  selecting columns 6
  specifying subsetting criteria 10
  specifying tables 9
  subqueries for subsetting data 131
  subsetting data using correlated subqueries 138
  subsetting data using noncorrelated subqueries 132
  subsetting rows using calculated values 11
  subsetting rows with conditional operators 13
  summarizing groups of data 19
  validating syntax 38
  viewing all columns 7
  views in 141
quotation marks
  macro quoting functions and 207

R

referencing macro variables indirectly 226
right outer join 78, 81
rows
  counting all 27
  counting number of 26
  duplicate 9, 101
  eliminating duplicates from output 9
  inserting in tables 51, 52, 54, 55
  joining tables with matching values 72
  limiting number displayed 37
  ordering 32, 33
  ordering by multiple columns 34
  ordering by position 34
  processing unique vs. duplicate 101
  restricting processing 36
  row numbers in output 38

S

SAS log
  %PUT statement 191
  displaying macro variable values 190, 191
  MCOMPILENOTE= option 233
  SYMBOLGEN system option 190
SASAUTOS= system option 264
security, table views 146
SELECT clause
  INSERT statement (SQL) 57
  SELECT statement (SQL) 6, 7, 9, 23
SELECT statement, SQL procedure
  creating new columns 8
  DISTINCT keyword 9
  FEEDBACK option 7
  FROM clause 9, 66
  functionality 5
  GROUP BY clause 19, 20, 22, 25, 30
  grouping data 20, 29
  HAVING clause 29, 30
  INTO clause 214
  NOPRINT option 214
  ORDER BY clause 32, 33, 34
  ordering by multiple columns 34
  ordering by position 34
  ordering rows 32, 33
  SELECT clause 6, 7, 9, 23
  selecting columns 6
  specifying subset criteria 10
  specifying tables 9
  summarizing groups of data 23
  syntax for inner join 68
  syntax for natural join 77
  syntax for outer join 79
  syntax for set operations 97
  VALIDATE keyword 39
  viewing all columns 7
  WHERE clause 10, 11, 12, 13
semicolon (;) in macro programs 234
session compiled macros 261
SET clause
  INSERT statement (SQL) 52, 53
set operations
  combining and overlaying columns 101
  defined 97
  EXCEPT set operator 96, 103, 106, 107
  INTERSECT set operator 96, 109, 110, 111, 112

modifying results via keywords 102
OUTER UNION set operator 96, 120
processing multiple operations 98, 100
processing single operations 98
processing unique vs. duplicate rows 101
UNION set operator 96, 114, 115, 116, 117
sorting
  ordering by multiple columns 34
  ordering by position 34
  ordering rows 32, 33
sounds-like conditional operator
  description 13
  syntax 18
special characters, masking
  %NRSTR function 209
  %STR function 208
  macro function support 207
spelling variations 18
SQL procedure
  accessing metadata 60
  creating macro variables 214
  FEEDBACK option 7
  functionality 4
  INOBS= option 36
  NOEXEC option 38
  NONUMBER option 38
  NUMBER option 38
  OUTOBS= option 36, 37
  selecting patterns 17
  specifying options 35
  syntax 86
statements
  %GLOBAL 242
  %IF-%THEN 247
  %LOCAL 243
  %MACRO 232
  %MEND 232
  %SYMDEL 192, 193
  ARRAY 274
  DO 277
  macro variable support 192, 193
storage
  in autocall libraries 262, 263, 264
  macro definitions in external files 259
  session compiled macros 261
subqueries
  comparison operator in 134
  correlated 132
  noncorrelated 132
  subsetting data 131
subsetting data
  correlated subqueries and 138
  noncorrelated subqueries and 132
  subqueries and 131

subsetting rows
  specifying criteria 10
  using calculated values 11
  using conditional operators 13
summarizing data
  GROUP BY clause, SELECT statement (SQL) 19, 22
  SELECT clause and 23
summary functions
  functionality 19
  GROUP BY clause and 25
  number of arguments 21
  on groups of data 22
  SELECT clause and 23
  with columns outside function 24
  with multiple arguments 24
  with single arguments 23
symbol tables
  %GLOBAL statement 242
  %LOCAL statement 243, 244
  global 240
  local 243
SYMBOLGEN system option 190
SYMPUTX routine
  DATA step variables and 219
  syntax 217
SYSDATE automatic macro variable 188
SYSDATE9 automatic macro variable 188, 200, 203, 204
SYSDAY automatic macro variable 188
SYSENV automatic macro variable 188
SYSERR automatic macro variable 189
SYSJOBID automatic macro variable 188
SYSLAST automatic macro variable 189
SYSPARM automatic macro variable 189
SYSSCP automatic macro variable 188
SYSTIME automatic macro variable 188, 203, 204
SYSVER automatic macro variable 188

T

table aliases, specifying 72
tables
  creating from query results 49
  creating like others 48
  displaying structure 59
  empty 48
  generating Cartesian products 66
  methods of creating 43
  specifying 9
  specifying data types 46
  views and 141, 146
  virtual 141
text, macro variable references and 193
tokens

percent sign and 209

U
UNION set operator
  ALL keyword and 115, 117
  CORR keyword and 116, 117
  functionality 96, 114
update process
  for views 146
UPDATE statement, SQL procedure
  updating views 146
  WHERE clause 146
user-defined macro variables
  %LET statement and 188
  global symbol table and 240
USING clause, CREATE VIEW statement (SQL) 145

V
VALIDATE keyword 39
VALUES clause, INSERT statement (SQL)
  functionality 54, 55
variables
  hash objects and 301
views
  benefits 141
  creating 141
  deleting 148
  displaying definitions 143
  dropping 148
  enhancing table security 146
  functionality 143
  in queries 141
  librefs and 144
  managing 144
  tables and 141, 146
  updating 146
virtual tables 141

W
WHERE clause
  SELECT statement (SQL) 10, 12, 13
  UPDATE statement (SQL) 146

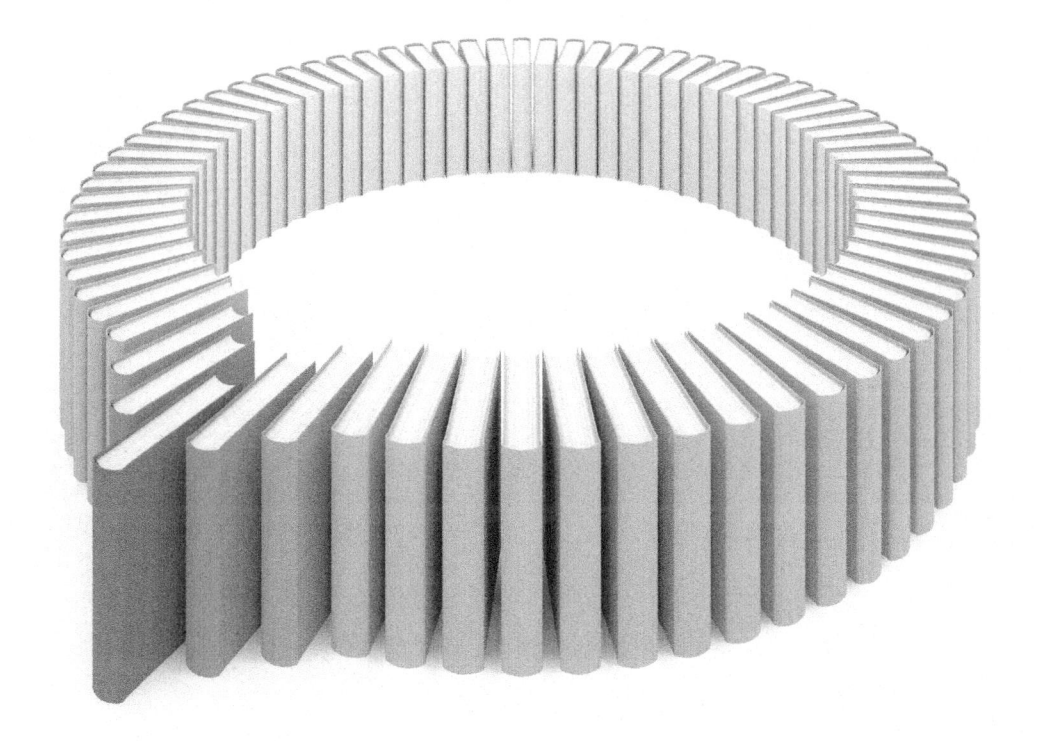

Gain Greater Insight into Your SAS® Software with SAS Books.

Discover all that you need on your journey to knowledge and empowerment.

support.sas.com/bookstore
for additional books and resources.

§.sas.
THE POWER TO KNOW®

SAS and all other SAS Institute Inc. product or service names are registered trademarks or trademarks of SAS Institute Inc. in the USA and other countries. ® indicates USA registration. Other brand and product names are trademarks of their respective companies. © 2013 SAS Institute Inc. All rights reserved. S107969US.0813

Made in the USA
Coppell, TX
02 June 2020

James Oglethorpe
Not for Self, but for Others

Torrey Maloof

Consultants

Regina Holland, Ed.S., *Henry County Schools*
Christina Noblet, Ed.S., *Paulding County School District*
Jennifer Troyer, *Paulding County Schools*
Michele M. Celani, M.S.Ed., *Baldwin County Public Schools*

Publishing Credits

Rachelle Cracchiolo, M.S.Ed., *Publisher*
Conni Medina, M.A.Ed., *Managing Editor*
Emily R. Smith, M.A.Ed., *Series Developer*
Diana Kenney, M.A.Ed., NBCT, *Content Director*
Torrey Maloof, *Editor*
Courtney Patterson, *Multimedia Designer*

Image Credits: Front cover: Clipart courtesy FCIT, Granger, NYC; pp.3,25 National Maritime Museum, Greenwich, London; pp.2,3,6,9,10,11,12,20 North Wind Picture Archives; p.8 Courtesy, Georgia Archives, RG 49-2-18, page 4; pp.5,11,13,18,19,22,23,32 Granger, NYC; p.17 Wikimedia Commons; pp.21,31 Courtesy of Hargrett Rare Book and Manuscript Library / University of Georgia Libraries; pp.6,14-15 Alamy Stock Photo; p.24 Ann Ronan Pictures/Print Collector/Getty Images; All other images from iStock and/or Shutterstock.

Library of Congress Cataloging-in-Publication Data

Names: Maloof, Torrey, author.
Title: James Oglethorpe : not for self, but for others / Torrey Maloof.
Description: Huntington Beach, CA : Teacher Created Materials, 2016. |
   Includes index.
Identifiers: LCCN 2015042467 | ISBN 9781493825554 (pbk.)
Subjects: LCSH: Oglethorpe, James, 1696-1785--Juvenile literature. |
   Georgia--History--Colonial period, ca. 1600-1775--Juvenile literature. |
   Governors--Georgia--Biography--Juvenile literature.
Classification: LCC F289.O37 M35 2016 | DDC 975.8/02--dc23
LC record available at http://lccn.loc.gov/2015042467

Teacher Created Materials

5301 Oceanus Drive
Huntington Beach, CA 92649-1030
http://www.tcmpub.com

ISBN 978-1-4938-2555-4
© 2017 Teacher Created Materials, Inc.

Table of Contents

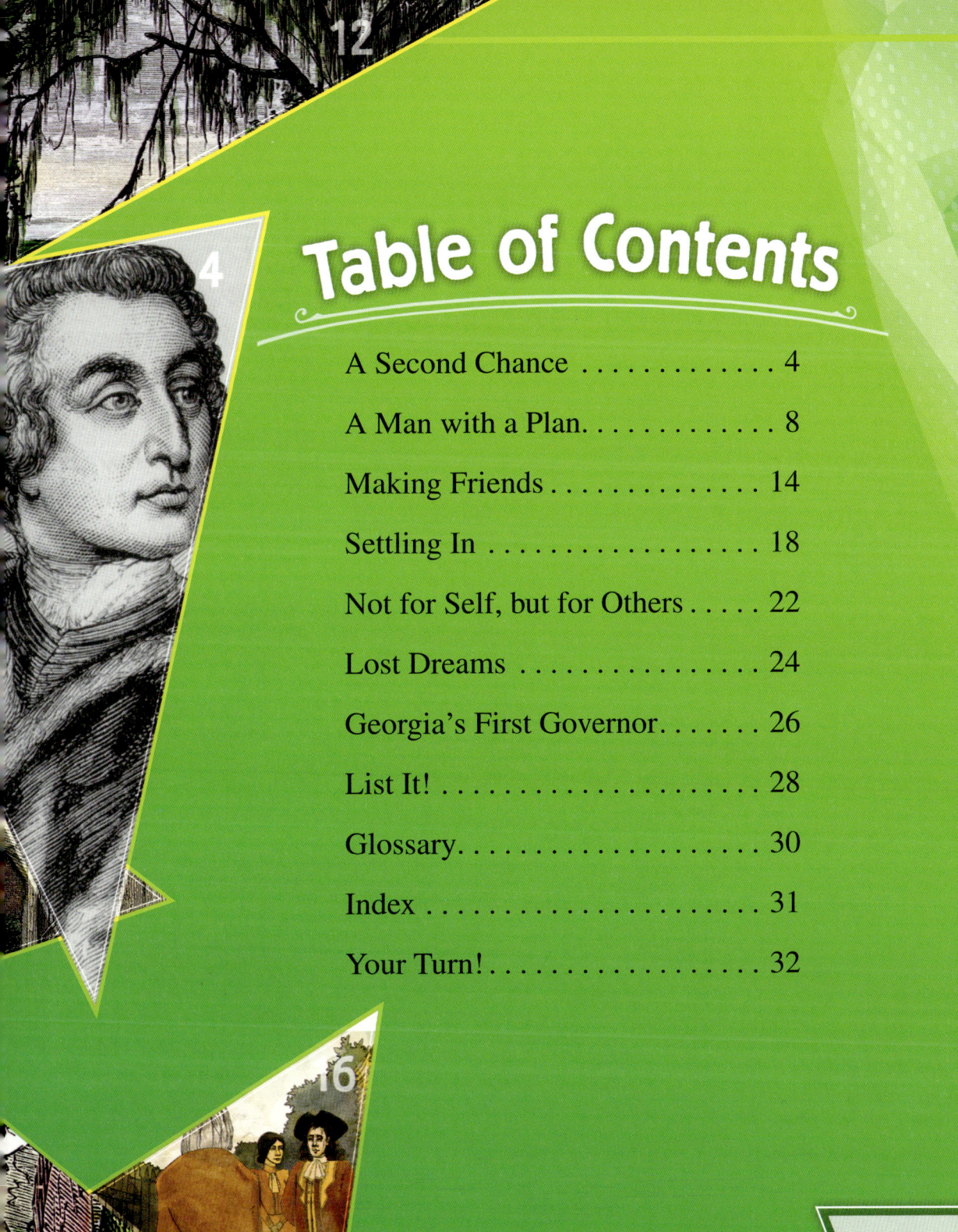

A Second Chance 4

A Man with a Plan. 8

Making Friends 14

Settling In 18

Not for Self, but for Others 22

Lost Dreams 24

Georgia's First Governor. 26

List It! 28

Glossary. 30

Index 31

Your Turn! 32

A Second Chance

Long ago, there was a man who wanted to help those in need in Great Britain. At the time, many people were being put in jail for not paying their **debts** (DETZ).

The man did not think this was fair. He thought they should get a second chance. That man's name was James Oglethorpe.

James Oglethorpe

A man sits in jail for not paying his debts.

Making a Difference

One of James's close friends died in jail. James wanted people to be able to make up for their wrongdoings in other ways.

James wanted to start a new **colony** (KAHL-uh-nee). It would be in the New World. It would be a place where people could start a new life.

James's plan was to bring some of the people who were in jail. He hoped the king would set them free. Then, they could travel to his new colony. They could help him settle the land.

King George II was in charge of the colonies.

Colonists settle in Massachusetts in 1621, more than 100 years before Georgia would be settled.

7

A Man with a Plan

First, James went to the king. He needed the king's permission. James told the king his plan.

The king gave James a **charter**. It said he could start the new colony. It would be the thirteenth colony in America. It would be called Georgia in honor of the king.

The Royal Charter

Map: Eastern North America, c. 1600s–1700s

the 13 colonies

New France (Canada)
- Ft. La Hontan 1680
- Sault Ste. Marie 1641
- Ft. Lake Pepin 1727
- Michilimackinac 1659
- Quebec 1608
- Ft. Richelieu 1642
- Montreal 1611
- 1673
- Toronto 1749
- Ft. Niagara 1726
- Ft. Detroit 1701
- Ft. St. Joseph 1679
- Ft. Kakionga 1660
- Ft. St. Louis 1682
- Ft. Crevecoeur 1680
- Cahokia 1700
- Ft. Vincennes 1735
- Ft. Kaskaskia 1695
- St. Louis 1764
- Ft. Chartres 1720
- Ft. Prudhomme 1682
- Ft. Assumption 1714
- Ft. Toulouse 1714
- Ft. Tombeckbee 1735
- Natchitoches 1717
- Ft. Rosalie 1714
- Mobile 1702
- Pensacola 1696
- New Orleans 1717

The 13 Colonies
- Pemaquid
- Falmouth 1632
- Dover 1623
- Portsmouth 1629
- Salem 1629
- Boston 1630
- Plymouth 1620
- Providence 1636
- Crown Pt.
- NEW HAMPSHIRE
- MASSACHUSETTS
- CONN.
- NEW YORK 1623
- N.J.
- CLAIMED BY PENN.
- Philadelphia 1682
- Wilmington 1732
- DELAWARE COUNTIES
- MD.
- Baltimore 1729
- St. Marys 1634
- VIRGINIA
- Williamsburg 1632
- NORTH CAROLINA
- SOUTH CAROLINA
- GEORGIA
- Charleston 1680
- Savannah 1733

Florida (Spanish)
- St. Augustine 1565

Other
- Marquette and all the tributaries
- Mississippi R.
- Lake Superior
- Lake Michigan
- Lake Huron
- Lake Erie
- L. Ontario
- Illinois R.
- Wabash R.
- Ohio R.
- ATLANTIC OCEAN
- GULF OF MEXICO

Area shown on large map

9

The king chose 20 people to help James with his plans. This group did not like all of James's ideas. They thought it was unwise to take people from jail.

The group said James should take people with more skills. They wanted people who could help the colony succeed. James was upset, but he agreed. They chose people such as farmers and carpenters.

Skills Needed!

New colonists were chosen for their skills. Farmers could grow food. Carpenters could build homes. Merchants could trade goods.

carpenter

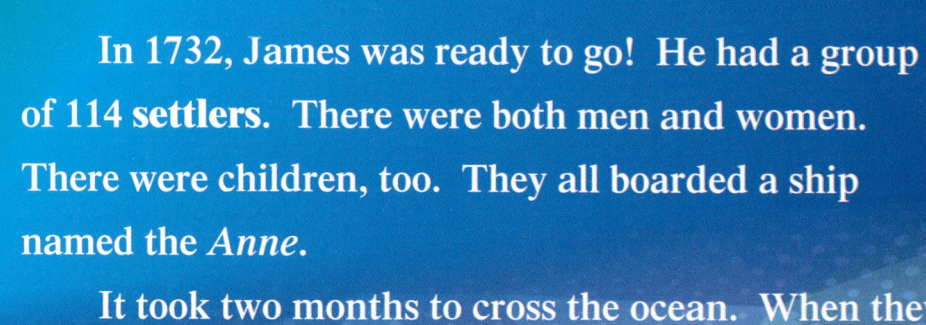

In 1732, James was ready to go! He had a group of 114 **settlers**. There were both men and women. There were children, too. They all boarded a ship named the *Anne*.

It took two months to cross the ocean. When they arrived, James looked for a place to settle. He found the perfect spot. But there was a problem. There were already people living there!

An American Indian paddles down the Savannah River.

Colonists sail to America on the *Anne*.

13

Making Friends

The Yamacraw (YAH-muh-kraw) were an American Indian **tribe**. They were living on the land James wanted. James did not want to upset them. He did not want to start a war.

James wanted to tell the tribe his plans. He wanted to talk to their chief, or leader. His name was Tomochichi. But he did not speak English. Luckily for James, there was a person who could help!

Tomochichi gives James a buffalo skin with symbols representing their new friendship.

Helpful Friends

The settlers didn't know how to grow food in Georgia's soil. The Yamacraw showed them how.

15

Mary Musgrove translates for James Oglethorpe and Tomochichi.

Mary Musgrove

Mary's father was British. Her mother was an American Indian. They taught her both languages.

Mary Musgrove spoke English. And she also knew how to speak with the Yamacraw. She helped James talk with their chief.

The two men signed a **treaty**, or a deal. They also became friends. They had a lot of respect for each other. James could now start his colony.

Tomochichi

Settling In

James chose a special place to build the first town in Georgia. It was on a **bluff** that overlooked a river. He named the river and the town Savannah.

He wanted the town to be orderly. He used a series of squares. The squares made a **grid**. The town had wide streets and lots of parks.

This plan shows streets and parks arranged in a grid, or pattern of lines that forms squares.

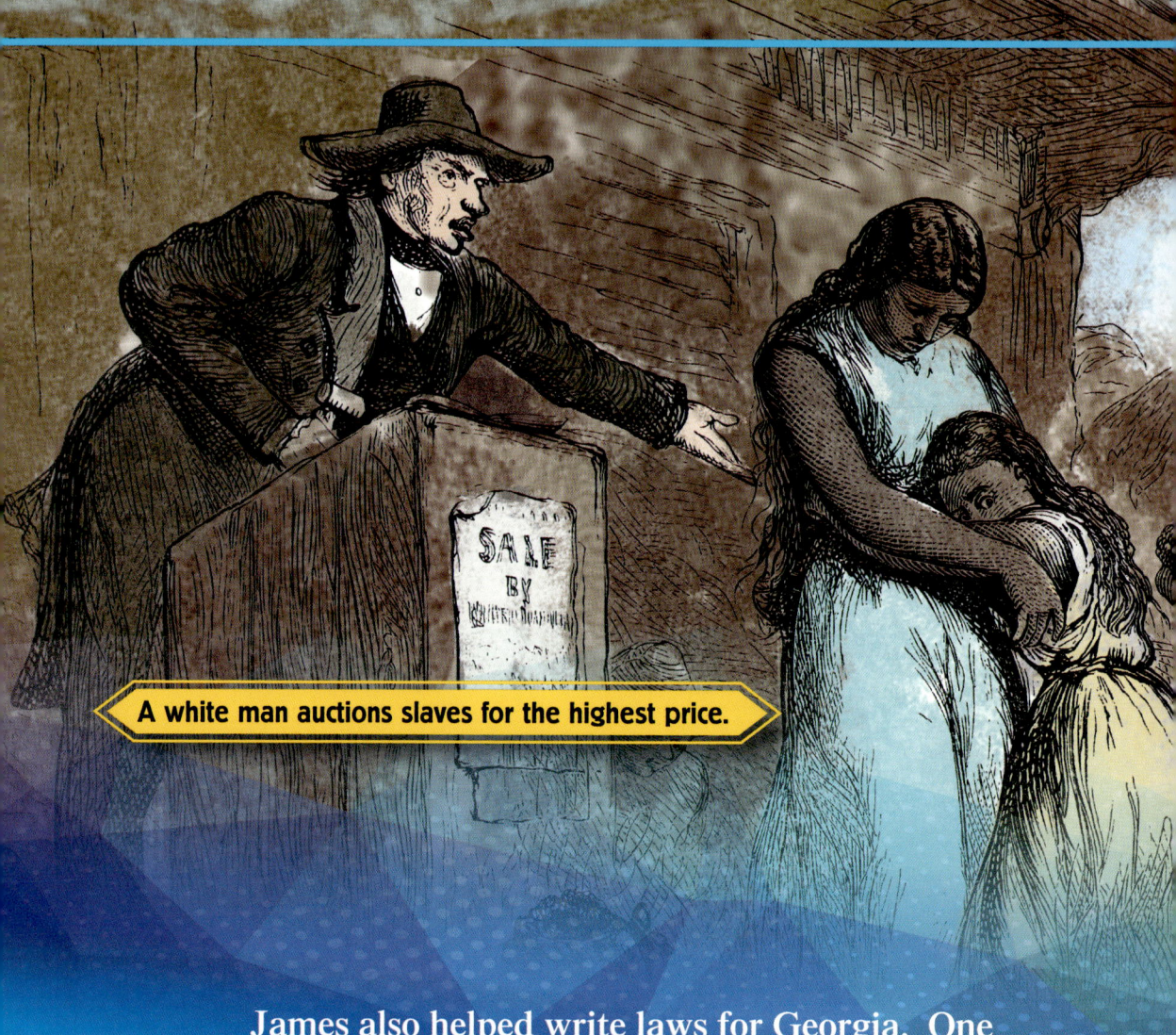

A white man auctions slaves for the highest price.

James also helped write laws for Georgia. One law said that people could not own slaves. Other colonies allowed it. People took slaves from their homes and forced them to work for free. Slave owners treated them very badly. They had no freedom.

But James did not like slavery. He thought it was wrong. He thought it would make colonists lazy.

In this 1733 journal, a colonist writes that laws against slavery make it hard for Georgia to be successful.

21

Not for Self, but for Others

People say James worked hard. He wanted to make Georgia successful. The colony's motto was "Not for self, but for others." James worked hard for others before working hard for himself.

This made him a strong leader. He helped the settlers in any way he could. He cut down trees. He helped build homes and roads. James also made trips to Great Britain. He went there to get more **funds** for Georgia.

Women's Roles

Colonial women worked very hard. They took care of the homes, raised the children, made clothes, and cooked.

23

Lost Dreams

Even though James tried to help, the settlers were having a hard time. They did not like the hot weather. They did not like the laws. They wanted slaves to do the hard work for them.

James was unhappy, too. Georgia was not turning out the way he had hoped. The other leaders in Georgia were making changes. James didn't agree with them. They made slavery **legal** in 1751.

John Reynolds

John Reynolds was made Georgia's first royal **governor** in 1754.

Georgia's First Governor

In time, James left Georgia. He went back to Great Britain. He lived there until he died in 1785. He was 88 years old.

James lived his life to help others. He was a good man. He had big dreams for Georgia. And he worked hard to make them come true. Today, many think of him as Georgia's first governor.

This monument of James Oglethorpe stands in Savannah, Georgia.

BULL ST.

OGLETHORPE AVE.

27

List It!

Good leaders have many qualities. They work hard. They are honest. They are responsible. They help others. James was a good leader. Think about the book. Make a list of his good qualities. Then, draw a picture that shows your favorite thing about James.

29

Glossary

bluff—a high, steep area of land

charter—a document that says a town, city, or school has been founded

colony—an area ruled by a faraway country

debts—amounts of money owed to someone

funds—money used for a special purpose

governor—the leader of a state or region

grid—a pattern of lines that cross each other to form squares

legal—based on the law or rules

settlers—people who go to live in a new place where there are few other people

treaty—a deal that is made between two or more countries or groups

tribe—a group of people who have the same language, customs, and beliefs

Index

American Indian, 12, 14, 16

Anne, 12–13

George II, King, 6

Great Britain, 4, 22, 26

Musgrove, Mary, 16–17

New World, 6

Reynolds, John, 25

Savannah, 18, 27

slaves, 20, 24

Tomochichi, 14, 16–17

Yamacraw, 14–15, 17

Your Turn!

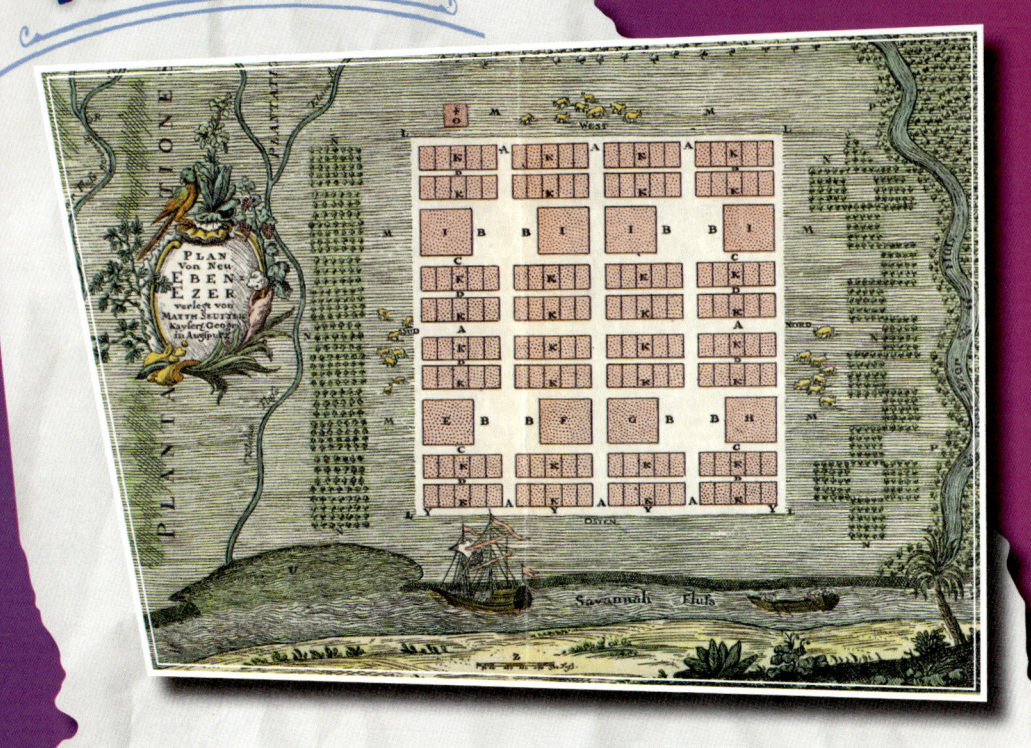

Your City

When a new city or town is built, there needs to be a plan. An artist can draw a town plan to show what the layout of the town should look like. Think about your city or town. What would you include in the town plan? Draw a plan for your city or town.